Doctor
to the
Front

Doctor to the Front

THE RECOLLECTIONS OF CONFEDERATE SURGEON THOMAS FANNING WOOD

1861–1865

Edited by

Donald B. Koonce

Voices of the Civil War
Frank L. Byrne
Series Editor

THE UNIVERSITY OF TENNESSEE PRESS / KNOXVILLE

The Voices of the Civil War series makes available a variety of primary source materials that illuminate issues on the battlefield, the homefront, and the western front, as well as other aspects of this historic era. The series contextualizes the personal accounts within the framework of the latest scholarship and expands established knowledge by offering new perspectives, new materials, and new voices.

Copyright © 2000 by The University of Tennessee Press / Knoxville.
All Rights Reserved. Manufactured in the United States of America.

Cloth: First printing, 2000.
Paper: First printing, 2016.

Library of Congress Cataloging-in-Publication Data

Wood, Thomas Fanning, 1841-1892.
Doctor to the front : the recollections of Confederate surgeon Thomas Fanning Wood, 1861-1865 / edited by Donald B. Koonce.
p. cm.—(Voices of the Civil War)
Includes bibliographical references and index.
ISBN 978-1-62190-158-7
1. Wood, Thomas Fanning, 1841-1892. 2. United States—History—Civil War, 1861-1865—Personal narratives, Confederate. 3. United States—History—Civil War, 1861-1865—Medical care. 4. Confederate States of America. Army—Surgeons—Biography. 5. Surgeons—Confederate States of America—Biography. I. Koonce, Donald B. II. Title. III. Voices of the Civil War series
E625 .W66 2000
973.7'75'092—dc21
99-050664

*To the memory of my great aunts
Maggie and Jeannie Wood,
who succeeded in keeping the
family history alive*

Contents

Foreword	ix
Frank L. Byrne, Series Editor	
Preface	xi
Acknowledgments	xxiii
The Recollections of Confederate Surgeon	
Thomas Fanning Wood, 1861–1865	
1. Mr. Erambert's Drugstore	3
2. Joining the Rifle Guards	11
3. The Regiment Moves to South Carolina	17
4. Virginia and The Seven Days Battles	23
5. Richmond	31
6. The New Assistant Surgeon	43
7. The Battle of Chancellorsville	73
8. The Gettysburg Campaign	91
9. The Winter of 1863 and the Turning Tide	115
10. The Wilderness Campaign	135
11. Early's March on Washington City	147
Notes	191
Bibliography	239
Index	243

Figures

Thomas Fanning Wood, M.D., c. 1886	xix
Robert Barclay Wood and His Sons, c. 1875–1877	xx
Bonitz Hotel, 1880s	5
Professor Otis Manson, M.D.	35
Wood's Appointment to Assistant Surgeon	44

Special Trouser Button Assembly from Wood's Memoirs	49
Thomas Fanning Wood, Assistant Surgeon	54
Captain John F. S. Van Bokkelen	55
Reverend George Patterson	57
Major William M. Parsley	60
Captain Edward H. Armstrong	62
Captain Richard F. Langdon	65
Map of the Battlefield of Chancellorsville Drawn by Wood, 1863	80
General Richard Ewell	93
General George Hume "Maryland" Steuart	94
Pocket Surgical Kit	98
Christian Benner Farmhouse and Barn	106
Layout of the Colonel's Cabin from Wood's Memoirs	131
Thomas Fanning Wood, c.1864	148
General Jubal "Old Jube" Early	149
General Robert Emmett Rodes	179
General Dodson Ramseur	187

Maps

Chimborazo Hospital Area of Richmond, 1863	33
Chancellorsville Battlefield, May 2, 1863	75
Chancellorsville Battlefield with Route of Jackson's Reconnaissance	77
Gettysburg Battlefield with Regimental Hospital	105
Wilderness Battle Line, May 6	139
Spotsylvania Battlefield with the Muleshoe and Steuart's Brigade	142
Route of Jubal Early's Raid on Washington, 1864	153

FOREWORD

Like all wars, the American Civil War resulted in losses for many and gains for a fortunate few. In the victorious North, non-participants laid the foundation for several postwar fortunes. Some who served in the Union Army developed valuable skills such as those of Wesley Brainerd, the engineer whose memoir constitutes an earlier volume in this series (Ed Malles, ed., *Bridge Building in Wartime*). Even in the defeated South, some among the high proportion of the population that went into the military were able to find opportunity which would have been unavailable in peacetime.

Such a lucky man was Thomas Fanning Wood, who herein gives an account of his wartime experiences. A North Carolinian of New England heritage, he was an ardent Southerner with the ethnic prejudices characteristic of his period. While his scientific interests inclined him toward a medical career, his family circumstances would likely have limited him to the Wilmington drugstore (of which he gives a good description). However, his service to the Confederacy brought him to the new nation's capital at a time when its desperate need for physicians created an opportunity for a well-connected soldier to attend medical lectures. Wood gives a good account of the Richmond medical school, and especially of the Confederate Army's procedure for examining prospective assistant surgeons.

Wood's report of his field service gives a non-combatant's view of such major battles as Chancellorsville, Gettysburg, and the Wilderness, and of life in the Virginia camps. Especially rich is his narration of Jubal Early's 1864 campaign in the Shenandoah Valley and to the outskirts of Washington. As ably edited by Donald B. Koonce, Wood's papers constitute a partial history of the officers, volunteers, and conscripts of the Third North Carolina Infantry Regiment. Students of military history will be interested in Wood's report of both the fighting and the field medicine. General readers familiar with modern lengthy and specialized medical schooling may be struck by the revelation of a time when it was possible largely through self-education to become a physician, indeed a published scientific scholar and one of a state's professional leaders. Still even today's nostalgics would most likely prefer to read Wood's writing rather than to submit themselves to his medical practice.

Frank L. Byrne
Kent State University

PREFACE

In the Spring of 1886, Dr. Thomas Fanning Wood, only 45 years old at the time, lay flat on his back in bed suffering from an acute aneurysm of the aorta. The treatment, following the traditions of the day, prescribed that he remain on his back for a period of eighteen months or more, regulating his diet to simple farinaceous food and milk and iodide of potassium. Being an active, energetic man with a keen wit and probing personality and pressured by his demanding medical practice, this drastic cure presented a regimen that was rather difficult to accept. As a medical man, however, he understood the implications of ignoring the treatment and, in an attempt to prolong his life and continue his work, he followed his doctor's advice to the letter.[1] He tried to keep busy, continuing to prescribe for his patients, researching new medical discoveries and writing articles for the state's medical journal, but there was still not enough to do in this reclined state to keep his restless mind occupied.[2] In late April of 1886, he decided to make a written record of his life for his children, and during the next two years this effort grew into three full volumes, most of which involved his service as a surgeon in the Confederate Army.[3]

Written some 21 years after the Civil War this account is remarkably accurate and detailed, especially regarding the descriptions of men with whom he served, a good many not surviving the conflict. His commentary is warm, human, often humorous, and frequently open to his own prejudices and introspections. His feelings for the Irish, Yankees, and most of his senior surgeons are a bias that is exhibited unashamed. The incidents described in his writings match quite closely with letters he wrote to his parents and siblings from the actual battlefield and it is difficult, in comparison, to discern the span of so many years. These recollections serve as the foundation for this book and are supplemented with his letters from the front, newspaper articles that he wrote during the war, medical experiments and observations that he transcribed during the early war years, and various writings by and about him which the editor has added in an attempt to fully portray the depth of character, personality, and intelligence of this man of medicine.

The Civil War was a brutal and tragic war that destroyed many lives and many families, both in the North and South, but there were those fortunate few whose lives were changed for the better. Thomas Fanning Wood was one of those fortunate ones, and his chance encounter with this violent conflict led him to realize his true calling in life and gave us, even for a short time, one of this country's most distinguished scientists. The chances taken and the lessons learned during the four long years of war helped build the talent and character of this remarkable man—a physician, pharmacist, botanist, genealogist, and editor. All in the brief life span of fifty-one years. This story goes much deeper than a battle-to-battle account of the war through the eyes of an inexperienced surgeon. It brings to life the colorful journey of a young man resolutely seeking his dream of becoming a physician and the education he received on one of history's most tragic training grounds.

Thomas Fanning Wood was born and raised in one of the busiest river port towns in the South—Wilmington, North Carolina. Wilmington in the 1840s was a bustling, colorful and thriving coastal crossroads for many different countries, cultures and beliefs—and the Wood family lived right in the middle of it all. Their first home was only three blocks from the Market Square and busy waterfront along the Cape Fear River. Tom's father, Robert Barclay Wood, a brick mason, moved to Wilmington in 1839 from Nantucket after the failure of the whaling industry and quickly became a prominent builder. He and his brother John C. had originally come to Wilmington to build St. James Episcopal Church. The thirty-year-old J.C. was the "principal mason," and R.B., at 24 years of age, was the "builder". The architect for the church was Thomas U. Walter, who is most famous for designing the dome of the U.S. Capitol in Washington, D.C. Shortly after the building of St. James, the brothers decided to start the construction firm of J.C. and R.B. Wood Builders and soon acquired the contract to design and build Wilmington's City Hall, as well as a number of other significant buildings and houses in the growing community. They also helped build the first railroad between Charleston, South Carolina, and Wilmington.[4]

As Thomas grew up he experienced all of the excitement and thrill of a thriving waterfront town. He frequented the tan yard, riding the horse which walked round and round the vat grinding bark; built forts in the brick yard his father and uncle owned on Smith's Creek, about 3 1/2 miles from Wilmington; and watched molasses being made across the river at Orton Plantation. He fished for Blue Perch from the rice dikes along the river, swam in Burnt Mill Creek and joined in the fun during the traditional tar-barrel bon fires on Market Street.

His father and uncle built the Carolina Hotel on Second and Market Streets in 1841 as a speculative venture. Their advertisement for lease or sale of the building describes it as "a very commodious Hotel to be fitted up in superior style, with generally single lodging rooms . . . four stories high, of fine brick." An 1851 insurance policy described the four story brick structure as being "42'x 45', with a 22' rear addition and 25 fireplaces, 6 of which had coal stoves." Receiving no offers for lease or sale, the brothers eventually decided to operate the hotel themselves, and R.B. became so thoroughly involved in the hotel business that in the 1850 census, he listed himself as a "hotel keeper."[5] He actually moved his family into the hotel for three or four years during the 1850s.[6]

This was a wonderful time for young Thomas because he had the opportunity to see and talk with many celebrities visiting or passing through—Madame Anna Bishop and the Parodi singers, Dr. Marshall Hall—the great English physiologist, Billy Bow Legs—the captured Chief of the Florida Indians, Joseph Jefferson—the actor, and Louis Kossuth—the famous Hungarian leader in exile. He also began to help teach the hotel barber, Richard Edens, a slave, to read. This had to be done after school in secret because in those days it was illegal to teach slaves to read, and this was quite a risk for a young boy. Unfortunately, the lessons were discovered (probably by his uncle or father), and Richard was to get thirty-nine lashes as punishment. However, instead, with the help of Thomas and his mother, Richard escaped to Canada and freedom.[7]

Thomas became fascinated with science through the study in school of what was called Natural Philosophy by Apparatus, later called physics. He began to read books on heat, light, electricity, gravity, pneumatics, hydrostatics, and chemistry. Most of his teachers supported his interests, especially a Mr. Levin Meginney, whose school he attended when he was fifteen. Mr. Meginney, a Marylander, had purchased the old Odd Fellows School in the early 1850s and lived in the dwelling with his family. He was recognized as one of the foremost educators of his day and his strong moral influence had a lasting impact on the community. Thomas spent a good deal of his free time at the old school house by himself, encouraged by Mr. Meginney, doing experiments with the philosophical apparatus. He also enjoyed French, drawing, and reading, and these studies opened up new ideas that were to prove very helpful later in life. Recognizing the boy's potential, Mr. Meginney gave Thomas a new chemistry experimental outfit which he hoped would create a spark that would lead to a more in-depth study of science. It did. Thomas read and studied everything he could get his hands on and became more and more interested in the science of medicine.

About this time, Thomas became quite interested in the possibility of attending the University of North Carolina and becoming a doctor, but his father would have none of it. Robert Barclay was opposed to college, especially the University of North Carolina, and believed that young men learned very little in college except how to "dress like gentlemen and act like rowdies." He also had a prejudice against Latin and Greek. He wanted both his sons to be engineers and consented that they could attend a polytechnic college.

This decision was taken out of R.B.'s hands, however, by hard financial times during 1857. Even though the Wood brothers were prominent builders and masons, their financial situation was grim. In an earlier letter to his mother, J.C.

wrote: "We are drove to death with work.... Money never was scarcer since the world was made." During the fifteen years they owned the Carolina Hotel, J.C. and R.B. used it as collateral for loans totaling an astounding sum, exceeding twenty-one thousand dollars. With mounting debts and money scarce, they eventually lost everything, and the firm of J.C. and R.B. Wood was dissolved.[8] J.C. had been taking jobs at Fort Caswell "to superintend the (repair) work" because the government pay was good. In 1859 R.B. was engaged by Major W.H. Whiting of the U.S. Engineer Corp to build a light house on Hunting Island about thirty miles east of Beaufort, South Carolina. Thomas accompanied his father and spent the summer on the island and nearby at "Coffin Point Plantation" owned by a cousin, Thomas A. Coffin. Here he first became interested in botany, spending his days wandering through the dunes and palmetto forests, making crude drawings of plants and trees. In mid summer his father suddenly came down with severe dysentery, and it was impossible to get a doctor in such a remote location. Tom knew nothing of diseases, having never read a line of medical practice, but something had to be done. He went to *Dunglison's Medical Dictionary*, which he had borrowed from a doctor in Wilmington, and looked up the word "dysentery." Based solely on his reading, he selected Dover's Powder because it had Opium in it. This powdered drug contained both opium and ipecac and was used to relieve pain and induce perspiration. He turned back to *Dunglison* and found the composition of the medicine and the dose. With this as a guide, he gave his father five gram doses every three hours, and soon the pain ceased, and his father became comfortable. In a few days, he was well again.[9]

Financially, things remained pretty discouraging after they returned to Wilmington, and Thomas's hope of a medical career was again put aside. His father and uncle had gone down to Federal Point to help R.B.'s employer, W. H. C. Whiting, build the new fortification at the mouth of the Cape Fear River to be named Fort Fisher. His older brother, Robert Barclay, Jr., went to work as Deputy Clerk of the County Court, and Thomas was also expected to find a job to help support the family. In the fall of 1859, Thomas found employment as a teacher at a country school five miles south of town. He was paid one hundred dollars for three months and found lodging with the family of Thomas H. Williams. He was put up in the shed room, which was small and drafty with little or no light to read by. After one night of this, he decided to walk the distance of ten miles a day rather than sleeping in the shed. He had still not given up on medicine and used his small salary to purchase medical books, and his collection grew—*Chiselden's Anatomy, Darwin's Zoonomia,* and *Draper's Physiology*.

After the school term was over, he found employment as a clerk for the attorney, Mr. Eli W. Hall. Hall had a large and successful practice in Wilmington and won fame in the courts as a ready and able debater. According to his clients and competitors alike, he was a courteous, honorable, well-read gentleman of strict integrity and warmly popular in all classes of society. He was elected to the North Carolina Senate in 1860, 1862 and again in 1864.[10] Thomas's salary was twenty-five dollars a month and he worked at night as a writer for the Methodist newspaper, "The Messenger," under the name Thomas Didymus.[11] He spent his free time across the street from the law office, at the offices of Dr. James F. McRee, Jr. where he continued to probe the mysteries of medical science. Dr. McRee was the son of the distinguished and beloved physician and botanist, Dr. James Fergus McRee, who had also served the community as Commissioner of Wilmington and magistrate of police. Old Dr. McRee had passed his practice along to his son, which included an abundant library of medical volumes.[12] In 1860, with Dr. McRee's help, Thomas secured a position in Mr. Louis B. Erambert's prescription drug store, located on the first floor of the Carolina Hotel, which gave him the opportunity to further his study of chemistry and pharmacy. He also found time to volunteer as the secretary for the newly formed "Committee of Safety," organized to defend a nervous community on the eve of war. It is at this point in Thomas's life that this book begins, giving details of his service with the Confederate Army and the beginnings of his medical career.

After the firing on Fort Sumter and the secession of South Carolina, numerous military organizations began to organize throughout the city of Wilmington, and Thomas began to drill with the Wilmington Rifle Guards. Once North Carolina seceded, the State Legislature ordered the formation of ten regiments of State troops, and the Wilmington Rifle Guards became part of first the 8th Volunteers and then the 18th North Carolina Regiment. They were assigned to non-violent duty at Fort Fisher, North Carolina, Coosahatchie, South Carolina, and Kinston, North Carolina, before experiencing their first real combat during the Seven Days Battles in front of Richmond. In these memoirs, Wood describes the almost vacation-like atmosphere of the early days in the army and the juvenile attitude of most of the soldiers. He records how the rank and file scoffed at discipline and how the men perceived it as a manly challenge to disobey orders. Their first real taste of war came during the Battle of Mechanicsville in Virginia, and it was a life-changing experience for most of the young men in the regiment. They would never again be able to return to the boyish lifestyle and carefree attitudes of just weeks before. They had met the beast and their lives would forever be changed. After the Battle of Hanover Court House, Tom came down with a severe case of Chickahominy Fever and was sent to the North Carolina hospital in Richmond. While recovering, he made the acquaintance of the Surgeon-in-Charge, Dr. Otis Manson, who recognized Tom's interest in medicine and put him in charge of one of the wards. It was an intelligent decision and, understanding that the young Confederacy had an acute shortage of surgeons for this escalating conflict, Dr. Manson encouraged Tom to attend lectures at the Virginia Medical College there in Richmond. It was the turning point in his life. This is one of the most interesting and poignant chapters in the book. For the first time in his life Tom actually sees the possibility of becoming a physician within his grasp and the writing is charged with eagerness and a sense of urgency. His descriptions of Moore Hospital and his duties there present a clear and concise picture of the crowded and unsanitary conditions in most hospitals in Richmond at the time. The acute shortage of medicines, inadequate transportation and insufficient training of medical staffs in the early years of the war was beginning to create serious problems by the time Tom began his studies at the Medical College.

In eight short months, he was invited to appear before the Army Board of Examiners and, after passing a grueling examination, was appointed Assistant Surgeon in the Confederate Army. Dr. Thomas Fanning Wood was ordered to report to the 3rd North Carolina Regiment, Stonewall Jackson's corps, just prior to the Battle of Chancellorsville. He was just a few hundred yards from General Jackson, tending Union wounded, when the North Carolina troops fired on the general's staff, critically wounding Jackson. Dr. Wood's ambulance driver transported the wounded general to the field hospital behind the lines. Dr. Wood tended the sick, wounded, and dying of the 3rd Regiment through the battles for Culp's Hill at Gettysburg and witnessed the total destruction of the 3rd Regiment during the desperate struggle for the "Muleshoe" at Spotsylvania. Desperately short of drugs and medical supplies, he did what he could for the sick and wounded of the now combined remnants of the 3rd and 1st North Carolina Regiments at Cold Harbor, and rode with Jubal Early on his daring raid to the Federal Capitol. He finally surrendered, marching near the front of the column as part of Gordon's corps, along with no more than thirty remaining members of the once formidable 3rd North Carolina, at Appomattox, Virginia, April 12, 1865. On April 13th he began his long journey home on foot—more than two hundred miles—tending to the sick and wounded along the way.

The life on the front lines for the young surgeon was often overwhelming. Most army physicians were so swamped with soldier-patients that they could only perform some kind of needed treatment as expeditiously as possible. Insufficient training, fear of infection, and impossible conditions forced many surgeons to resort to the speedier and supposedly more reliable option of amputation. The majority of amputations were performed at so-called "field hospitals" a mile or two behind enemy lines. This is where Dr. Wood spent a good deal of his time, especially after the Gettysburg Campaign. These medical stations were often hastily selected locations. On the front porch or in the yard of abandoned farmhouses, the surgeons grimly went about their work treating badly wounded men. Operating tables ranged from the tailgate of a wagon to a door laid atop two barrels. An incredibly large number of battlefield operations, especially in the South, took place with no painkillers at all. Patients already unconscious from shock were often regarded as naturally prepped for surgery. In some cases, surgeons came to believe that pain was an appropriate combatant against shock.[13]

The facts speak for themselves and paint a horrifying picture of what the Civil War physician had to face every day. Between 1861 and 1865 approximately 620,000 men perished from battle wounds and sickness; more than in all of the nation's other wars combined.[14] American medical knowledge lagged a generation behind that in Europe. Stethoscopes and microscopes were rare instruments in the United States at the time of the war and no more than ten thermometers were used in all of the Confederate armies. Few surgeons North or South had any idea that unseen organisms called germs played any part in infection.[15] Diseases ravaged the troops in the field. One of the largest military hospitals in Richmond recorded 47,176 admissions over a two-year period. Of these, only 6,740 were wounded soldiers. Only 17,845 were returned to duty. The 3,031 deaths during that same time-span included only 377 men who succumbed to wounds.[16]

Dr. Wood transcribed his experiences during the war in an attempt to leave for his children a personal account of his involvement in the greatest and most deadly conflict ever to take place on American soil. It is assumed that out of consideration for his audience, he avoided the details of daily medical duty that illustrate the full horror of this war but instead focused on the personality and character of his life as an assistant surgeon in the 3rd North Carolina Regiment. His role in this conflict could certainly not be as casual as he sometimes describes it and the scenes he witnessed must have haunted his dreams for the rest of his life.

The war had taken its toll, and a good number of Dr. Wood's Wilmington friends did not return home, but for him the war had firmly set his course. He had just experienced his residency by fire and was fully prepared to take on the medical needs of his community. Dr. Wood returned to Lumberton, North Carolina, where his family had taken up residence during the war. It is not certain whether he actually practiced medicine in Lumberton but on February 22, 1866, he married Adelia Powell Fuller of Lumberton. They had a son Thomas Powell Wood in February of 1867, but he died a little over two months later. Thomas and Adelia moved to Wilmington in 1868 and had a second son, John Fuller Wood. Adelia died in July, 1870, at 26 years of age, followed by her second son nine months later.[17] It is assumed that all three perished from disease, which probably increased Dr Wood's passionate commitment to public health.

Dr. Wood began the practice of medicine in Wilmington in August of 1865, while still living in Lumberton, and was quickly placed in charge of the small pox hospital, managing the troublesome epidemic brought to the city by the war, and which had prevailed for nearly a year. Dr. Wood's intense interest in the study of small pox and the non-traditional use of the cowpox virus, in vaccination form, as a preventative measure against the disease, was a direct result of his work at Moore's Hospital during the war.[18] This hospital, under the guidance of Dr. Wood, cared for hundreds of patients, and the experience in caring for the poor and suffering in his hometown became his schooling in public health. In 1866 he was granted a medical license from the Board of Medical Examiners, in their first meeting since 1861, and in 1868 an Honorary Degree of M.D. was conferred on him by The University of Maryland.[19] He never forgot his role in the war nor his strong feelings of loyalty to the South. As a result of disagreements with Federal authorities over local medical practices, he refused to work in a Federal hospital unless he could wear his Confederate uniform.[20]

His experience with the small pox epidemic intensified his study of viral diseases and increased his concern for the general health and welfare of the people in the state, leading him to begin the formation of a State Board of Health. After repeated petition by Dr. Wood, the legislature of North Carolina enacted the first law in 1877 creating a State Board of Health and making the North Carolina State Medical Society the first Board with an annual appropriation of one hundred dollars for its operations.[21] It wasn't much but it was a beginning, and he immediately set about planning for the future development of this new Board of Health. A colleague, Dr. George M. Cooper, said of Dr. Wood, "It is readily seen that Dr. Wood's great pioneer work was not done for selfish reason or personal or professional aggrandizement but for his deep love for human welfare, which is exemplified in every act of his life."[22]

Doctor Wood was the twenty-second member of the newly formed North Carolina Medical Society to sign its Constitution in 1867 and from that moment until his death, he was one of the most powerful influences for good works in the Society. He was made the first secretary of the Medical Society, and in 1882 and again in 1891, was elected president. He was elected to the Board of Medical Examiners in 1878 and appointed by the legislature to the office of Secretary of the State Board of Health, the organization he had founded. He served in that capacity until his death.[23]

Thomas Fanning Wood never forgot his experiences during the war and dedicated the rest of his life to using the lessons he had learned in the field hospitals and on the front lines to fight disease and illness. He began to insist on the application of army policies concerning sanitation and hygiene to civilian health issues and was later instrumental in helping bring about medical reform in the United States. He promoted better hospital ventilation and called on his experiences at Moore Hospital to help perfect the ward

Thomas Fanning Wood, M.D., c. 1886. About the time of his illness. Thomas Fanning Wood Collection, Wilmington, N.C.

system. He supported the efforts to make dietary needs an important part of patient treatment and spent a great deal of time in researching the prevention and treatment of infectious disease.

Committed to spreading the word about the importance of good hygiene and cleanliness, as well as promoting the good works of the Medical Society and the State Board of Health, he began editing and publishing the *North Carolina Medical Journal* in 1878 as a private publication. Several of his wartime friends and associates numbered among the advisors to this journal, including Dr. Hunter McGuire, the former Medical Director for the Army of Northern Virginia, Dr. Otis Manson, his old mentor in Richmond, and Dr. John Wellford, his professor at the Medical College of Virginia.[24] The *Medical Journal* had originally been started by Dr. Edward Warren, a distinguished physician from Edenton, North Carolina, but had ceased publication at the beginning of the war.[25] Dr. Wood revived the *Medical Journal* and continued as self-imposed editor for the next fifteen years, furnishing to the North Carolina medical profession a medium of regular communication and keeping alive the interests of human welfare.

He was elected a member of the Committee of Revision of the Pharmacopoeia of the United States for the decade 1880 to 1890 and then again from

1890 to 1900. In 1891 he was elected first vice-president of the American Public Health Association, and the University of North Carolina conferred upon him the honorary degree of LL.D. in 1888.

He continued his passion for botany and collected plants throughout the rest of his life. He was especially interested in insectivorous plants growing around Wilmington, such as the Venus Fly Trap, and wrote numerous articles for scientific societies throughout the country. In 1886 he co-authored a book with Gerald McCarthy about plants growing about the Wilmington area, entitled *Wilmington Flora: A List of Plants Growing About Wilmington, North Carolina*. A newspaper article written in the 1940s mentions that Dr. Wood had catalogued over 1,202 species of plants growing within a radius of ten miles of Wilmington.[26]

In November of 1875, he married Mary Kennedy Sprunt and they had five children. One of his sons, Edward Jenner, was destined to carry on his father's legacy, becoming a renowned physician in his own right. He received the degree of Doctor of Tropical Medicine at the Royal College of Physicians and Surgeons of London and among his many notable achievements was the cure for the tropical diseases of Pellagra and Sprue.

In the spring of 1885, while accompanying penitentiary officials on a tour of convict camps, Dr. Thomas Fanning Wood experienced a stabbing pain in

Robert Barclay Wood and his sons in 1875–77. Left to Right: Robert Barclay Wood, Thomas Fanning Wood, M.D., Alfred Vincent Wood, Robert Barclay Wood, Jr. Courtesy, Cape Fear Museum, A. Jarvis Wood, Jr. Collection.

his right side. At the request of medical friends in Wilmington, he went to New York for a check-up. The diagnosis was an aneurysm of the aorta and the treatment was his exile to bed for almost two years.[27]

In July of 1888, Dr. Wood finally decided to cease his confinement, got out of bed, and continued with his medical profession. He soon became as active as ever in political and scientific matters concerning the health of the people in North Carolina. However, his own health problems were not relieved, and he began to suffer once again from his weakened heart. He knew that the end was near, and this knowledge drove him even harder to accomplish the goals which he had set for himself. At approximately 2:00 A.M. on August 22, 1892, he died at the age of fifty-one. Those fifty-one years had changed the course of public health in North Carolina.

At the time of his death, the president of the Board of Medical Examiners and State Board of Health made the following statement: "In all that elevates and ennobles the human race, Dr. Thomas Fanning Wood was a shining example. He was one of those rare men who stand out in the history of a century to show that the grace of God does, even now, conform fallen man to his divine likeness. The mainspring of his character was charity—that God given inspiration, which raises man to the level of the angels, and stamps the perfect type of enlightened civilization—a Christian gentleman."[28]

This edition of Dr. Wood's reminiscences, letters, articles, and comments seeks to preserve the legacy of the Doctor's valuable service to mankind and present a brief glimpse of his role as a surgeon on the field during one of this country's most tragic conflicts. The three volumes, comprising his remembrances of the Civil War, contained in this book are part of a collection now housed at the William Madison Randall Library of the University of North Carolina at Wilmington. This collection also includes the five letters he wrote anonymously as a correspondent for the *Wilmington Journal* during Jubal Early's campaign in the Valley and the raid on Washington. He signed these letters or articles with the initials, "U.U.D." No records have been found to explain the strange signature on these letters unless he felt that his identity would violate the Confederate government's warning to soldiers not to write home about sensitive military matters. The initials could be translated as "double U. D." or "WD" for wood. Some twenty letters, which Dr. Wood wrote to members of his family during the war, survived in the hands of his older brother Robert B. Wood, Jr. These letters were destroyed after his death in 1920. In the late 1980s a notebook containing copies of these letters was found among the papers of Alfred V. Wood, Jr. which were apparently made for his historical collection prior to the destruction of the originals. These letters, except for one, now belong to the family of Arthur Jarvis Wood, Jr. One letter, the only original letter surviving, addressed to "Dear Lydia" and dated June 10, 1864, was found in a trunk in Charleston, South Carolina, some years ago and is in a private collection. Seventeen of these letters are part of this book and present an interesting contrast between the forty-five year-old veteran physician, remembering the war some twenty-three years later, and the twenty-one year old, newly appointed assistant surgeon mired in the middle of this deadly conflict. At the same time, they also offer a surprisingly clear and detailed connection with the everyday actions and emotions of the men who shared this unforgettable experience.

In recognition of the value of Dr. Wood's natural writing style, editorial comments, corrections, insertions, and deletions have been kept to a minimum except to clarify specific events or references. Dr. Wood's spelling, with the exception of geographic places and individual person's names has generally been preserved. He spelled General George Hume Steuart's name in various ways throughout his memoirs, including Stewart and Stuart. Since there was a William F. Stewart in the 3rd North Carolina Regiment and certainly General J. E. B. Stuart as the illustrious cavalry commander, the spelling has been corrected to avoid confusion. Dr. Wood also spelled Colonel Stephen Decatur Thruston's name as Thurston. The Official Records, North Carolina Troops and the Southern Historical Society Papers spell his name as Thruston. Several Wilmington newspapers in April 1863 have official notices from the Headquarters, 3rd Reg't N.C. Inf'y that were signed "S.D. Thruston, Lt. Col. Comd'g". Because Thruston's name appears so many times in this book, and because there was a Thurston on the regimental staff of the 3rd North Carolina as well as a William Thurston in Wilmington, the spelling has been corrected to allow for easier reading. He also misspells John C. Breckinridge's name as Breckenridge which the editor has corrected in the text. Illuminatory notes to set events in context are inserted in italics in appropriate places in the text, and explanatory details relating to people, places, and times are footnoted. Bracketed inserts are used for additional identification of: an item, place, or individual, correction for accuracy, word or an additional word to make a sentence grammatically intelligible. All insertions in parentheses were added by Thomas Fanning Wood. Commas have been added where needed and paragraphs included to break excessively long narrative passages. Chapter breaks have been devised by the editor in accordance with Dr. Wood's style and subject changes. In all, however, editorial impositions have been used sparingly to preserve the character and personality of Dr. Wood's unique remembrances.

Dr. Thomas Fanning Wood was not only a unique and talented physician, his writings show that he was also an extremely colorful character with an enlightened wit—occasionally careless and opinionated—but still a brilliant mixture of energy, creativity, ambition, courage and ability. He was one of a select group of doctors that clearly understood the need for change in medical science and helped pioneer a new approach to public health. This is his story.

ACKNOWLEDGMENTS

Since I was a young boy, the image of my great-grandfather, the Civil War hero, loomed over me as a mystical icon to be properly revered by old men and small boys. When my second grade teacher mentioned his name, I was told to stand up and tell the class all I knew about the grand doctor who was my ancestor. Sadly, I knew very little to tell them. My parents mentioned his name frequently but seldom explained who he was or what he did to merit such acclaim. In my vivid imagination he became the valiant soldier who stormed breastworks and captured gun emplacements against overwhelming odds. He was the striking and ramrod-straight general, leading his men through the wall of bullets to break the Yankee lines. I can remember the times that I became him as I stormed those impregnable Yankee entrenchment's in my back yard.

When I was about eleven, my father destroyed that image by explaining that Thomas Fanning Wood was a regimental assistant surgeon during the war and did not even carry a gun. As a non-combatant, he didn't even carry a sword that could be passed down to his ever-loyal great-grandson. What a crushing blow. The heroic image that I had created passed into oblivion and did not surface again for many years. When he did surface again, I was in college and as a history major, studying the Civil War, he demanded my attention. For the first time I began to truly understand the contribution surgeons made during that terrible conflict and the danger he faced as a front-line physician, armed with only his wits and his compassion. His memory sustained my growing interest in the Civil War and medicine. Once again Thomas Fanning Wood, M.D. became the hero of my childhood but with far more substance and character. I began to make a study of his life and promised myself that one day I would do something significant to honor his memory.

I had heard rumors, in the family, that he had written a memoir of his war experiences and that his daughters Maggie and Jeannie had carefully protected it and passed it on to his grandson, Thomas Fanning Wood, III. In 1993, I had the opportunity to read a version of these memoirs, that had been typed by his daughter Maggie, and realized that it was a valuable piece of Civil War history and should be shared with the public. After the death of Thomas Fanning Wood, III, in 1994, the original memoir came into my hands, and I realized that I finally had the opportunity to make good on my promise to do something significant to honor his memory.

The editing of Thomas Fanning Wood's memoirs and the assembly of this book have been a rewarding personal experience, but I certainly could not have done it without the help of many people. My sincere thanks go to all of the wonderful friends that I have made and who have generously helped me through this project. David Moltke-Hansen, director of the Center for the Study of the American South, encouraged me to pursue the project and sent the rough manuscript to Dr. Gary Gallagher who in turn recommended that I send it to the University of Tennessee Press. I am especially grateful to Gerald Parnell, archivist at the Randall Library, University of North Carolina at Wilmington, who was always there when I needed help and spent countless hours researching elusive connections to TFW. Jerry is the new curator for the Thomas Fanning Wood Collection which has been donated to the University of North Carolina at Wilmington. My sincere thanks also go to Dr. Chris E. Fonvielle Jr. for his valued friendship and support and for his eagerness to take time from his own projects to root out answers to my often bizarre research questions.

Janet Seapker, executive director of the Cape Fear Museum was always there and willing to share information about early Wilmington and TFW's early life. Patricia LaPointe with the Memphis County Library graciously filled in some gaps regarding the Reverend George Patterson and his life after the war. John Heiser and Gregory Coco with the National Military Park at Gettysburg have supported me in my efforts from the very beginning and were extremely helpful in identifying TFW's field dressing station during the Battle of Gettysburg. I am very grateful to Robert Krick with Richmond National Battlefield Park for his efforts to help me locate Moore Hospital and expand my knowledge of the medical environment in Richmond during the war. Donald Pfanz, with the Fredericksburg and Spotsylvania National Military Park, was always eager to help me locate field hospitals, sort out sometimes confusing troop movements and decipher TFW's battlefield descriptions. Julie Reid illustrated the wonderful maps in this book and her patience with my sometimes vague descriptions and my last minute changes after visiting battlefield sites, is greatly appreciated. My very sincere thanks go to Debbie Hinkle for her continuous support and for the many hours spent, in various libraries and book stores, trying find more information for me on wartime Richmond. Much gratitude goes to Jennifer Siler with the University of Tennessee Press for her patience, help, and encouragement, and to Dr. Frank Cooling, Dr. Frank Byrne, and Dr. Gary Gallagher for reading the early manuscript and offering their valuable guidance.

Dr. Thomas Fanning Wood penned his memoirs for his children as a recollection of his life with an emphasis on his Civil War experiences and the men with whom he served. He did not spend a great deal of time focusing on his responsibilities or experiences as a battlefield surgeon but concentrated on his relationships and personal encounters as a member of the Army of Northern Virginia. I felt that it was important to support these recollections with a description of the duties and heavy responsibilities he faced every day as a battlefield surgeon. A number of talented and dedicated people helped me fill in the medical side of this account, and I am eternally grateful to all of them. I am especially grateful to Dr. Josephine Newell, founder and curator of the Country Doctor Museum, a beautiful and talented lady who offered continuous encouragement and support and endless hours of help in sorting out TFW's fascinating medical background. Jackson Marshall with the North Carolina Museum of History was also very helpful and always available to answer my medical queries. Alex Peck with Antique Scientifica provided valuable information concerning the Civil War surgeon's pocket kit. I am extremely grateful to Dr. Joe Nance for helping me identify medical terminology and references from TFW's early experiments and writings. My personal thanks go to Dr. Jack Lynch and Dr. Joe Hooper for reviewing the manuscript and offering their thoughts.

I am blessed with a remarkable family that has not only supported my efforts in this project but have been equally dedicated to the preservation of our family's legacy. My first cousin Francis Loughlin has been a constant source of encouragement and support. My cousins Jenner Wood and niece Dudley MacFarlane have always been there when I need them. My late uncle's wife, Fran, has been interested in this project from the start and is that special someone I can always lean on for support. Thanks to my wonderful children, Stacey and Brock, who have been a constant source of inspiration and motivation and no longer have to begin every conversation with, "Well Dad, is it done?" To all of my family I express my sincere personal thanks for your patience and love and for trying to understand why it has taken so long to finish this book.

And finally, it would be impossible to express the gratitude I feel for my wife, B.J., and her unending support of this book. She has cheerfully endured countless hours of proofing manuscripts or listening to the latest research breakthrough, or following me through old battlefields in search of troop dispositions or field hospitals. She has patiently waited for this book to be finished—for the last time—so I can return from the Civil War to the twenty-first century, if only for a brief time. She is definitely my inspiration and without her love and support, this book would not have been possible.

Doctor to the Front

THE RECOLLECTIONS OF
CONFEDERATE SURGEON
THOMAS FANNING WOOD

1861–1865

ONE

MR. ERAMBERT'S DRUGSTORE

By 1860 tensions in Wilmington, North Carolina, were increasing steadily and there was already talk of secession. The political and business leaders in the city and throughout the state were seriously divided on the issue, and many friendships became strained. Thomas Fanning Wood's father was a firm Unionist while his brother J.C. fiercely believed in secession. Later in 1860, at the age of 45, R.B. changed his loyalties and joined a special company of mounted horse guards for home defense.[1]

Very little documentation exists to explain the split between the Wood brothers over their loyalty to the Union, but it probably had something to do with their religious commitments. Both families tended to divide their worship between the Presbyterian, Methodist and Episcopal churches. R.B. often turned to St. James Episcopal Church, which he helped build. St. James was a conservative congregation with few secessionists and a tolerance for Unionist sentiments. The Reverend D. Drane was a Northern man. It was an atmosphere that could have easily preserved R.B.'s loyal feelings for his New England roots. Little is known of J.C.'s religious affiliations but it was most likely with the Front Street Methodist Church, which the brothers also helped to build. This was known as the people's church and spiritual direction tended to follow the will of the people and the climate of the times. This was a difficult time for the two brothers. The business had failed, and both men were forced to seek employment building the new fortifications at the mouth of the Cape Fear River. It is not unreasonable to assume that the troubles in the business could have helped contribute to the brothers' split in allegiances.[2] There is no evidence that the Woods owned slaves, but they could have rented them, and this arrangement, especially in the construction business, was acceptable in antebellum Wilmington. In addition to slaves, many free blacks worked in the construction trades.[3]

Thomas himself was drawn to the Front Street Methodist Church by friends during the religious revival of 1857. He left St. James and joined the Methodist church at the age of sixteen, and it was here that he began to follow many other young people in their growing belief in secessionism.[4]

The town was deeply troubled and old friendships were straining. People waited for the politicians in Washington to sort out the differences between the North and South, but the gap was widening every day. Thomas Fanning Wood, in an attempt to help relieve the financial burden on his family after the tough year of 1857, had worked as a teacher and a law clerk but was still in serious financial straits. He needed a better-paying job badly and had all but given up on his hopes of a medical career. Fortunately, his friend, Dr. James McRee, helped him secure a position in a new prescription drug store owned by a devout secessionist, Mr. Louis Erambert. The drug store was often the headquarters for Mr. Erambert's secessionist friends, and the meeting place to share news of the growing unrest in the state.[5]

The year 1860 found me 19 years of age and as financially bad off as ever. I agreed to take a situation in a new prescription drug store just started by Louis B. Erambert. [6] The conditions were that I was to keep store during his absence, and employ my time in study to suit myself otherwise. He also bought me quite a good outfit of apparatus to pursue the study of chemistry.

It was a great disappointment to have to give up school lectures again but I soon got interested in my close attention in pharmacy and chemistry, and I believe now it was a lasting benefit to me in many ways. My first contribution to a medical journal was while engaged at the drug store. Oxide of silver was in much repute as a remedy, and several times it had been observed that spontaneous combustion or explosion took place. The druggists did not know why, some attributing it to the honey used, and some claiming to remedy it by the use of ext. [extract of] gentian.[7] I undertook the study, and contributed the results to the North Carolina Medical Journal, then edited by Dr. Edward Warren at Edenton.[8] My point was this, that oxide of silver precipitated from the solution of the nitrate by ammonia was explosive and that precipitated by a fixed alkali like soda or lime was not. I used to think that this was an original discovery, but I saw it in Paroira's Therapeutics and Mat. Mad.[9] of a date prior to 1859, so I must have obtained it there. At any rate, I found it to be new or rather that it was a piece of forgotten information quite applicable to a wide spread inquiry. This was my first contribution (I signed it, Medical student) and I was greatly delighted when I saw my work actually in print in a Medical Journal. I must confess though that I kept the secret of my authorship to myself until many years afterwards.[10]

I saw for the first time during those days the application of a surgical splint, which afterwards came into universal use during the war. It was "Smith's Anterior Splint." The old splint used for fractured thigh was a simple long outside splint, confining the patient to his back for six months, almost always resulting in bed sores, and making the treatment a great ordeal from which the patient frequently succumbed. The introduction of the splint

The Bonitz Hotel, owned by J. H. William Bonitz in the 1880s. Located on the corner of Market and Second Streets in Wilmington, it was formerly the Carolina Hotel, owned by Robert Barclay and John Coffin Wood. Erambert's Drug Store was on the right corner at street level. Courtesy, Cape Fear Museum, McCoy Collection.

was noteworthy. Dr. McRee applied it after directions and illustration from the Maryland and Virginia Medical Journal to Ned Glavin, an employee at the W. and W.R.R. The first form of the splint was of wood and made by the master carpenter of the road, John Wright. By means of the splint the patient could change his position quite freely in bed, something entirely new and very desirable. The case was a fracture of the leg and not a test one, but the principal as here introduced was for the first time applied in North Carolina. It helped Confederate Surgeons greatly during the war.[11]

I liked my work in the drug store, and spent most of my time reading and informing myself about the qualities of drugs. A sad disaster to Mr. Erambert brought upon me the full work of the establishment. It seems that a number of Chapel Hill students collected in the store on Saturday night after I had started home. The young men were in various degrees of intoxication. Mr. Erambert was at the dispensing scales cleaning his pistol. Some words ensued between a young man named "Pink" Shelly and he fired, shooting Jack Costin in the fleshy part of the buttocks. Mr. Erambert by this time had his pistol loaded. He went to the front door, pistol in hand, and he and Shelly must have fired at the same time. Mr. Erambert fell to the pavement with his thigh broken.[12] I heard the firing and returned to the store, and found matters in great disorder. The wounded were carried home, Mr. Erambert to be confined for six months. This left me in the possession of the business, and as I had no experience as a drug merchant, and as Mr. Erambert was too sick to talk business, I was in some trouble. I had to go to the store after breakfast and stay until 9 o'clock at night, closely confined.

In the meantime the loud talk of war had culminated in the secession of South Carolina, and the firing of the State Militia on Fort Sumpter.[13] The excitement was great in Wilmington. North Carolina had not seceded, and was in no hurry to take the step. Town meetings were held to discuss the questions. Dr. James H. Dickson made a very warm speech in favor of the union, and advised the people to be not hasty, in following South Carolina. That during the war of the Revolution our friends were the Virginians and Marylanders, and that we had better wait. If Virginia seceded we had no choice by reason of our geographical condition, but until then nothing as rash as secession should be attempted.

Dr. Dickson was an elderly physician of great reputation as a practitioner, and of a rapidly growing reputation as a Belles Lettres scholar. He had made several addresses at the University in 1855 and afterwards one before the public in the interests of the Wilmington Library Association. He was the president of that association and with the assistance of Mr. George Davis, was responsible for collecting the funds to establish it. Dr. Dickson was a very studious man. When not interrupted he read absorbedly in the intervals of his visits. When physicians abandoned the keeping of medicines in their offices he got more time and begun the collection of a professional library. At the time, about '59, there was no decent medical library in town. I saw for the first time, in this collection, books beyond the ordinary text books. "Bennetts Practice", "Bowman's Cyc. of Anatomy" and a few others.

Dr. Dickson was a very consistent member of, and an elder in the Presbyterian Church. In his latter years he was noted for his great punctuality at church notwithstanding he did the largest practice in town. He was universally relied upon both as a citizen and a physician. His council was sought upon the most varied topics. He was a strong Whig and adhered to his party friends "through thick and thin", and many are the instances I have heard of his helping hand to struggling young men in the community. In the sick room he was quiet, non-committal, reserved and cold until he was warmed up by cases of interest either professionally or those which drew out his sympathy by reasons of distressing circumstances of his patient. He was a man who placed the proper estimate upon the seriousness of our lives. He did all he did with earnestness and devotion to duty, and his Christian example remains to this day as a precious legacy.

In 1862 the Yellow Fever was brought into Wilmington on the steamer Kate from Nassau. The first cases were not recognized as Yellow Fever—it was the first visitation during the memory of any of our doctors. Dr. Dickson was taken and died with the fever in September of 1862.[14]

After the total failure of the "Peace Conference" in Washington, in 1861, it was evident that war must come pretty soon. Never-the-less, many good citizens desired and hoped to secure the Union.[15] I was a secessionist. It seemed to me that the North would not let slavery alone until we had a war, and the sooner begun the better. My father was a firm Unionist, and spoke his mind so freely that I only talked secession among my friends away from home. Mr. Erambert was a secessionist and his store was headquarters for the news. He was a Lt. [Lieutenant] in the Light Infantry and prided himself on his knowledge of tactics and studied books on that subject very attentively. The young men wore secession rosettes made of small pine "burs".

A company of about 25 men, supporting the Union, known as the "Cape Fear Minute Men", was formed as an imitation of a like organization in the Revolutionary War. They were fire eaters even in a town where it was no longer safe to talk against secession and when Lincoln's call for 75,000 men was sent out, nearly the entire community went over to the Secession Party. Dr. J. B. Carr, a New York dentist, very unpopular, at the time of the trouble was carrying on a dairy farm, and was accused of some ugly transactions in connection with that business. He was an officious "Minute Man" and wore the blue ribbon on his coat "CFMM".[16] Nearly every northern man was suspected of not being truly southern if he had not enlisted in some sort of military company. My father although over 45 years joined a company of mounted horse-guards for home defense. Shortly after this and before this company had fully organized, he was taken with sciatica—a most painful disease of the muscles and nerves of the fleshy part of the thigh. I remember how he suffered and how intolerant his stomach was to laudanum and morphine. He had a hard time of it but finally recovered. During his confinement, a elderly carpenter by the name of Rose, a CFMM fire-eater, spread the word that my father was not a true southerner and his sickness was feigned. It did not damage his reputation, however, for he had friends among many people higher in the social scale than Mr. Rose, who knew very well that my father would do his duty in whatever cause he undertook. Although he saw the revolution going on with pain and gloomy foreboding for the future, he gave all of his energies, from first to last, to the southern cause. None had the principle of defense to the bitter end more deeply ingrained than my father.

I met with a terrible accident to my eyes during my stay at Mr. Erambert's. I had a call for Granville's Lotion in haste. It was to be made with stronger ammonia. This chemical is bottled cold and labeled with a caution that it must not be opened until it has been cooled to a certain temperature. The old Negro woman hurried me so saying, "Marse John was mighty bad off," that I disregarded the precaution given and as I knocked off the putty from the glass stopper, the caustic gas escaped in my face, and I went one way and the old woman the other. I was fearfully strangled and blinded, and rushed to the door and into the middle of the street, throwing up my arms in the agony of suffocation, and then darted for the Carolina Hotel which was next door. I remember seeing old Mr. William C. Bettencourt in the front part, but in seeing me he pictured a crazy man and got out of my way. Only one man had the sense to help me and he led me to the back part of the Hotel to a bucket of water. I ducked my head in the bucket and opened my eyes freely to wash out all the hartshorn [ammonia] and soon was taken home. This accident gave me bad inflammation of the eyes with which I suffered for several weeks, passing most of the time in a dark room, where only a little taper floating in oil kept burning day and night furnished the light I could stand. It was a very lonely confinement but Ma and my sister Agnes nursed me faithfully.[17] I can remember how difficult it was for me to walk when I first got up and I was very weak owing to the confinement in that dark room. Luckily, my eyes were not permanently damaged by the accident.

Everything kept for sale in drugstores, and in fact all kinds of shopkeepers' merchandise, became at once very valuable. The South had no foreign trade, and all drugs came from the North. I made a grand mistake for Mr. E. about this time. He was wounded and could give me no advice, and I found that his stock was running quite low. I made up an invoice largely in excess of anything he was in the habit of ordering. I recollect that when he saw the bill he looked frightened. One of the items was a gross of chamois skins, which seemed to be big elephants. It was discovered, at an early date, that chamois was in demand for sword covers, and that in fact everything found a ready sale. What would have been a blunder was a fortunate adventure—for as the intercourse was quickly suspended with the North, everything in the drug store was in demand. It was not long before merchants, especially Jews, were ransacking the country to pick up anything they could find, to hold for higher prices. An editor of one of the papers said that they would bottle up air to hold for a rise if they could.

TWO

JOINING THE
RIFLE GUARDS

In January of 1861, alarmed over the conditions in Charleston Harbor, the leaders in Wilmington decided to risk no further delays. A meeting of the citizens was held in the courthouse, and the Committee of Safety was charged with organizing various volunteer companies into a temporary defense of the city. At that time Thomas Fanning Wood, at 20 years old, was serving as secretary for the Committee of Safety.[1] On January 9, 1861, the Committee of Safety sent the Wilmington Light Infantry and newly formed Wilmington Rifle Guards under the command of Major John J. Hedrick to take possession of Fort Johnston and Fort Caswell at the mouth of the Cape Fear River. Fort Johnston, at Smithville, was surrendered by Sergeant Reilly, and Fort Caswell was surrendered by Sgt. Frederick Dardingkiller. More volunteers were sent to reinforce the fort and prepare for any attack up the river. On January 13, the Governor of North Carolina, John W. Ellis, nervous over the relationship between the US Government and the state of North Carolina, sent Col. John L. Cantwell, commanding the 13th Regiment North Carolina Militia, with the order that Fort Caswell be restored to the possession of the authorities of the United States. Soon after the firing on Fort Sumter, Col. Cantwell was ordered to take possession of all defenses along the Cape Fear.[2]

During all the excitement, I joined a military company of young men. The average was twenty and a half years for the whole company. It was called the "Wilmington Rifle Guards," and was commanded by Capt. O.P. Meares. I had no time to drill although I kept up my membership. North Carolina seceded 20 May, 1861 and troops were ordered to Fort Caswell, and when the 18th Regiment was organized under the Colonelcy of James S. Radcliffe,[3] Capt. Meares was made Lt. Col.[4] and the regiment was ordered to encamp on Confederate Point (changed from Federal Point). The companies were "Light Infantry," Capt. Henry Savage, "Wilmington Rifle Guards," Capt. Robert Williams, "Wilmington Scotch Boys," Capt. Malloy from Laurinburg, "German Volunteers," Capt. Cornehlson from Wilmington, two companies by Capts. George and Robert Tate [Tait] from Bladen, Capt. Norment's company from Robeson County, Capt. Gore's company from Whiteville, and Capt. Hawes' company from Long Creek.

The promotion of Capt. George Tate [Tait][5] to the majority made Capt. Purdy Commander of Company K. I did not enlist for some months because of the confinement of Mr. E. [Erambert] and so had six or seven months of hard and confining work in the drug store. I remember on one occasion that the crowd came into the drug store after night to talk over the news. The news was that the "Harriet Lane" a little Revenue Cutter had been sent to reinforce Fort Caswell.[6] The crowd was greatly stirred. I was in the act of putting a cork in a poor green glass bottle and twisted the neck off, cutting my middle finger through the nail, which has left a scar to this day. The "Harriet Lane" did not come and the Fort was surrendered by Sgt. Reilly to some volunteers. Reilly afterwards became a Major of Artillery in the Confederate Army.[7]

In 1861 Wilmington stood in a peculiar relation to the rest of the state. Charleston, our near neighbor had opened the war and it was evident that we had to follow. The state was trying to adhere to the Union. The town saw the necessity and borrowed $100,000 from the banks to put defenses in order and buy supplies for the troops already mustered at the mouth of the river. Repeated applications to the Governor were not heeded and one of the "Military Committee" appointed to aid Gov. Ellis who was then rapidly declining with consumption. Warren Winslow, replied that "the Wilmington people must not become panic stricken."

Owing to Mr. Erambert's wound, I was confined to the store without exercise in the open air, until I was very thin and poor, and had a bad attack of dyspepsia. I did not join my regiment until September 1861. My friends were expecting me but I was not legally a soldier until I had been mustered in.

There was a Jew by the name of Mason Loeb who was trying to get out of the company so that he might go into some money making enterprise. He proposed that if I be enrolled on a certain day that our Capt. would be willing to sign his release and in that event I would have his pay which had accumulated since April to about $66. This I agreed to and the boys were very much amused at the transaction, calling me a Jew's substitute.

At Fort Fisher we were encamped near Craig's on Federal Point.[8] From this camp, we marched out every morning to practice with the heavy guns, about half a mile or more away.[9] At that time they were just building the casement guns and those we exercised upon were old Columbiad "en barbette." Ammunition was very scarce and ordinance officers were not numerous, for in fact we were all learning. The exercise was pretty severe for me and for many days I was so much overworked that I twitched at night. The food we had, though varied, was not suited to my dyspeptic condition at first; but after a while I found that I had an appetite for anything, and took part with the boys in everything. Our camp life was more like a big holiday excursion. We were under lax discipline. We had to answer roll call at reveille (about day break) but after this we went most everywhere except the few who were detailed for camp guard. This guard was not at all strict, and many times the sentinel spent his time playing drafts with anyone who might come along. Sometimes we would fall in at reveille with our fishing lines in hand, half dressed, and as soon as we broke ranks would dash across the sand dunes for the sea beach and fish for drums and whiting until breakfast time.[10]

My company L was formed by combining with the "Scotch Boys." The company was composed of young men, all acquaintances with the exception of a few from Duplin County, so that all sorts of frolics usual to school boys were indulged in. We shot marbles, danced, played ball, played cards, chess, back-gammon, drafts, etc. All sorts of practical jokes were played on one another of course. Singular to say though it did not fall to my lot to drill in the manual of arms all this time, but the rest of the company were well drilled.

I had no choice of selection of my tent-mates. There was one vacancy, each tent holding six. In my tent was Mr. Jack Mallard (now a harness dealer, then the oldest man in the company), John N. Bowden (a conductor on the R.R.), John L. Jacobs (an old school-mate and cousin of Bowden's), Phil Carpenter (son of the Superintendent of the W.C.R.R.), Jeff Smith (a R.R. locomotive engineer), and myself. Many of the tents had written over them some motto or device like, "Bogue Pt. Braves," etc. but I adopted for ours, "Les Elites." Our mess was a lazy one, if not the laziest, and when the French pronunciation was given to it (lazaleet) it was accepted as a very well selected emblem.

At last my time came to cook. I was left in charge of the raw material as the boys went off to the guns at the Fort. The main feature of the meal was biscuit, and I considered myself perfectly competent for the task. I put in all the ingredients, flour, salt, a little soda, and water and kneaded it together with a good will. But the dough was tough and crumbly and hard to work, but I kept on persevering, and finally it came to the point of rolling out the biscuit. I tried in vain, for the pieces would not adhere to each other. I discovered that I had put in too little water, and tried to add to it, but it wouldn't mix. My time was growing short and soon the boys would be back, ready for their breakfast. After a fashion I made some rather crumbly looking biscuits, put them into the iron oven, built a good fire underneath and on top, and left them to struggle on with another batch of dough. After laboring for some time, for it was labor, I attempted to work in some water, and made up another batch, and thinking the first lot about done, I took off the iron top with a stick, when lo, there came a big puff of smoke, a smell of burnt bread, and my poor biscuits were burnt to a coal. What could I do, for the hungry boys were in sight, and my bread ruined. Fortunately for me, a good natured darkey, the cook of another mess, came to my relief. In a very short time he had some hot biscuits on the table. The boys were willing to let me try at something else than cooking after that.

A practical joke was played on one of our men Bridgers. He was rather a stupid, gullible fellow, with a plenty of self conceit. One morning, just after reveille, one of the men beckoned to Bridgers to come and bring his gun, that there were some ducks swimming in the edge of the river among the rushes. He had chopped up a bullet in lieu of shot. Bridgers was very much excited by the sight of the ducks for there was a good flock of them, large and fat, busily feeding and quacking and enjoying themselves. The water was pretty cold but as our friend got more and more excited, he waded in to get close in on his game. He fired at close range and brought down four fat English ducks. Great was his triumph when he came into camp wet and muddy from his wade, but fairly gleaming at his good shooting and the toothsomeness of the game. The boys smiled a smile of satisfaction, and something more. Bridger's mess had a feast of fat ducks and had in their friends to enjoy them.

The next day, Mr. Henry Howard who lived near the camp came with a complaint to the Capt. that someone had stolen his ducks and the proof was that he found the feathers. A search showed that the feathers were from Bridgers' "wild ducks". He acknowledged the shooting and asserted with great vehemence that they were wild and he had a right to shoot them. The whole matter of Bridgers amused the boys very much, and it was pretty generally known that he had been "taken in" by one of the company. Howard demanded a dollar apiece for his ducks, and the Capt. required Bridgers to pay it. And then the shout went up in camp at the expense of the luckless nimrod. This is but one of the many examples of the practical jokes perpetuated by "the boys". They were sometimes very cruel as the following will show.

We had a Colonel [Colonel James D. Radcliffe] who had been a pedagogue, but had also had good training as a soldier at the Citadel College in Charleston. He was some what of a peacock, and assumed airs of importance which were not very well disguised. He was very fond of having the "long roll" beaten (this was the alarm for rapid assembly of troops in time of danger) and always for false alarms. The boys said the Colonel was generally under the excitement of liquor, (but this I don't know) when he summoned the regiment by the long roll. He rode a small black horse, a prancing, glossy, inferior animal and a "wind-sucker" making a sort of display a General would in parade. This night they stretched a rope across the street of the "Staff" just about high enough to catch the Colonel under the chin when mounted. He came tearing through to the parade ground to be in his place at long roll, when the line caught him under the chin and threw him off his horse. It was a wonder it didn't break his neck. The perpetrators were never discovered.[11]

Sunday in camp was inspection day. The Col. and his staff would go around with the Capt. and examine every tent and knapsack and everything about the camp, after examining the guns of the men. So that Sunday was a busier day than any other. Sometimes we had preaching by our chaplain, a Rev. Colin Shaw, but there seemed to be little attraction to him. In our mess Mr. Mallard was a singer. He had a little fine tenor, but could read music, and he taught us something about it, and we used to spend many hours in this innocent way. But camp life was ruinous to religion, especially to those feeble Christians who made but little advancement in the divine life. In the early years of the war it was worse than ever after that. I had more harm done to me in these few months than I would have believed.

My Uncle John C. Wood was at Fort Fisher during my stay there, building casements of palmetto logs.[12] He was a fierce secessionist in his language, and by his actions did all he could to aid the Confederacy. He was a naturalist almost by instinct, and made a good collection of sea-mosses while off duty, from the water of New Inlet. The laborers were principally Negro slaves, sent from all parts of the country. The work was immense for the difficulties were great, but for nearly three years they worked on unmolested at the Fort. It was mostly of sand-turfed over with grass sod, (course salt grasses mostly) to prevent the winds from demolishing them. At this writing the whole of the immense forts are leveled just by the action of the wind. Dr. Haigh and I visited them in 1880, and found them nearly demolished. Our regiment was ordered from Fort Fisher to Coosawhatchie, S.C., in November or December 1861 and at that time there was not a gun mounted in the case-mates at the Fort, and we left no one to take our places, except Capt. Purdy's Company K. for a short time.[13]

Among friends I made after the war broke out was a young man Pierre Agostini, from Morsilio, Corsica. He was the brother of an old adopted citizen F. M. Agostini, also a fruit dealer.[14] I had great desire to speak French well. Agostini had a shop just across from the drug store, and as I was fond of candy and anxious to learn French, I saw a great deal of him. He had been in the French army, and was a drilled man, and showed on many occasions his skill in this way. I was too poorly from long confinement to enter into his gymnastic feats, but I picked up every word of French.

Dr. John deRosset was about at this time, and he spoke French and German with grammatical accuracy and fluency.[15] There was also a young Mississippian named Saunders just back from Paris, who also talked French. French was all the go with Southern people, and we at an early period of the struggle hoped to get the same sympathy for us from them (as they showed in the Revolution) for the whole country. I know now that Agostini's friendship was no advantage to me except for the little French I got. I found myself unconsciously losing my hold upon the sanctity of Sunday, and looking with favorable eye upon the pleasant way religious people in France were able to spend their Sundays. This French idea of Sunday was in accord with the growing looseness of Sunday observance which pervaded the whole country soon after war was declared, and for some months before war broke out. As soon as the earliest commissions were issued and the gray uniforms were settled upon, the churches were dotted with officers in their new gray uniforms. Some of the officers from civil life, especially paraded their uniforms on all occasions, and followed inflexibly the army rules of turning Sunday in the camp into the busiest of all the days. This neglect of Sunday I think from the date of this writing (Nov. 1886) did young men more harm than anything I know of, surely it was so in my case. Drinking liquor was not a wide spread evil in our camps, the officers were more at fault than the men in this. I am sure that the failure to respect Sunday as the Lord's day, as Sabbath, is a most fearful risk to the soul of any person. It lets Satan into the heart in a way that nothing else can, it seems to me. It dulls the sensitive conscience, and tempts us to make light of sins which we would have shunned. Satan enables us to make a great many excuses for violating this day made holy by the resurrection of our blessed savior, and when Monday comes we are not refreshed in spirit but go about our duties with a lowered moral tone. I am not surer of anything that I know than this.[16]

THREE

The Regiment Moves to South Carolina

      About this time the state authorities decided to change the numbering system for volunteer regiments. The numbered units one through ten would be changed to eleven through twenty so the 8th Volunteers became the 18th North Carolina Regiment. On November 7, the regiment received orders to move to Port Royal, South Carolina, to reinforce the Confederate troops defending the area. There were unexpected delays in readying the regiment for movement and more delays with transportation at Wilmington, which resulted in a temporary change of orders to Charleston, South Carolina. While at Charleston, they learned of the fall of Beaufort and Port Royal to Union forces on November 7, 1861.[1]

    All of this moving around still bore little relationship to real warfare, and the boredom and loneliness continued for the men in the ranks. They had yet to understand the importance of discipline, and they searched for every opportunity to bypass army law. Their boyish pranks and immature escapades continued, driven by boredom and uncertainty about their future, but the fun seemed to take on a harder edge now, and even a calculated cruelty began to develop. Slowly but surely they began to understand that the time was coming when each of them would have to face death. Their carefree boyhood was about to end.

The breaking up of camp on Federal (then Confederate) Point was a great undertaking. The amount of "plunder" accumulated was very great, and the men did not know how far their rights of transportation extended. Every camp stool, pot, bottle, table, etc. was indispensable to its owner, and all means were devised to keep possessions. Large bundles of things were wrapped up in tents to get them transported. We were carried by steamer to Wilmington and were treated as veterans by the people at home. The cause of our removal to Charleston was the attack by Federals on Port Royal in Beaufort, S.C. Charleston was thus threatened by the back door, as it were.

It was a large regiment and made quite a good show in Charleston. The regiment was divided and breakfasted at the hotels, and then marched to the American Hotel,[2] which was emptied and the regiment put in quarters there. In the excitement and lack of organization of Commissary Departments, no food was prepared for the regiment but strict orders were given that no one should be allowed to leave the hotel. The officers enjoyed the privilege of course, but the private was not so fortunate. As officers and privates in our regiment were schoolmates and friends, all from the same walk in life, the distinction was very galling to the men, and they at once set about to devise ways to get at large, and get some food.

One or two of my comrades suggested that we should try an untried way of escape. We mounted to the roof and made our way across the roofs of the adjoining houses until we came to a cupola. We had no idea where we were or whose house it was, but we made some noises at the windows, when a very polite old Negro servant came, and we told him very frankly what we were doing there and asked permission to go down through the house to the street. He at once asked us down and seemed to enter into the fun with us. We were soon at liberty and on the street, (three of us) and were laughing and enjoying the adventure. We had not gone far before we met Maj. George Tattoo, (now a seedsman in Norfolk, Va.) of the regiment. He very considerately turned his head away so as not to see us, and we made our way to the restaurant for breakfast.

The next day we were moved to James Island and put into bivouac, in order to keep the regiment together. The Ashley River was now between us and Charleston, but the inconveniences of camp were still greater. The connection between us and the city was a ferry boat. At the time, Cousin Henry S. Haines was Superintendent of the Charleston and Savannah Railroad and was busied making preparations to transport us to the Coosawhatchie.[3] We had become very much straitened for something to eat, and a party of us determined to try to get to the city. I found Cousin Henry busy at his work on our side of the river. I told him what I wanted to do and he playfully remarked, "I told your Colonel that I would let none of you boys go over without a pass." I promptly replied "well, if that is all," and at the same time put my fingers in my vest pocket. But he did not wait to see the pass, (which I really did not have) but blew a whistle for his men to pull us across in his boat. We soon found our way to breakfast and stayed until after dinner. We went to the Charleston Hotel to see our Sergeant Major T.W. Brown (afterwards Captain in the regiment but the poor fellow was a constitutional— well, not a warrior. After the war a newspaperman in N.Y. then an Episcopal minister, now hopelessly insane at the asylum at Raleigh). His uniform was of that gaudy pattern which did not survive the first year of the war among the troops in the field. As we were coming down the stairs and about to enter the office of the hotel, we spied our little Colonel [Radcliffe] strutting like a turkey cock, and evidently full to the brim of a good dinner. We were truants and thought that he was aware of it, but we made bold and gave a salute, and I believe he showed his friendship by shaking hands with us enjoining us to be at camp by sunset as the regiment would leave that night. Delighted with our "escape" we went to camp and found that hundreds had deserted camp as we had and were straggling in, in groups, recounting with more or less merriment the adventures of the day. The boys had all evidently enjoyed Charleston.

The regiment was transferred to Coosawhatchie, a station on the Charleston and Savannah R.R. on flat cars.[4] We went into camp permanently at or near the plantation of Mr. Huguinin [Huguenin], a very wealthy planter, on the Coosaw River about six miles from the railroad.[5] From the reports, we expected to form a line of battle as soon as we got off the cars, but such rumors were then very common and we paid little heed to them.[6]

The camp selected was a low flat land near the Coosaw river, and none of the precautions which would now be considered necessary for health were attended to. We had an abundance of beef of a poor sort, and were furnished with lard and flour and a plenty of plain food, but the beef was so uninviting and our knowledge of cooking so primitive, that much of it was wasted—thrown out to decay near the camp. We were visited quite often by the Negroes of the adjoining plantations who came with "nuttin but de dry tatter so, Morser," as they replied to us. But we did get something better than dry potatoes. There was one man, an overseer and a confidential servant of Mr. Huguenin who offered us a good and varied bill of fare. He had rather a mysterious air about him, half confidential and self important, at the same time a desire not to let his offers be known to but a few of the "gentle men" in camp. "What can you give us for a supper on such and such a night?" "Let's see, I can give you roast pig and sweet potatoes and rice." And so on through a considerable list, until it got so large we would have to reduce the bill.

But soldiers in camp were not to be satisfied with a dinner without something to drink, and after a confidential chat they always managed to get something from the overseer who must have robbed his master's wine cellar.

An exciting and (now) amusing incident occurred while in this camp. Our Colonel did not know that there were other Confederate troops on the Coosaw and conceived the idea that he would make some discoveries about his surroundings. He procured a yawl boat from a steamer that had been run up the river near our camp for safe keeping from the enemy. He took with him Louis Howard, Ed Brown and others whose names I do not remember, and rowed down the river. A Tennessee regiment was stationed below and on the side of the river opposite us. They had directions to fire on any boat going down the river, to prevent the escape of slaves, and other persons going towards the enemy at Beaufort.

Radcliffe knew nothing about this and being ordered to halt by the Tennessee picket, they shot a volley into the boat. It created quite a panic among all except one or two, and the man who was expected to be the bravest got the lowest down under the gunwales. Those who had presence of mind, backed-water, and got to shore opposite out of reach of the Tennesseans. Two or three deserted the boat taking to the marsh to escape and get back. It was after night when the news reached camp, and there was a general litter of excitement, especially at the discomfiture of the Colonel. The whole story was so foolish—the assumption of authority, the lack of soldierly qualities of precaution and presence of mind, and lack of courage made it all appear ludicrous.

The Adjutant of the regiment, Charles D. Myers, called for volunteers and we soon manned the yawl and pulled down to the scene of conflict and rescued all who had not taken flight across the marsh back to camp. Ed Brown, was shot through the cap but none of the others was touched. So ended what the boys called the "Battle of Coosaw River."

One incident will show how much lack of discipline there was in the regiment (18th N.C.) and how much freedom was allowed to the officers. It was agreed upon that Christmas day 1861 should witness the parade. John D. Barry, a private in Company L, a Wilmington boy, and one of the brightest and most polite of our set, was the quiet manager.[7] Gus Lippitt, of Company G, a Wilmington boy was to be Colonel, having the requisites as exhibited in the part of "Bones", which he took in the regimental Negro minstrel show. He procured a little donkey from "Donkey Island" as his charger for the occasion. A list of general and special orders was written out, I believe by Barry, Willie Wooster[8] and Charley Flanner, which was nothing but sharp satire on the officers, the management of camp and the grievances of the men. It was a wonder that such a paper should have been allowed, but it was. A miserable drunken, little Irishman, Ned Stanton, the only one in the regiment, was made Sergeant of the mock regiment and the surgeon (Dr. J.A. Miller[9] who enjoyed the fun as much as anybody) lent him his green sash for the occasion.

After reading the orders, the regiment started out to drill. The Colonel came to a puddle in the road and the donkey refused to go on. The Colonel dismounted and with the assistance of a man lifted the donkey over the bad place, remounted and rode off. Lt. Col. O.P. Meares was greatly offended at this exhibition of quiet insubordination, but the Col. [Radcliffe] shut his eyes to it. Not having started with disciplinary restraint it was too late now to curb the school-boy pranks of the young men, many of whom were his social equals and had been his pupils only a year or so before.

One of the amusing experiences of my camp life at Coosawhatchie was my first picket experience. I was placed on post at a point near that is known as Boyd's Landing on the Coosaw. We were constantly getting messages, by couriers of the Charleston Dragoons, that gun boats were approaching. The excited Colonel would have the "long roll" beat and trot us off eight miles without rest to this point. I believe nearly all of those were "false alarms", gotten up to teach us the duties of soldiers. What a gun boat was, no one seemed to know, except that it was a terrible naval vessel with demolishing armament, equal to all occasions of war, and to be dreaded. With all of these vague ideas before me, I went on post with careful instructions from the officers. Two of us were on post and kept watch all night, I believe without relief. Towards day, when I was very sleepy, I heard an unearthly chorus of sounds, peal upon peal from the direction of the river. It was a new sound to me. Could it be a gun boat? No, for surely that would approach with a rush of steam and a splashing of wheels in the water. My comrade, D. Julee Rumpell, and I listened with some degree of excitement, until at last we heard the noise reduced to the braying of single donkeys. Analyzing the sound, we found that the unearthly chorus came from a colony of donkeys which had been planted on Donkey Island. They had been introduced to this part of the state as plow animals, but the experiment had been a failure, and they were all sent to this island where their number had greatly increased. It was from this point that "Col." Gus Lippitt got his donkey for the mock Christmas parade.

I don't like to tell of a "scrape" I got into by insubordination, but I will. It was on the very occasion of the visit to Boyd's landing. Our Capt. Bob Williams[10] was very lazy and good-natured, but had no idea of what was required of men on the march. In this 8 mile march homeward, no halt was made and the Capt. got tired and dropped out to make his way at leisure. The command devolved upon 1st Lt. Mat Laspeyre,[11] and his old companion, but who was considerably elevated by his office. He determined to show us what he knew about commanding on a march, and requiring the company to march "close order" as if we were on drill.

It was warm and the road was uneven and I was tired and afflicted with an annoying ailment, so that I could not march without irritation. When I came to a bad place in the road, I would fall out and pick my way. This irritated our strict Lt. and he ordered the company to halt and for me to "fall in." This I did and we went on as before and I, as before, falling out when we got to heavy road or deep sand. This being repeated two or three times by me, Laspeyre became very much exasperated, drawing his sword in a threatening manner upon me. At this, I drew my bayonet and we stood confronting each other. We both cooled off, the Lt. ordering the company forward and I marched to camp.

I was ordered in arrest when we reached camp, and after remaining in the guard tent all night, and no charges being brought by the Lt., I was released. I had the sympathy of the company in the matter and Laspeyre was looked upon as a tyrant, but he had the law on his side and could have made the matter very serious if he had court martialed me. I was surely wrong in disobeying orders, but he should have been more reasonable and have inquired into the cause of my disobedience. So I thought. But the incident shows what a poor idea we all had of our duties as soldiers.

I believe such a state of things existed in all regiments except the first seven regiments. These were organized for war, on strict army rules, and were commanded by West Point men. General R.E. Lee was in command of the department at Coosawhatchie but I only saw him once, and then he had an iron gray mustache.

The selection of our camping was bad. There was no drainage and all sorts of abuses were allowed until sickness broke out to an alarming extent, and our camp was moved to a few miles off, to a better location, near a good spring.

The new camp was called Camp Stephens. The health of the men improved somewhat, but it was still not good. There was no personal instruction about health and the men were imprudent. Dr. William James Harris[s] Bellamy[12] was a private in the same company of which I was a member [Company I] but he was not then a doctor. We used to read medical books when we could, and both longed for the time when we could attend college and get our degree. He was taken sick with camp fever here and was furloughed to complete his convalescence. I was seldom called upon to assist the doctor now, but did some friendly nursing now and then among the sick in the hospital.

On one of my visits to Coosawhatchie, I heard of my old friend, Mr. John Fripp, whose hospitality I had enjoyed at Morgan Island.[13] The fall of Port Royal had placed his estate in the hands of the enemy and he had offered his services to the Confederacy as a nurse. He was destitute, having only $10 which I believe he had offered to the village blacksmith to whom he owed it. The blacksmith declined it. The estate was never returned to the family and as the Negroes were all freed, it was worth very little.

FOUR

VIRGINIA AND THE SEVEN DAYS BATTLES

In the spring, the regiment was given orders to join other North Carolina troops at New Bern, North Carolina, but passing through Wilmington, they heard the news that New Bern had fallen to Federal forces. The regiment proceeded to Kinston where they joined the New Bern garrison. All North Carolina troops were formed into two brigades, the 1st commanded by General Robert Ransom and the 2nd by General Lawrence O'Bryan Branch. General Branch's brigade was composed of the 7th, 18th, 28th, 33rd, and 37th North Carolina Regiments, and was assigned to guard the Virginia Central Railroad, Richmond's main link with the Shenandoah Valley. His forces were posted near Peake's Crossing on the railroad four miles southwest of Hanover Courthouse.[1]

About this time, Union General George McClellan was presenting his "grand plan" for the offensive on Richmond. Taking advantage of Federal seapower, he planned to move his army down the Rappahannock to Urbanna and then march to the York River which would cut off enemy forces holding the lower Virginia peninsula between the York and the James. A rapid move up the peninsula would position the army to take the Confederate Capitol. His move would also flank the Rebel army at Manassas and Centreville and force it to abandon its threat on Washington. General McClellan presented his plan to a council of General officers on March 7, 1862, so a final decision could be made concerning his grand strategy. Circumstances concerning logistics would force him to alter his plan but his basic concept remained intact and March 8, 1862 would mark the official birth of the Peninsula Campaign.[2]

The news of the fall of New Bern brought an order for us to return to N.C. I don't know the date, but it was before April 1862 [March 14, 1862]. We were carried to Goldsborough and then to Kinston. All along we heard the disgrace of some of our regiments in the Battle of New Bern. They were raw troops and their officers were incompetent. Some of the regiments were decidedly good, particularly the 7th [North Carolina] under Col. Campbell.[3]

When the troops all assembled in Kinston, there was a lively time. I believe we had the 28th., 18th., 33rd., 37th., 7th., 26th., and the regiment that Col. Sinclair (the fighting cowardly Scotch parson) commanded.[4] We considered ourselves the best drilled regiment in the brigade. We were drilled in the Hardee tactics and they in Scott's.[5] Our movements were all at quick time and showed to best advantage. General Branch was put in command of the first five regiments above mentioned.

We had no sooner settled in camp than the all-absorbing topic was the expiration of the term for which we had enlisted—a year.[6] Men and officers were equally excited and there was to be a mustering out of men whose terms had expired, and election for field and company officers. I was now given more work in the medical department, made a sort of brigade hospital steward by Dr. Miller, regimental and brigade surgeon.[7]

The camp was in constant turmoil. Our Lt. Col. [O. P. Meares] thought it was a good time to make one of his indiscreet speeches to the men on the cowardice of going home before the war was over. He defeated his own election and that of the Colonel and Major John D. Barry, a private in our company was a principal wire-worker and succeeded in being made Captain of the company [Company I]. At a late hour I thought of running for Lieutenant, but was beaten by a man that I greatly disliked. Many of the men went home on the expiration of their terms. Col. R.H. Cowan[8] at the time Lt. Col. of the 3rd N.C. Regiment Inf. was elected Col.; Capt. Purdy,[9] Lt.Col., and Capt. Forney George,[10] Major.

Our camp was in constant confusion and turmoil by the discontent caused by the prospects of the mustering out of all who had enlisted on or before April 15th, 1861, and by the electioneering, of those to be retained, for the officers. I was greatly in hopes that I would have been allowed to go home as

I had substituted a man who had enlisted from April 1861. During the excitement, I believe that the Confederate Congress, finding that men were not re-enlisting, passed a law conscripting all whose terms had expired, but most of the men had gone home.

A singular thing now happened to me. I was apprenticed by Col. Cowan as orderly sergeant of Company I. I knew less than any man in the company about drill, and did not desire the place at all. B.A. Hallett, of Wilmington, (afterward my friend and patient, now living at Mt. Olive) was chosen orderly sergeant for the Light Infantry Company G. We were the only orderly sergeants not examined as to drill. Hallett was well drilled. I knew very little.

The duty of the orderly sergeant was to form the company in the company street and turn it over to the Captain. I got along all right until I ordered the company to "right face." No one moved. I then ordered them "left face." No one moved, but the men commenced to smile. The new Captain [John D. Barry] came down and saw my dilemma, that the company was at "order arms" and could not move, suggested I should command "shoulder arms" which I did. I turned the company over to the Captain and we went out to drill. I could not get into it though and never did make any headway.

In one of my visits into Kinston, I found a stock of drugs owned by Mr. or Dr. Pollock for sale. The disaster at New Bern made matters right uncertain and an offer was made to sell all at N.Y. list price. I took him up without consulting Mr. Erambert (my old druggist friend) and bought the lot. It turned out to be a good purchase, as all kinds of drugs were very scarce. Kinston was getting to be quite a pleasant place and everything settled down into quiet. But it was all too comfortable to last long and we got an order, probably in June [May 2, 1862] to go to Richmond.

Our whole regiment was taken at one load, number in all about 800 men. Soldiers were no new things in Richmond and when we got there early in the morning, the city was sleeping as quietly as though McClelland's army was not encircling its eastern limits only a few miles away. We were put in camp at Howard's Grove, a place afterwards occupied as a smallpox hospital. After a few days here, we took the train for Gordonsville and thence to Swift Run Gap in the Blue Ridge, to reinforce Stonewall Jackson. When we reached the Gap we were countermarched to Gordonsville and took the train for Hanover Courthouse, in Virginia, where we rested a day or two until the Battle of Hanover Court House.[11]

I will never forget the impressions of the battle. The regiment had settled down into an idea that the war would soon be over and we would never see a battle or "get into one." It was now over a year since the regiment was organized and we had never been near an enemy. I remember with what interest we questioned Captain Sikes, an old veteran of the Mexican War, who commanded one of our companies. He looked upon fighting as a serious business, and his accounts of what he had witnessed in Mexico did not tend to sharpen our appetites for it. The next day, the poor fellow was instantly killed in battle.[12]

I believe it was the night before the battle our whole company was put on guard with orders to patrol a certain part of the railroad, all night, without relief. It seemed to me then unreasonable, and I know now that it was due entirely to a lack of experience of our officers who so far had seen nothing of the practical duties of our soldier life. The men all did their part well with some grumbling and pretty sharp criticism which seemed to be the rights of all Confederate soldiers. Every man was more or less an authority on military matters, and had his own opinion of how a campaign should be conducted.

It rained very hard the night and day before the battle (May 26, 1862). The ground was thoroughly soaked and the small streams were full. To this day, I don't know anything about the topography of the country. In the afternoon the regiment was hurried out of camp and pretty soon we heard the fire of artillery. Our company (I) was detached as skirmishers and deployed after a run of about a mile. I remember I had on a fancy knapsack which was sent out as a pattern for the Wilmington Light Infantry, a civil military company existing before the war. The knapsack consisted of a slender white pine frame covered with patent leather and made a snug square parcel, with a place on top for a blanket. It was only suited for holiday soldiering but I was too proud of the appearance it made to give it up for the poor rag of a thing the men had. I had a very fine pair of white blankets which Ma had given me when I left home. As we were running into the battle, my knapsack got too heavy—I was very thirsty—and confident that we would return the same road when the fight was over, I threw my precious knapsack into a tangle of smilax vines and went on, now and then stopping to scoop up water from the cart-ruts which were running with muddy water. But it was the best we could do. I was hot and excited from running and the firing in our front.

Just as we neared the battlefield, I saw the first wounded man I had ever seen in battle. He was coming along the road we were traveling, between two men. He had been shot in the bowels, and was pale and a horrible sight. This was very sickening but only a few steps further there were several dead and wounded horses of our artillery (Captain Latham's) that had been knocked down by the enemy and silenced. The impressions were more and more serious as we advanced. Our Captain was directed to take the left side of the road, and deploy as skirmishers. Just where our line extended there was a deep grade in the road, so that when we were deployed, the right of the company where I was at the edge of the steep bank looking down on the road. Cord wood was stacked about in the piece of woods we occupied, and we could hear the patter of lead from the enemy on the trees, but could see no one before us, and here we were ordered to lie down and await orders.

The battle raged hotly to our right, and in the midst of it, our junior 2nd Lt. Bridgers gave me the order very excitedly to "deploy"—that is—extend the company line to the right. To do this we would have been obliged to get down a steep bank, pass a road being scoured with artillery, and climb another bank, then dividing the company into parts. The Lt. kept repeating the order, but finally the Capt. overhearing it bade me not to mind and silenced our would be "general."

I don't know why, but we came hastily off the field about sundown, and discovered that our regiments were moving rapidly away and that the 7th N.C. was bringing up the rear of the defeated Brigade. We had to cross a field under a sweeping fire, and move right lively to rejoin our command, and so rejoin a retreating line.[13] We picked up on the way that we had been attacked by General Fitz John Porter, and after making a good fight we had to retreat through Hanover Slashes, the neighborhood of Henry Clay's birthplace, and that we were going to Ashland, a little village nearer Richmond. On the road, I picked up a new Enfield rifle which I exchanged for mine, an old fashioned Springfield percussion musket. I heard that one of our regiments acted badly in the fight, and that the 12th Regiment (Sol Williams) which joined us on the road, was utterly worthless.

I ought to go back and relate an incident which had a bearing on my career. Before we took train for Richmond previous to the battle, we encamped at Gordonville. We had a battalion drill and I went on drill as O. Sergt. [Orderly Sergeant] for the first time. I knew nothing of drill and it was my duty and that of the Captain to see that the proper interval was kept between our company and the one before it, so that when we wheeled into line there would be no space and no overlapping. I missed it every time and it worried Col. Cowan very much. When the drill was over he sent for me, and in a half-humorous way he scolded me for spoiling his drill. I could make no defense except that I hadn't had the opportunity to drill. Dr. Miller was standing by and heard the conversation. The Col. ended his conversation by inviting me not to go on his drill again, if I could find anything else to do. Dr. Miller spoke for him to turn me over to his department, so that every now and then I was detailed to help him.

I was among the first to get into Ashland, of our regiment, and set about looking after the wounded. But I found that there was great confusion and little to do, and slept very soundly on the hospital floor, rejoining my regiment the next day. We then moved to Brook Church near Richmond and went into camp. It was a very pretty site, and the best camp we had during the war. We remained here some time and were in camp when the exciting news came that General J.E.B. Stuart had marched around McClelland's rear.[14] With our little knowledge of things, it looked like we were now in a fair way to have a decided victory and end the war. The news came in, too, of Stonewall Jackson's brilliant battles in the Valley of Virginia over Banks and Shields, and others. Our newspapers were full of it, and in one newspaper we read Ben Wood's speech delivered in Congress, I believe on the subject of *peace*. Put all the news together our prospects were bright, and little did we know that in a few weeks the great "7 days battle before Richmond" would take place.

From this camp we were occasionally on picket duty at Chickahominy Swamp. There was a flock of sheep between us and the enemy's picket in a meadow. Both sides wanted the sheep, and at last commenced firing at each other when a party from one side or the other ventured too far. This brought on a sharp picket skirmish, the first one since Hanover, and the only time we had seen the "blue-coats". No one was hurt. While on picket, two well-dressed gentlemen came to my station to cross the Chickahominy. They were dressed as sports men and had double barrel fowling pieces. They had passes from the highest authorities, and after submitting them to the Captain they were allowed to cross. In a few days after we heard the booming of the guns at Seven Pines, and expected to be engaged ourselves, but were not.

We returned to our camp at Brook Church after picket service. I got along pretty well in camp, but my duties as Orderly Sergeant made me some enemies in the performance of my duties as arbiter between men. I had a chicken for a pet. He got so tame that he perched about in my tent and on my shoulders while I was writing. One day news came to strike tents, cook three days' rations and be prepared for march. Poor chicken. It was too bad, but all sentiment disappeared before the necessities of war, and I had a fat chicken for the next day.

We moved out on Brook Turnpike and made our way to Meadow Bridge, the 7th N.C. deployed in front. All signs pointed to a great battle. Wounded men were being brought to the rear, a sight that we afterwards became so accustomed. We took an occasional prisoner from the Michigan Cavalry regiment which picketed in our front, while we were in the meadow on duty. It was nearly sunset, when as we were marching along the road, firing quite heavy in our front, there was a tremendous rumbling sound coming directly down upon us. I never could explain it, or how it came about, but a panic seized the regiment, and I believe that most of them jumped the fence and cleared the road in a minute. It proved to be one of our ambulances with run-away horses coming down the road with a tremendous crash. The regiment soon recovered itself, was in line, and was never after known to do anything but the very best work as soldiers. I have talked this matter over with the survivors of the 18th regiment, but none could account for it, that a regiment that had always behaved well under fire did such a foolish thing as this. It was not long after this that we charged across the bridge and up the hill at Mechanicsville, under very heavy fire and took our position in the line of battle. It had been a hard day's fight but we were up all night. We were ordered to charge several times and had the order countermanded, and then we slept for a short time upon our arms.[15]

We saw Jackson coming in towards Mechanicsville as we were going into battle. The next day he appeared upon McClellan's flank and the works in front of us were evacuated. The next day I was decidedly unwell, but there were many others who were on the complaining list, and I did not want to be considered a coward. But at last I submitted my case to the doctor and he gave me a pass to the rear and I made my way to Richmond.[16] I could have gone further but I was so weak that I thought there were signs of fever coming on and I sought the house of Captain Sam W. Skinner who then lived on Church Hill. He was a brother-in-law of Louis Erambert, and treated me very kindly. He sent for his family physician, Dr. Knox, who had me under treatment for several days. All day and all night we could see and hear in Richmond signs of the raging battle. I was sick about two or three weeks, and determined to start for my regiment when Lt. Bridgers [Bridger][17] of my company was brought to my neighborhood wounded. I nursed him until he was convalescent. Seeing an order for all convalescents from N.C. to report to the N.C. hospital, I reported.[18]

FIVE

RICHMOND

By the time Thomas Fanning Wood arrived in Richmond for convalescence, the city was in turmoil. The Seven Days Battles had filled every hospital and private home with wounded and ill men. Desperate shortages of medical supplies and trained personnel plagued the Confederate army so that both the Medical Department and Congress were compelled to give considerable attention to the establishment of an effective and efficient hospital program. It was suggested that most of the hardships suffered by soldiers while in hospitals grew out of the practice of mixing up soldiers from all sections of the Confederacy in the same hospital and scattering men from the same area and regiment in many different institutions. A new bill provided that hospitals be identified by state and, when feasible, sick and wounded be assigned to hospitals representing their states. Governor Zebulon B. Vance was then, in his own mind, presiding over the destiny of North Carolina and was committed to providing unmatched care for the state's troops in the field and for the wounded of her army in the hospitals. It was determined that a hospital be established for North Carolina soldiers in Richmond, and a warehouse for the Harwood Factory, located on South Main Street just below the large Chimborazo Hospital, was selected as the site. This is the hospital to which Thomas Fanning Wood was sent to recover.[1]

This hospital was named Moore Hospital after Surgeon General S.P. Moore, who disliked the compliment expecting to have a larger one named after him. For this reason he ordered all hospitals in the city to be numbered, and it was known as General Hospital No. 24, but the name had already been painted on the front and there it remained.[2]

I found Dr. Otis F. Manson in charge. He was a North Carolinian who had been well known in our state, as an active member of the state society (medical) and a member of the Board of Medical Examiners.[3] The building was an old tobacco factory, the property of Captain Lebby who lived on Church Hill. It was just above "Rockets" [Rocketts] at the S. Bend in Main Street. It was three stories high, with a considerable basement. The first floor was occupied as follows. On the left the office of the Sergeant; on the right the office of the Steward. Beyond this the floor was divided into rooms. On the left were sleeping apartments for the officers, and in the center a general dining room. The second and third floors except small rooms, divided off for dispensary, linen and bath rooms, were large open wards for the sick men the hospital having the capacity for about 70 or 80 men.

When I reported at the hospital I expected to be examined and returned to my regiment. I found matters in the unsettled state of a new institution, with more work on hand than they could manage. The surgeon in charge, Dr. Manson, was earnestly at work giving his attention to all the details of the organization, besides the medical and surgical services so numerous and pressing after several battles. Dr. Sherrod of N.C., and Dr. Hussey of N.C., were his assistants. There was also a doctor who acted as an apothecary. These two last named, after a short service, decided to return to their homes and this was the condition of things when I reached the hospital. Dr. Manson found out I was a medical student, a pupil of Dr. W.G. Thomas, of Wilmington, an old medical society friend, and he put me to work.[4] I was glad indeed to find something suited to my tastes, and a comfortable place to work in, but felt uneasy about the long absence from my command. I told the whole affair to Dr. Manson. He promised to make it all right, and sure enough he got from the Secretary of War an order detailing me for duty at the hospital with the privilege of attending lectures at the Virginia Medical College.[5] This opened a new field for me, and I hailed it with delight. The difference between a home—a fixed abiding place in a hospital, a comfortable bed, good fare, congenial companions about me, and the hardships of the battle field were very great. I thought that my Captain and Colonel would oppose it, but they all agreed and after a while seemed somewhat pleased.

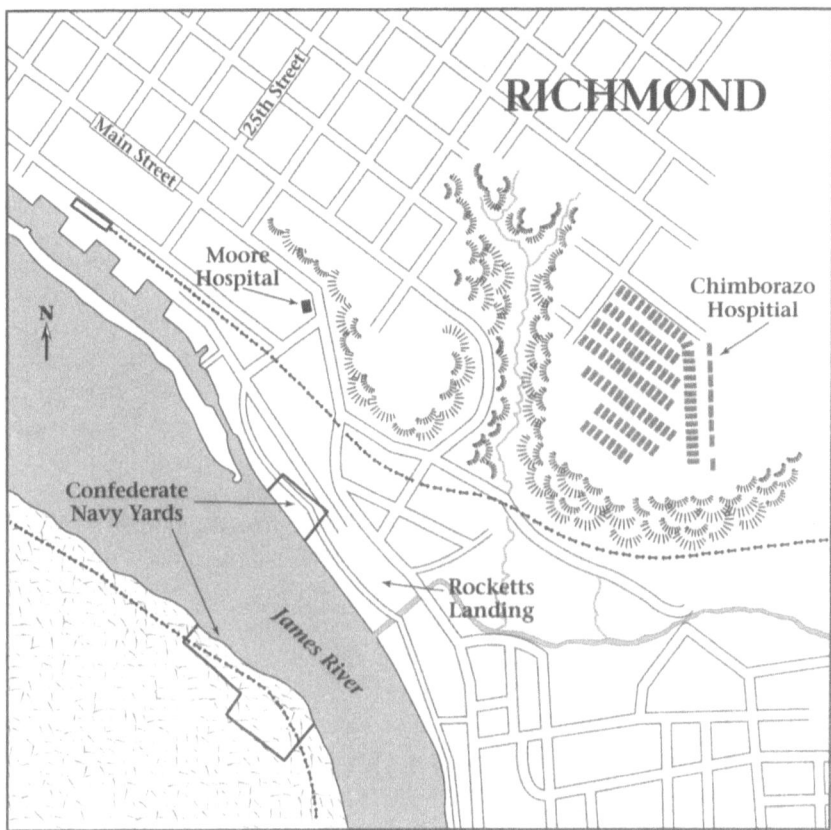

The east end of the city of Richmond showing Moore Hospital on Main Street, Chimborazo Hospital, Rocketts Landing and the Confederate Navy Yard. Based on a U.S. Corps of Engineers Map, 1865.

I found pretty soon that Dr. Manson expected work and that my stay there depended on making myself useful. I was put in charge of the second floor, first ward as ward master and apothecary.[6] It was a large room with about 50 beds with a platform extending out of the West window for convalescents to promenade and lounge. It gave a view of the James River and Manchester. The dispensary was a small room cut off from the ward, by a partition. There were few drugs ready made, and I was put to work to make the usual preparations of the pharmacopoeia. I had under my call all the nurses of the ward, 5 or 6, including the night relief. I also kept a "case book" with name, disease, dates, and medicines of each patient.[7] The ward was kept scrupulously clean. It was scoured with a mop every morning, and dry scoured every afternoon. The floors were very white, although it was hard to keep the soldiers habitually in mind of clean habits. One anecdote connected with my ward I ought to tell. One afternoon some gentlemen came in to my ward smoking and spitting on the floor, with their hats on. I could not imagine who they could be, without they were gamblers who often visited us, and were very liberal with their money among the sick—they were the only people, except Marylanders who wore citizens' clothes. As soon as I noticed their disregard for the rules of the ward I administered a mild rebuke by calling a Negro nurse to mop up the place where the men spat. They didn't notice me, though, but went on talking and laughing, quite at home, still smoking. I was getting quite out of patience not knowing what to do next. Pretty soon my anxiety was relieved by the surgeon in charge, who came up and addressed one of the gentlemen who had on a silk hat, as Governor. It turned out to be Governor Vance and Dr. Edward Warren[8] and I believe Dr. Grissom. I was, of course willing to let the Governor off, but I did not like it. The officers of the hospital had the laugh on me, they thought.

Dr. Manson had moved his family to Richmond, after assuming his duties as Surgeon, and brought his library with him, placing it in his office at the hospital. He invited me several times to his office, and when he found that I was interested in his books he gave me free access to them. French medicine was then in the ascendancy. He had all the best of these authors—Andral, Louis, Trousseau, and Pidoux, Grissolle, and a great many more that I had never seen but had heard of and seen noted in my text books. Particularly I noticed that he had Lebert's famous work on pathology in three large folio volumes.[9] This was a very remarkable possession for a country doctor's library. It seems that Dr. Manson had always been a student, and made choice collections of books. His practice had been good in Granville County, N.C. and he married a rich wife. He was always proud of his profession and studied and wrote well. His enthusiasm often led him into a style that was quite ornate, and out of keeping with strict scientific usage, but his composition was not devoid of good descriptions founded upon actual experience. This he was always able to fortify by reference to books in French and English and Latin. Some of the theory and practice as regards malarial fever, were commented on as extravagant, especially as to dosage of quinine, but I noticed that not many years after, the same opponents and critics, were imitating Dr. Manson very closely.[10]

His father was a builder in Richmond, and gave the Doctor a medical education, he graduated at the Virginia Medical College. Soon after graduating, he went to Granville County (Townesville) and became a candidate for practice. He was then a spare built young man with slightly round (stooping) shoulders, and bright black eyes, and black hair and moustache. He dressed very neatly, always, and attracted much attention by his almost dandy-like appearance. For some time he had not much to do, as is the usual lot of young beginners. Fortunately for him he had an early opportunity to show what stuff he was made of.

Professor Otis Frederick Manson, M.D., eminent physician and distinguished author. Courtesy of the North Carolina Collection, University of North Carolina at Chapel Hill.

That year Smallpox broke out among the negroes on one or two plantations near town and created quite an excitement. The older physicians did not like to be taxed with work which would make their other patients afraid of them, but still the negroes were valuable property and could not be neglected, to say nothing of the principles of mercy. Dr. Manson was applied to and responded and although having the appearance of a fastidious lady's man he entered into the work with so much courage, diligence, and knowledge of his professional duties, that he at once took a stand among the older doctors besides gaining some very good fees, at the time so much needed. This spirit actuated him through his career. When he undertook work, nothing deterred him from doing his best.[11]

But to return to the library. I had never seen such a sight and my delight was very great when I found that I had the privelege of reading. I remember two of the books that I took in hand pretty soon, Louis' "La Fiever Typhoide" and Magnus Huss on "Enteric Fever". This subject was most interesting as the greater part of my cases were typhoid or as we call it typhoid-malarial fever. I had to brush up on my French for one of the books but I enjoyed it.

There was a matron in the hospital, a sister of Dr. Robert Gibbon of Charlotte, who had left her home to minister to the sick. She had a good deal of zeal but little knowledge of her duties. In fact many ladies wanted to imitate Florence Nightingale, but who had not prepared themselves by study or practice in art of nursing, and who having some success at home nursing a single patient, were greatly at sea when they undertook to look after numbers of rough soldiers, with few of the appliances at home. Miss Gibbon was very kind to me in many little ways. I had sent home for my citizen clothes feeling somewhat secure that I would not be molested in the pursuit of my avocation for some time to come. She kept my white clothes neatly mended without my knowledge for a long time and was the friend to whom I was indebted. I was very much pained to learn some time after my separation from the hospital that she left the city under a cloud. Her brother was General Gibbon, of the U.S. Army.[12]

There were two other wardmasters. Dr. Bellamy of Warrenton, N.C. and Mr. Roberts of Granville. The Hospital had secured at its foundation all the crockery and wares of the steamer "Curtis Peck" which formerly plied between Richmond and Norfolk, and another valuable acquisition Captain Freeman of the steamer to be chief of the cooking department. He was a most excellent provider, and our meals were of the very best. No hotel in Richmond set out such meals in 1862 and 1863 as we had. The officers' table was separate from the general table, but the food was excellent. The state of N.C. provided for the Hospital in a very generous way, and private donations came in abundantly from ladies of the state. Our store-room was well filled with every delicacy. So bountiful was our supply, that Surgeon General Moore made a written requisition upon our Hospital to distribute among other less favored hospitals. The demand created an angry controversy, which was for a long time kept up. One incident will show how far the Surgeon General allowed his feelings to carry him. Dr. Grissom, then Captain Grissom, of the 20th or 30 N.C. Regiment was wounded severely in the Seven Days Battle Before Richmond, was promoted to be Major and Surgeon in the N.C. troops by the Governor.[13] He came to Richmond with a Major's uniform, which displeased the Surgeon General, Dr. Grissom having no commission from the Confederate Government but from the State. The quarrel ended by the triumph of Governor Vance, who was at the time in Richmond, and Dr. Grissom was allowed to wear the uniform of a surgeon. I believe that Dr. G. was on the staff of the Governor, or on the staff of the Surgeon General of N.C., Dr. Edward Warren.

While at the Hospital I made many acquaintances and among others that of Professor Dimitry. He was a great linguist. A native of New Orleans, had been U.S. Minister to Central America. He resided with his family near our Hospital. I believe at the time he was Government interpreter. He translated Hugo's

Les Miserables, carefully surpressing all those parts referring to slavery, as the tone of the book was against this institution, and in the South all books were unlawful or at any rate excluded by common consent (1862) if opposed to slavery. I believe that Fantine and Cosette were the work of Mr. Dimitry. He had two daughters who made us frequent visits and we found them quite lively.[14]

My interest in French had attracted the attention of Dr. Manson, and he increased my facilities for study. I was allowed many more privileges than any of the other young men. At last Fall came (1862), and the Medical College was opened. I was given night charge of the ward only, and sleeping in the Dispensary with its partition reaching not half to the wall, I could hear the slightest sound and so keep the nurses at their duty. I matriculated at the College in October, took out my tickets with $115 sent from home by my father. I had been a medical student since 1856, but this was my first opportunity to attend lectures. The class was quite large, and composed of men who were on duty in some capacity in the various hospitals in the city. I made no acquaintances among them, but kept my own counsel, hoping that something would turn up to enable me to get my commission as Assistant Surgeon, by the end of the term, although I knew that I could not graduate, two sessions being requisite to accomplish this.[15]

Dr. Manson had a son 10 or 12 years old, William. He conceived the idea that this little fellow must attend lectures and drink medicine in, just as a child would learn a foreign language. Dr. M. had a German music teacher who took out tickets at the College, and daily performed the duties of a school-master, leading little Willie daily to the College by the hand. The little man was of course dubbed "Doctor" by the students, and was quite a curiosity, as he was probably the youngest student on record. His first day in the anatomical lecture room was marked by a scene of crying on the part of Esculapius[16] and coaxing by his German teacher, until finally the boy got seasoned to all the sights and smells, and made his daily visits to the lectures. Dr. M. was not successful in his theory of educating the boy, for he acquired the greatest aversion to medicine, and today is a merchant. When I last saw him in New Orleans he was reviewing this part of his life, and thought his father had pursued the right plan to disgust him with medicine, and he was glad he had made the escape.

The professors, at the time, lecturing at the Medical College were Dr. David Tucker, Dr. Charles Bell Gibson, Dr. L.J. Joynes, Dr. McCaw, Dr. Peticolas, and Dr. B. Wellford, and Dr. Conway.

Dr. Gibson was an excellent lecturer in surgery. He was the son of Dr. William Gibson of Philadelphia, the author of a work on surgery. The father quoted the son freely and the son the father, so that the students always knew what was coming when certain subjects were mentioned. Dr. Gibson illustrated his lectures with beautiful paintings done for or by his father. He was able to make his class understand his teaching, using at all times the most select words, and pronouncing them distinctly. He was a very successful teacher, and was indeed the attraction of the College before the war—during the war there was no other choice, all the Colleges, Charleston, Mobile, New Orleans, Nashville, University of Virginia, had closed their doors after the first year of the war.

Dr. McCaw[17] the lecturer in chemistry was the next best teacher, having the ability to teach the generally neglected subject in such a way that his lectures were always well attended.

Dr. Joynes, (physiology) was a good lecturer, but teaching physiology by the old method, with scarcely a demonstration, there was little to interest. He was esteemed the most learned man in the faculty.

Dr. Peticolas taught anatomy with success. He had an excellent demonstrator, Dr. Howard, who prepared his subjects in a very thorough way and the classes were small enough for everyone to have a good view.

Dr. Tucker (practice) was a practical lecturer, but was sometimes course in his jokes—repeating many of the old jokes of Dr. N. Chapman, of Philadelphia, and always an applause from his class.

Dr. Wellford was from Fredericksburg. A fine, modest, old gentleman, but a very prosy lecturer. He illustrated his subject with good drawings and articles of materia medica, but his lectures occuring at the time when my services were needed at the Hospital, I seldom heard him, but followed him by reading the U.S. Dispensatory.

Dr. Conway was a very prosy lecturer. He was given to bad habits (we heard) and sometimes came to the lecture desk without reading his lecture. His branch, obstetrics, was little cared for just then, as all the instruction desired was to enable one to pass the Board of Army Examiners.

[Thomas Fanning Wood was very dedicated to his personal correspondence. The letters in this publication were all written by him during the war and were found many years later among the papers of his brother Alfred V. Wood. These letters reflect the youthful outlook of the twenty-one year old just preparing for one of the most dramatic adventures of his lifetime. The text of his memoirs, written twenty-one years later, compare with surprising accuracy to these letters from the war. In the following letter to his older brother Robert Barclay Wood, Jr., he tries to explain his excitement over being invited to appear before the Board of Medical Examiners to take the exam for appointment as assistant surgeon in the Confederate Army.]

Richmond Va. Jany 3d 1863

Dear Bobby:

It seems like I have been the recipient of a "perfect streak of luck" for the past six months. I owe it in no small measure to all my friends, and particularly to Drs. Thomas & Manson. I have been in a comfortable house, enjoying privileges which above all others I coveted more earnestly than any in the world. At the same time I have caused you at home, from time to time, to be uneasy and be at expense for me. But we must bear with each other in these frailties of our human nature. Today I carried a letter to the Surgeon General, asking my appointment as Asst. Surgeon, waiving the examination, at present until I should have had time to verse myself in the "minutiae of the Science". This last clause did not meet the approval of the Surgn. General as it was against the fixed rules of his department. After endorsing Dr. Manson's letter in my own writing, he remarked, "your invitation will be sent to you." So in a few days I will be summoned to appear before the "dreaded tribunal." I have only a few days to prepare in, and you must not expect to hear from me again until I fail or succeed, be that short or long.

The letter of Dr. Manson's was flattering to me and of course tickled my vanity. He has so much confidence in me as to trust the charge of the Hospital to me during the Holidays. But while I am elated at my past success there is a dread for the future which I can't avoid. If I fail I lose nothing. But if there is any virtue in studying, or if I have accomplished anything by a long attention to studies it will be proved. If I fail I will have one more chance in two months. Don't expect too much of me.

I received a letter today from you and one from Agnes.[18] My last letter acknowledges the receipt of a letter from Pa and Mary[19] and the nice time I had at Christmas. I would rather by far have spent it with you.

I send you some vaccine matter on shreds, to be used in this way. With the point of your knife or lancet make an incision and insert a piece of thread. Stick on it a piece of courtplaster. We are having small pox here every few days. Ned Moore[20] & Rich. Lloyd[21] are in the hospital on the other side of the street, wounded. They are improving. I have a great deal more to write, but must get to my books. Love to all. Thank you for the money, until you are better paid. Saw Bob McRae [MacRae][22] today.

> Affectionately your bro.
> Thomas F. Wood

I must confess that I was not diligent at lectures except on interesting subjects, but I tried to make up at the Hospital by reading textbooks. In

January 1862 I got an invitation from the Surgeon General of the Army to appear before the Board of Medical Examiners at Richmond, for the appointment as Assistant Surgeon. I was quite sure that this was at the instance of my friend Dr. Manson. This was my first course of lectures, and the term would not be over until March, three months after my examination. I had just two months to prepare in, and knowing that it was known that I was not a graduate, one of my professors, Dr. Peticolas being on the Army Board, and knowing that if I failed that I would be conscribed and sent to the Army as a private, I studied very hard. I received the encouragement of everyone connected with the Hospital, and allowed all the time I wanted to study.

The Richmond Board was very strict. I could hear every week of men rejected, some of them old doctors, and some fresh from College. I was kept in a feverish state for these two months. In order to continue my studies late into the night I would resort to wetting my head in ice cold water, and other means, but after 10 o'clock I could do little or nothing.

During my course or earlier, my friend and former fellow student, Dr. Hugh Walker Gardner[23] was brought to the Officers' Hospital (No. 10) and died there with abcess of the liver. He had had a very hard time. He presented himself to the Goldsborough Examining Board for Assistant Surgeon and had the mortification of being rejected. That Board was the easiest of all to pass I had always heard but they rejected my accomplished friend. Three months later he applied to the Richmond Board and passed such a good examination that he was made a Surgeon. From the issue of his appointment he had been unpleasantly associated but at the time was assigned to a battery of artillery. He took the Chickahominy Fever after the "Seven Days Battle" ending. Poor fellow, he suffered greatly. His poor mother was there, but so great was the stench of gangrene of his lungs, (the abcess bursting upward through them) that she could not stay in the room to see him die.[24] I closed his eyes and heard his dying testimony that his trust was in Jesus. John DeRosset was an assistant in the Hospital and attended Gardner through his sickness.[25] DeRosset encouraged me greatly to persevere for an appointment as Assistant Surgeon, knowing the difficulties of the situation. I saw him occasionally as he was the Inspector of Hospitals of the Department of Henrico, including Richmond.

> [During his studies at the Medical College and in his work at the hospital, especially in the "fever ward," Thomas Fanning Wood kept a written record of the illnesses, diseases, and injuries he witnessed accompanied by his observations of the various treatments involved. He carefully noted the similarities between typhoid fever and typhus when most of the eminent physicians of the day had concluded that they were very different diseases. He wrote that even though there is a marked difference in the symptoms, the

diseases themselves are different only in degrees of the same pathological disturbance. He examined individual cases and the diagnoses that supported this belief.

He discussed a case involving a young man admitted to the hospital with weak pulse and irregular heart beat. The man was in the artillery and believed that his ailment was due to firing heavy ordinance. The diagnosis was enlargement of the heart, but TFW noted that there was no mention of the fact that the man probably had a diseased heart before he became an artillerist.

He also discussed what he calls "Army Rubeola" or Measles. He notes: "This disease has occured [sic] in our army to a great extent among raw troops. It differs from the ordinary form of the disease in occuring [sic] the second time." At that time doctors had not recognized the difference between regular measles and German measles which would account for the second occurrence.

These notes were a great help to him in sorting out symptoms and causes of disease, as well as an understanding of the proper treatment. These notes were also the beginning of his dedication to written case studies and formed the basis for his later medical journal.][26]

The great day in February came and I was to appear before the Board.[27] It was very cold—my moustache was stiff with ice, when I reached the place on Main Street above the old American Hotel.[28] I was shown into a dark, cold and dirty looking room in the 2nd story. There were two little boys (ushers) who sat on high stools in the room, one or the other being always on duty for messages and to watch the candidates that they did not speak to each other, or bring any book or paper into the room. The custom was to examine two candidates at a time, and my colleague at the time was a middle aged Doctor from Alabama. I don't remember his name. He had been in practice for some years. He was a little deaf. We had little to say to each other, our thoughts being too much occupied with the trial which was before us. We had not long been seated in the cold room—no fire at all—before a boy brought in a blank sheet of fools-cap with the name of the subject written on the first line, and upon this subject we were expected to write. I don't know if the boy gave me mine by chance or not, but my subject was "Typhoid Fever", and that of my friend "Compression and Concussion of the Brain". I was fortunate because I had charge of fever cases for months and had kept records of my cases. In addition I was saturated with the writings of Louis and Huss. The French school being in great favor I made use of all the quotations I could from the great masters, and I thought I did very well. I had not finished my paper before my colleague who being undergoing his examination in another room, came back where I was in a state of excitement showing that he had been rejected. This did not tend to raise my spirits, but I felt safe on my "Typhoid Fever" paper.

I was pretty soon called to go before the Board for oral examination. There was a good fire in this room and I was cold and shivering from cold and excitement. Dr. H.F. Campbell, of Augusta, Georgia, was first to question me. He saw that I was cold and asked me to be seated at the fire and warm myself and not get excited. His manner was very kind. He seemed to know exactly what I wanted to be questioned upon, for he took me up on the diseases of the chest, beginning with the physical signs. For these I gave the simplified terms, in use by J. Hughes Bennett in his Clinical Medicine. I saw that Dr. Campbell was pleased with my answers. He also examined me on the action of medicines in diseases of the chest. I was after a while quite at ease, but I don't think I would have been had I known that Dr. Peticolas (my professor and member of the Board) was amusing himself sketching me, as was his custom, I learned. I think I went from Dr. Campbell to Dr. Peticolas for examination in anatomy. He examined me on the physical and general anatomy of the arteries, and was very particular, knowing I suppose that I was an undergraduate. From Dr. Peticolas, I was taken in hand by Dr. St. George Peachy, on surgery. His plan seemed to be to go on until he stalled (or "stumped" as the college boys say) the candidate. He took me all over the field of fractures until he finally came to the fracture of the lower jaw. I described the fracture and the apparatus, and often this was asked, "how I would feed my patient?" I thought of milk baths, enemata of nutritious substances, and at last gave it up. He suggested either extracting a tooth before applying the apparatus, or passing a tube around behind the last molar tooth, and feeding the patient on fluids. During the examination I found I was right in an answer and that Dr. Peachy was wrong, and that Dr. Peachy sustained me. I don't know how long I was in this examination, but it seemed like a long time. I left the room with a feeling that I had succeeded, although there was no intimation of it from any member of the Board.

I returned to the Hospital in this state of uncertainty, and so remained for a few days, when one morning an official note reached me through the mail, directed to "Assistant Surgeon Thomas F. Wood", announcing that I had passed my examinations successfully and must report to the Surgeon General for orders.

SIX

THE NEW ASSISTANT SURGEON

D r. Thomas Fanning Wood was thrilled to have the new title "Assistant Surgeon" but was totally unaware of the burdens and responsibilities that accompanied that title. He hoped for an assignment in wartime Richmond but soon found he had a tougher job ahead of him than expected. A shortage of surgeons was a constant drain on everyone in the armies. The Confederacy never had more than 3,200 physicians in the field, an average of one surgeon per 312 soldiers. Neither side in this war possessed physicians with experience to deal with large numbers of incapacitated men. As the war progressed, the growing number of casualties forced many examining boards to relax their criteria and license assistant surgeons with minimal training, depending on the battlefield to provide much needed experience. Ignorance and assumption too often prevailed where understanding and education would one day exist.[1] The dedicated but poorly trained new assistant surgeon, Dr. Wood, was assigned to the field and would face a brutal and bloody challenge in the upcoming Chancellorsville Campaign.

My friends at the hospital were quite jubilant and gave me supper and made other manifestations. Dr. Manson at the time had only one Assistant Surgeon having rid himself of a Maryland doctor, who was very incompetent. He fully expected that I would be assigned to him, and requested the Surgeon General to that effect. I reported to the Surgeon General's office for orders requesting a leave of absence to procure a uniform, etc. This was granted with the addition, "and at the expiration of which time he will report where he is."

I paid little attention to the meaning of the order, but came home, (Wilmington) and found the family on the Sound (Masonboro Sound at the Fowler's) where Pa had gone to make salt, and where the family took refuge during the yellow fever epidemic which began in August 1862, and continued until October or November of that year.[2] My stay was very short and I found outside of the family very few persons I knew, or who cared that I had achieved what (to me) was a very important feat. The family of course was very glad, but principally, I believe because of the exemption from danger, which the new office brought. I was now 22 years old, rather an unripe specimen of a doctor, with but a young moustache, and not much external evidence of wisdom and skill, but my appointment was a great source of internal satisfaction.

Richmond at the time of my residence there was a very busy city. The streets were crowded with soldiers and strangers from all parts of the South, and from Maryland. The Confederate authorities were particularly tender of the feelings of the Marylanders, as in that state there was a large secession element, and we were all anxious that Maryland would go with us.[3] Negro minstrels, gamblers, gentlemen-at-large, handsomely dressed in citizens' clothes were nearly always Marylanders. Many of them were in the service, but more of them were seeking their fortunes, with the new government. Every day on the street, I saw someone I knew from North Carolina. Our Congressmen visited us occasionally to see how the sick and wounded were doing at the Hospital. We had a good laugh at one visit. Honorable Mr. George Davis was then Senator from North Carolina and Mr. Thomas McDowell (Bladen County) a Representative from my district. They made me an early visit before the Surgeon in charge had come down, and I did the honors, showing them the cooking arrangements, dining room, etc., etc., on the first floor. We then started up stairs to the first ward. I had forgotten that a case of small-pox had broken out the night before in this ward, and it occurred to me when we were half way up stairs that I had better announce the fact to the gentlemen, lest they might have some fear of the disease. Accordingly I did so, and it did not take more than a simple statement before they were making a hasty retreat, for the front door. Some of "the boys" looked upon it as a joke but I had no idea of perpetrating a joke upon such distinguished men.

The appearance of small-pox in our hospital was the beginning of my

Official appointment of Thomas Fanning Wood as assistant surgeon in the North Carolina Troops of the Army of the Confederacy, April 1, 1862. Thomas Fanning Wood Collection, Wilmington, N.C.

interest in a subject which was always after an absorbing one. Small-pox was quite plentyful in Rocket[t]s among children. Vaccine was not of a good quality, and had been greatly deteriorated by private maccinations by the means of vaccine crusts or "scabs".[4] Small-pox patients were at the time sent to Howard's Grove Hospital.[5] On the appearance of the disease, the subordinate in the Hospital had agreed that if one of us should be taken with small-pox we would nurse him privately and not send him to Howard's Grove. Shortly after I was taken with fever, pain in the back and head, and symptoms which looked very much like small-pox. I had been vaccinated about three years and since, but the last time gave no characteristic evidences of "taking."[6] I was not at all alarmed, but I was put into a room by myself and quarantined. The "boys" were faithful to their word, but I noticed that when they came in it was not for more than a moment, until after three days of fever and lonesomeness on my part, no eruption having shown itself I was gradually restored to my duty. Vaccination had saved me.

I got a little practice in Rocket[t]s,[7] which was of service to me if not to the patients. On one occasion a woman sent for me who had a large absess under her chin, extending across the neck as far as the carotids. It was from a blow from her husband, and of course she was an Irish woman. I remember how puzzled I was, whether I had a bloody tumor or an absess, and what danger there was in putting my lancet in it. What if I opened the large mass and a carotid should pump away and cause death. This was before the day of examination with grooved exploring needles or hypodermic syringes or aspirators, and no wonder I dismayed. At any rate I ventured, made a free incision in the middle line and out poured the pus and the woman was made happy as well as the embryo "doctor." I was highly applauded by the demonstrative Irish woman, but got no pay. In fact she saw by this time that I was practicing for glory, a thing very hard for a young doctor to keep to himself.

On another occasion I was called to see an Irish baby, that had been "given up" by Dr. Wellford. Either the child was so sick that Dr. W did not think it worth while to call again, or else he was too hard pressed to give his attention. At any rate I was accepted as the "doctor" and took the case in hand. I was not far enough advanced to know a case of pneumonia or bronchitis especially in a child so near death, as this one seemed to be. So I looked wise, did very little and waited to see what would happen, not a bad way under such circumstances for anybody. In a few days my patient was convalescent, and finally got well. This gave me great credit, all attributing it to my skill with that narrow sightedness which would under opposite circumstances have condemned me for failure. Much to my surprise, a few days after being Christmas, a very nice dinner was sent to me in compliment to my success and we all enjoyed it.

All articles of clothing were very high in Richmond, and Confederate money was beginning to decline in value. I remember one incident which will show the state of affairs. I took a walk with Mr. Warner L. Fleming (a native of Goochland, Virginia) steward of our Hospital up to Broad Street, high up, and strolled into a dry goods store. We found a piece of beaver cloth, heavy, black, shaggy on the inside. It had been on hand some time and was held at the very high price of $15.00 a yard, 5 yards for $45.00. It was considered very extravagant but I bought three yards with the trimmings costing about $5.00 more, took it to a tailor, who made it for $18.00. The overcoat cost then $68.00 and was considered in that day, a very handsome garment. I appeared with it on the street for the first time in the Winter of '62–'63, and had offers to sell it for sums which were very much more than I gave, but the eager manner of the would-be purchaser showed how scarce such common articles were. This coat served me excellently. It had a large rolling collar which I could turn up over my ears, and a long skirt with which to keep my legs warm.

This coat had a further history. When we were in the Valley of Virginia with

General Early I came near being arrested as a spy.[8] We made a march at night through a bridle path in the mountain, and with the greatest secrecy and caution, and about daybreak, a cold frosty morning, we debouched upon a plain where we waited the appearance of some picked cavalry who were to capture the ememy's outpost. It was given out that there was a spy in camp wearing a black overcoat. I was very cold and was walking up and down near my brigade (then that of General W.R. Cox of North Carolina, formerly Ramseur's)[9] and walked into the lines of Butler's Brigade, when Col. Forsythe arrested me. I thought it was a joke at first, but although I knew the Colonel, I had to show my credentials before he would believe he had not caught the right man. It was just daybreak and it was not easy to discern features. This old coat was a good friend though, and served as a blanket and dress coat, was very durable and warm and easily cleaned of mud and clay after a campaign.

Richmond was very early in the war put under martial law, so that persons coming in and going out had to have a "pass", from the Provost Martial.[10] Guards were stationed all about in the busiest streets to demand the "pass" or passport from the authorities. The guards were from the soldiers who had seen service, and seemed to delight in arresting anyone without, especially if he happened to be well dressed, for in the latter case, the evidence was that he was shirking his duty and ought to be put in the field. Sometimes the guard was unfortunate enough not to know how to read and had to call upon his superior officer to pass upon the authenticity of the passport. While I was attending lectures I greatly enjoyed wearing citizens' clothes, and felt free to do so bearing the order of the Secretary of War—James Seddon, I believe.[11] I remember one morning walking pretty briskly on Main Street towards the College, feeling quite proud and perhaps showing it in my carriage, I was considered the right sort of chap to arrest; "take in out of the dew" as the army slang went. The poor fellow could not read however, and had to call upon his Lieutenant to read my "pass", as it differed from the brown paper of the usual passport. I suppose that not being able to read he had been relying on the color of the paper as the genuineness of the "pass", and mine being in the form of a special order from the Secretary of War it was too much for his limited education. Such men made good soldiers though, and they were in ernest doing their duty, for the war was a life and death struggle, and the South required every man to do his share in whatever place he was called serve. To return to my guard. I was of course allowed to pass, but every few days I had to undergo the same scrutiny, and of course everyone else did. Especially was it bothersome when one wore citizens' clothes, for near every man throughout the South wore a uniform of some sort, and indeed after the second year of the war, I doubt if you could have bought enough black or any other sort than gray cloth of which to make a suit.

In Richmond the Jews were especially the active merchants. At first they volunteered in considerable numbers, but the thirst of money-making induced most of them to get out of the Army upon one pretext or another. Wilmington from 1862 to 1865 was headquarters of the Confederacy for goods of all sorts, brought in through the blockade. At auction sales Jews and Gentiles, too gathered and the prices brought were fabulous. At one sale of Cronly and Morris (the chief auctioneers) the sales amounted to four million dollars, and their deposits at the bank were so large that it was refused except as a special deposit—they did not have clerks to count it. Money kept declining in value and goods kept going up, so that whatever went from one person to another increased always in price from day to day. Everything was saleable. Course crockery, pins, corsets, cutlery, calico, etc., etc., much of which was of English manufacture coming through Nassau. I remember one very ingenious device, that of a patent button sent to me while I was in the field. It consisted of two parts. With a sharp stick you made a hole in your pants, pushed a little peg like this with a sharp tip, through the cloth and screw the round top or button proper on to it. This was a great convenience as bottons were always coming off, and no mother or sister at hand to put them on.

Another device was a sheet of paper with a flap, which could be so folded as to make a neat self-sealing envelope. This was English too, and a somewhat similar plan has been adopted (1886) by the Post Office Department. These were novelties and only a very few ever saw them. Pa and Brother Bob were both in Cronly and Morris auction store, and were always on the lookout for my comfort. From them I got a complete suit of rubber with a broad cape, coat, leggings, hat and gloves, so that I was completely weather-proof. But unfortunately in the Army it was as hard to keep such things as it was to get them.

The Confederate Congress met in Richmond, and was almost always in session even in the sound of the battlefield, I was told. I remember a story told by one of our men, A.B. Cook, that he went to a farm house to get something to eat, and being successful he was seated at the table with a lot of officers and one man they all called Mr. President. Cook did not know who he was but he heard the officers speaking in high praises of troops from all states but North Carolina, where upon Cook boiled over and joined in the conversation reminding them that North Carolina troops were in those fights although no one had said a word about it. He had his "say" out, which amused the party very much. Cook afterwards learned that he was giving his opinion to the President of the Confederacy.

The hotels in Richmond were the "American" and "Spottswood"[12] on Main Street and "Ballard's Exchange" on Franklin Street.[13] The patronage was great but after 1862 the fare was bad. There was no such thing as a genuine cup of coffee to be seen at the tables, only the miserable substitutes of rye, etc. The crockery was of a mixed sort, hardly half a dozen cups in sight were of the same pattern, and although of the coursest, heaviest ware, was chipped and cracked. The fare was expensive, far above the reach of private

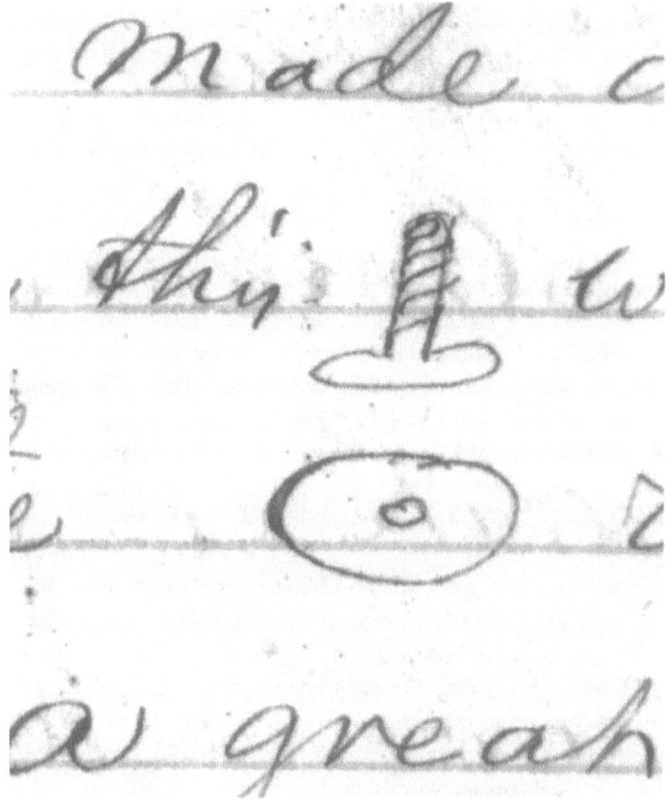

New quick repair trouser button assembly from Thomas Fanning Wood's Memoirs, book 2, page 47. (Drawn approximately 1886.) Thomas Fanning Wood Collection, Wilmington, N.C.

soldiers who got $11 a month, and after a late day in the war, seldom one was to be seen at the tables. The men generally carried their rations with them, or depended upon the wayside peddlers for food. After a while all these disappeared, and some of the states fitted up a "soldiers' home" near the depot where soldiers going to and from the Army were well fed, and the officers were charged a nominal sum. The home was under the care of Dr. Manson, and immediately superintended by Dr. S.W. Murphy, a recent graduate of the Virginia Medical College.[14]

    Dr. Murphy came to Richmond from Baltimore and was given a position as ward master at the Moore Hospital during my residence there. He had lived in North Carolina formerly and may have been born there. His father and his brothers were Episcopal ministers. Dr. Murphy had a good classical education and took up the notion of studying medicine after coming into the Confederacy. I don't think that he had any real tastes for the study, but it seemed to be the best he could do. We were a great deal together and he was quite companionable.

During my stay in Richmond I had an abundant time to go to church. Church going was much neglected in those days, as all parades, and inspections and movements of troops seemed to be done on Sundays. I am quite sure I did not do my whole duty, not connecting myself with any church during my stay there. But matters were very uncertain, and from week to week I hardly knew what would happen, and unfortunately I became careless with the rest and shamefully neglected my previleges. I attended sometimes Broad Street Methodist[15] and sometimes a Methodist Church at the foot of Church Hill. I made no acquaintances at either of them. Christian people though were actively engaged looking after the spiritual interests of the soldiers. They visited the hospitals, took the sick and wounded into their homes, and were full of patriotism and hope for our success. In fact in those days if anyone ever dreamed of failure, it was seldom if ever hinted at by persons in conversation.

I attended the organization of the Army and Navy Surgeons Medical Association.[16] It took place in one of the rooms of the Virginia Medical College. I was but a looker on, attracted by a sight of the men whose names I had often heard. I heard Dr. J.J. Chisholm, Dr. M. Michael, Dr. E.S. Galliard, and others speak, and saw the Surgeon General S.P. Moore and many others there. I think the subject of the discussion was "when should a gun shot wound be treated as a simple incised wound and closed up"—if this was not the thesis, the subject took that range. The majority of speakers were inclined only in the rarest cases to close these wounds, but allow free suppuration,[17]—drainage and antiseptics were of course not employed. The application of cold water and frequent renewal of dressings was the routine.

This society begun the issue of a medical journal under the title of the "Army and Navy Surgeons' Medical Journal", a complete copy of which I have in my library with a note from its editor, Dr. M. Michel, on the history of some of the later issues. It is at this date a rarity and will be very rare in a few years.

Before my time (10 days) were up I presented myself at the Surgeon General's office at Richmond. I knew his reputation for abruptness, but I put on a bold face. He kept me standing a long time before he would notice me, but when I got the opportunity I presented my orders, and after looking at the paper, he said in a very cross manner, "what are you doing here, you were ordered to report where you were?" I replied that I understood the order to mean to report where I was at the end of my leave and that I did so accordingly. My chief object was to get to Richmond and so increase my hopes of getting into the Moore Hospital, as Dr. Manson's Assistant. I was ordered to report on a certain day to the Surgeon General's office for orders. I was promptly on hand, and my orders were very short to report to Medical Director LaFayette Guild,[18] Army of Northern Virginia in the field. So ended my hope of being stationed in Richmond. I had been there in all about eight months, and had become so used to the comparative luxury of the life, I did not relish the idea of going into the field. But there was no hope otherwise and from what I now know, it was the turning point in my life.

It was very disagreeable weather in February 1863 when I started to report to Army Headquarters. I took the train for Hamilton's Crossing,[19] a station on the Richmond and Fredericksburg Railroad and on alighting I found that Medical Director Guild's quarters were two or three miles from the station, and the snow was quite deep. There was nothing to do but plunge out into the snow, or go back to Richmond, for there was no place of public entertainment any where near. After a long drag through the melting snow I arrived at Dr. Guild's tent, and was shown without ceremony into the tent. He was an old Army officer, comfortably housed in a large marquie tent, with a broad open fireplace, which seemed quite snug and comfortable to me who had been out in the disagreeable weather. Dr. Guild was sick with gout, sitting up in a chair with his disabled feet carefully swaddled in red flannel, on a camp stool. He gave me a right cheerful welcome and ordered a hot toddy for me. "What brought you out in such weather. You must be an old soldier", were his complimentary remarks. I soon entered into an agreeable conversation, and explained that I would like to be assigned to the 3rd or 18th North Carolina Regiments. He replied that he would do the best he could, to assign me to Jackson's Corps, and he had no doubt that Dr. Hunter McGuire[20] would let me go where I desired if there was a vacancy.

After a pleasant hour passed in conversation, I returned to the station. By this time it was nearly night, and I had no where to go, and no prospect of a lodging even under a tent. I determined to strike out for Marye House,[21] but they politely declined being over run with company. I struck out then in search of a place and finally arrived at Captain Allsops [Alsop][22] about late suppertime. Here my fine new overcoat got me into trouble. I rapped anxiously at the door, and the proprietor himself came to the door, when I told my story and made quite an urgent request for entertainment, I was very prompt and bluntly refused. But while the old captain stood with the door half opened one of my old friends, Major Wood[23] of the 10th, 23rd or 37th Virginia Regiment overheard my conversation, and called out, just as the Captain was shutting the door, "Why that's Dr. Wood." I was very thankful for this interposition, for as soon as I was recognized as a Confederate the old Captain gave me a warm welcome, and I was soon installed in his home, where he had many officers as guests. He explained jokingly that he took me for a "d—— Yankee" judging by my fine clothes. That spies were prowling about and that he had no idea of letting them under his roof. Captain Allsop's house was at a place near Fredericksburg called "The Summit", situated on a high hill overlooking the town. His hospitality was very cordial, and when the time of departure came I was pressed to stay. But I left the next day, and made my way to Guiney's station,[24] where I expected to get some way to Jackson's Corps, then stationed at the Corbin House[25] and towards Port Royal, but meeting some old friends there I went to Richmond.

While there I met Dr. Josh C. Walker.[26] He was just from home and had been recently married, was on his way to the 3rd Regiment, wanted some one to take his place that he might go back to Wilmington to take charge of the Marine Hospital in the military district of his brother-in-law, General W.H.C. Whiting.[27] I went back to the army and took up my quarters with the 3rd N.C. regiment (February 1863) then stationed at Skinker's Neck.[28] I found there the Rev. Mr. Patterson who had lately arrived in camp to assume his duties as Chaplain. I joined the mess at Captain John F.S. Van Bokkelen's quarters. It was a large one, composed of Captain Van Bokkelen, Dr. Walker (Assistant Surgeon), Lieutenant James I. Metts, Lieutenant William H. Barr, Dr. James Clark, Reverend Mr. Patterson, John Cowan, Ned Armstrong and myself.

My next anxiety was to get assigned to this regiment and borrowed a horse to make the rounds to Medical Director McGuire. The horse I rode belonged to Captain Rhodes[29] who was killed at Sharpsburg. He had no proper care, and the mules in search of salt, which was very scarce, had eaten the hair off his tail, leaving nothing but the bare stump. On my way to Dr. McGuire's I had to pass through the camps of several brigades, and the men crowded to the roadside amused at the appearance of my horse, and cheered and annoyed me with all sorts of jeering remarks.[30] A comic song was in vogue " Mister here's your mule", and the favorite salutation was "Here's your mule, here's your mule." I had to stand it, for it was no use to show one's temper before two or three thousand soldiers bent on having fun.

I found Dr. Mcguire at his tent, and for the first time saw Stonewall Jackson. He had his new uniform on, given to him by the ladies after the Battle of Fredericksburg. Dr. McGuire was very kind and assigned me to Trimble's Division. Dr. Coleman was Chief Surgeon of that Division, but I had to delay my visit to his headquarters until another day. Dr. Coleman was not inclined to be so accomodating as his superiors and wanted to assign me to Nichol's Louisana Brigade, but at another visit to his quarters got his clerk to assign me to Taliaferro's Brigade in the 3rd Regiment.[31] My assignment enabled Dr. Walker to return to N.C. where he was installed as Surgeon in charge of the Marine Hospital.[32] Dr. James F. McRee, Jr., was the surgeon of the 3rd Regiment at the time.[33] He was my first preceptor, and treated me with kindness, and set me to work. Dr. McRee did little or nothing towards the work of the Regiment except when he was called upon specially or was required by his office. He was very fond of his ease and read novels and entertained old friends nearly all of his extensive leisure.

Hd. Quarters 3d Regt.
near Guineys' Sta. Va.

Dear Pa,

I am at last in the field, but I am agreeably surprised at finding everything here so comfortable. In my new position the field is quite as pleasant as it could be anywhere *except* in the Hospital. But the difference between this & the hospital is much less than when I left the field. We have little to do—comfortable quarters, substantial fare (no sweet potatoes though) and good company. If I succeed in getting in this Regt., which Drs. McRee and Walker will make an effort, you will not hear me grunt again until the war is over. Or if I even get into any Regt. as good as this I will be satisfied. I forgot to explain to the girls[34] the reason they did not get the things they wrote to me for. Tell them I have been so busy preparing for camp that I have had but little opportunity and that they shall have them by express soon. I wish if Joe Jacobs[35] is at home that they will ask him to stop at the Hospital in Richmond for a package for me.

The weather up here is quite cold, but I feel all the better for it provided we can be free from rain. The roads are better now, but have been in terrible condition. It took us five hours to come 11 miles by wagon from Guiney's to camp. The army news is of no importance. Dr. McGuire, Med. Director for Jackson's Corps told me he thought there would be a movement soon.

Every one of the boys from Wilmington are well. Send me some potatoes etc., and if you will let me know, I will send you down transportation to Richmond for it.

With love to all

I am affectionally, Your son
Thomas

The Hospital Steward of the Regt. was George W. Williams,[36] a brother of Captain Williams of the Regt. who was killed at Sharpsburg. George Williams was a medical student in Wilmington at one time, was good natured, attended to his duties, rather indolent, and fond of pulling teeth. One of his peculiarities was to carry his extracted teeth in a bag, and whatever else might be lost, he clung to his trophies.

I well remember my first service at Surgeon's call.[37] The Regiment now under the command of Major Thruston,[38] was quite full and the sick were numerous. I got along well at the first sick call, but discovered at once, that my chief difficulty would be learning the men before I could rely upon their

Dr. Thomas Fanning Wood, newly appointed Assistant Surgeon, 3rd North Carolina Regiment. Thomas Fanning Wood Collection, Wilmington, N.C.

statements as to their ailments. The judgement of the Assistant Surgeon, as to the ability of a man claiming to be sick settled the matter for that day, and upon the doctor's statement of his condition the man was put on duty or excused. The Orderly Sargeant selected his details for duty for the day upon the authority of the doctor, and it was necessary therefore that justice should be done. In camp there were always men who relied upon an excuse from the Surgeon to get off duty. These men were known as "Hospital Rats", and were very troublesome to sargeants and surgeons. I remember on one occasion a case of doubtful sort was referred to Dr. McRee for his judgement and decision. He directed a Hospital Steward to give him a cup of castor oil. It was administered from a large tin cup on the spot, and was intended of course as a rebuke for the malingerer. But he was not to be defeated by such tactics, and gravely wiping his greasy lips with his coat sleeve remarked, "he would be obliged to get a full dose of *ile*[39] if there was any to spare", passing back his cup for another dose.

An incident of my first Surgeon's call will show how far on I had gotten in medicine—in ready diagnosis. A patient presented himself with an eruption of clear large vesicles[40] about his waist on both sides. I was puzzled, not having seen it before. I noticed that the man was somewhat concerned and spoke of it as the "Shingles."[41] He was alarmed by the tradition that it was fatal, if the eruption extended around the girdle, and on this account it attracted some attention. Fortunately in military practice, the doctor was not expected to enter into explanations and soothing assurances, therefore I prescribed a lotion and dismissed the case. I went to my tent and found a copy of *Watson's Practice*, and read up on

Captain John F. S. Van Bokkelen, commander Company D, 3rd North Carolina Infantry. Thomas Fanning Wood Collection, Wilmington, N.C.

the case of shingles and ever after that I made it a rule to keep my own council upon doubtful matters, and resort to the silent and wise counsellors—good books—that treat the wise and the unwise alike, if they come with industry to consult them. After this in all my professional life I made it a duty to study my cases, even though I considered myself quite familiar with them.

My stay in the Skinker's Neck camp was a pleasant one. I had the opportunity to become acquainted with the men, and to prepare for the Spring Campaign. Not very much skill could be displayed in a camp practice, where men as soon as they became seriously sick were sent to the field hospital. My practice was principally in diagnosis and treatment of simple ailments, a good introduction to practice, and one that served me a good purpose in after life. Young men usually going into practice from civil life have to wait for patients, and get into practice very slowly. In my case I had an abundance of involuntary patients, from whom I could gather valuable information. I seldom referred to the Surgeon (Dr. McRee) as I desired at once to become self reliant and gain the confidence of the men and officers.

CAPTAIN JOHN F. S. VAN BOKKELEN

In this Regiment were many old friends whom I had not seen during the war. John Van Bokkelen, Captain of Company D, was the son of Mr. A.H. Van Bokkelen of Wilmington. He was about 22 or 23, a handsome young man, with bright expressive black eyes. He was either a Harvard College graduate or was a student there when the war broke out. His father clothed and cared for his men at first before the Confederate Government made arrangements to care for the troops.

The first Captain to the Company was Captain Edward Savage of Wilmington who was promoted to Lt. Colonel on the promotion of Col. Cowan and the death of Col. Gaston Meares, the first Colonel of the Regiment. Col. Meares was killed at Malvern Hill. Col. Savage had resigned before I reached the Regiment. Van Bokkelen succeeded him, and had an excellent company under good discipline, but thoroughly in love with their Captain. He was firm and lenient where he could be. He looked after the comfort of his men, and saw that the laggers and skulkers did not impose upon the true and willing men; looked after their quarters and clothing; saw that they were promptly cared for when sick, and exercised a paternal care over them, although he was young as the youngest man in ranks. At home the wives and children of every man in his company was provided for by his patriot father, Mr. A.H. Van Bokkelen and this was an additional bond which united his men to him. Captain Van Bokkelen was well educated, had a fine literary taste, very healthful and permeating all who came in contact with him. He had several good books in camp, and reading was indulged in to some purpose. The fewness of the books made them all the more sought after, and made all read more diligently perhaps. When I joined his mess, Bulwer's *Strange Story* had just come out in the G.S. [Editor's note: TFW probably intended "G.S." to be "C.S." for Confederate States.][42] It was the custom at the mess table to discuss which was being read, the *Strange Story* was then in full blast. I had not read the book, but I sat every day for an hour or so at camp dinner with no dessert but the discussion of the *Strange Story*, until I thought I knew it by heart.

In these discussions, Van Bokkelen, Jim Clark, Rev. Mr. Patterson joined Dr. Walker having no turn that way, Bill Barr not interested, and I not knowing anything of the book. During this Winter we did not play cards at all that I remember, although "whist"[43] playing was quite common in a certain set, and poker playing, too prevalent in another set. VanBokkelen's mess was the headquarters of literary tastes, and in this he was sustained by Mr. Patterson.

Reverend Mr. Patterson, Our Chaplain

This last named gentleman (now Rev. Dr. G. Patterson living in Memphis, Tennessee) was an Episcopal minister, and had been Chaplain to the plantation of Mr. Josiah Collins of Scuppernong Lake in Tywell County in Eastern North Carolina. His citizen's costume consisted of a tall, soft hat, an overcoat made of Scotish shawl stuff black and gray, and made with long flowing sleeves, somewhat like the cut now called by the ladies a Dollman.[44] He was an old bachelor, fond of the society of young men, but a most exclusive Churchman of the strict construction school. Mr. Patterson's general

Reverend George Patterson, Chaplain, 3rd North Carolina Infantry. Thomas Fanning Wood Collection, Wilmington, N.C.

appearance was most peculiar. He had a clumsy shuffling gait at times, owing to the clumsy shoes he always chose, was a little round shouldered and this was increased by the peculiar set of his unmilitary Dollman overcoat. He was near-sighted and went smooth-shaven and his hair cropped pretty close. He brought great spirit and animation into the mess, and was ready always to discuss the topic of the day. Few of the men were Episcopalians, but quite a number of the officers were, and so were some of the officers of the 1st North Carolina, so intimately associated with us all during the war, and together it was possible to get up quite a good assemblage at Sunday services. We had daily short prayers each day in our mess with reading of the scriptures. Mr. Patterson had some peculiar ideas about his ecclesiastical jurisdiction in the regiment, and forbade the distribution of religious tracts by colporteurs without his permission and in this Lt. Col. Thruston sustained him. But the service of the Episcopal Church was not popular with the men and I don't think that a single man was ever attracted to it although several officers were. Mr. P. was very useful towards the men, and proved his Christian love by his daily intercourse, but he was not esteemed tolerant enough of the church-leaning of those not of his faith, to win any to his way of thinking.[45]

COLONEL THRUSTON

Lt. Col. Stephen Decatur Thruston (he was promoted to this rank about or after the Battle of Fredericksburg) was a native of Virginia but moved to

Smithville, North Carolina,[46] when he was a young man, shortly he graduated in medicine.[47] He attended lectures at the University of Virginia, and graduated at the University of Pennsylvania as M.D. When he moved to Smithville the small town did not afford enough support for him and his competitor, Dr. Walter G. Curtis, and Dr. Thruston supplemented his living by teaching school. He married Dr. Everitt's daughter. Dr. Everitt of Smithville, the eccentric old physician, a man of much reputation for his roughness and a certain sort of success, especially in accumulating quite a fortune. He at one time lived in Wilmington, owning the house once the residence of Governor E.B. Dudley, now the residence of Pembroke Jones.[48] When the war cloud was gathering, Dr. Thruston was one of the foremost men in his section to advocate secession and I think he was one of the party that took forceable possession of Fort Caswell, in advance of the secession of the State. In a campaign (political) in which secession was the issue he made earnest secession speeches. I remember his telling me of his great embarrassment during one of his attempts. There was a very eccentric and witty lady living at or near Smithville. She was very bright and the public generally acceded to her liberties of speech quite uncommon among the members of her sex. On the occasion referred to, Dr. Thruston was enumerating the causes for secession when he was interrupted by an undertone voice, quite distinct to him, "That's a lie! That's a lie!" It did not quite disconcert him, but he said that he could scarcely hold his ground.

When the call from President Lincoln came for 75,000 men, all the state flew to arms, and John Badger Brown and Dr. Thruston raised a company in Duplin County. Brown probably raised the company, and having no military experience he yielded the highest office to Thruston. This Company was made a part of the 3rd regiment which was mustered into service on the 16th of May, 1861. Captain Thruston took to military life as one trained to it. He was subordinate, alert, faithful and commanded as he obeyed. He was cool, decisive and of a bright and bouyant disposition. In 1863 he probably was 39 years of age, rather below the average size. He was a good judge of human nature, read character instinctively, was a walking reference file of what was going on in the army and what was going to be. Where he got it all, nobody ever knew, but we were never surprised when Thruston told us what we were going to do, as he either knew, or had the military introspection which enabled him to forecast some likely probabilities. I had some misgivings as to how Thruston would receive me as his Assistant Surgeon knowing as he did that I entered the profession by the side door, and had not had any experience; but he became my friend (officially) at once. One matter in connection with Col. Thruston's career gave me much trouble on account of a friend and this I will speak of hereafter as it is a long story. In camp the Colonel was a good disciplinarian. The regiment had been raised on a war footing. Although the men were volunteers, they were enlisted for the war, and were from the uneducated class of farmers generally.

There were no companies, without I might mention Captain Craig's [Craige] Company from Washington and Albritton's from Gran. [Granville] County, that could be called gentlemen—that is men and officers all of the same class or set in civil life. The men were treated at once with the strict discipline of the regular army. Colonel Gaston Meares[49] was a West Point soldier, and he instilled this spirit of discipline in the first year of the war before they had been under fire. This beginning was strenuously maintained until the end, and made the Regiment what it was, one of the best of the North Carolina troops.

One incident will illustrate. There was a law allowing regiments to elect their officers when a vacancy occured. This was a bad law for the 3rd, as an election from among the men in many instances would have given for officers those who were merely popular, and popularity with the majority of soldiers would have its foundation in the leniency and indulgence in the man about to be promoted. The officers were strongly opposed to the law and determined to circumvent it. The first occasion was that in Captain Savage's Company [I]. An election for Junior 2nd Lieutenent had been ordered. It was freely discussed at regimental headquarters, and the whole matter was referred to Major W.L. deRosset[50] who instructed Lt. William Quince[51] what to do. The company was ordered out in the company "street" by the Sergeant and Lt. Quince took charge.

Lt. Quince announced, "Men, this is an election for the office of Junior 2nd Lieutenant. There are two names before you—all in favor of so-and-so (the man chosen by the Colonel) will shoulder arms—Company, shoulder arms!" Of course the company would not disobey such an order, and their compliance with the order was recorded as their unanimous vote. After this there was no further trouble—the Colonel nominated officers to the Governor of N.C., and he issued commissions accordingly. The policy of the regiment was not to confine itself to its own command, but wherever they could get a good man they selected him, and so there was no great degeneration of the "esprit du corps" of the organization.

Major Parsley

Major William Murdock Parsley was the Major when I joined the regiment. His father, Mr. O.G. Parsley was an old and prominent citizen of Wilmington, and when the war broke out was President of the Commercial Bank. He fitted out a company at his own expense. It was known as the Mechanics

Major (Lieutenant Colonel in this picture) William Murdock Parsley, Regimental Staff, 3rd North Carolina Infantry. Thomas Fanning Wood Collection, Wilmington, N.C.

Riflemen, and William Parsley was made Captain. R.S. Radcliffe, Tobe Garrison, and Henry Potter (all brickmasons) were Lieutenants. Parsley was not quite 21. He was undersize, but manly and a true gentleman, very much respected by his men and his superior officers. His father, like Mr. Van Bokkelen, was very good to the families of the men in his son's company. By the promotion of Major Thruston to the Lt. Colonelcy, Captain Parsley was made Major about the end of 1862.[52]

CAPTAIN JOHN B. BROWN

The promotion of Thruston to be Major, promoted Brown to be Captain of his own Company. John Badger Brown was from Kenansville, Duplin County.[53] He was a dry-goods merchant when the war broke out, and about 21 years old. He was quite handsome and neat in his appearance, but knew nothing whatever of military life except the education he got in the "3rd." He had an excellent company, and had his men well under control. Brown was fussy about the rights of his men, and always saw that they were well supplied with food and clothing if it could be had. He was not satisfied that the men had clothing but they must have well-fitting clothes. There was a warm attachment between him and his men. Brown developed soldierly qualities surprisingly. It was astonishing to his old friends who knew him as the somewhat exquisite city man, always neat and apparantly effeminate, to fall into military life as though he had been trained to it. His health was good, he was always at his post, he knew his rights and privileges, and maintained self-respect to a degree that made him a prominent officer. The old friendship of Thruston and Brown was interpreted by his rivals into partiality of the new Lt. Col. for the new Captain.

Captain H. W. Horne

Captain H. W. Horne, commanded Company C from Fayetteville.[54] Lt. Charles P. Mallett was his 1st. Officer, Lt. Graham, his 2nd. Horne was a lawyer, rather a small man, half bald, unmilitary in his appearance, and unambitious. He was exceedingly shrewd and had much of the knowledge of passing events that characterized Thruston. Like the Lt. Col. he was fond of the draw-poker and the two indulged in it more than was good for either. Co.C had good men, but not being well officered it lacked a good deal of the spirit of the other companies. Lt. Mallett was a good officer but was not enough in command of his company to counteract the laxity of his superior.[55] Mallett too, was young, and did not take seriously to the cares of his situation. He was brave and devoted, though, and was relied upon. I never could quite understand why Horne never thoroughly amalgamated with the other officers, without he was disappointed in his regimental assignment and would have preferred another regiment. He was well read and was very entertaining in his conversation, and especially when he warmed up in argument—he being a strong Calvinist—with Mr. Patterson on the Apostolic Succession. In the heat of argument one day, Horne told Mr. Patterson had he been born in the days of the Inquisition he would have been chief Inquisitor, and we had about the same opinion of Horne.

Captain Tom Armstrong

Captain Thomas E. Armstrong commanded Company K from New Hanover. Captain Williams was the original Captain. He was killed at Sharpsburg[56] and was a man of the most exceptional gallantry. He was rather an elder man when he served in the Regiment. Tom Armstrong succeeded him having Lt. Kitchen Powers and Ormsby as his Lieutenants. This was an excellent Company and was as good as the best in the army. I did not know Tom Armstrong intimately as he was a new acquaintance and was killed within a few months after I joined the Regiment.

Captain Ned Armstrong

Captain E.H. Armstrong commanded Company G, from Onslow County, raised by Captain Rhodes.[57] He was a young man about 21, a graduate, or a student of the University of N.C. He was beardless, fat, of a florid complexion, fresh and plump as a girl, and having much of the gentleness of a girl. He was a man of the

Captain Edward H. Armstrong, commander, Company G, 3rd North Carolina Infantry. The Thomas J. Armstrong and Family Private Papers, 1859–68, Manuscript Collection, William Madison Randall Library, University of North Carolina at Wilmington.

most rigid adherence to his duty. While amiable and affectionate and careful of the feelings of others, he never hesitated to do his duty however disagreeable. He was very brave, but strange to say he was not a secessionist, did not believe that we could secede against the North, and didn't consider it desirable if we could because of the dissensions which would spring up in the new Confederacy, but always deported himself in battle with the coolest courage. Of course he kept his opinions for his intimate friends. He was remarkably fortunate in battle having gone through every battle of his Regiment to the 10th of May, 1864 at Spotsylvania without a scratch.

Captain William Thomas Ennett

Company E was commanded by an old friend Captain W.T. Ennett.[58] He was born at Stump Sound, Onslow County, was a graduate of the University of N.C. He was about 22, and succeeded Captain Red the original captain of his Company. Red was sheriff of Onslow but made a poor Captain and resigned early in the war, leaving Ennett his successor. Captain Ennett got all his military training in the Regiment, and thoroughly imbibed the spirit of the organization. He was very popular with his men, and had them well under command, besides being kind as a friend. His company material was excellent. The men were sounders of the uneducated class, but tough, witty, and brave. Ennett had the respect of his superiors for his close attention to his duties, and his bravery. He was not a very strong man, and camp life developed rheumatism, but for all that he was faithful during the four years, seldom absent from the Regiment, and commanded the Brigade at Appomattox.

Lt. Cicero H. Craig [Craige]

Company I was raised in Washington, by Captain Arch. Craig[e]. He offered a commission of Lt. to his nephew Cicero Craig[e], who accepted it in 1862.[59] Cicero Craig[e] was a school mate of mine. His father John Craig[e] was a tailor. Cicero was rather a singular lad—somewhat weakly, not disposed to study, did not show any considerable intellectual capacity, except that he wrote a beautiful hand—most rapidly, and could cipher quickly and accurately. In 1860 he was before the U.S. District Court for enlisting a "fillabuster expedition with the Knights of the Golden Circle", whose design was to capture Nicraugua. I forget the sentence of the court, but Cicero went out to Memphis then, and was assistant in the County Court Clerk's office, and when the war broke out he joined the Oglethorpe Light Infantry of Augusta, Georgia and was in the campaign under General Lee in the battles fought in West Virginia.

Craig[e]'s accounts of these battles and the diagrams of the fields were very interesting and showed considerable acquired ability above that which I knew of him as a timid school boy. This campaign awoke in him a military ambition and daring which never deserted him. This calls to mind that he had no official connection with his Uncle's Company I (3rd Regiment) until the Battle of Sharpsburg. He won his appointment by volunteering to burn a barn in which the enemy's sharpshooters were lodged. In this act I think James Clark was also a volunteer and for which he was promoted.

Craig[e] had few intimates in the Regiment. He kept closely in his quarters, read and wrote a great deal, and studied most thoroughly tactics and army regulations. He was greatly animated by the adventures of the conspicuous men in the war, and built a great many castles and devised many schemes of enterprises for the dull months of Winter. None of these plans saw the light, but the more he made of them the more impatient he was of camp restraint. I don't know what was the original cause of Craig[e]'s dislike of Thruston, but I know that Craig[e] was irreconcilable, and insubordinate. I know that he was put in arrest after a tour of picket duty the Regiment made at Port Royal, while we were still in camp at Skinker's. Craig[e] was charged with leaving his post, and his defense involved the gentlemanly deportment of the Colonel. All the remaining days of the Winter were spent by Craig[e] in arrest in his quarters, during which time he was active in writing his defense and studying military law. I visited him often and was surprised in these conversations with the restlessness he displayed.

LT. ARMOND L. DEROSSET

Company H was raised by Captain Theodore Sikes, a dentist from Bladen County.[60] I heard that he had proven himself a very poor and untrustworthy soldier, and had resigned, I believe. This put Armond deRosset in command of the Company—as first Lt. and Bob Lyon as 2nd. I saw but little of Armond in camp as he was wounded at Sharpsburg and did not return to camp until Chancellorsville Campaign begun, May 1863.

LT. TOBE GARRISON

Garrison was a young mechanic who succeeded Radcliffe, who suceeded Parsley in command of Company F, the Wilmington Mechanics Riflemen.[61] He was a brave fellow, uneducated, and not at all a favorite in his Company. Henry Potter was another Lieutenent in the same Company. Altogether this Company was the poorest officered in the Regiment.

CAPTAIN ALBRITTON

Company A was one of the best in the Regiment.[62] There was a greater majority of educated men than in any other. From its ranks its officers were generally selected. Walter Clarke, the excellent Regimental Ordinance Sergeant was chosen from it. Albritton's 1st Lieutenant was Lane, a very gentlemanly officer who was captured at Spotsylvania.

ADJUTANT THEODORE C. JAMES

By the promotion of Adjutant W.A. Cumming to be Captain, there was a vacancy and Theodore Calhoun James who was at the time a private in the "3rd" Cavalry, was chosen to fill the vacancy.[63] James entered the service as a private in the Wilmington Light Infantry of the 18th Regiment, and was mustered out at the expiration of his 12 months term. He was a very conscientious, ambitious and brave young man. He had a high conception of honor, and lived up to his model as faithfully as most men. He was an ardent Confederate, and entered upon his duties with enthusiasm. His addition to the corps of officers was a most excellent acquisition for while he had never been in an engagement, his courage was undoubted. As an Adjutant he was impartial, and undisguidedly

Captain Richard F. Langdon, Quartermaster, 3rd North Carolina Infantry. Courtesy Cape Fear Museum, Wilmington, North Carolina.

impatient of the shortcomings of his brother officers. James was rather tart sometimes, but the cause was usually the lack of conscientious duty on the part of others, for when he trusted a man, it was hard to shake his confidence. In fact Theodore carried his likes and dislikes farther than this—his friends could do no wrong. At the time he joined the Regiment he was a ruddy, fair cheeked boy, about 22, considerably under size, but vigorous and alert, fond of camp life, and the friends he fell among in his new post were mostly all friends, and just such company as he would have chosen. He became a favorite and a "pet" officer from the first. This does not mean that he did not have some strong enemies, because to say this would be to say that the Regiment had no officers fond of neglecting their irksome duties of camp. I had known Theodore all his life. I had been at school with him, and saw him frequently, as a soldier, and personally his arrival was a welcome to me, and he from the first gave me his confidence as a friend, and what was still stranger, as a patient, for he had known nothing of me as a doctor. He settled down into his duties very easily as well he might, with nearly everything in his favor.

Captain R. F. Langdon

Captain Richard F. Langdon, was promoted from Lieutenent of the 1st.[64] to be Quartermaster of our Regiment.[65] He was a native of Wilmington and had served through the Sharpsburg Campaign in the line. His selection was a good one. He had good business habits and camp life suited his particular disposition. In camp he was the central figure in card parties and good times generally. He had been in California during the prevalence of the "gold fever" and had had some rough experiences. He could tell very entertaining stories, was well read, and a sharp man of the world. He knew his duties and prerogatives as a Quartermaster, and gave general satisfaction in that capacity.

I believe I have written enough of the military family of the "3rd" to give an idea of its officers. The whole regiment was under different discipline from that I remembered in the "18th"—all the difference between a "regular" and a "volunteer" regiment. Privates were required to be respectful to non-commissioned officers and officers, and it was quite habitual in our camp. Such was the habit, too, between officers. Although I might "mess"—eat and sleep with the Colonel, I would be as quickly reproved for not being on hand at Surgeons' Call (5:00 or 6:00 in the morning in the winter) as though I had been on the most formal relations.

The Ambulance Corps

The rule in force (1863) was that two, two-mule or two-horse ambulances were allotted to each regiment.[66] The ambulances were plain spring wagons without cushions, the bedding for the wounded men being such straw or hay as the driver was able to collect in the emergency. The driver had a seat in front on a box, and in this box he carried his possessions. The driver of one of our ambulances was Thomas Jefferson Capps, from Onslow County of the other ward from Greene County. These ambulances were under the control of the medical officers of the regiment. The ambulance corps consisted of twenty men—two from each company. These men were selected with care, generally because of the physical strength and personal courage of the men. They were relieved of general camp duty, and instead did irregular duties as were assigned them. They all willingly assisted the doctors in their personal matters. Each regiment was allowed a hospital cook and a medical knapsack bearer. Dr. McRee had selected from the ambulance corps one of the strongest men they had, Bishop, from Company C, as cook, and he held the place for a long time. Morton was my knapsack bearer. He was a young man from Onslow County. He was a short, stout boy, about 23 and carried the hospital knapsack and his own with perfect ease, and was always ready to do extra duty when called upon.[67] He was a picture of smiling good nature, under the most trying circumstances. Food might be scarce but Morton always had something for the Surgeon's Mess. Between Bishop and Morton we could always count on having all that was going—a good camp, food for ourselves and horses, a good camp fire and all the news of the day.

My first duty on the march was to answer to an alarm sounded at the threatening of cavalry at the ford of the Rappahannock at Port Royal. When we arrived there it happened that the enemy had abandoned their efforts, and the Brigade stacked arms to rest. I rode to the head of the line to get permission from the Colonel to look for something to eat and to see the village. When the men of another regiment perceiving that I was a new officer by my new uniform, saluted me as I rode along the line, "no danger now, Doctor to the front," and seemed to enjoy my confusion very much. There was no way to stop it of course and I, like many other man endured it. This was the custom in our army, and sometimes extended to the officers of the same regiment by the men. After I was fairly initiated though, I seldom had to stand such taunts. I have known the like to be done to a General. On one occasion General George H. Stuart [Steuart],[68] commanded his own and a Louisana Brigade. When they halted in camp one night special orders were sent out that no fence rails were to be burnt. Stuart's [Steuart's] own Brigade obeyed his command but the Louisanaians' helped themselves quite freely to the rails of the fences. The next day he ascertained the names of the companies and regiment and ordered that the expense of the rails be paid by them. In a few days Stuart [Steuart] was relieved from the command by the arrival of General Nichols, and as Stuart [Steuart] rode past this Louisana Brigade, the men called out "Rails." At first he turned in his saddle to mark the men to demand their punishment, but pretty soon it was taken up by so many voices—"rails", "rails", "rails", that he had to beat a retreat, and complain to General Nichols, which amounted to nothing, for Nichols had not control over his men in such things. Discipline was very poor in his Brigade, but the men fought very well; after the battles they were largely plunderers. They were composed of about three regiments of Irish Catholics to one of Protestants.

Outpost Picket Station
Morton's Ford, Rapid Ann [Rapidan] River[69]
April 4th 1863

My Dear Mother:

You see by the heading of my letter that I am on picket. If I dared, I would look back at the comfortable old rocking chair, the blazing and cheerful hearth, and plenty of good books, far, far away. But I control such retrospective glances, and in a few hours after I got into camp I learned to look upon home and all its happy appliances as a romantic little spot, having existence only in the imagination; and the happy faces there, as my guardian spirits, they too have existence in the imagination. I hope to prove their real existence though in six months, or at any rate when our family circle can again be restored entire, without the loss of one single face. But to come to *real* things, the rain is falling fast. It has been snowing and sleeting. You have already imagined we have not brought our cabins down with us, but are protected by a tent, with a large log fire in front. The ground was sloppy before we pitched, and the only use the tent is, is to keep the rain from wetting us.

I wish I could draw well. I would show you our circle. The Col. sits opposite me on the ground with his arms clasped around his knees, chewing tobacco and looking gloomily out towards the lines. Capt. Brown is to my right on his blanket reading "Rory O'Moore." Theo James has taken up his position like a duck in rainy times, favorable to shedding rain, and with a comfortable fire before him commenting upon the *poetry* of his situation. Every thing is so wet we can't get up a game of whist or even raise a song. We will remain in this delightful place eight days! But of course we will have some good weather.

I declare! I enjoyed a cup of tea at dinner hugely. I had some corn bread and nice raw pork, and with an appetite sharpened with exposure and exercise, who would want a better meal? The Government is treating us very nicely now. We are getting one ration a day, which we share with our boys: the ration consisting of one pound of meal, four ounces of meat, with *occasionally* a *little* sugar and molasses. This is really insufficient rations. I bragged, as you all remember during my visit home, of our good fare in the army, and would be the last to complain. But since the passage of the late law about rations we don't have enough to eat. Now I know how hard it is to get something to eat at home, but if you ever do have any surplus, please remember me occasionally. Dr. Patterson got a box by having it sent to Raleigh when it will be forwarded by Dr. Ed. Warren, Surgeon Genl. of N. Caro. to the army.

We reached camp on the night of Thursday, having missed connection at Petersburg & Richmond. Mr. Patterson preached yesterday a most excellent sermon, and had service in the afternoon; but it gave him a great deal of pain. I don't know how he will stand it until he gets his shelter built. I hope then it will not be so much labor for him to preach. Major Collins and Capt. Walker Anderson were over to preaching and dined with us.

The prospect for an early opening of the campaign seems not to be near at hand. The weather is quite bad and we have rain and snow every day or so.

Everyone admires my new shirts, and I believe I could *give away* a quantity of them; for if shirts were selling for ten cents apiece, very few would be able to buy a collar. The army has not been paid off in some time; all waiting for the new issue.

Our party from Wilmington to Weldon got a seat in the lady's car—next to us was a party of ladies. Mrs. Tom Colville with her little boy being one of them; and Miss Alice Beale another. I thought I recognized Mrs. C. but could not recall her face; even if I had, I had passed the lady on the street once and she did not speak, although I tried to be very polite. In short I missed getting acquainted with a pretty girl by not having my wits about me. John Cowan[70] however was not idle, but commenced by scraping an acquaintance with the little boy by dint of sugar cakes and peanuts; then with his mother; and before we got to Goldsborough the little Captain made the acquaintance of this pretty young lady, who was now alone.

Upon the whole, barring the trouble I had with the baggage of the party, I had a delightful time, especially in Richmond. I called upon several old friends, and was received cordially, and asked to dine & sup etc.

I forgot to mention to Pa about the pantaloons. If he gets them, do have some broadcloth stripes put upon them, and edged with gold lace. I would also like very much to have some more of that good tea. Now if you make up your mind, (*and have anything to send*) you can do so as I have directed, via Raleigh.

I am so sorry to write home so soon for anything, when I was so liberally supplied.

I am well and expect to get fatter than ever if I get a chance. Give my love to all. Explain to Mary[71] & Co. the reason I didn't get the things. The Col. is waiting for the pen and ink.

Affectionally your Son
Thomas F.

The old Blue Ridge with its snow capped summit looms up on the horizon. I am glad to sniff the free bracing air of the Virginia Hills.

Head Quarters 3d. N.C.T.
Colston's Brigade
Trimble's Division
Near Port Royal
April 14th 1863

Dear Nat & Agnes,[72]

I have at last received a letter from home, from Mary, the first and of course very acceptable. Our chaplain and I have just returned from the "Moss Neck" one of our picket stations. You wouldn't credit the stories of scarce provisions if you could see the lively groups of soldiers along the road in the different brigades, scaling the nice herrings and shad. Anyone would be surprised to see our men looking so well. There is little or no sickness, except among the conscripts. And now in this beautiful part of Virginia, everything is springing up fresh and green. Our Regt. went down on picket day before yesterday. The Yankees were very communicative. They are constantly amusing themselves, perpetrating bad jokes on us. One of them remarked yesterday that he understood we had a new Genl. in Richmond. We inquired, who? Whereupon we received the reply—General Starvation! They seem elated at what they call the Richmond bread riot.[73] Three men left us on Saturday night for the Yankees, and I'm glad to say that two of them drowned in their attempt to swim the Rappahanock. I saw the Philadelphia Enquirer of the 10th which gave a diagram of the Yankee position at Washington, N.C. It seems that there are societies forming for resisting the conscript act, and that several leaders have been arrested.[74] The Northwest question seems with them to be growing more serious daily. The Yankee pickets were very anxious for us to come over, i.e. desert. They are quite mistaken about our discontent, etc. Although occasionally we have desertions, we have given very few to the enemy. The contrivance for communicating with the pickets is quite novel. No doubt Tim and Herbert would enjoy it.[75] They make little boats of shingles, board or anything with paper sails, then loading them with a plug of tobacco; in this way the men amuse themselves when the wind is not too high. There was a grand review of the entire "Army of the Potomac" on the other side yesterday. A part only of the army could be seen as it defiled past our picket post. The papers say that "Abe" has been paying his pet "Army of the Potomac" a visit. The movements on the other shore have been quite strange. For a day or two there were no Yankee pickets from A.P. Hill's Division to the extreme right. They have returned though now, and our Regt. has another tour of picket duty down there tomorrow. I don't have to go, but will go tomorrow to enjoy the fishing, and hear what the Yankees have to say. I have an invitation out to church next Sunday with some boys of the "18th". "They say" that there will be some fine girls who attend the church regularly. You know the sight of a lady up here is "good for sore eyes". Actually a lady rode up on horseback near our Regt. one day, to see a dress parade, and the men—who are gentlemen at home—almost surrounded her as though she was some rare animal. About sun-down every evening the brass band of the 10th Va. on dress parade, plays quite prettily. It is just far enough off to sound well. We unassuming N. Carolinians are content with having the best Regt. in the Brigade, and a fife and drum. Poor Craig[76] is yet under arrest, awaiting the decision of his courtmartial. He has the sympathy of a majority of the men and officers of the Regt. He makes such an excellent officer, it would be a great pity for him to be dismissed, and then too he will soon be Capt. if not dropped. I see by the papers that R.B.W., Jr. is Deputy C & M.[77] Before I left Richmond I left my books in charge of a friend in the No. Ca. Depot, so that they are quite as safe as they can be anywhere. I think R.[78] is as safe at Lumberton at present. I am sorry the girls did not hear from the articles they wanted. I will write to R. and find out about them.

We have some interesting "cricket matches" introduced by our Sgt. May, a plenty of the Waverly novels,[79] and just enough sick to keep me from forgetting where the "pulse is." Kiss that boy[80] for his Uncle Tom. Give my love to all.

      Affectionately your Brother,
      Thomas

SEVEN

THE BATTLE OF CHANCELLORSVILLE

As Dr. Thomas Fanning Wood settled into his uncertain future as Assistant Surgeon of the 3rd North Carolina Regiment, General Robert E. Lee made plans to open the spring campaign. Heralded victories at the Seven Days Battles, Second Manassas, and Fredericksburg brought the officers and men of Lee's army into the spring of 1863 with abundant faith in their commander and the belief that the Army of Northern Virginia was almost invincible.

The Army of the Potomac was also ready under the command of its controversial and volatile new leader, Maj. General Joseph "Fighting Joe" Hooker. Hooker had brought the army out of the doldrums of the Fredericksburg disaster, through the mud and ice of the Virginia winter and into the warm sunshine of April as a large, well-trained, well-organized fighting force fully prepared to face Lee on his own ground. Hooker planned a bold strategic move to defeat Lee's army. He envisioned marching the bulk of his army up the Rappahannock River and crossing in a turn around Lee's left. If all went well, Lee would be caught between Hooker's powerful flanking movement and General Sedgwick's troops in his front. But, as usual, Lee refused to follow the script, responding instead with a series of unpredictable moves. Assigning some ten thousand men under General Jubal A. Early to watch Sedgwick at Fredericksburg, Lee and Stonewall Jackson moved quickly with the rest of the Army of Northern Virginia westward to stop Hooker. This was the beginning of one of the most classic battles of the Civil War, and it was also to be a frightening baptism for one of the Confederate army's new and inexperienced assistant surgeons.

Spring is now opening beautifully. In order to supplement the monotonous food of soldiers and prevent scurvy,[1] the ambulance corps was sent out to collect wild onions for the men and also water-cress. The theory was good but the practice was not successful. But Spring was far advanced when we received orders to cook three days' rations and prepare for a march, which we knew to be the opening of the Spring Campaign. One of the shrewd officers smelt (scented) the battle afar off, and got on the sick list before I had the slightest intimation that a Campaign was to open, thus throwing me off my guard entirely. This trick was well-known in the Regiment, and loudly complained of by his men, as his absence from a battle was not only unjust to the men but his company and the officers below him. The Regiment was quite well prepared for the Campaign, having pretty full ranks, deducting the men lost in the bloody battle of Sharpsburg. The men and officers were all in fine spirits. After several changes, Gen. R.E. Colston,[2] formerly a professor at the Virginia Military Institute, and an officer who was at the first battle of Mannassas, was put in command.[3] He was a very courteous officer and well skilled in military tactics.

We took up our line of march in the direction of Fredericksburg,[4] joining other commands in the march until the whole of Jackson's corps had gathered on the Rappahannock in a broad plain in sight of Hooker's army on the opposite shore. We were expecting an immediate battle and everything was in readiness, but after watching Hooker's movements for a day or so, our whole corps was moved from in front of the enemy with bands playing and colors flying, and were soon marching at a brisk pace in the direction of Chancellorsville.[5] The movement was shrouded in mystery to officers and men. The strictest orders and details of march were kept up. After a march of an hour, a 5 or 10 minute halt was made for rest. The men were not allowed to get out of ranks for water, but the ambulance corps collected canteens filling and returning them. The Assistant Surgeon rode at the rear of the Regiment with the Major,[6] and his duty was to examine and prescribe for men complaining and to write permits for men disabled. A man found straggling without this permit was arrested by the rear guard which marched at the rear of every Brigade and brought them up in time of battle. Genl. Jackson's directions for marching were imperative, and were carried out to schedule.

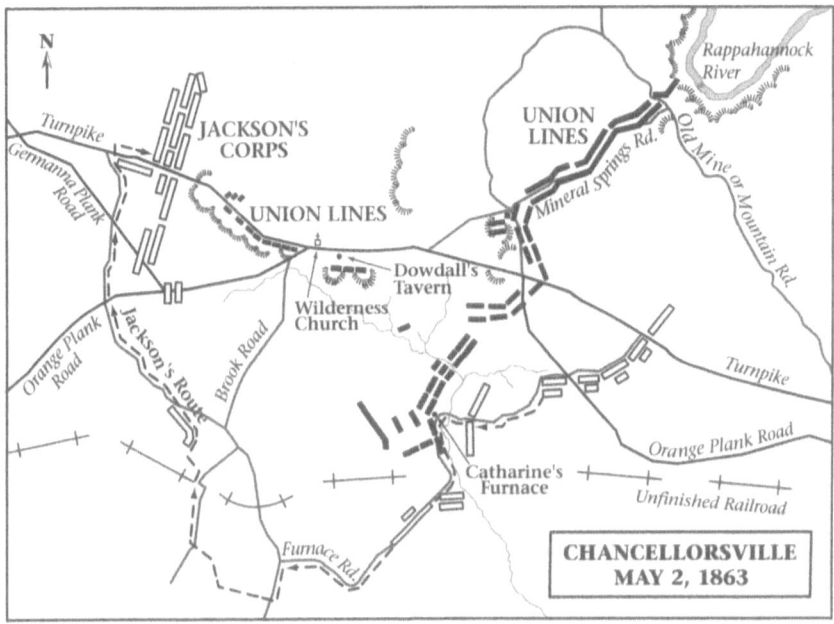

The Battlefield at Chancellorsville on May 2, 1863 showing Stonewall Jackson's flanking march around the right of General Hooker's lines.

None of us knew where we were going. Every man was taxed to the utmost of his strength to keep up. I was quite hot for the season and many were overcome by diarrhoea and exhaustion owing to the sudden change from inactive camp life with unchanged food, to great exertion and drinking too much water—and water of any kind that the ambulance corps could get. It was estimated that on the last day of our march around Hooker's right flank we made 25 miles.[7] It was Jackson's rule to strike a blow at the time he appointed if his ranks were ever so much reduced by straggling. It seemed to me from the men who fell out that about one third of our corps was left on the roadside. It was late in the day when we were formed into line of battle. Our Brigade was composed of the 10th, 23rd, and 37th Virginia and 1st and 3rd N.C. Regiments.[8] No enemy was visible and no preliminary skirmish fire announced an approach of battle, but line after line was formed in the narrow roadway and on each side of the Old Plank road. The men went in with a yell which was very noisy and exciting and it could be heard above the rattle of musketry. The woods on each side of the roads was a perfect wilderness of small trees, so close together that it was impossible to maintain a line. As I followed up the line I noticed that there was very little return of fire. Soon prisoners began pouring in the rear. They were mostly Germans even to the officers, and I heard for the first time, what afterwards became an Army byword, "We fights mit Siegel [Segal] and runs mit Howard".[9] It turned out that we had struck Howard's Army Corps, completely surprising them, and with very little loss of life on either side, secured a large number of prisoners and a great deal of camp plunder. I dressed sabre wounds, inflicted on some of our cavalry, for the first and only time I saw any during the war.

My duties as Assistant Surgeon were to go along with the Regiment on the field, and dress the wounds of the men as they fell out and came to the rear. Only those cases needing immediate attention ever applied, but in stopping to dress the wounds we got pretty well to the rear, and so we were not subjected to the hottest firing. Surgical appliances were very simple. My ambulance man carried a canteen of whiskey and one of water. We had sponges, bandages, ligatures, and necessary medicines—usually morphine and opium. Surgical instruments were so scarce that it was not every Assistant Surgeon who had a pocket case, so that having none myself, I secured a very poor one.[10] Dr. L.C. Coke of the 1st N.C.[11] and I went together on the field and mutually assisted each other being drawn more together by reason of being both attached to N.C. Regiments. It was all we could do to keep anywhere within reach of the Brigade, so rapidly did they move to the front. Their only obstacle seemed to be the tangle of wilderness. Finding beef on the fire and coffee in the pots, as they went through the enemy's camp they snatched food and ate as they ran, for they were all desperately hungry. At night there was a halt to reform the confused lines and Coke and I went on the field with a lantern to look after the wounded and to take note of the dead of our Regiments. We found none, but attended to all we came across, of friends and foes.[12]

Just as we were turning over a badly wounded or dead man, the artillery opened in the clearing at a tremendous rate. The clear space on each side of the road was very narrow, perhaps not more than 100 yards—and all the artillery was concentrated there. Shells and shrapnel rattled around us for awhile so that we were obliged to lie down until it was all over. This firing we now know was the fatal engagement brought on by General Jackson's imprudent reconnaissance in person. He was wounded and is well known fatally.

> [*General Jackson, concerned about the rapidly increasing darkness and slowing of the Confederate attack, moved out ahead of his lines with his staff to find out exactly where the enemy lines were. He had ordered Colonel Brown of the 1st and Colonel Thruston of the 3rd to fire at anything coming from the direction of the enemy. He decided that he must press the attack, regardless of the darkness and turned back towards his lines. General A. P. Hill had seen Jackson pass in front of the lines and considered it his duty to follow with his staff. Confederate troops, predominantly the 18th North Carolina Regiment, nervous and keyed*

up for an attack, and probably provoked by a single shot from the Union side, opened fire as they saw silhouettes in the darkness. The horsemen were ripped apart. Jackson and his staff were on the Mountain Road about two hundred fifty yards in front of the lines and Hill's group were some sixty yards behind Jackson near the Van Wert house. Four of the ten people in A. P. Hill's group were struck by bullets, killing three. Three were taken prisoner. Three of the nine people in Jackson's group were hit. Only the signal corps courier, William E. Cunliffe was killed. Jackson was hit three times, twice in the left arm and once in the right hand but stayed in his saddle and Little Sorrel carried him from the field in a wild and painful ride. (Gallagher, Chancellorsville: The Battle and Its Aftermath, 116–29)]

That night we spent under a tree in the yard of a little house by the roadside, attending the wounded and finally lying down to sleep for a short while. I was awake very early and found that I had been lying down next to a dead man, and that the dead and wounded were all around me. The battle opened on Saturday evening. General Trimble, our Division Commander, was disabled by old wounds, and his command divolved on General Colston our Brigadier, and our Brigade fell to the command of Col. E.T.H. Warren of the

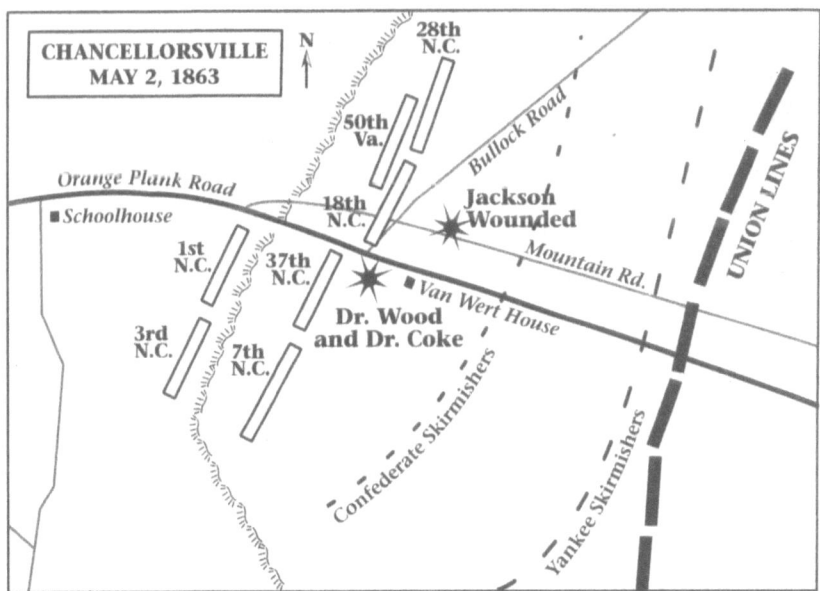

The area of the Orange Plank Road and Mountain Road where General Jackson and his staff were fired upon on May 2, 1863, and also showing the approximate position of Dr. Wood and Dr. Coke at the time.

10th Va. who was wounded on the afternoon of Saturday.[13] During the night of Saturday the enemy had thrown up some strong field works. I went all over it after the battle, and the one attacked by our Brigade was on the right of the road looking towards Chancellorsville. They felled a number of trees and twined telegraph wire among them in front of their works, and in trying to make my way over the "abattis"—felled trees with their sharpened trunks and limbs—I found it was difficult to do. What must it have been to men under fierce fire. The wounded came to the rear in large numbers from the 3rd and only one ambulance could be found. Ward's—Capp's had disappeared.[14] It turned out that after Jackson was wounded, an officer went to the rear to get an ambulance to volunteer to go to the front to bring off an officer. The name of the officer was not made known for had it been, there would have been numerous volunteers.[15] It was thought best not to make it known that the army had met with such a disaster. Capps, my ambulance driver, volunteered and drove down the plank road under fierce fire I have spoken of as occuring Saturday night, and brought Genl. Jackson off the field, and carried him far to the rear.[16] Those who knew the particulars considered Capps' undertaking a very brave act. As Jackson was brought off the field no one was allowed to know who it was.[17]

Sunday morning, it was found that their works had to be taken, and here the hottest of the fight took place. It was not known then by many that Jackson was wounded. Sunday's battle was fought under the leadership of General J.E.B. Stuart, A.P. Hill, the next in command being wounded, and Stuart being the senior. The conflict although bloody was not long.[18] Capt. Tom Armstrong was killed, Col. Thruston was wounded in the foot, and Maj. Parsley struck in the chest. As the wounded were now pouring in and our medical force was entirely insufficient, I was very fatigued. In the midst of it, I got an order from the Surgeon, Dr. McRee to come to the field hospital near the Lacy House to assist him. It was two miles to the rear.[19] I found the improvised hospital to consist of a few small houses and a number of hospital tents. Dr. McRee was the senior Surgeon of the Brigade, and conceived it to be his office to superintend the other Surgeons, and that my duty was at the hospital in his place as Surgeon and not upon the field. This opinion of his met with much opposition, and caused him with other things to resign after the battle was over. It afforded me the opportunity to do some surgery which usually fell to the lot of the Surgeon. My first case was amputation just below the shoulder joint. There was no escape from it and it was necessary to save the man's life. I had for an assistant—not Dr. McRee, nor did I get his council in any helpful way—my assistant was an old hospital man, Arnett, and the hospital steward of the 1st. I succeeded quite well, but for many years after I was worried as to the final results, of this my first amputation. After the war my doubts were overcome. An old man named Everett came regularly to sell us oysters. I did not remember him exactly, but he knew me very well. I ventured to ask him who amputated his arm, when he replied, "I think you ought to know, you done it yourself." Although amputation near the shoulder is not a remarkable piece of surgery, then or now few young surgeons in the war ever knew how their maiden cases turned out, and I was very pleased to discover that my first one had recovered and survived the war over 20 years. This was my real introduction into surgery and a trying one it was, as I had to rely upon ready wit more than to assistance from my superiors, who were far too busy to look after me.[20]

[By the third day of fighting, field hospitals were a nightmare for soldiers and surgeons alike. Operations took place on any available surface, including porches, doors laid atop barrels or stumps. Underneath were tubs to catch the blood. Water was always scarce and heat and flies were overwhelming. Amid the groans and screams of mangled soldiers awaiting their turn, surgeons worked hour after hour with scalpel and saw, with the only anesthesia often being a drink of whisky. The shortage of linen and cotton material resulted in old bandages being used again and again after being rinsed in bloody water. Pieces of shirts, filthy handkerchiefs, discarded socks were all used as tourniquets to control the bleeding. Infections such as osteomyelitis, erysipelas, gangrene and pyemia were widespread. This was the training ground where TFW did his residency and had his first experience with amputation. It was a brutal training course but one that would be of benefit to him for the rest of his life. (Gallagher, Chancellorsville: The Battle and Its Aftermath, 176–91)]

One incident of the Sunday's battle, (3rd May) was told by Ned Armstrong which I think worth relating. One of the guns of a battery in front of our line was disabled. It seemed to be a favorite piece, and a party of 4 gunners came up under fire, dismounted it from the carriage and carried it off the field. I asked Capt. Armstrong what he did then. He said that he was so lost in admiration at the act that the men ceased firing for a moment. I believe they got their piece safely away.

Our field hospital was moved to Caledonia Mine, an abandoned mine, expecting that we would have more wounded but the enemy retreated by way of Ely's or U.S. Fords on the Rappahannock, and we were left on the field.[21]

An incident in this battle was remarkable. In one of the charges of one of our Regiments on Sunday morning (May 3rd) they were repulsed and the color bearer Butler of Company C was wounded and fell within the enemy lines. He tore his flag from the staff and held it under his clothes. In another charge the enemy was driven, and the advancing line met Butler coming to the rear mounted on a horse being led by a captured Federal. There was great rejoicing at the recapture of Butler, and the safety of the flag. In this

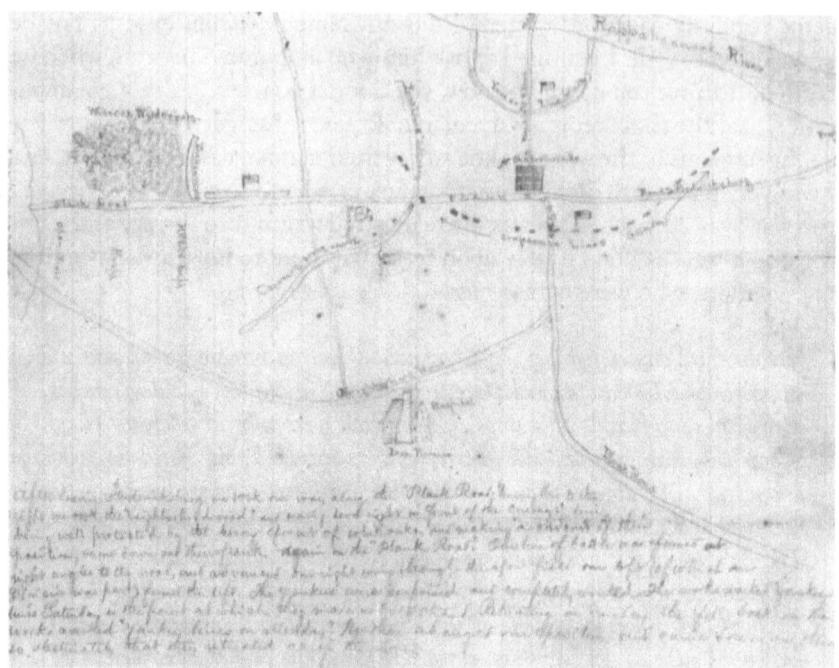

Above is a map of the Chancellorsville battlefield, drawn in pencil by Dr. Wood on May 6, 1863. On the back of the map are the words: "Sketch of Chancellorsville Battlefield made on the ground by T.F.W., May 6, 1863." This map was found folded in a copy of Life and Letters of Stonewall Jackson, by his Wife, 1892. Thomas Fanning Wood Collection, Wilmington, N.C. Below is the text accompanying the map.

"After leaving Fredricksburg we took our way along the "Plank Road". Leaving this to the right we took the "Neighborhood Road" [better known as Furnace Road] and coming down right in front of the enemy's line, being protected by the heavy forest of whiteoaks, and making a circuit of this position, came down on their flank again on the "Plank Road". Our line of battle was formed at right angles to the road, and advanced our right wing through the open field on our left (of which our Division was part) formed the left. The Yankees were surprised and completely routed. The works marked "Yankee lines Saturday" is the front at which they made a bold stand. Retreating on Sunday they fell back on the works marked "Yankee lines on Monday". We then changed our position and came down on them so obstinately that they retreated across the river."

charge, Lt. afterwards Capt. E. Porter, now Dr. Porter, was seriously wounded with a fracture of the right thigh.[22]

When the battle ceased we heard of the serious wounding of Jackson and his death a week later—the 10th May, 1863. This date was afterwards selected as the one for decorating of graves of those who were killed or died of disease during the war, and is observed as "Memorial Day", to this day.[23]

Our Brigade was badly crippled in this fight, and at its close, Maj. H.A. Brown of the 1st was left in charge, and the Brigade in charge of the battlefield.[24] In this way I had a chance to go over it, and learn items which could not be ascertained during the battle. I was surprised to notice how nearly our whole corps passed to the enemy's line at Caledonia Forge,[25] in our march around the flank of Hooker. The most appalling sight was the wounded in the burnt woods. In a small space the woods caught fire from our shelling and a number of killed and wounded were lying there. Some of them had been carried off, but some of the badly wounded who could not get away were charred in the very agony of their contortions. It was a sickening sight. Dead horses and dead men, that had only been slightly covered had been washed bare by the heavy rains that occured after the battle. The road from the Chancellor House was strewn with dead horses and abandoned wagons, etc., etc. The temporary earthwork thrown up about the Chancellor House had for its basis the knapsacks of the soldiers, and when it was discovered the plunderers were busy enough demolishing the works. Large quantities of medicines packed beautifully were captured, and especially from one well near an old saw-pit.[26] We recovered chloroform, ether, etc., etc., in metal cases with screw tops from the laboratory of E.R. Squibb of Brooklyn, it was the first I had seen of his now famous chemicals, although I knew of his reputation, and of his severe accident from the explosion of an ether retort some time in 1859.[27]

It was determined that there should be an exchange of the wounded, and our Brigade was put in charge of the exchange. I went down to the ford, (U.S. or Ely's or between the two)[28] and saw Hooker's Pontoon Corps throw a pontoon bridge over the river. It was done in a very short time. Every man knew his duty and his position and they went through the drill more lively because of the spectators from our Brigade. We were then all under a flag of truce. As soon as the bridge was laid, almost 200 new ambulances were driven over and parked on our side of the Rappahannock. They were under the command of a Capt. and Sergts. and made enough display to put our Confederate appliances to shame. Dr. Morris J. Asche, Assistant Surgeon U.S.A. came over as the medical officer in command, and we had frequent conversations.[29] It was hard to make him and other Federals believe that Stonewall Jackson was dead. They had so often heard this on other occasions and found the next thing that he was booming away on their flanks or rear, that they considered the news as a *ruse de guerre*. Dr. Asche was very pleasant. He had a copy of Stephen Smith's manual of surgery and a little book of instructions about minor operations in the field, for which I exchanged a copy of our Confederate States Medical Regulations. Their exchange party was provided with everything needful, and removal of the wounded did not take but two or three days.

A characteristic scene occured during this exchange between Rev. Mr. Patterson and Judge Wright of Lowell, Mass who came over to recover the body of his son who was mortally wounded and afterwards died in our hospital. Mr. Patterson had shown him some attention during his dying hours, and they retired into one of the ambulances to talk it over. Towards the last the conversation grew louder and louder, until we overheard Judge Wright say, "Oh, Mr. Patterson he was a glorious boy and he died in a glorious cause." Mr. Patterson replied and came back out of the ambulance, "excuse me, sir, but the cause of the Devil." Judge Wright followed him up with tearful eyes, and soon a reconciliation occured and the pair were soon again engaged in conversation. The intercourse between the officers on both sides was generally of a very pleasant sort, and little reference of a disagreeable sort was made to the affairs of war.

The stench about the old battlefield in a week was awful owing to the dead horses, which had been bared by the rain. It was very remarkable that there were no buzzards seen.

In one of our strolls over the old field I took a cow path and followed it to examine into the nature of the dense woods and wilderness. I there discovered a dead Confederate, in a half recumbent position with a haversack full of biscuits. The poor fellow had evidently wandered after he was wounded and lost himself in the maze of forest. His name was on some part of his trappings but it has been so long I have forgotten it.

Bivouac near "United States Ford" Va.
May 11th 1863

Dear Pa,

I received one of your ever welcome letters during the confusion and labor of the battle of Chancellorsville, and it was so badly marked with blood stains that it could scarcely undergo a second reading. As I write, my headquarters are in an ambulance. Our tents were all left for want of transportation. However, my quarters are very comfortable, having our chaplain, Mr. Patterson, as my guest. I was very much interested in your letter about home affairs. I have no doubt you will have a good crop. The real independence of the farmer is pretty well demonstrated in this war. And I hope you may make enough to rank you as a farmer.

The late battle has proved again Genl. Lee's superior ability as a leader. He made a circuit of the enemy lines, and instead of attacking him in his front, he came down on the enemy's flank and whipped him badly. For obstinancy and resoluteness the Yankees only seconded their Richmond contest. For brilliancy of design the execution of this battle has no equal, except perhaps that of Harper's Ferry. If you could see the eight lines of entrenchments which the enemy had between Chancellorsville and the "Ford" you would only wonder that he was ever defeated. The impetuous charges of our men can't be stood by the Yankees. Every private and officer believed in the invincibility of Genl. Lee and their determination increases as their hardships increase. So emense was the slaughter of the Yankees, that even now they are not all buried. I was amused at the "Confeds" who for keenness are considered second to their enemy. The Yankees in making their entrenchments threw in their knapsacks, and covered them over, to keep them from the booty they contained. But with their usual instinctive cunning, as soon as the day's hot pursuit was over, they set to work with spade and pick, and soon secured everything. Greenbacks[30] and a thousand-and-one other "notions." Nearly every "Confed" can show you a dollar or more in "Greenbacks."

It is currently reported in our camp that Genl. Jackson is dead. I regard it mearly as a rumor. The army will not receive it with that degree of sadness which it would have caused among them one year ago. They still confide in the old hero, but they think they are safe as long as Lee is our Captain. I suppose you know that it was the old Branch Brigade[31] who fired into him through mistake. Our Generals, especially the Brigadiers, expose themselves too much. Poor Col. Purdie no doubt lost his life by undue exposure.[32]

Dr. McRee left us on Sunday and says he will not return. I have no doubt that several Surgeons will try to obtain his vacated position. I would like to do it, and intend to correspond with him on the subject. Nearly everyone expects me to be his successor. If I succeed in getting an invitation, I shall ask for it at Charleston in order that I may make you a visit, and do the necessary study at home.

The weather here is very hot but the nights are so cool that one can enjoy his sleep. I forgot to tell you that Joe Hooker had, among other great preparations, a gutta-percha telegraph from his rear across the river. It being gutta-percha and consequently insulated he attached it to the tree without the aid of the glass.[33] Instead though of bringing over his commissary and Q. Master's team to fall in our hands, he was keen enough only to bring what he wanted on pack mules. Good for "Fighting Joe"!

I went in company with Mr. Patterson, Col. James & Capt. Ned Armstrong to Capt. Tom Armstrong's grave to pay the last tribute of respect to him. We met a paroled Yankee there from Boston who said that they had given up all idea of ever getting to Richmond. To use his expression, "Methusaleh would be a young man to me if I lived until we get to Richmond."

I think there is a reaction going on among our men in the army for good. A good many of them are endeavoring to be better men.

     With love to all, I am affectionately
       Your Son
       Thomas F. Wood

When we changed camp we moved to the neighborhood of Fredricksburg, near to Capt. Allsop's [Alsop's]—the old gentleman at whose house I was formerly entertained. Here our ranks were recruited by the return of many of our officers and men, and our ranks were soon respectable although at our best we did not have but a little over 100.[34] The camp chosen was a healthy one, and everything was done to secure the health of the men. Dr. McRee was now retired from the Regiment, and I was left in charge until Dr. M's vacancy was filled by a newly appointed Surgeon Dr. Walker Washington.[35] Up to this time he had been a country doctor, and had no experience with soldiers or military surgery and was rather too old for active campaigning. He was born and lived all his life near Fredricksburg—Woodpecker was his farm or his post office—and he was an old bachelor until late in life. He was exceedingly anxious to do the right thing, but was little disposed to put any confidence in those under him—and most of all he suspected every soldier who claimed to be sick, of trying to shirk duty. He was therefore very unpopular, and it made my duties all the more burdensome. I knew the men and they would rather suffer than have him examine them.

        Head Quarters Medical Dept.
        In Ambulance, Near Hamilton's
           May 22d 1863

Dear Bobby:

Your Letter of the 17th came to hand this morning and found us once again settled in camp near Hamilton's Crossing. We are pleasantly camped, our whole brigade on the knolls of two or three beautiful hills. I have taken a ravine under our Regt. and expect to enjoy a few months of quiet. Our whole army is lodged within an area of 3 miles square, forming a very pleasing view. The camps are on the summits of the hills: while the wagons occupy the plains convenient to grazing and water. The Chaplain and I now mess alone, and having no tent, take up our abode in one of our ambulances. We have plenty of books: plenty of good company, and plenty of eatables at an extra price.

Camp dysentary is the only disease, and I have put that under the thumb of my Hospital Steward.[36]

I was not much surprised to hear of Dan's marriage,[37] as Pa prepared me for it. Congratulate him for me, and wish him much joy. Our relatives, by-the-way, have a strange way of slighting their poor soldier friends. They know best their own affairs though. Perhaps such information "is inconsistent with the exigencies of the service", as they say in the army. Since I wrote to you last I have had an interview with some Yankee Surgeons, at the U.S. Ford, and made some exchanges of books with them. It is impossible to realize how we ever lived as long as we did with these fellows. Their accent, inclinations, etc. are distinctly separate from ours, as between us and the darkies. Their cool impudence, insinuating address on all occasions is calculated to overcome many of our simple minded men.[38] By-the-by 80 out of 800 of our late prisoners took the oath,[39] one of the men was from our Regt. He was a man who fought very bravely. From the cooresponded of "Nemo" (our Chaplain) to the Wil. Journal,[40] you will see that our ensigns (for we have two) acted with great bravery. Every officer spoke enthusiastically of their conduct. We have left, of our N.C. Flag, about 3/4ths of it.

The loss of Genl. Jackson is great, but the whole army agrees that Genl. A.P. Hill is his *able* successor. It is not a well known fact, outside of the army, that Genl. Jackson was not esteemed by Genl. Lee as the people did. His loss twelve months ago would have been much more serious than it now is. Jackson certainly died at the right time to live forever in the hearts of the people.[41] We get no Wil. papers now for some irregularity of the mails. Maj. Parsley and a Lt. Clarke[42] were baptized last Sunday by our Chaplains.

The books have been shipped by express—so a friend to whom I entrusted the duty informs me. Look out for them. I thought to be able to eat green peas with you this Spring, but under the circumstances without I obtain an invitation to go before the "Board",[43] I will not be able to do so.

>With love to all, I am affectionately
>brother
>Thomas F. Wood

My respects to Chas. Banks,[44] Dan H.[45] and all W. friends, also to Thally[46] when you write to him. Also love to Aunt Nancy[47] & Children.

May 25th 1863

I went to Fredricksburg to-day to visit with Mr. Patterson, Capt. Love of Hillsboro and saw David Thally with his Regt. I expect to visit him in a few days. Did you get the pipe Craig[e] sent?
T.

Camp 3d N.C. Regt. near Hamilton's
June 2nd 1863

Dear Pa,

The excitement of the battles having died away, everything has relaxed into indolence and monotony. We have nothing to disturb our quiet, and are left to our good companions—books. In spite of inadequate transportation we have constantly in camp something to read which is always of a standard author. I consider myself quite fortunate in being in such good company as that I now enjoy. Very frequently in this war, we are necessarily thrown into the company of persons uncongenial and even objectionable; with whom you might associate a life time and not learn one thing worth knowing. Fortunately though my associates here are men of accomplished educations. I refer more particularly to our Chaplain. He is an elegant *belles-lettres* scholar, and is very instructive in his conversation. So I take his valuable hints and make up for a part of my education in which I am deficient. We (the Chaplain & I) "bunk" together and "mess" together. He is a man of very much wit: so gay and worldly that you scarcely take him for a priest, except that he wears a long cassock and keeps his hair cut in the style of the Roman priests; but withal he is a strict churchman: observes studiously every fast and feast of his church, and is so much of a bigot that he really believes and even preaches that none except those regularly baptized by a clergyman of the "Apostolic Succession" can be saved. He is a warm friend of mine, and urges, sometimes indiscreetly, my promotion. I give you this little sketch of our Chaplain, as I speak often of him in my letters.

Some time ago I wrote you that I had a horse. I am in possession of him upon singular terms, but wish if I can make any arrangements, to purchase him. I can't get along without a horse, and this one has stood a long and severe campaign, and is just the horse. He belongs to E.M.F. Rhodes, Adm. of Capt. Rhodes. With my means I can't raise enough money at one time to buy him, although by economy I can in a short time. I want to ask you to assist me. The price of the horse is $350 and with my

$110 per month less my "mess bill" it will take me so long to buy the horse the owner will be out of patience. However I would rather forego the pleasure of owning the animal to putting you to any inconvenience. I can raise $200 in a short time.

In my last letter I wrote that Dr. Herndon[48] had been assigned to the regt. as Surgeon. Since that time Dr. Washington has been assigned to relieve Dr. H. Dr. W. is a Virginian and belongs to the great Washington family from Westmoreland County. The chances for promotion for me at present are not good. But I am not just ready for it yet. They are talking of me in Richmond quite agreeably in connection with a hospital there, and as I am so well contented as I am, I shall not let a desire for promotion make me forget that it is always best to "let well enough alone."[49] I have already succeeded far beyond my expectations and shall let the future make its own revelations. Of course I would not refuse a position in a General Hospital.

I was down at Fredricksburg yesterday to visit David Thally. He was well and in a good regiment with a fair chance of promotion. The town is badly torn up with shot and shell. The Yankees are very plainly seen on the other side. Our men have been in the habit of fishing and swimming in the Rappahannock. A few days ago the Yankees planted some siege pieces and told our men that if they didn't quit fishing they would fire upon them. They don't swim down there, but I understand still continue to fish. Two or three Yankee horses swam the river a few days ago while their hostlers were watering them. They had the impudence to send over for them, which was of course refused.

Since I last wrote home Genl. Colston to whom we had become very much attached has been ordered away, and Genl. Steuart of Md. sent to take his place: all because we asked to be put in a N. Caro. Regt. Of course we held a meeting and expressed our opinion to Genl. Lee.[50] Genl. Pender, who is acknowledged a fine Brigadier, and who was senior Brigadier in command of A.P. Hill's Division, has been removed, we all are jealous enough to think because he was from N.C. and would succeed A.P. Hill. So much for the wire-pulling in the army. I am confident that Genl. Lee is doing all of this for the best. I saw him on review last week, and was within a few feet of him. Genls. A.P. Hill, Early, and (Alleghany) Johnson, our Maj. Genl. were with him. These men would impress anyone favorably. There was no gaudy uniform or any of the pomp of the general officers with them. Genl. Lee wore a Col's uniform. He remarked of our Regt. that it was the best in the Brigade, a remark made of no other regiment in the Division, as I was close to him.

Our army is now better clothed and fed than it has been, except for a few months in the early part of the war. The health is good; the drones have been removed, and we are more formidable than ever. The anticipation of a forward move is given up; and I think we will not fight again until Stewart does something.[51]

Today's papers have just come in, and I will leave you. We get them every morning by 11 o'clock. I heard from Drs. Thomas & Love a few days ago, and will answer them soon.

If you are having the weather with you that we are, the prospect of bountiful harvest is good.

Affectionately your Son
Thomas

Direct
Stewart's [Steuart] Brigade, Johnson's Division
near Hamilton's Crossing

Head Quarters Medical Dept.
3d Regt. N.C. Troops
near Hamilton's Crossing

Dear Mary:

I believe that I owe you at least one besides the letter received from you today. I often think that if it was not for the mail up here, that we would relapse into a state of sullenness that a battle could scarcely drive away. More than that we would forget our homes and only feel like wandering vagrants. I have been spending some time with our new Surgeon, and find him to be a very clever gentleman of about 40 years rather precise, but conscientious with regard to his duty and not afraid to relieve his assistant of duty. I judge from your letter that you are having a pleasant time in Wilm. The old place really looked dreary when I was at home. It certainly must change very much before I could consent to make it my home.[52] No one can tell though what it might be, or what we may be when this war ends. I am glad to hear that Pa is accumulating stock etc. for his farm. That is the only pleasant way of securing a plenty to eat. If everybody would make something to eat, we would have nothing to fear. I am glad to hear that you are getting fat on the country fare. I hope Ma is getting strong and hearty. The field certainly agrees with me now. When I came up here I weighed about 140—now I weigh 153—more than I ever weighed before. We are getting pretty good fare now. Every day we have butter, milk, eggs, lettuce, asparagus, green tea & coffee etc.—always some of these things besides our regular army diet. Strawberries can't be bought here just now, but we get green peas & lima beans. Perhaps we live too well—but our Parson believes in it, and I am not one to oppose anything of the sort.

I am glad to hear that Dan Haines has such a nice wife. If she succeeds in making of him what Henry's wife did of him, she will be worth having. Their poor relation in the army seems to be forgotten in their honey-moon. But he assures them of his well wishes. Speaking of getting married, I think it would be well for Bobby perhaps, but for me, I am destined to live a long time before I will be so crazy. Married indeed! A young sprout of the medical profession, without income, without practice, even without a horse, to stick himself down for life with a girl, and not be able to make a decent support. You mistake this brother of yours. He has gone through the ordeal that all young susceptable boys of 20 go through. This was all romance, and I hope won't be remembered a year longer. But when a poor young man wants to take a stand, to take a diploma with credit, to finish his education in Paris, to be above the herd, the last thing he thinks of is marriage. Then you remember "Tim"[53] has to be taken special care of. He will want a better education than usual, and I am particularly desirous of seeing him on the right track. This will all seem new to you, but as I have built but few air castles which have fallen I hope one day to realize all.

As for my furlough, they keep me moving about so much that I don't get time to think much of home, or rather of a furlough.

We received orders this morning to cook up our rations and prepare to march at a moment's notice. Whether backward, forward, or sideways we don't know. Neither is it a soldier's duty to ask. Genl. Lee keeps us well enough employed to keep us satisfied. I have no doubt I would enjoy the high living at L.[54] but will wait until next Fall, when sausages, sweet potatoes, etc. will be so abundant. I would much prefer though coming back into W. with the tattered flags of the 3d & 18th, and for peace to be the terms. I *hope* too this is not far distant, while I at the same time *think* that Lincoln's terms will conclude it.

Speaking of huckleberries there are quantities in the rear of my tent, but they are not near ripe. The fruit up here you know is always excellent and usually plenty, when the money is.

I thought last night, that after I had made me a nice bunk, and enjoyed such good nights rests, and had "taken root" generally (a sign of which is the accumulation of books & bottles & boxes) then comes the cruel order, and breaks up our comforts, and we put once more on the wing in search of the Yankees. Well, I will only be better suited for the laborious life of a physician after the war.

Let me advise you & Lydia[55] *not to forget your books*. Don't imagine that the existence of the war will be any excuse for a young lady's ignorance. You should take the children in hand and by schooling them, you are very much improved. Of course you will say you are too busy, and that you have no time, or don't know where to commence. But, by spending a sufficient time at home and select profitable books, such as History etc. together with your old school books, you will do well. I know that girls would rather have advice to be married and in the mean time forget to make themselves fit by neglecting their intellectual cultivation.

I will write to Lydia & Nat & Agnes soon. With love to all of Uncle John's[56] folks and all of others,

       I am, affectionately your brother.
       Thomas F.W.

Address:
Stewart's [Steuart's] Brigade, Johnson's Division
Richmond, Va.

EIGHT

The Gettysburg Campaign

Just as Thomas Fanning Wood and his fellow combatants in the 3rd North Carolina were settling into the relative calm of routine camp life at Hamilton's Crossing, the orders came to move again into the jaws of the lion. It had been more than a month since Chancellorsville and the depleted units had just begun to build back up and stabilize. Illness had dropped off dramatically as soldiers developed a more healthy diet in camp and surgeons had time to attend to the details of sanitation and nutrition. They were a victorious army, the gallant defenders of the new Confederacy. From the high command down to the private soldier, there was a feeling that this Army of Northern Virginia was invincible. But now it was time to begin the cycle of killing again, and this time it would be more terrible than anyone could ever imagine.

As General Lee's army sat stationary near Fredericksburg facing Joe Hooker's Army of the Potomac located across the Rappahannock, it was clear that he had three possible options. He could attack Hooker across the river, which would surely cause problems. He could assume the defensive as he had at Fredericksburg in December 1862 and force the Union army to come after him, or he could undertake a raid into the North. The danger of the defensive option was the risk that Hooker would decide to move on Richmond, and Lee would have to retreat to defend the city. Lee believed that an offensive move into Union territory would disrupt the enemy's war plans and throw Hooker off balance, diverting pressure on Richmond. It might very well delay the renewed Federal invasion until the following year. By moving north and then east and threatening Philadelphia and Baltimore, possibly cutting off Washington's lines of communications with the rest of the North, it would force Hooker to attack him—once again on Lee's terms. It might also help increase the growing opposition to the war by northern people and force an early truce. Fully conscious of his numerical disadvantage and the serious strain it would have on his army to operate so far from its base, he was nonetheless convinced it was the only alternative.

He decided to divide his army into three corps. The Confederate First Corps would remain under the command of General Longstreet. Lieutenant General Richard S. Ewell would take Jackson's place and head up the Second Corps. To lead the new Third Corps, Lee chose Lieutenant General Ambrose Powell Hill, the high-strung, impatient but highly competent fighting man. Major General Edward Johnson was assigned to command the Stonewall division in the Second Corps and General George H. Steuart would lead Colston's brigade. The First Brigade or the "Stonewall brigade," was commanded by General Elisha Franklin "Bull" Paxton and the Second Brigade commanded by General John Marshall Jones. Lt. Col. William Murdock Parsley commanded the 3rd North Carolina Regiment.[1]

The rest was not a very long one but a very much desired one, and I enjoyed it heartily—to change the din of battle and the hardships for comparative ease in camp. We got together some books although our baggage had been sent on to Richmond and stored, as was our custom when the Spring campaign was about to commence. The rest was broken after a while by an order to examine all the men in camp and send to the hospital all not able to march.

After I had completed the examination, the Surgeon, Dr. Washington, noticing how large the list was, went over my examinations and struck some of my excused men from the list and among the number was Captain VanBokkelen.[2] He with the others was obliged to travel in the ambulances. In the case of VanBokkelen it was found that his malady had increased so much since he left camp that he had to be left at Woodville, a small village on our line of march. He was afterward carried to Richmond where he died.

General Richard Stoddert Ewell replaced Stonewall Jackson as head of the Confederate Second Corps and had the responsibility for Lee's left flank at Gettysburg. The 3rd North Carolina Regiment was part of the Second Corps. Massachusetts Commandery Military Order of the Loyal Legion and the U.S. Army Military History Institute.

Dr. Washington was hardly to blame for his mis-judgement in this matter, but his desire to be scrupulously conscientious in what he did caused him to distrust the opinion of others, and his experience in field work was insufficient, and besides he was not acquainted with the officers and men individually.

The march was begun sometime in June.³ Great changes had taken place in our army organization. Lt. Col. Parsley was in command of the Regiment. Genl. George H. Steuart of Maryland was in command of the Brigade. Maj. Genl. Edward Johnson, of the Division and Lt. Genl. Ewell, of the Corps in place of Jackson. Genl. Colston was relieved of his command because of his bad management in the Battle of Chancellorsville as a Division Commander.

General Steuart was an excellent organizer and disciplinarian. He was a Capt. of Cavalry in the regular army, and in his new position gave great attention to the physical well-being of man and beast. His camps were always models of cleanliness, and his horses and mules were always in good condition, his men well clothed, and the greatest order prevailed in everything. On the march he was very strict, and noticed the slightest irregularity of officers.

We reached the neighborhood of Winchester, and then found that we had to have a battle with Milroy. Our Brigade was marched around to Stevenson's Station and the attack was commenced on the other side of the town, by the Stonewall and J.M. Jones's Brigades and Early's Division.

About this time I believe, a price had been set upon the head of President Davis, and Milroy was particularly offensive to the Confederates and they determined to capture him if possible. Steuart's Brigade was stationed at the point

General George Hume "Maryland" Steuart led a brigade in Edward Johnson's division of the Confederate Second Corps. Massachusetts Commandery Military Order of the Loyal Legion and the U.S. Army Military History Institute.

by which he was expected to escape. Sure enough after a short contest Milroy was dislodged from Winchester and his retreating army driven towards our command. The fighting for a short while was very hot. The artillery of a section had become disabled and matters were about to go badly with us, when the Lieutenant of the 1st Regiment volunteered with other men, and fought the guns with great effect.[4] Milroy escaped and we lost men in killed and wounded,[5] as well as many others—and all were taken to Jordan's Spring. This was a place of Summer resort, but during the war was not occupied, and it made an excellent hospital. We had quite a rest here for a few days.

The Assistant Surgeon's place was behind the Regiment, now stopping to write a rear pass for some poor fellow overcome by fatigue, carry a canteen of water to one fellow by the wayside, and by aid of his knapsack-bearer, break a few boughs and spread over the exhausted man to break the fierce rays of the sun until something better could be done for him;[6] make a few powders of opium & camphor[7] on the pummel of his saddle for the ones who had the prevailing disease of all poor Confederates when they had any ailments at all, these were some of the constant duties on the march. It would have been a lesson to the most able city druggist of the day, to have seen the Asst. Surgeon handle his powder papers with no counter but his saddle, with no scale but his eyes, but with the nimbleness of a Spaniard rolling his cigarette, he went through the most perfunctory duty of giving of necessity, his almost certain dose of either quinine, morphine, opium, or Dover's powder to the very willing patient. The slim canteen of whiskey which for safety must be worn over the shoulder of the weary doctor and under his head at night for security of its contents, was his reserve force, his special dose, for well enough he knew his supply once exhausted, to renew it was the most difficult feat. Whiskey was popular, more so with the well than the sick, but it was very, very scarce, and very, very weak. I have known the tumbler of whiskey to come back from the purveyors, with only the faintest reminder of the ardent. It got its dosing of water from the time it left Richmond, and when the ambulance driver & his friends got all they wanted, and had substituted canteen of water for canteen of whiskey all the way from Orange Court House, the poor Assistant Surgeon and his friends could think of Dr. Holmes' famous rum dilution of the lakes Wener & Wetter.[8]

> Jordan's Springs, near Winchester, Va.
> June 15th 1863

Dear Pa,

While on the march I wrote a letter home, but since that time I have not had an opportunity. I received your letter dated ———— last evening during the battle. We had a pleasant journey over the Blue Ridge, and are now nicely ensconced in Hospl. near Winchester. The people in the mountains and valley were very enthusiastic and treated us as well as they could such a large body of troops. Tubs of ice water were placed at our disposal on the road, and such other courtesies extended as made it quite comfortable. I have not time to give you an account of our journey, but will subsequently. We attacked Winchester—Milroy being fortified strongly on a high hill commanding the whole country—and this morning the enemy are in full retreat, i.e. all who are "left". We captured 3 or 4,000 of the Yankees, which was more than one third of their force. Winchester is strewn with Sutlers' Stores. Cicero Craig[e] lies on the bed that I am writing on—wounded in the right arm. The artery was thought to be severed and amputation necessary, but since then we are in hopes we can save the arm. Lt. Kitchen Powers,[9] Co. K, was wounded also, not seriously. Three or four killed, among them Geo. Rouse.[10] We are in hopes to demolish Milroy, and are in pursuit. The 1st N.C. is mounted today as scouts. The stores captured are large, and among them some horses. Thank God for victory.

The wounded are waiting for my attention. I must tell you good-bye until I am at leisure.

With love to all. I am affectionately.

Your Son
Thomas F. Wood

Please ask Bobby to communicate with Lt. Powers at Sills Creek.

I had a practical joke played upon me here which I must tell you about. I wanted to take a bath, and looking in the bath room found that the tanks were empty, and I would have to pump water for my own use. This I did, first hanging my haversack in the bath room very confidently. This haversack was not for food, as was usually the case, but a satchel containing all my toilet articles—tooth brush, towels, comb, soap, Bible and prayer book, writing material, needle and thread, buttons, pins, collars etc. and a bottle of brandy sent from Wilmington, to be used in case of need. I pumped pretty hard and was in a way to enjoy my bath, when lo, upon descending the platform steps to the bath room, I found that the door was shut and that someone was inside enjoying a bath at my expense. Such pranks were so frequently played that I was not surprised, and taking my seat at the foot of a large tree, where I could detect the rogue. Fatigue of the night before had tired me out, and while on watch fell asleep and he escaped from the room carrying off my "haversack". It was a considerable loss as none of the articles could be bought, and from Winchester to Gettysburg and back again I had to resort to the primitive plan of the country people, and make my *"bresh"* from a twig.

The horse I began the campaign with, had a sore back and had to be led, leaving me a-foot. I thought I had secured a horse from one of our Colonels. I did not go around on the flank with the Brigade, but after the battle came directly through town. There I met Col. B. having a good saddle horse he had captured. The Col. was under the influence of liquor and was in search of whiskey and gave me the horse for a canteen of whiskey. The horse was a good one but did not serve me long, as a quartermaster found it out, and took charge of him. I was therefore obliged to pursue my journey on foot.

I believe there were altogether 800 horses and mules captured, and many prisoners.[11] After the defeat of Milroy and the enemy was in full retreat, Col. Brown[12] of the 1st N.C. conceived this idea of following up the victory by pursuit, and so mounted his men on all sorts of horses without saddles. But the men were so unused to riding and began falling out one by one until the pursuit was abandoned as fruitless.

From Winchester we marched to Shepardstown, crossing the Potomac River there.[13] When we had gone into camp, Mr. Patterson conceived the idea of going back into Shepardstown to call upon the Rev. Dr. (somebody), an Episcopal minister, thinking that by the ministerial brotherhood we would be invited to take supper. It was a miscalculated visit, for the Rev. Dr. was a violent Unionist, and extended no civilities whatsoever, and the disappointed parson and I took up our journey campward. As we reached the river a tremendous thunder storm came up, and by the time we had forded the river we were thoroughly wet. I had no other clothes, and had to ring [wring] mine out and lie down between a pair of borrowed blankets hoping to have some tolerably dry garments by day.

All was excitement now in the army. We had come on a campaign of invasion and every thing was hopeful. The army was in fine condition. The poorly men and stragglers and camp followers were pretty well sifted out, and all the commands I had knowledge of, were in excellent condition. We made an accession to our Brigade of the Maryland Battalion. It was a fine command composed of Md. Secessionists who had come South, and with the exception of Capt. Torsch's company of Irish Catholics, they were in the best sense of the word, gentlemen. I heard that the Regt. opposed being brigaded with N.C. troops, and were not in any good humor about it when they saw it was inevitable.

The day after we arrived in Maryland we halted a day near Sharpsburg and had an opportunity of seeing parts of the battlefield. It was a most bloody field for our Regt. "3" N.C. (17th Sept. 1862) losing as we did 23 out of 27 officers and many men.[14] The march of invasion was welcomed by some Southern sympathizers, but they were very few. The old theory that Maryland would rise in revolt, join the Confederates, was no longer indulged in.[15]

You will hardly believe how badly equipped Asst. Surgeons were on the field. I had now been a medical officer since February, and although I had made requisitions for a case of surgical instruments such as doctors know, as a pocket case, but the Confederacy was too poor to honor my demand. It had therefore been necessary to chum it with brother saw bones of the 1st N.C., Lucas [Lucius] Coke, and do the minor surgery off the field. It became necessary therefore to replenish my empty canteen with whiskey and get a pocket case. I had found my way to the nearest Federal field hospital[16] and made my demand upon the medical officer on duty and carried off his pocket case, this being the first set owned by the glorious 3rd.

Nothing illustrates more completely than this the poverty of our medical department. My surgical outfit then consisted of bandages, lint, limited amounts of Chloroform, sponges, some surgeon silk & needles & adhesive plaster. It is

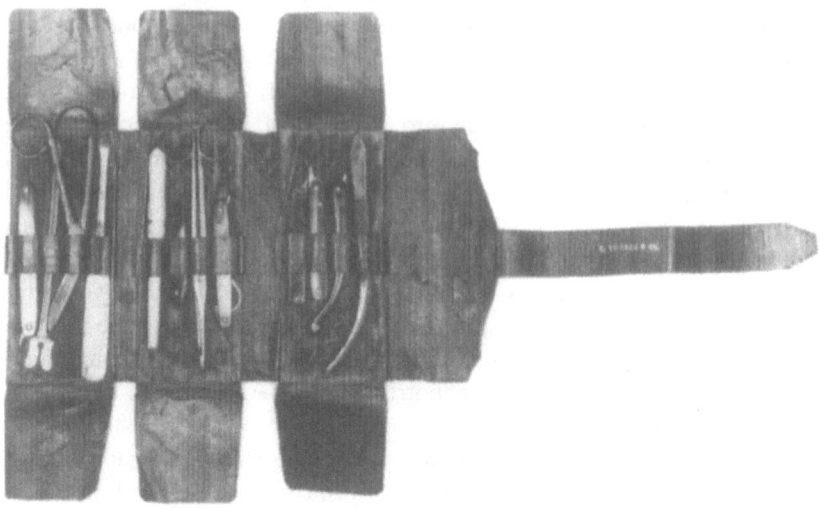

This is a Union pocket surgeon's case similar to the one that TFW took from a Federal surgeon after the Battle of Winchester. Most Federal pocket cases contained: folding lancets and vaccinators, grooved director with tongue tie for cutting tongue frenulum, straight and angular scissors, spatula with elevator for spreading plasters, probe with eye, finger saw for amputations, silver catheters in sections, various types of forceps, suturing needles, and possibly a variety of scalpels for incisions and dissections. Courtesy of Alex Peck, Antique Scientifica, Charleston, Ill.

true the whole art of surgery has been revolutionized since that day, but the complete outfit of all the field surgeons of a brigade in that day, would not suffice for the dressing of one wound of any extent now, according to the antiseptic plan.[17] Although the best we could, as we thought, was to cleanse a wound, stop bleeding & bandage it, and commence at once the application of cold water, our bandages were new and would not easily take up the water. One single item which we now possess would have saved the Confederacy an immense expense of labor, and put our surgeons in possession of the very best dressing that more modern experience has denied. I refer to the making of absorbent cotton. It would have been necessary to boil the cotton in strong lye to rid it of the natural oil in the fiber, and would have taken the place of the nasty sponges we had to use over and over again, unwittingly infesting the wounded with each other's poison. The same cotton would have been the very best anticeptic protection, by simply medicating it with borax on powdered rosin, or any one of the many native products we now know to exist.[18]

Then remember too, that the hypodermic syringe with which we now certainly & quickly assuage pain, produce instantaneous vomiting, stimulate a flagging heart, arrest some forms of hemorrhage, and do many wonders, all now carried in a little case in the pocket of every doctor was not heard of then. In fact, the doctor now in his daily rounds carries more in his satchel than Jackson's Corps could muster altogether at the Battle of Winchester.[19]

General Lee issued the strictest orders about our march. No plundering was allowed, and no straggling. The people were to be treated courteously, and when it was necessary for the army, authorized agents were to seize what was wanted and either give Confederate money or a receipt for such property.[20] The people had no use for our money and preferred receipts, these receipts after the war were evidences of the property captured by the enemy and were paid for, I believe, by the U.S. Our men treated the citizens with marked kindness. I do not remember a case of wanton destruction or indecency by our men, although there may have been some. If citizens remained quietly at home they would not be molested. If they hid their property it was considered lawful capture, but if not it was to be paid for in the way above stated.

Most of the men composing our army were from the country, but they were surprised at the neat and orderly appearances of the farms, and particularly of the excellent condition of the turnpikes. At nearly every farm house the wagons had only three wheels and the horses had been driven away except now and then, an old worn out plow horse—heavy, clumsy old animals that were of no use to us. Our marching was very easy over the smooth roads, and food was abundant. We traveled unmolested for many days, until just before we reached Chambersburg (Pa.) our Brigade was detached to attack a body of Pa. militia supposed to be hanging on our flanks in a small village, McConnellsburg. We made 27 miles that day, part of which was up the mountain. I felt the march very much, as I was on foot, my poor old horse still being led, on account of his sore back. The scenery was beautiful as we ascended the mountain, and here and there slight obstacles had been placed across the road, but the militia fled on our approach, and there was no resistance. We camped on the side of the mountain above the town, and the next morning marched towards Chambersburg.

An amusing thing occured as we started off. The people were driven from necessity of making tar from the mountain pines and a few barrels were lying on the road side. As soon as the N.C. soldiers spied the tar, like a lot of school children they commenced to cheer as though some great event had happened. Poor fellows, the sight and smell of tar reminded them of homes which many of them had seen for the last time. Our N.C. soldiers already had the nick name of "tar-heels", but it is not known how it came about, but probably due to the fact that the best known commodity of the state was tar, (pitch and turpentine) and associating this with the tenacity of our men in battle, and the number of them on every field in Virginia the name originated. I remember on one occasion, one night when we were marching around Hooker's flank[21] we went into bivouac, and had already lighted our camp fires, when an Alabama regt. or brigade came upon the ground near by. As soon as they discovered that we were North Carolinians they commenced derisively crying out "Tar Heels". Unfortunately for the Alabamians, the 6th Ala., behaved badly in one of the battles, before Richmond, and poured to the rear, their Col. foremost in the race yelling out "steady 6th Alabama". It did not take our men long to find out who their new friends were, and they set up the cry "Steady, 6th Alabama, here's your good old Colonel behind a stump."[22] This latter half of the clause had been added to the story, but it silenced the taunters of the "Tar Heels" very efficiently. Our men always took the nick name very good naturedly, and became very proud of it, as their repeated acts of valour gained for them good reputation as soldiers.

The presence of an army in the quiet and peaceful settlement of Pa. created quite a stir, although the inhabitants were stolid and undemonstrative, generally being concerned chiefly about their horses, and cows and spring houses. Ascending the mountain on our march, McConnellsburg looked like a miniature village, as though you could throw your hat over it and cover it. The road was beautiful and at the top was a fine spring from which the water was carried in wooden troughs to the village at the foot of the mountains. We saw only the women in these little villages, and many of them were on their front porches, barefooted, and amused the men very much by calling them "rebels" and "tramps". I saw a doctor's sign here, and went in thinking that I might get some medicine for a sick man, but was pretty frankly refused. The settlers here are of German descent, and many of them speak among themselves "Pennsylvania Dutch". They are excellent farmers, and their fine barns and rather poor squatly houses, and large out-of-doors ovens were a continual cause of remark by our men. In the villages the houses were mostly of brick, and far ahead of the homes of the majority of our farmer-soldiers. It looked like a pity that there was a necessity for it, but I saw a whole battalion of artillery driven into a fine field of ripe timothy and clover to get their fill for the night. Our ambulance drivers and our wagon drivers were required to pull grass for the mules and horses at every hours rest, and they were sleek and fat as compared to their condition in Va.

I remember that some old farmers came to Genl. Steuart complaining that their horses had been taken—it seems they had been secreted in the mountains and were claimed by us as war captures. The General was very sharp to them and they went off without getting much satisfaction. Steuart and all the men, especially the Md. Battalion had hopes that we were going right into Baltimore, and were very jubilant. We marched through Chambersburg and on towards Carlisle. Early's Division was in advance, and reached Carlisle but we did not stay long.

Head Quarters near Carlisle Penna.
June 29th Sunday 1863

My dear Parents,

Long since you have been informed that our army had assumed the offensive, and that instead of hugging Richmond as we did last year, we have pierced the central part of Penna. and stand at or near the threshold of the Capital. Had I been a seeker of pleasure, instead of a soldier, I would have enjoyed this trip through the most delightful portions of Maryland and Penna. as far as agriculture is concerned. On the evening of Friday June 18th our army crossed the Potomac, and encamped on the old battle field of Sharpsburg or Antietam, during Sunday and on the next day made a march through to the Penna. line, via Sharpsburg to Middleburg. The line between Penna & Md. passes through this little village. Every one of these little burgs had a Sunday look, all the houses of business, stores, etc. being closed. In Sharpsburg and Middleburg we received our last wave of the handkerchief. Some few ladies waved their handkerchiefs behind their closed windows for fear of being badly used by their Union friends. I was amused on the march the other day, some Penna. women cheered us. I suppose they mistook us, veterans of the Army of N. Va. for their own militia. From Middleburg we went to Greencastle and from the last named town to McConnellsburg, across the Cove Mountains. At Greencastle, which by the way is quite a town, the people were exceedingly sour. I forgot to mention that we passed through Hagerstown on our way from Sharpsburg. It is a delightful little town, elegantly built, and pleasantly located. The public buildings which are quite more numerous than in our small towns, are built with a great deal of taste. You remember the lamented Dr. Drane was a native of this town.[23] I enquired of his family, but he seemed to have gone out of the knowledge of the citizens. To say which part of the route I consider the prettiest would be hard, but I must say from Mercersburg to McConnellsburg across the mountains was delightful. The militia were reported at the last named place but we only saw traces of them.

On the summit of the mountain they had barracaded the narrow road with stones, but they coudn't stand the advance of the "Rebels". The little children in Maryland towns were very eager to procure "sesesh" buttons, and would have stripped us, had we been willing. The majority of Md. is against us, in the part of the state we passed through. The Penna. people look distainly upon us, or wear very long faces. It certainly delights me to realize that we are visiting upon these people what they have so long scourged us with. For the good of the service we take supplies at their market price and pay them in Confederate money, although our corps captured at Winchester $100,000 in Greenbacks. The order is for us to leave a sufficiency for the use of these citizens: their surplus horses and cattle we take on these terms. Everyone remarks on the odd appearance of the magnificant barns in this country, built near houses very inferior to them. Every field here is groaning under the burden of immense crops, which we are in hopes to eat. Fruit with the exception of cherries is still green but very abundant. Gooseberries and currants are just turning. Quinces, pears and such fruit as Yankee land abounds in is quite plenty. So that we are in a land teeming with plenty, that our brave army may recruit itself, both with fat horses & men. Our march over the Cove Mountains was very wet. We were suspended for several hours in the clouds. From McConnellsburg we went by way of Louden and Campbellton to Chambersburg. We arrived at Springfield from Chambersburg day before yesterday, and last night encamped near Carlisle. We heard from the front that Rodes was occupying the barracks built for Yankee troops. Genl. A.P. Hill's Corps is at Gettysburg, between Baltimore & Pittsburg; the position of Longstreet not known. Genl. Lee is at Chambersburg or there abouts. What can be the design of this bold move of our army is only known to our almost worshipped General Lee. They flocked (the Pa. citizens) around him, crowding him almost to suffocation. Our ambulances, which by the way are marked "U.S." were also marked Steuart's Brigade, Johnson's Division, which combination of great names excited everyone's curiosity to see Genls. Jo. Johnston and Jeb Stuart. The towns through which we passed have furnished us abundant stores, except shoes and clothes. Many of our men are barefooted but they stand up bravely to a hard march over rocky turnpikes. I am employed nearly all day on the march, providing some plan to assist them in my ambulances, so that they may not straggle. At Mercersburg some abolition women tried to induce one of our officer's servants to run away. But he said he was too well pleased with his own master to a Yankee one, and came and told his master about it. John Cowan's boy Peter asked at a house to buy some bread. The woman replied that she "didn't cook for nasty niggers". All of our negroes are not at all prepossessed with their Yankee brethren, and I don't suppose one in the Regt. could be induced to leave.

We enjoy this rich valley. Butter, milk, etc. are plenty, and we luxuriate in them. We can buy butter for a Pa. shilling a pound in Confederate money. It is the proudest thing of my life to see our peaceful army going triumphantly through a country which has furnished such vandals to desolate our soil. The people expected us to come burning and stealing as their troops did, but find instead, that we not only are courteous and respectful, but allow the people to express their opinions as they please. They show us a good many acts of reluctant kindness in order, it seems, to conciliate us.

But I have gone the length of my time, and must bid you good bye. I am thankful for a letter from Aggie recd. last night.

Remember me with much love to all

Affectionately your son
Thomas

We went into camp every day at 5 or 6 o'clock, and my knapsack bearer always had a few fat hens at his griddle, and we enjoyed a chicken stew, some good Penn. bread and butter, and I believe some real coffee. Mr. Patterson, Dr. Washington and I went into mess together. On one occasion despatching this meal, which was dinner and supper, Dr. W. called up Morton; "where did you get these chickens, Morton?" "I flank 'em, Sir." The Doctor had not learned many of the army phrases, was a strict constructionist and a matter-of-fact sort of an old gentleman and was not to be fooled with. "What do you mean by flanking them?" Morton could only repeat what he had already said, when the Doctor burst upon him in a storm of indignation, "You mean you stole them, Sir?" etc. etc. Morton only smiled and made no defense when Mr. Patterson came to his relief, "Doctor", said he in a somewhat quizzical way—"Isn't it a little singular that you only found out you had stolen chicken for dinner after you have enjoyed a hearty meal?", and more such pungent remarks, and our dapper little Surgeon quieted down into a little more serene spirit—more like a man who had enjoyed a good meal at a "crack" hotel.

We received orders to countermarch, retracing our steps until we reached Fayetteville, or Fairfield, finding Longstreet's corps there in camp.[24] We marched through Thad Stevens' Coal or Iron Mines in Caledonia Pass in the mountains. Stevens was a very violent politician, a member of the U.S. Senate at the time. His coal pits had been set on fire by our cavalry, I think. About the time of our march the papers were full of the treatment of the New Orleans ladies by General B.F. Butler, calling him "Beast" because of his outrageous conduct towards the ladies of the captured city.[25] The La. Brigade incensed by this, stripped the gardens of vegetable, carrying off every thing they could and destroying the rest. These were petty acts of retaliation, but were as bad as anything I saw during the march of invasion, and I felt proud of the self-control of our soldiers.[26] When we got beyond Caledonia Forge, we heard the fire of artillery before us. I reckoned by this that it was the 1st or 2nd of July [July 1, 1863]. The firing was from A.P. Hill's Corps, and the whole command quickened its pace towards the sound of battle. When we reached the battlefield the fight was over, and a large crowd of prisoners showed that our arms were successful. Someone showed me the photograph of Maj. Genl. Reynolds, U.S., picked up on the field where he was killed. The sun was not down but there was great activity among our troops. Our Division now commanded by Genl. Ed Johnson, of Va.,[27] was marched nearly to Gettysburg, then to the left around the town, and put in position on the extreme left of our army.[28]

It was after dark before we got into position, and on our march an incident occured which is characteristic of the ways of soldiers. Quite a number of barrels of whiskey were captured and in order to keep them from the men they were rolled into a stable and the heads knocked in. This was intended to spoil the liquor so that the men would not drink it, but the practice did not sustain the theory. The men waded into it, and dipped up in their cup as fast as they could, some filling their canteens, and quite a number of some regiments were hilarious. My knapsack bearer among others availed himself of this alcoholic solution of cow manure, and offered me a drink from his canteen with the gusto of a man who had something good. He was a little exhilerated but not drunk.

I forgot to mention an incident out of the usual course in our march. Lt. James I. Metts was baptized by immersion in the Potomac River, by the Rev. Mr. Patterson. Metts' parents were Baptists, and while he preferred this form of baptism he united himself with the Episcopal Church!

At last after marching and countermarching a line was established on Culp's Hill. In company with Dr. Coke of the 1st. I established a field dressing station at the foot of a hill in an abandoned farm house. There was a large spring at the door of the house, and everything was adapted to our purpose, and especially we were secure from the fire from the front lines.[29] Wounded men no less than Surgeons get rather nervous over a fire of a line of battle, and it is hard to keep them until their wounds are dressed as it is for the doctor to do his work cooly.

Dr. Washington our Surgeon had never seen a battle and was anxious to see how such things went. We had received through the ambulance corps word that firing would begin at a certain hour, but we did not mention it to Dr. W. He rode up on the hill, saying that he would select a better location near the line. In about a half an hour we saw Dr. W. coming down the side of the hill under heavy artillery fire. Dr. Coke spied him, and as he was not of his regiment, he got some fun out of the incident. Coke had a very loud voice, and hailed the doctor just after a shell burst in the ground just ahead

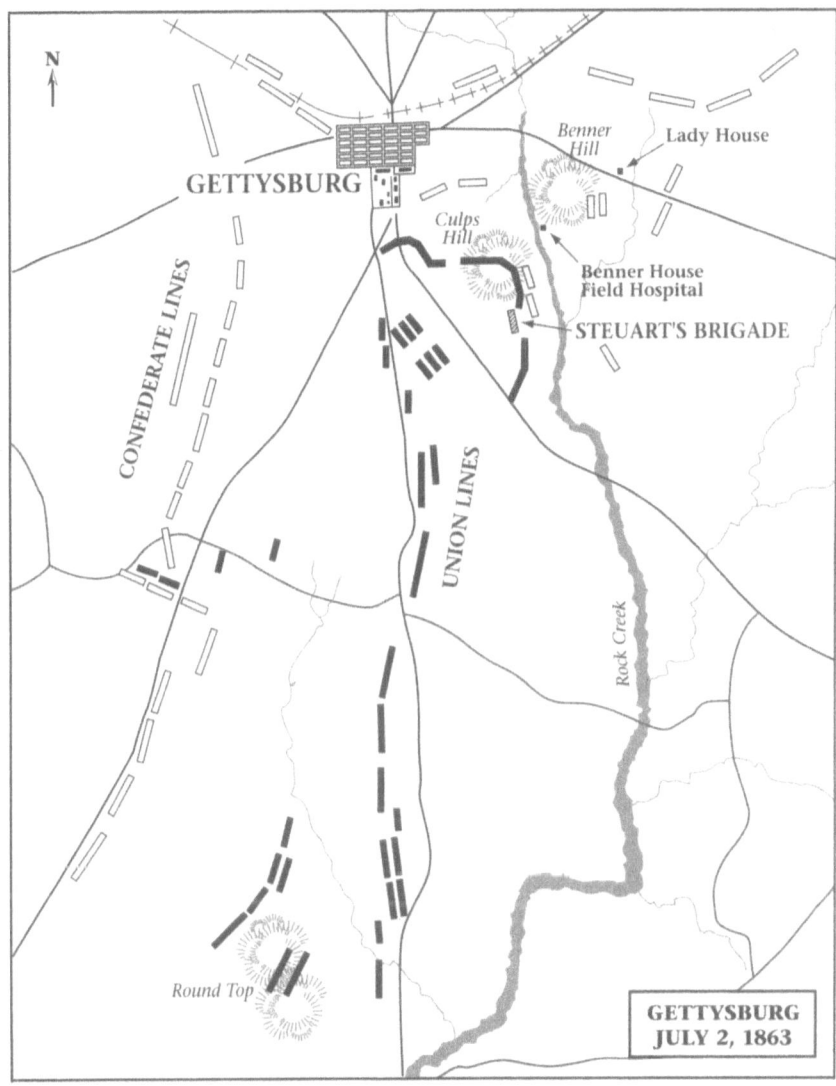

The battlefield at Gettysburg on July 2, 1863, showing the Union and Confederate lines around Cemetery Hill. It also shows the location of the Christian Benner Farm, TFW's field dressing station and the Daniel Lady Farm, the location of Ewell's HQ and hospital.

of him. Dr. W. seemed to be relieved to know that he was near such a good place as our dressing station, and came in with a grim smile on his face, agreeing that it was a pretty good place, and quite near enough. This firing was the great artillery drill of the 2nd day of the Battle of Gettysburg, and our hands were busy attending to the wounded of the artillery battalion—Latimer's, I believe[30]—just on the crest over our hospital.[31]

The proprietor of the farm house had been frightened away from home by the battle of the 1st day, and left his affairs in the hands of a boy. I don't remember the name of the farm,[32] it was small, but in this country we always found a dairy, and we were not disappointed here. The spring house was well supplied with milk and cream, and I set my ambulance men at work, in the quiet morning of the 2nd day, to churn. I had $2.00 in greenbacks which I gave the lad for the privileges of the house, consisting of buttermilk and a "crock" of quince marmalade. This was our meal, for as usual we were not supplied with rations at the proper time. At my leisure I looked around this house which we had plundered a good deal, and I found stored away a box marked, "T.C. McIlhenny, Gettysburg." It was the name of a friend in Wilmington.[33] The goods being secreted I opened two boxes and found one filled with felt hats, and the other with shoes for children. My hat was pretty bad and I exchanged it for a new one, got one for Mr. Patterson and gave one to the ambulance Sergeant. The rest I sent to General Steuart.

In the rear of our station was a line of battle. Among them were some La. soldiers. They completed the sacking of this house, even to the bee hives. They took a hive of bees in the open day between two of them, marching straight

The field dressing station set up by TFW at the foot of Culp's Hill was probably at the Christian Benner Farm. This is a photograph of the back of the house showing the barn in the background. Photographed by the author in June 1999.

through a bivouac of men, the infuriated bees flying in every direction. After the bees had quit the hive, the plunderers sat down and destroyed the honey.

My overcoat again was the cause of some trouble. A chaplain came into the farm house and spied my coat which I was obliged to keep on my arm. He seemed to be anxious about the plunderers, and I suppose he took me for one and entered into a conversation about my overcoat, and seemed disappointed that he could not take it away from me and restore it to its rightful owner.

The firing of the day was tremendous from one end of the line to the other, and nearly 200 pieces of artillery being engaged.[34] It is not easy to describe such a scene, but in this mountainous country it was grand. Shortly after it ceased the infantry were engaged, our brigade charging up the hills taking the lines of the enemy, and penetrating as far as Spangler's Spring in the flank and rear of the enemy and were obliged to retire. We had about 300 men when they went into line and we lost 180 killed and wounded 200, and a few prisoners, so that when the Regiment was withdrawn on the 4th we had 77 men in line. Lieuts. Garrison and Potter were killed, Lieuts. Kelly and Metts were shot through the lungs, the former died, the latter survived, and the number of wounded was very great.[35] Coke and I were kept busy with the wounded, day and night, until we were exhausted, and when our lines were withdrawn we went to the rear to the Division Hospital and found our old friend Washington fussing about and quite glad to see me, thinking he was going to get some work out of me—but instead I abandoned myself to a short refreshment in sleep.[36] The doctor ventured to ask what I had been doing, that his time had been fully occupied, and that he needed my help, etc. I did not explain, but when I got rested, helped him out. He had little ability to manage, and had to depend largely on Henkel and other Surgeons. Indeed we had the largest number of wounded, and the Maryland Regt. next. I administered to Col. Herbert and Maj. Goldsborough of the Maryland Regt. on the field and also Genl. J.M. Jones, who were all wounded, and were sent away to the rear in an ambulance.[37]

During the night after the battle of the second day, an Assistant Surgeon U.S. straggled into our lines, and was taken prisoner. He was allowed all the priveleges of our mess. I am sorry that I have forgotten his name. When he had been with us a day or so, he got Willie, Mr. Patterson's mulatto servant, a slave of course, to black his boots. Willie was very polite and did as he was requested. Mr. Patterson found it out and opened on the astonished Dr. "Don't do that any more, Willie, you are Dr.'s equal and not his servant. Let him wait on himself. He is fighting against us to make white people your masters, the same as negroes etc. etc. I don't think the Doctor applied for such service again. The conversation of course amused the by standers, but made some of us feel very badly, the prisoner being under our protection, and as likely as not far from being an abolitionist as any of us.

The scene at the Division Hospital was very distressing. I was sent to report the number of wounded and indicate all who were able to march or be transported in wagons. The men were not slow to find out that we were preparing to fall back, and leave them as prisoners. I knew the men well by this time, and they greatly desired that I remain with them, but Dr. Dabney Herndon, of Fredricksburg, Surgeon in an La. regiment was detailed for the purpose, and in a few days abandoned the men, I heard, and went over to Baltimore. Lt. Metts was shot through the right lung, and I was obliged to tell him I thought he would die, and Lt. Tom Kelly, also wounded in the lungs I thought would get well. The reverse was the case.

The retreat from Gettysburg was begun in the rain which continued without cessation for some days.[38] Every empty wagon was loaded with wounded men, and the roads leading toward the Potomac were full of troops, stragglers, slightly wounded men, making their way as they could. But there was no panic. We were followed up by the enemy but not with much vigor. The most annoying thing was the wild firing of stragglers as we were crossing South Mountain.[39]

The retreat was very fatiguing, and many men laid down for sleep, and were captured. The rain had greatly swollen the Potomac, and our army was without ammunition, even our reserve wagons being empty. General Lee formed a line of battle at Hagerstown, building good entrenchments, and here our men had an opportunity to rest, but there was no food.[40] A pontoon bridge had been thrown across the river, but no wagons or men were allowed to cross until the ordinance wagons were safely over. Maj. Harry Miller, our Brigade Commissary officer was always active in supplying us with food, and knowing how strict the orders were against admitting any but ordinance wagons over the river, supplied himself with a black ordinance wagon, and brought over to us our needed supply of food. We were fed probably in advance of all other commands by this *ruse*.[41]

While we were in the trenches at Hagerstown, an accident happened to Capt. Ned Armstrong. He was examining a little Smith & Wessons, and it went off shooting him through the palm of his hand. This excellent officer had been the most fortunate of our regiment—had not had a scratch in all the hard battles, and had never missed a battle. One of his friends joked him about it, and it mortified him greatly. Some of the trifling men had a trick of deliberately shooting off a finger or thumb, so as to avoid the battles, and a joking insinuation of this sort was hard to bear.

Armstrong bore his suffering patiently, but after a few hours the pain was so great and such rapid inflamation ensued, that I had to take him in charge. He made a good recovery and was soon back at his post.

The distance from our lines to the river was about four miles and when we took up our march to cross it, we were before sun set of one day, until daybreak the next crossing the river. We would march a few steps and then halt, and this was repeated all night long—just enough marching to keep the men awake. I was on horseback this time, and wearied out I determined to seek the piazza of a house by the roadside and turn in for a few hours of sleep. It was very dark, and tying the halter to my wrist I jumped the baluster, and in doing so planted both feet into some sleeping fellow, who had conceived the same brilliant idea as mine, but many hours in advance. I was glad enough to scramble out of the crowd, and mount my horse and take it along at the former sleepy pace.

When I got to the river I saw what the difficulty was. Our men were attempting to ford the Potomac. It was very much swollen, and each man had to secure his rations and his ammunition and keep his gun dry. It was all right for the tall men, but the short ones could hardly keep their footing, so they divided up into groups, short men between two tall ones and so on. This caused long delays, but by daybreak we were safely over the river without an accident. Being mounted I had to ride into the bed of the canal, and horses balked there so much that an officer on each side with a drawn sword struck your animal on his rump with the flat of his sword, and forward went the horse, and sometimes down went the horse as mine did, but he soon recovered and scrambled forward.

When we got into Virginia we were re-inforced by the arrival of men, from hospitals, until our regiment looked more like a regiment than it had done, but our ranks were painfully thin. We had an uneventful march until we were safely back on the Rapidan again and went into camp. Our camp was near Orange Court House[42] and was beautifully situated, still we had a good deal of sickness. Dr. Washington resigned, and I was again in charge.

The failure of the Gettysburg Campaign had set up a cry in N.C. for peace, in some of the middle and western counties, and W.W. Holden, an old politician and rank secessionist, who after signing the secession resolution in the General Assembly, waved his pen over his head saying that he would hand it down to his children as their proudest legacy—also that he "pledged the last man and the last dollar" in the cause—this man began to write Union articles for his paper. This was distributed in our camp secretly.[43]

A dissatisfaction ensued which cost some brave men their lives. Ten of our men who had been noted for their courage, determined to return home with their guns and their equipment. When it was discovered, a party of soldiers, also North Carolinians, were sent to interrupt them and arrest them. They did so near Ashland, I believe. A fight ensued, resulting in the killing of Lt. Mallett of Fayetteville, commanding the party. Seven of the men were captured and returned to the regiment. Three escaped. I have always rejoiced that I was absent at the time on leave when the Court Martial assembled, and the men condemned to be shot. Dr. William F. Stuart,[44] who had by this time succeeded Dr. Washington, witnessed the execution, which would have devolved on me had

I been present. The seven men were tied down to stakes and shot. Of the three who escaped, one died of small-pox in "Castle Thunder" a military prison in Richmond, one was pardoned by the President, and one was never captured. His name was Horrell and after the close of the war was *rewarded* for his conduct by making him deputy sheriff of New Hanover County (North Carolina). This whole affair was a very sad thing for us all, but the remedy seemed to be necessary to stop desertions. After this it became necessary to scrutinize all the mail coming to camp. It stopped desertion for a long time, and nothing disagreeable happened. We had regular services in camp every Sunday, and our minister had listeners from other regiments. We were quiet until October from some time in July, during which time our regiment was considerably recruited.

Camp near Orange C. House
August 24th 1863

Dear Mary & Lydia,

  This is a beautiful Fall morning, but reminds me of the fever and ague weather of our country. We are here in full view of the Blue Ridge, and the sharp early morning air comes down off the mountain and gives me a good appetite for breakfast. For now, since we are so nicely fixed in camp they wake me up at six o'clock to examine my sick. Our Surgeon, an elderly gentleman, from Baltimore, insists on sharing my duties (something unknown in this Regt. before) and gets up with me. I am very fortunate in being with such a clever gentleman as Dr. Steuart [Stewart]. He is an exile from Maryland. He was for a long time in charge of the Md. State Hospital. He is a martyr to Southern rights, and has done great good to our cause. Although the duties are light in camp, I find little or nothing to do with his assistance.

  Genl. Lee has issued an order granting furloughs to staff officers when the Brigade commanders approve it. I think of making an application. The limit for N. Carolinians is 18 days; so that if I am fortunate enough to get leave of absence I want to spend most of it at L.[45] or where ever Ma & the rest of you are. I will be obliged too to visit Raleigh before my return. I shall never forget how I felt when I visited W.[46] last. I got the "blues" on landing, and didn't feel right until I got to the city of L. which you seem to dislike so much.

  Fast day here was kept more rigidly than I ever knew on a former occasion. Mr. P.[47] had service three times during the day. Some ladies attended the services which were held at Genl. Steuart's H. Qrs. These were the first ladies I had seen in some time—so much so that they were natural curiosities. We have considerable company here now and then. The Rev. Mr. Smith (of course) of the Episcopal Church preached here yesterday. We had thirteen visitors to entertain at dinner yesterday, or rather our entire party was 13. But if you think we are scared in camp by crowds just see what we had for dinner. Roast ducks & geese, stewed beef, fried and broiled chicken, vegetables, Irish potatoes, tomatoes, corn, cucumbers, onions, wheat & corn bread & Laguyra Coffee. And for pastry—bread and syrup. All completed by a good smoke. It is rare though to find a party in which there were fewer smokers than among our company. As a general thing everyone smokes in the army, black & white.

Our friends of the 18th are quite neighborly. I paid them a visit last week. Quite a number of the old men are returning; but I am heartly glad that I am not in Col. Barry's Regt. Not that Barry is not a good Col., but that his Regt does not compare to this now in discipline. You spoke in your letter something about shoes. I don't know how you ever imagined that I had shoes for you; when I told you expressly that I didn't get any in Pa. because I didn't think it right. I could have done so, but failed to bring out of Pa. any trophy except my horse & hat. Send me your sizes by next letter. Ask Bobby what are the chances to get a horse from Weldon home by R.R. As I have a letter to write Bobby I must bid you good-bye.

                    Affectionately Your Brother
                      Thomas

                              Bivouac near Raccoon Ford
                              Rapidan River, near Orange
                                      Sept. 23rd 1863

Dear Pa,

I arrived here yesterday morning and found my Brigade in bivouac behind their extensive works on the Rapidan River. I was delayed in R.[48] several days, because I found Mr. Patterson quite sick, and because I wished to make the arrangements for my transfer. Dr. Manson according to promise made the application which I carried to the Department in person. The Med. Director informed me that I was out of his Dept. and that I would be obliged to send up my papers regularly through Genl. Lee's Medical Director.[49] I have not yet determined to make the application. I am almost sure that at present I would not succeed, for the reason that there is no unassigned Asst. Surgn. in this Divn. which was the difficulty that Dr. Walker labored under. I think it would be well for none of you to say anything about it; in the meantime I will watch my chances.

I spent my time in R. most agreeably. Mr. Patterson introduced me to his friends Mr. & Mrs. Mordecai,[50] two venerable inhabitants of R., both of them authors. The former a Jew and author of a book entitled "Richmond in By-Gone Days". The latter authoress of "The Secret of a Heart, or the Account of My Conversion to the Christian Religion". Mr. M. is a man of great wealth and has lived in R. through three generations; he interested me very much by several little anecdotes which are not contained in his book. They apologized for not extending the hospitalities of their house, because that Mrs. Mordecai (a lady of 98 yrs.), the mother of Mr. M. was very low. I stayed with my friends Drs. Murphy & Sherrod,[51] overstaying my furlough three or four days. Fortunately on my arrival here, Genl. Steuart was in command of the Divn. and I reported to the Sen. Col. During my stay in R. Dr. Sherrod invited me to attend a meeting of the Med. Soc. of Army & Navy Surgeons. Surgn. Genl. Moore is President, and Dr. Michel of Charleston Vice Pres. I had the pleasure of hearing Drs. Galliard, Chisholm, Campbell, etc., men of the first standing in the profession engaged in a debate. I have never before had an opportunity of being in such an assembly, and was very much instructed thereby.

I didn't find my horse at the R.R. the day I arrived, and so was obliged to walk 14 miles to camp. My feet were very sore, so I made bad progress. I fortunately found Capt. Langdon's H. Qrs.[52] at a convenient distance, and so divided the journey between two days, regaling myself with a good dinner and a sleep at Capt. L's. I found everyone without tents here, and though there had been frost for two nights we have been sleeping outdoors. The sudden change has given me a little cold, which will wear off after the frost falls on me a few times more.

Now, up here, we are enjoying a plenty of bread and beef; I tell you sweet potatoes would go well up here, and that barrel which you wished to send me last year would be very acceptable. I have asked Ma to pick me some scuppernong grapes on the bunch and send them here. If you will direct to me in care of Dr. G.W. Murphy, N.C. Soldiers Home, Richmond, I will get it.

Our position here is a very good one. We have entrenched upon the hills overlooking the river, and all before our works is a vast meadow. Our troops are in good spirits. I am sure that if we wait here for the Yankees to fight us, there will be no fight here until next Spring. There was heavy firing upon the right of the Army towards Madison C.H. The Yankees were trying to turn our flank, but I suppose they were repulsed as there was no firing today.

I hope that all the folks are better. The medicine I prescribed for Tim & Aggy[53] can be taken without any regard to other medicine prescribed. I find no one sick here.

We are just ordered off. Good bye, Love to all,

      Affectionately your son,
      Thomas

You will observe this was written in bivouac on my knee. Direct as before, Steuart's Brigade, Johnson's Divn. Ewell's Corps, 3rd Regt. N.C.T. Richmond, Va. If you do send the barrel please send me a peck or so of salt.

      Camp 3d. Regt. N.C. Troops
      near Mitchell's Ford, Va.
      Sept. 29th 1863

Dear Ma,

I wrote you a short letter from R. and one to Pa from this camp, which I suppose have been received some time since. We are yet quiet in camp waiting orders, with "two days rations" in our haversacks, and prepared to march at moments warning. The news for to-day if true will alter the appearance of things in this army for some time. It is reported, with seeming truth, that A.P. Hill's Corps is to go to reinforce another department.[54] If so I infer that the Yankees don't intend anything serious against us for some time. I hope the fighting in this army is at an end, and that a few decisive battles in the West will accomplish everything. We are not in a very desirable place for Winter quarters: being 20 miles from the R.R. and in such a country as this, with our usually bad Winter roads, we will fare but poorly.[55] But we may be some time yet going into quarters, and will perhaps be nearer the road. There is no doubt that if our Corps (Ewell's) is left for the sole defense of R. that we will change our base, and occupy a shorter line of defenses. Also, if Hill's Corps does go West, many of the hospitals in Richmond will necessarily be broken up, and my chances for transfer will entirely fail. I am not disappointed, but really as contented and happy as one can well be. I must always have an "iron in the fire", and have another project in view, the result of which is so doubtful that I can't mention it. I find in camp that it is always best now and then to build some little "castles in the air" to while away the time; always provided that one makes himself accustomed to see them fall occasionally. In this way we fill up the little leisure minutes that otherwise would hang so heavily.

I don't know what I would have done but for the books I brought in camp. Genl. Stewart [Stuart], or rather Genl. Lee, has stopped the furlough of officers for the present, in consequence of the change going on. I hope though by February to be able to get another chance to visit you. The execution of those men of our Regt. was said to be an awful scene. There is one yet to be shot, but Genl. Lee has ordered his execution to be suspended until further notice.

I wish you would ask Bobby to inquire if McCormick has any stout French Cassimere of which he could make me a suit, and what coat, pants and vest would cost. I must have a suit, and I am tired of military. If he can't get Fr. Cass., see if he has any cloth such as that Capt. Van Bokkelen and Capt. Brown had a suit from.

I am told that Rhodes now refuses to take $350 for his horse, and that I have not bought him. "Many a slip, etc.". One thing is certain, I have his horse and he can't get him. He was valued by the Committee the other day at $450. They always undervalue. I have a *conditional* offer of $250 (one fifth in silver) for my colt. As he has distemper, I think I will sell. I expect to get a saddle for Pa in a few days if we are not moved.

I am calculating upon that barrel of ———. Remember the diet of camp *now* is not variable. *Why doesn't some one write to me?* I am anxious about the sick ones I left.

Give my love to all. Kiss Bertie[56] for Uncle Tom.

Affectionately your son
Thomas

NINE

THE WINTER OF 1863 AND THE TURNING TIDE

The setbacks of the summer of 1863 had taken a serious toll on the Army of Northern Virginia, and they were suffering through a hard winter with short rations. Manpower was stretched frighteningly thin. The Confederate Congress abolished the privilege of substitution and required soldiers with upcoming expiration of their three-year enlistment to remain in the army. They also stretched the upper and lower age limits for enlistments to fifty and seventeen. Despite all these efforts to rebuild the army's strength, the Confederate forces still numbered less than half of the Federal troops in the field. The Union manpower was also stretched tight due to the need for occupation forces to police one hundred thousand square miles of conquered territory. Invading armies had to devote significant numbers to guard supply lines and wagon trains against rebel cavalry raids. These subtractions somewhat reduced the odds against the Confederate forces, but decisions were being made on the Federal side that would bring the beginning of the end for the Confederacy. President Lincoln promoted U. S. Grant to Lieutenant General with the title of General in Chief and Henry W. Halleck was reassigned to the post of Chief of Staff. Grant designated Sherman to command the western armies and came east to make his headquarters with the Army of the Potomac. General Meade remained in charge of the Army of the Potomac but was to operate according to Grant's strategic orders. Phil Sheridan also came east to take command of the Union cavalry. Grant's new strategic plan involved the destruction of the Confederate armies in the field and preventing them from reinforcing each other. His instruction to Meade was "Lee's army will be your objective point. . . . wherever Lee goes, there will you go also." This rumpled and rather shabby-looking man had piercing steel-blue eyes and a bearing that communicated a firm determination not to play the game according to Lee's rules the way his predecessors had done. This war had taken a new turn, and the future was not encouraging for the Army of Northern Virginia.

Despite this and the hardships following the defeat at Gettysburg, the morale of the Army of Northern Virginia remained high. These were battle-hardened veterans and many had re-enlisted even before Congress required them to do so. Their devotion to Lee was unwavering and they were ready to follow him regardless of the consequences.

In the Fall of 1863, General Lee had settled on a defensive line behind the Rapidan River near Brandy Station and was looking for an opportunity to catch Grant unaware. Following the Union defeat at Chickamauga in September, Meade had sent the Eleventh and Twelfth Corps to reinforce Rosecrans, thus weakening the Army of the Potomac. Lee, still dramatically outnumbered, saw his opportunity to flank Meade's army and drive him from the western part of Virginia. The Confederate army crossed the Rapidan on October 10 and moved north towards Centreville. Meade abandoned his line north of Culpepper Court House and fell back towards Warrenton. A. P. Hill and Ewell moved to intercept him near Greenwich, but at Bristoe Station on October 14, Hill became overanxious and pushed to attack without sufficient reconnaissance or reinforcements. With two brigades led by General William Kirkland and General John Cooke, he blundered into a hole in the line of Union General George Sykes's Fifth Corps. General Governor Warren's Second Corps suddenly appeared along a railroad cut on Hill's right and cut down his attacking force. This was the Battle of Bristoe Station, and even though Ewell's corps was not engaged, the defeat had a serious effect on the morale of Lee's entire army.[1]

In October the whole army was in motion for a flank movement upon Meade. We went through Warrenton and on through Bristoe Station without fighting on our part. As we approached the heavy firing, we were halted but were not engaged and the battle was all over. We were bivouacked on the field of battle and it was an awful sight. It seems that A.P. Hill had struck the enemy in the wrong place contrary to orders. Cook's and Kirkland's N.C. Brigades went into action at the Station. The enemy posted men behind the Railroad, and threw out skirmishers *in their rear*. These two brigades were led on into the ambush, and when within easy gunshot they all rose from behind the embankment and mowed our men down mercilessly. After this the enemy retreated, but this was a terrible blow to the two Brigades. Our regiments were not engaged. The field of battle was a sickening sight, the losses having fallen entirely upon our men. It was said, and I think it was true, that General Lee came upon the field and General A.P. Hill asked for instructions, and General Lee replied, "Your lines are too long and too thin, let your men stack arms and bury the dead."[2]

As in all the battles, North Carolina was a prominent figure; in all the battlefields the dead from our state were abundant. At Gettysburg we passed over the field often, the first day's fight and I saw there the men of General Ivenson's N.C. Brigade[3] lying dead as though they had been cut down with a scythe. Next to N.C. were the dead Georgians, and it seemed as if these two states furnished a large part of the army. Virginia, though, abounded in cavalry soldiers and artillery. Our state had six cavalry regiments, but only 1st, 2nd and probably 3rd won distinction. The 1st and 2nd were as good soldiers as ever went from any state.

Monday, Oct. 18th 1863
Camp near Culpepper C.H.

My Dear Pa & Ma,

Some time has elapsed since I wrote you last. During that time I have been on the march. We left our encampment near Mitchell's Ford[4] on the 8th having had previous information that the enemy was much weakened and about to fall back on Washington. Genl. Lee's whole design, as has since transpired, was to separate their column, cut off an enemy corps or so with its train, and pursue the remnant to their entrenchments. The design was admirable, showing much of Genl. Lee's ability, but the execution was miserable. Although comparatively this campaign was a short one, its failure is more signal than any during the war, although not *disastrous*. I saw very much of Genl. Lee during this march, and his face indicated good humor and high spirits. I never saw the General look better. He superintended in person the fording of the Rapidan. Genl. Ewell's Corps marched on a by-road to the left of Cedar Mountain, and having accomplished the flanking of the mountain with a considerable cavalry fight, we rested on the first day behind the mountain. The cavalry then pursued the enemy, after a brisk fight at Brandy Station, to Warrenton Springs Ford, where another desperate cavalry engagement ensued. The Yankees fought stubbornly and fell back on Warrenton. That night we encamped at Warrenton Springs. This was once, as you remember, a fashionable place of resort—the most beautiful perhaps in Virginia. The buildings and groves were magnificent. The enemy saw fit though, because they had a few hundred dollars worth of stores there, to burn the whole establishment except one small building. We passed through Warrenton on the morning of the 14th. This was a beautiful little town with more real handsome houses and ladies than I have seen before in Va. except Shepardstown. The ladies are noted for their enthusiasm and beauty. A Confederate looks forward to a visit there with pleasure. Refreshments were distributed very freely. The discipline is so exact now on our Division that the men were not allowed to leave ranks, and in that way we missed a great many things intended for them. You can readily imagine that such treatment at this advanced state of the war, in these evil times when a soldier is buffeted & spit on by the extortioner and out-of-the-war people— that such a reception by so many bright and beautiful faces was cheering. We encamped outside of W.[5] and the next day at sunrise we were saluted by the boom of the cannon. During all this time the enemy was leaving Culpepper by the Orange R.R. and the turnpike; we were gradually converging towards the R.R.

Bristoe Station is one on the R.R.[6] On both sides considerable eminences. The eminence on the left side commanding a plain in front of it; and on each flank of the plain two hills commanding the one on the other side. Genl. D. H. Hill knew the enemy to be at or about the road. Having placed his battery on the hill commanding the plain in his front *he advanced his line of battle without the precaution* of skirmishers in his front. The Yankees in order to entrap our men threw out skirmishers in the *rear* of their line of battle, to make it appear that their line of battle was farther off than it really was. Genls. Cook [Cooke] & Kirkland of N.C. were ordered forward. They advanced only a short distance when they found themselves upon the enemy. The Yankees poured in a terrible volley and repulsed our line with great slaughter. In the mean time their batteries (six in number)were planted on eminences on the opposite side of the road.[7] Their fire completely enfiladed our batteries (one of which was a N.C. battery) and their infantry support being repulsed, we lost the entire battery of six pieces. Genl. Heth was the division commander who thus murdered our brave men, and suffered unavoidable retreat.[8] The object of Genl. Hill was to throw his left around and in this way encircle the enemy. But, his right attacking too soon, and without precaution, the left had no time to take position. In this way we lost our game. Genls. Hill & Heth are both highly blameable, but are not under arrest as is reported. The fruits of the whole adventure is about 3 or 4,000 prisoners, and driving the Yankees away from R.[9] Genl. Lee no doubt feels badly; but the men look much more so, for they were calculating upon overcoats & blankets for the Winter. As it is they will await the slow process of being supplied by the Q.M. Dept. C.S.[10]

I never saw horses so badly mutilated as those killed in Manly's Battery. And the most sickening scene of the war on so small a battlefield was the brains of a man scattered all over the ground. We congratulate ourselves, after failing to do what our Genl. desired, that we have freed the country from the enemy for some time, with small loss. The prospect is that now we are to be quiet, perhaps to go into Winter quarters. It is supposed, too, that two Divisions will be sent to reinforce Bragg and further that Rhodes and Anderson will be the men. I am in hopes that the A. N. Va.[11] is destined to enjoy peaceful occupation of W. Qrs. until Spring sets in. We have torn up the R.R. from Mannassas to Culpepper, and are now near Culpepper, in the neighborhood of that arch traitor and Unionist, J. Minor Botts. While the other citizens around him have suffered, his plantation remains untouched.[12]

I received your letter as we were falling back from Mannassas. The pleasant strain of Pa's letter made me feel quite like home.

Henry Flanner[13] has just called to see me. Love to all.

       Affectionately your Son,
       Thomas

              Camp near Brandy Station[14]
              Tuesday, October 27th 1863

Dear Mary & Lydia,

I received your letters—Lydia's while I was on picket & Mary's before I got up this morning, but in consequence of our unsettled condition, they were a long time getting here. They were none the less acceptable, as uninteresting as you thought them to be yourselves. We located here last Sunday, but were not permitted to stay long enough to make ourselves comfortable. It is the design of our Genls. that we take up Winter quarters here. Consequently we are making preparations to build houses. We are all glad enough to change our vocation of arms to that of peaceful labor, even for a short time. And should no demonstrations be made by the enemy, will be quite comfortable in about a week. We are about five miles from the Rappahannock River, and about one mile from the R.R. station (Brandy's). The prospect therefore for something to eat this Winter is better than last, at least as far as commissary stores are concerned.

The country surrounding us though is little better than the plains of Mannassas; nothing at all can be bought. The few scattered houses showing that they had once been nice residences and happy homes, have idle fields all around them, with scarcely a panel of fence in sight. We had some unpleasant duty to perform yesterday. General Ewell took Johnson's Division out beyond our outposts to gather the R.R. iron of the O &A[15] R.R. still remaining. The Yankee cavalry was obstinate in the matter and showed fight. We had a sharp fight, and after securing about three miles of iron, returned. I thought at one time that we would have a heavy fight. Our Brigade was ordered to flank a battery, but the Yankees saw our object and withdrew. We had four or five killed and about twenty wounded; some though from our Regt.

The weather here is unusually cold. The ride yesterday, returning from our adventure, was almost cold enough to freeze. I was green enough to come away from home without gloves; and in riding, my hands and arms almost froze. Ask Ma while she is in W.[16] to buy me a pair of gauntlets. I am willing to pay a big price for them. You all seem to be very anxious about the grapes Ma sent me. I don't think I am bound to tell anyone what I did with them, as I wanted them for a *"particular purpose"*. As *"farmer"* I don't think that my sister Mrs. Mary has any right to say "there is no use in sending potatoes *if* grapes didn't reach me." Send them as I asked, as soon as you can, as I asked—care of Dr. F.W. Murphy, Soldiers Home, Richmond, Va. You can remind Miss Ellen G. before you send them about that "big turnip". She understands.

I have several letters to write today, and must let this answer til next time.

Affectionately your Brother,
Thomas F.

Hd Qrs. 3d Regt. C.S. Troops
Oct. 30th 1863

Dear Pa,

Capt. R.F. Langdon, A.Q.M.[17] of this Regt., leaves tomorrow for Raleigh for clothing for officers and men. He will probably remain until the next arrival of a steamer; if so I will be able to buy a pr. of blankets, $10., one of shoes or boots at $———; cloth at $10 per yd., overcoats $40., shirts $8. or $10. per pair and other things. As I am nearly threadbare I will have to keep the cloth; but as I write to Bobby, you can divide the other things between you. I am entitled to one each only. It does not amount to much but I thought if you wanted them I would secure them for you. I will let you know positively in a few days what we can get and at what price.

I am going over to see Col. B.[18] tomorrow or *soon*. The saddle I thought to get is not as good as I expected, so I will wait another chance. I can buy for $125 at the Govt. Ord. Dept. an excellent saddle, bridle and everything complete; but it would not suit you. I will watch my chance, as a good many officers will send their horses off. My horses are looking finely. I expect to sell my pony in a short time.

I have not time to write you a letter. Love to all. I am not very well.

Affectionately your son,
Thomas F.

We returned to camp near the Rapidan and again went into Winter quarters, as I supposed because it was about November. The rigors of the march had used up our Surgeon Dr. William F. Steuart [Stewart], and he was obliged to ask for duty at a post. Dr. Steuart [Stewart] was first cousin of our General George H. Steuart. He was apparently 50 when he came to us. He had been sent out of the lines from Baltimore, his home because of his implication in aid to the South. He told me of some of the adventures of some of the Southern sympathizers in Baltimore. They had an organization which had to be maintained with great secrecy as their movements were very closely watched by the U.S. authorities. On one occasion he sent a raft of patent gate-posts across the Potomac River. The posts were hollow, and filled with percussion gun caps. I believe this venture was successful. One of Dr. Steuart's [Stewart] sons was arrested for his Southern sympathy and put in prison. He bribed the guard with a gold watch to let him escape, but when he attempted it he was shot dead. While lying dead in prison his father and mother were sent for to come and see him. The shock was very great, but it only inflamed to a higher degree, the animosity of his parents. I don't remember what particular act was fastened upon Dr. Steuart [Stewart], but he was sent out of the lines after a few day's notice. Dr. and Mrs. Steuart [Stewart] made preparations by turning all their valuables into money. As they were allowed only a hundred pounds of luggage and a given sum of money they restored to the subterfuge of preparing a turkey, and rolling up some bills of exchange in oil silk and sewing it up in the place of the "stuffing". Mrs. S. had a traveling suit prepared with a great many rows of buttons which were $50 gold pieces, covered with cloth. So the Dr. reached the Confederacy with about $20,000 and put it all in Confederate bonds, so sure was he of Southern success. He was very kind to me, and for a month would not allow me to get up to Surgeon's call as he wanted to relieve me of duty, which I had done without relief for so long, and he wanted to learn the condition of the men. He was very kind and was esteemed by officers and men. The hardships of camp were too hard for him and he was forced to ask for assignment to post duty.[19]

Dr. B.M. Cromwell of Ga., formerly of the 1st N.C. was assigned to succeed him.[20] His service was at the "Battle of Payne's Farm". We were then on Mine Run, near the Rapidan in November 1863, when the enemy attempted to surprise our Division—Genl. Ed. Johnson's—when in return we surprised him and drove him across the river. It was a very sudden and unexpected fight. We were marching along the road not knowing that there was an enemy about, when the snapping of caps by the men (a preliminary precaution to dry out the gun barrels which was very common among our soldiers) showed that some one had spied the enemy. Capt. Ned Armstrong, as usual, handed me a note to his folks, his money and watch to be sent home if he was killed, etc., but still I did not understand the urgency of these preparations. "Rise in your stirrups and look over the trees," says he, and as I did I spied a large body of "Blue Coats". It was a hasty line we formed, but so well arranged was it, that one of our Brigades, the "Stonewall", was put in on the flank of the enemy, and the battle was decided very soon against them.[21]

Brigade Hospl. Nov. 30th 1863
(near Mountain Run, Va.)[22]

My Dear Brother & Sister,

We left our camp on Thursday night and bivouacked in the rear of our entrenchments at or near "W. Qrs.".[23] On Friday morning we started by the left flank towards a mill, and passing the mill-stream turned a little to the left. We had gone only a few miles before the Yankees opened their musketry upon us, taking us entirely by surprise. Our ambulances and wagons were all in the road. It would have taken but little to have caused a panic. There were Yankees in force, only a few hundred yards from us, and no guns loaded. Our men were soon loaded. The men were very much amused at the Doctors, who were right up with the line of battle (their usual place being several miles—sometimes—to the rear) and sung out at them "We've got you now Sawbones." I dismounted and as they say in the army "I limbered to the rear." Our ambulances were soon parked in the rear of the line of battle—nobody knowing where the rear was; there was firing in the rear, in the front, and the flanks—everywhere. An amusing scene occured at the Hospl. which was temporarily established. As the Asst. Surgn. came running to the Chf. Surgn. Division, singing out *"Doctor, Doctor, this is no place for Doctors; a horse got shot in the yard just now, and a stick was knocked out of the ambulance wheel!"*[24]

The confusion soon subsided. The enemy was endeavoring to turn our flank; but as soon as his object was seen—after a considerable battle we changed our line, where we are now entrenched. We lost in the battle about 76 men, among them Lt. Oates of Onslow was killed.[25] None of the Wilmn. men were killed, and none that you know wounded.

There is a prospect of battle this afternoon. The enemy has certainly to fight, as he has crossed his force.

Nothing can be told of course of the result of the battle; but the men are confident.

Affectionately your brother,
Thos. F.

This was the first battle of Sergt. Maj. Robert McRee. He was the son of Dr. James F. McRee, our former Surgeon. He was just 18 years old and had been a student up to the time he left the University of N.C. He was a student at the Jesuit College near Georgetown, D.C. when the war broke out, and returning home at that time was sent to the University of N.C. at Chapel Hill. When he reached 18 years, the time for enlistment, instead of remaining at home and securing an easy place, he went at once to the scene of war and enlisted in the 3rd Regt. He was made Sgt. Maj. and was serving in this capacity at the Battle of Payne's Farm. McRee came to our camp with his citizens clothes—all that he could get—and he was an odity to look at. He wore a broad-brimmed straw hat, and was unmilitary looking as a Quaker. His blanket was a thin white one, not at all suited for field life, but the best he could get. McRee was a Chesterfield in politeness, and his knowledge of the world was in strong contrast with his knowledge of books. He was well versed in literature, and Shelley and Poe were his favorites. These two authors he had thoroughly mastered, and he read them with good effect especially Poe's "Raven" and the "Bells." But to return to the battle, McRee saw a tempting opportunity to get a blanket and a canteen from a dead prisoner, but not being skillful in the art of disposing the dead of their property as others, and having compunctions as his military right, sought the Col. (Thruston commanded in this fight) saluted him and asked permission to secure the prizes he so much coveted.

We went into permanent Winter camp after this battle. We lost very few in the fight. During our Winter encampment the state of N.C. sent us quite a number of conscripts principally men from Surry and Stoke's counties. They were evidently the last drainings of the back woods. Holden, the editor of the "Sentinel" said that N.C. and the Confederacy "robbed the cradle and the grave" to recruit our army, and it came near being a literal fact.[26] One of the lot of men was a very intelligent fellow, and claimed that after he got to our camp that he was a "friend" (Quaker) and that it was against his conscience to fight. The Col. told him there was a law providing for such cases, that he could have settled it in Raleigh at the Camp of Instruction, that now it was too late and he would have to fight. In this Battle of Payne's Farm he tried to maintain his assumed Quaker principles, and would not load. He was put under guard, but as soon as he stood before one volley he loaded and fired like a good fellow and showed so much skill as a marksman and coolness and courage he was afterwards promoted to be Sgt. Some of the "conscripts" sent were not so good.

One half-witted fellow named Hinshaw was assigned to Co. H. On our return from the Bristoe Campaign we had to ford the Rapidan at a very rocky ford in the night, and the footing was not secure for men or horses as the current was swift. It was in October and the water was cold. In crossing the river Hinshaw got behind the Adj. Genl. of the Brigade, and supported himself by placing one hand on the rump of the horse. Growing more confident he asked Capt. Williamson to carry his gun. The request was so innocent and so reasonable Capt. W. took it and carried it across the stream. When his company had crossed, the Captain forgot to whom the gun belonged, and poor Hinshaw had no idea who had his gun. But being informed that he must find his gun, he went in search. The Col. (Thruston) had not learned the conscripts by sight and the only semblance of uniform this poor conscript had was a letter H on his hat. The Col. discovered a strange fellow poking around his bivouac and hailed him—"look here sir, where did you come from, what is your name?" Deliberately taking his hat from his head to refresh himself about the letter of his company he drawled, "I belong to figger H. company—has you seed anything of my gun?" The Col. was quite amazed at his simplicity and found out that he was one of the new conscripts. "Don't you know," says he, "if you lose your gun you will have to pay for it?" He did not know that until his Captain told him, and he was now looking for it. "I gin it to a man on a critter last night when we was a-wadin' that river, and I thought he was in favor of the war as he was a-riding of a critter." This conversation let in a flood of light upon the attitude of the conscripts. They came from the western counties, were opposed to a war they had no interest in, and had taken up the belief of the new party of Union men in our state who started the cry that "it was a rich man's war and a poor man's fight," and so to this conscript any one so well off as to ride a horse was having a good thing of it and must be "in favor of the war." The conscript had apparently come against his will. The men "chaffed" him a good deal. "You say you are so poor Hinshaw, what did you get married for then?" His ready reply was, "I got married to save my oats crop." A remark which showed at least that the poor fellow could reason well on some subject. He was almost cruelly treated by the practical jokers of the Regiment so that it is not strange that he should have been driven to attempt to desert as the following narrative shows.

On one occasion we were on our way to the picket station, and the men commenced teasing Hinshaw telling him that he had better go over to the Yankees, he was only eating up the rations of some good men. So exasperated was he that as soon as he got to the station, and before our Regiment had relieved the Virginia Regiment on picket, he went down to the river with gun and cartridge box and all his belongings and started across the river. "Halt" says the Virginian, "where are you going?" Hinshaw's dispairing reply was, "I am going over to the enemy, my country rickermended me to go." He was arrested and put in handcuffs. As soon as we got back to camp I found that Genl. Steuart had determined to apply the full force of the law to this poor fellow, but we succeeded in making out a clear case of feeble mind before the court martial, and he was out I think.[27] Genl. Steuart was unreasonable with offenders against the law, and his guard house made as uncomfortable as possible, and I had the occasion to plead for some of the poor fellows to secure for them proper shelter.

But to return to the conscripts, most of them soon learned the way of soldiers and did good service. The period of seasoning with these poor fellows was very severe. They had to learn to accomodate themselves to the new mode of life and in a few weeks, which had taken their veteran comrades two or three years to learn. To cook for themselves with only a gum cloth for a kneading trough, and bake bread in a skillet, or frying pan, as it happened for utensils were scarce, and make the small ration of four ounces of meat (only approximately 4 oz. for it was only guessed at) and a pound of flour answer all the demands of hunger for a day, required skill and economy, which the conscript although brought from a rural and primitive condition of life had to learn by hard licks. To protect himself from rain before he had been on the battlefield to capture a shelter tent (two pieces of cotton cloth with buttons on one side and button holes on the other, so as to stretch over an improvised ridge pole set upon forked sticks) to take care of gun and ammunition, were all easy compared with the trials which his change of life brought upon him.[28] His veteran comrades had little sympathy for men who had to be dragged into war, for which they had volunteered, and they treated them as inferiors. Bad water, badly cooked food, unventilated quarters (in Winter) always disturbed their bowels and they were in majority upon the sick list. Coming from the country, where the most of them had lived with out ever having seen a town larger than the "store town", the cross road village with a hundred inhabitants, remote from railroads therefore uncommunicable with the outside world, the trials which usually come to children, they escaped, and measles and small pox were usually their fate. I have known almost the entire 57th N.C. Regiment (conscripts), to be sick at one time with the measles, and it was so with most of the regiments enlisted from the country as most of them were in N.C.[29] But few of the conscripts contributed to regiments in an active campaign were able to hold out for the reasons stated, although some of them did and became identified with the regiment and acquired some *esprit du corps.*

The remaining months from November to April 1863 were spent in camp near Orange C.H.[30] We had the usual quarters—log houses with daubed chinks, stick chimneys covered with clay, and the only opening being a door, as the thin clap board roof was sufficiently ventilating. Some quarters achieved the distinction of having a glass window, and other a substitute of greased writing paper to let in a little more light. Left to such inactive lives many were the means undertaken to while away the time. Some of the officers gambled, but I only knew of this from heresay, as I do not remember of having seen more than one game of *poker*—the universal gambling game. I account for this by the fact that my opinion of gambling was known to my friends and the gamblers always avoided such persons when they wanted to have a game. This of course may have grown out of a lesson taught by Maj. W.L. DeRossett [deRossett] before I joined the "3rd." Gambling among the officers was running pretty high, and the Col. [Meares] determined to break it up. He deputed Maj. DeRossett to execute the plan. He waited until the party was in the midst of an exciting game, and about $300 was up on the table as stakes, (it was before the depreciation of our money, in 1862) and walking in on them suddenly he took up the money from the table. The players and by standers took it for a joke and were annoyed at the interference but the Maj. informed the excited players that he would give them their choice, either to stand a court-martial for violation of the army regulations, or let the money go to the sick at the hospital. The money was handed over to the hospital, but it did not suppress gambling. I think after this that none but "players" were invited to be present at games.

Whist[31] playing though, was indulged in a good deal, and our small stock of books was soon exhausted. Some of the officers resorted to athletic games of jumping and wrestling, but I selected whist as more to my notion. I never did care about the science of the game and complied just enough within the rules to be within bounds. I liked only the luck of it and enjoyed that; but no money was ever bet on these games by us or any players. I was surprised at one thing that keeping score of games played steadily through the Winter, discarding "honors", both parties had won about the same number of games.

Mr. Patterson was still with us, and we had nightly prayers at the Col's. quarters, and no matter how frugal our meal was in camp or elsewhere we always had "grace." This much of the outer forms of religion were observed, and among most of the officers there was a compliance with the decencies of religion. A few of them were exemplary Christians, and oaths were seldom heard among the officers esteemed irreligious. The Bible was in nearly every man's hands, but I can't say there was much devotional reading of it. My house or "shanty" served as the dispensary of the regiment, and also as my quarters. Lt. Cicero Craig[e], I invited to share luck with me, for brave man as he was, he was just enough insubordinate at times to excite Col. Thruston's anger. What incensed Craig[e] most was that the Col. gambled with Lt. Stone,[32] Craig's subordinate, and preferred him above Craig. Stone was a well educated man, and well connected, but was a black sheep, coming into the army just in time to wipe away some stain upon his character which his conduct had brought upon him. Craig[e] knew all this and avoided the Col. and all his friends. To add to all his troubles he was desperately ragged, so much so that the Col. had to excuse him from dress parade. His friends at home were poor, and his father having married again he was alienated from them. Only one friend at home adhered to him—Capt. Tom Craig a pilot of a blockader. He heard of Craig[e]'s condition and bought for him in Nassau an outfit consisting of under clothes, uniform, boots and hat. The news of this valuable present cheered this poor fellow up, for with this he could not only make a good appearance, but be the envy even of the Col. himself. This would be better understood if one could know how difficult it was to get clothes even with an abundance of money.

Finally a letter came that a new out fit in a sole-leather valise had been entrusted to a corporal of the regiment, not willing to risk such a valuable package by the other means of transportation. The express companies did not deliver goods to the army. Like a little child Craig[e] was all expectancy and the morning came that Corporal Sellars was to arrive. Sure enough he did arrive, but where was the valise? Sellars was a brave fellow to deliver the message. His story ran, that while he was at Weldon waiting for the train to connect with that from Richmond, for security he put the valise under his head for safe keeping, and when he awoke the valise was gone. But one piece of comfort he had for the Lieutenant, he delivered *the key*. Think of the anger and disappointment and here was poor Craig[e] too ragged to go on duty, expecting a long delayed promotion to captaincy, refusing a leave of absence until he was promoted, and so he abandoned himself to a closer seclusion in my quarters dreaming of the revenge he was going to wreck upon his enemies by a promotion on the field for gallantry. All his thoughts seemed to be concentrated on this one desire—military glory. Craig[e]'s abilities had been noticed by Genl. Steuart and he made him Captain of his Brigade sharp shooters. This was a great relief from his contact with his Col. as now he was to get his orders from Brigade Head Quarters and all that he did would be under the eye of the Brig. and Div. Commander. After all Craig[e] was superseded by the appointment of Stone to be Captain, but Craig[e] was glad to have his new command, and it suited his peculiar form of ambition.

Armstrong[33] came frequently to my quarters, and his visits were always pleasant. His disposition was so happy, he seemed to live to do his duty because of the pleasure it gave him. He was firmly settled in his belief that the war was to end disastrously to us, but he was always the same, apparently very little distressed when he went into battle. Craig[e] and Armstrong were the opposites to each other, and had many a stiff argument over the conduct of the war. Armstrong didn't smoke, nor did I, and we heard that our quarters were to be visited by smoking comrades, to inaugurate some of their Chapel Hill[34] pranks, and smoke us out. The visit was first made to Armstrong. His cabin was like mine. One by one officers came in with tobacco and pipes. His little cabin was soon filled, every man armed with a pipe and smoking vigorously. That soon resorted to the more vigorous plan of blowing through the pipe to burn up the tobacco fast and to create a big smoke. All the time A. [Armstrong] waited on his friends when their pipes were empty. Friends on the outside seeing so much smoke escaping from the roof, threw a blanket over, while another climbed to the chimney, threw down tobacco into the fire, and covered the flue with a board. The smoke was very dense, but Captain A held out. After a while some gave it up and left, reducing the party to two. These tried to escape, still A. kept them from it, and they were forced to lie down upon the floor, for a more diluted air. These were finally compelled to beg Armstrong to let them go, and so the smokers were smoked. A. was terribly wilted the next day by the bad dosing of tobacco smoke he got, but his victory was complete, and the silly practice was never repeated notwithstanding I was threatened. This little incident shows how childish were the amusements of grown men in camp.

The mania of wrestling among certain officers was considerable. Parsley and Cantwell (Captain of Co. F), Maj. Ennett and others.[35] I always avoided it because I was not active and spry, and didn't care to have my ankle sprained or arm broken. Parsley and Ennett were particularly anxious to get at it. One day very unexpectedly Parsley watched his chance and boy-like ran in and took his hold, and to my surprise and his I threw him down. It was such a good joke on Parsley that Ennett came to his assistance and in attempting to pull me off, I seized at an opportune time, and he fell and I had them both down. Ennett was thrown by his own spurs.

Captain John L. Cantwell was formerly Col. of the 64th Regiment. He was a volunteer soldier in the Mexican War, in the Palmetto Regiment and received a medal for gallantry. He came to Wilmington from Charleston as the first officer of the Adam's Express Company (1850?). He was the leader in the civilian military co. known as the Wilmington Light Infantry, its Captain at one time, and when the war broke out he was Colonel of militia, and took temporary command of troops until other organizations were formed. He was left out in making up new regiments, and served as a volunteer private until 1862 or 1863, then he was made Col. of the 64th Regiment of N.C. This regiment was not of the best material, and jealousies arose. Col. C. was a strict disciplinarian in one sense, a stickler for little things, and was enthusiastic in modelling his regiment into good discipline. The men were not disposed to submit to strict discipline, and took the first opportunity to get a charge against the Col., which was for drunkeness. The matter did not come to a trial, he resigned, and our regiment, always on the lookout for good officers, offered the Captaincy of Co. F to Cantwell and he accepted. It was not without some degree of humiliation that he accepted a much lower rank, but he was moved entirely by his patriotism. He was one of our best and bravest officers.[36] He was very peculiar though, and such a stickler for army regulations that he was annoying sometimes. On one occasion he was Officer for the Day. My quarters served as sleeping apartments, office, dispensary, and most everything else pertaining to sick men from Surgeons Call until all the medicine was prepared for the sick which took until a late hour of the day. Cantwell came in and finding my quarters in bad condition, looked at his watch and said that he would return at a certain other hour to inspect me. He came punctually and finding my quarters still out of order turned to me and said that I would be reported to the Col. I cared very little for it indeed, and I knew that the Col. would care less, for he knew exactly under what difficulties I maintained my quarters as they were. Pretty soon Col. Thruston came to my quarters laughing, and asked me what was the matter with Cantwell. I told him and he had a laugh and sat down a while and talked. Cantwell had done his literal duty but it was not mixed with discretion, and there fore was with out weight. This was but a sample of much of his strict construction actions as an officer, so that his merits lay in the fact that he knew how to obey, and was brave.

Letter-writing and receiving letters was one of our great pleasures. Postage stamps were scarce in camp, and indeed we were allowed the privilege of "franking", by writing our name in the right upper corner of the envelope.[37] The mails were looked for with great anxiety in camp, and many were the long letters I wrote home, and the record against me is that I always wanted something. I have to say if I always wanted something, I almost always got what I wrote for if unfortunately the articles were not lost in transportation. The rail roads were badly out of repair. The cars were worn and dilapitated so that one could hardly go from one place to another without getting vermin on them. Freight to the army always took precedence, and it was only by special favor that a package could get through. Should it be favored with shipment it ran through another risk of being lost at the warehouse and at the army end of the route of being robbed. Frequently packages were opened and robbed, but as the blame could not be charged upon any one person, but upon many from the wagon driver who brought the package, through the guard (who was charged every little while), and the railroad agent. On one occasion though, when food was right scarce, I got a dressed turkey from home. It was fat and tender, and as we had nothing to cook with it but rice, four of us "sot our faces" to it, and when we had satisfied our appetites, the poor cook had only the bones for his share. I don't know the weight of the turkey, but it was large enough to have served less hungry people even to a good sized family. Food got so scarce sometimes that we were glad to have any addition to one pound of flour and four ounces of fat bacon.[38] Officers were allowed the privelege of buying a ration in addition, and this I did as often as the commissary allowed it, as my horse was often in lack of the meal I didn't eat. The horses seldom got enough and it took a man all his time looking after providing not only what was his due for his horse, but to keep it after you got it. Some of the men had a way of eking out their scanty rations with "big hominy." I often wondered where they got it but was informed by the knowing ones that they picked up the corn dropped by the Quartermaster and the Wagon Master when feeding the mules, and it was very likely that the mules were robbed of their scanty food. To prepare "big hominy" was difficult. They made strong lye and soaked the corn until the husk loosened, then the husk was separated from the grain, and the grain washed and boiled until it was soft and eatable. It was really a dainty dish as compared with some of our bread. Onions and cowpeas were the extras that we could generally get in Winter quarters by sending to Orange C.H.[39] Onions sold for $2 a dozen and cowpeas were about $.50 per quart, the difficulty generally in the way was to get a messenger. The ambulance man of our Regiment was at the Surgn's command until after the Battle of Chancellorsville. All ambulances were kept in park under the control of the Brigade Surgeon.

According to army regulations a regiment of a thousand men was allowed ten gallons of whiskey a month. The size of our regiment and the scarcity of whiskey reduced the amount, so we only got five gallons. Its arrival was a great nusiance. It was intended for the sick, but no sooner did it come than the officers came boldly up and upon some pretext or other got it all, and when the real necessity arose there was none for the sick. When I was the Officer in Charge I after a while declined to make the requisition for it, as I had to certify that it was "used for the sick of the army alone", and this I could not do. There were no drunkards in our regiment, and if there had been the compulsory abstinence would have cured him, as nothing like a regular supply of liquor could be had even for the sick. When liquor could be had though, so great was the rarity of it, the men who scarcely ever touched a drop at home would indulge for the temporary excitement.

I recollect what a great surprise I had in camp one night. I had been in bed some hours when the Col. had his orderly have me come at once to his quarters. It was cold but the distance was short. I dressed and went over. The Col., Lt. Col., Maj., Adjt., had a cabin built in the same manner but of different shape from the quarters of the other staff officers.

I found Col. Thruston sitting at his fire place. He pretended to be greatly surprised at my coming and paid no attention to me. After a little while he said, "who sent for you?" I told him he had. He denied it and teased me in this way until I was about to go back to my quarters considering myself a victim of a practical joke, when two or three came in and we crossed over into the Lt. Col's. quarters, and there to my surprise I saw a table upon which was spread cakes, lemons, sardines, crushed sugar, brandy, whiskey, pipes and tobacco of the famous Durham brand.

There were other dainties besides but I don't remember them. I rubbed my eyes to assure myself that it was not all a dream, and after a meal we all adjourned. The next night a party of Brigade officers including General Steuart assembled by invitation to a feast, and the like probably was not seen on the line that Winter. The party did not adjourn until 2 o'clock that morning. The next day we were ordered on a tour of picket duty, and when I met the General on the road, he expressed himself as very much pleased with the

Pencil sketch of Colonel Thruston's cabin from TFW's memoirs. (Drawn in 1886) Thomas Fanning Wood Collection, Wilmington, N.C.

entertainment, but he was of the opinion that it might very well have been divided into two feasts. So uncertain were we when we left a camp if we ever saw it again, it was the custom to consume everything not easily carried.

Camp 3d. Regt. N.C. Troops
December 24th 1863

Dear Pa & Ma,

I greet you all Merry Christmas, and hope it will really be a pleasant day for you. I will enjoy the day in imagination though, even if we will be on duty on the bleak outposts. I have nothing to complain of though, for I was awoke last night about 11 o'clock by a summons to attend—not a poor sick fellow with aches and pains—but a real genuine old time feast. They had received some boxes from home at H. Qrs. and Craig[e] & I were invited to the "soiree" or whatever you choose to call it. They had cake, oranges, peanuts and "sperrits". It was quite as pleasant a dream as I ever anticipated or realized. I hope this will be but a fore-taste of what I will get yet for Christmas. An ambulance went today to Orange, with instructions about turkeys and the like.

Capt. Langdon arrived in good time with his clothes etc. I am obliged to you for the bundle. It contained what I wanted and things that could not be bought here. I succeeded yesterday in procuring some drawers, pants, jackets & blankets from the QM Dept. so that I am well prepared for the coming Winter. I will send the jackets home. One of them I wish you would have made up into a military vest for me; the other you can make a jacket of for "Tim".[40] I tried to get some good pants that would do for him, but they were all so course that I concluded that they wouldn't do. All these things sell very cheap and are a great accommodation to the officers. We can wear our course clothes around camp, and in this way cheat the extortioners out of their high prices for uniforms.

We go on picket the day after Christmas to stay five days, and then we are to move our Winter quarters to within 6 miles of Orange, which will be our permanent location until next May. It will be quite severe on us to break up here; we will necessarily be obliged to bivouac for a couple of weeks before we can build again.

When I was at home I tried to get some silk braid wide enough to bind my heavy black overcoat, and some buttons to match. If such a thing is to be bought in W.[41] I wish you would send enough for a coat. We have a tailor here who can put it on. I want my vest cut in military of course; I have no buttons for it, so I will get you to get me a set. I suppose I can have it cut by Bobby's[42] measure and made at home.

I received Bobby's letter by Capt. L.[43] and will answer it in a few days.

A Merry Christmas to you all!!

Affectionately your son
Thomas F.

Ask Bobby to ask Maj. Ennett to call at Genl. Hospl. 24 on Main St. 25 & 26th St.[44] for a small package for me when he returns. If he will write word of the exact day he will be in Orange I will send an ambulance to meet him. He can telegraph from Wilm.

T.F.W.

Have concluded to have vest made in camp. Please send me 18 staff buttons for vest by Maj. Ennett or anyone coming.

T.F.W.

Among the amusing incidents of this camp was the appearance of the Major in the Lieut. Col's. uniform. Parsley and Ennett had returned to camp at the same time with new uniforms made by the same tailor, the only difference was that of the insignia of rank. The Major had a single star on the collar. The Lt. Col. two stars on the collar. Maj. Ennett was to go on dress parade and in his hurry to be on time he put on Parsley's coat. P. saw the mistake and humored it and let him go through with it and when it was all over he congratulated him as "Col." Ennett—didn't see the blunder even then until he got back to his quarters and saw his own coat hanging on its peg. Little incidents like this furnished amusement for the camp for several days.

On one occasion Maj. Ennett was hard up for clothes. The fashion was to wear long coats, but the more military fashion of short coats prevailed after General "Stonewall" Jackson appeared in his new uniform of short pattern. The seat of his[45] pants were in need of patches, but where to get the cloth was the difficulty. The idea struck him that he could reduce the length of his coat tails, and use it to patch his pantaloons. So he called up the best skilled man with the needle and set him to work, first cutting off one skirt. The scheme was a good one but unfortunately the long roll beat,[46] and the Major followed up the column in his right place in the rear, with a well patched pair of breeches, but one skirt of one length and one of another.

Col. Parsley on his return of leave, Winter 1863, brought a present of a box of a dozen bottles of Scotch whiskey. This was as clear as water. En route Parsley had emptied one bottle, and when he got to camp he filled it with water. The officers assembled at his quarters to welcome him, and to get a drink. Parsley was always ready for a joke, and put out the bottle of water asking the oldest captain first. As there was only one tin cup to drink out of, the first Captain poured a big drink and drank it off. He of course discovered that it was water, but did not care about having the joke on him, he rushed to the water bucket to get a drink to drown the strong liquor. Another and another did the same, until it came to an officer who had too little wit to humor the joke. He tasted his drink and turned to the Colonel and said, "why Colonel, it's nothing but water." Of course everyone yelled at the discomfiture of the "green" fellow, and then the Col. offered them the real stuff. This whiskey came in by the blockade from Scotland. I saw a similar joke played at a dinner party, by a lady, Mrs. McNair. She was very fond of young people, and they assembled at her house. Food was not plentiful and luxuries unknown. But at a dining when I was present, after giving us a good dinner she served a tart to each place and what I supposed to be a glass of wine. A lady sat by me and I proposed to her "health", and tasted my "wine" which turned out to be a concoction of persimmon bark, very astringent and bitter. I saw the joke at once and took another sip without betraying what I had discovered. The trap seemed to be set for a rather ill-contrived batchelor at the table rather than for me. I went on eating which under the circumstances was not enjoyable, as I did not find that apple tarts and persimmon tea were at all compatible. In a few minutes though, Mr. Callins, for whom the trap was set took a drink of his wine, and such a sputtering and spitting and a growling, and such a peal of merriment from the girls, repaid me for the badness of the dose.

To return to camp. During the Winter my principal books were the "Spectator", and the "Tattler" [Tatler] and "Guardian",[47] books I had never read before. The truth is, as I have stated elsewhere, I had never had an opportunity to do any reading outside of medicine, and in English literature I was deficient. Such books I read therefore with avidity, although much of the matter in these volumes had references to political and historical and social events to which I had no key. Poor Craig[e] wrote hundreds of pages of his unjust treatment by the Col. and set on foot a correspondence between himself and the Adjt. Genl. of N.C., which made it very uncomfortable for Col. Thruston, but all without effect, when the campaign opened Craig[e] was 1st Lt., Com. [Commander of] Sharpshooters of Steuart's Brigade.

TEN

THE WILDERNESS CAMPAIGN

Since November the Army of Northern Virginia and the Army of the Potomac had camped on opposite sides of the Rapidan River, near Orange Courthouse, surrounded by the battlefields—Chancellorsville, Fredericksburg, Brandy Station, Cedar Mountain, Mine Run—where they had fought each other for the past three years. General Ulysses S. Grant had been commissioned a lieutenant general and given command of all Union armies. Rather than become embroiled in the politics of Washington, he decided to make his headquarters with Meade's Army of the Potomac. As spring approached it was clear that Grant was preparing to launch an offensive against Lee's ever shrinking army. Critical shortages in men and supplies had forced General Lee to wait uncharacteristically for Grant to make his move. In this fourth year of the war, the resources of the Confederacy had been stretched to the point that Lee's only option lay in trying outguess his opponent with whom he was more unfamiliar than most of the other Federal leaders sent against him.[1]

The weather looked promising and the army was prepared to execute any plan that General Lee decided on, but acute shortages and the unfortunate encounters with the enemy in the Fall at Bristoe Station and Payne's Farm and a thwarted Union attack across the Rapidan in February at Morton's Ford, had created a strong sense of foreboding throughout the camps that this new season would be the most frightening and tragic for the Army of Northern Virginia. In a letter to his father, on March 30, TFW's friend Captain Edward Armstrong communicates this feeling of dread. "Last week we had a snow about 12 inches deep but it is nevertheless very acceptable to us as it defers the commencement of the Spring campaign which will undoubtedly prove the bloodiest of the war. Blood must flow in torrents. Many a gallant man must offer his life as a sacrifice in less than 60 days."[2] A few weeks later he writes, "All seem to be of the opinion that the campaign will open about the 18th or 28th. Some think that Gen. Grant will cross near our present position, say Morton's Ford, but others think he will try Hooker's route—via Chancellorsville. All seem to dread the approaching struggle. Though they feel hopeful of success. We all feel that though Grant may be driven back beyond the Rapidan yet our lives may be lost in the struggle. I should hate very much to fall now after so many battles have been fought but perhaps it may be as well now as any time."[3] Many Confederate soldiers felt this sense of foreboding, but most firmly believed in their commanding general and were more than willing to trust him to bring them through this campaign as victors. After Gettysburg, religious revivals became far more intense and spread through both armies. Southerners began to suspect the punishment of God at work in their military misfortunes. Moreover, the war was nowhere near an end and death lurked closer than ever. It was time for atonement and soldiers flocked to chapels and religious services. In February, TFW and a number of other members of the regiment were baptized by Rev. George Patterson.

Lee agreed with Armstrong and predicted that Grant would cross the river at the Wilderness using two fords, Germana and Ely. He had to be cautious in case Meade decided to move around the Confederate left instead of moving towards Fredericksburg. Using his instinct, he made preparations to counter Grant's move putting General Ewell's Second Corps in motion towards the Wilderness. Ewell's three divisions were to move eastward along the old stone turnpike, parallel to the river and enter the Wilderness on Grant's predicted line of march. Lee held Hill's corps in camps near Orange Court House and Longstreet's corps at Gordonsville, until he could be certain of Grant's intentions. Lee's basic plan was to intercept the Federal army at its most vulnerable point—the passage through the Wilderness. His plan depended upon a slow movement of the Union force, restricted by wagon trains, cattle and artillery that would spread the troops out along the narrow roads. This would expose the long columns to attacks on their flanks. If Meade sacrificed his support services and pushed his troops rapidly through the Wilderness, he would cross Lee's front and place himself between Lee's army and Richmond. Lee would be in serious trouble.[4]

On May 4, 1864, General Meade crossed the Rapidan at Germana and Ely Fords, as Lee had predicted, with a combined force of 125,000 men, and Lee moved to meet him with eight divisions totaling some 65,000 men. General Hancock's Second Corps crossed at Ely's Ford and reached Chancellorsville in the late afternoon. Warren's Fifth Corps crossed at Germana Ford and camped near Wilderness Tavern the evening of May 4. Meade planned to continue moving towards Lee early on May 5 but he had made two serious errors. By halting early on May 4, he had been forced to camp in the dense growth of the Wilderness. He also assumed that Lee could not reach the Wilderness until late on the 5th and acting on that assumption, failed to ensure that the roads were adequately patrolled. He seemed to content himself with moving slowly through the Wilderness with the full expectation of overpowering Lee's army when they met.[5]

Grant was playing right into Lee's hands, just as other federal generals had in the past, but Grant was a different kind of general, and Lee was to learn a very hard lesson about persistence during this campaign.

When the campaign began in 1864, we were in General Ewell's Corps (Jackson's formerly), Ed Johnson's Div., Steuart's Brigade. Steuart had devised some original badges for his men, of colored cloth, so that at a glance it could be told the Brigade, Regt., Co. of the man, the number of engagements he had been in, whether he was a Sharpshooter or an Ambulance Man, etc. Our Brigade was in excellent condition and when moved out in to the road, our line was direct for the Wilderness, our old field of battle.[6] Genl. J.M. Jones' Va. Brigade in front, Steuart's next and so on.

I must before I forget it tell of an incident at church which happened at Orange C.H. before the campaign opened. It was at the Episcopal Church. It was a solemn communion before the beginning of the "Grant Campaign." The church was crowded with men and officers, and I believe most of our prominent Generals were there. I saw General Lee. He was dressed in a very plain uniform and took a very inconspicuous seat. I am not sure if he had any insignia of rank, if he had it was nothing more than three stars on the collar. After the services had begun all eyes were turned to a person who came clattering up the aisle with his jingling spurs, and it proved to be Genl. Jeb Stuart the Cavalry Commander. He was handsomely dressed for a Confederate, with buff coat facings and collar and embroidered wreath around the three stars on his collar, full gold braid on his sleeves, and a bouquet in his button hole. His felt hat adorned with a plume he carried on his arm in a conspicuous way, and was altogether "loud." I had never seen Jeb Stuart before and was not surprised from what I had heard of him. Many poor fellows met around the table of the Lord who were to partake of the sacrament for the last time.

"J.M. Jones" Brigade was composed of Virginians.[7] It did not have a good record, the Genl. preceeding J.M. Jones being also General Jones, so that the new commander insisted on "J.M. Jones" being put on everything belonging to the Brigade. The scene along our line of march gave tokens of a battle. It was the 4th of May, 1864 when we left camp. On the morning of the 5th the road was strewn with playing cards which the men had thrown away. There was a good deal of card playing in camp, but the men had a superstition about having playing cards in their pockets when going into battle. So far there had been no signs of the enemy and how the men were so quick to find it out puzzled me. The symptoms in this instance proved correct and pretty soon J.M. Jones struck the enemy on the turnpike near Locust Grove (near Wilderness Run) and the whole Division was put in line. Jones' Brigade broke and the General in attempting to rally them was killed.[8] Mr. Patterson and I were standing near Steuart when he gave the command and all the regiments moved forward to the command *"Forward guide center."* In our front was a wilderness of small old-field pine trees, with branches near the ground, that were much lower than the mens' heads. We received a heavy volley before we saw the enemy, and before a volley was returned. One of our men stooped down and could see the legs of the enemy and close at hand. Evidently we were not discovered, but the hint was at once taken, the whole of the regiments delivering the fire kneeling. It was a killing fire which told, and the whole brigade pressed forward. There were only two pieces of artillery on the line and these were in the hands of the enemy and just in our front.[9] In the charge, the 146 N.Y. surrendered in a body, and the two pieces captured by the 1st and the 3rd. N.C. Battle's Brigade came up in our rear to support, and made a bad line of it, but had the courage to mark the two guns captured, "Battle's Brigade," we soon had this corrected. Our men won the day, having struck the head of Grant's column, and this was the first experience our men had had against Grant. The advantage gained by us over the enemy was not great, but it opened the campaign in good style.[10]

Our men knowing their weakness, did what they had never done before, built breastworks in front of their lines. It was surprising to see what tools were used. There were not more than two picks to a regiment, and not more than a spade or so, but they improvised tools by bursting a canteen with

The Wilderness Campaign   139

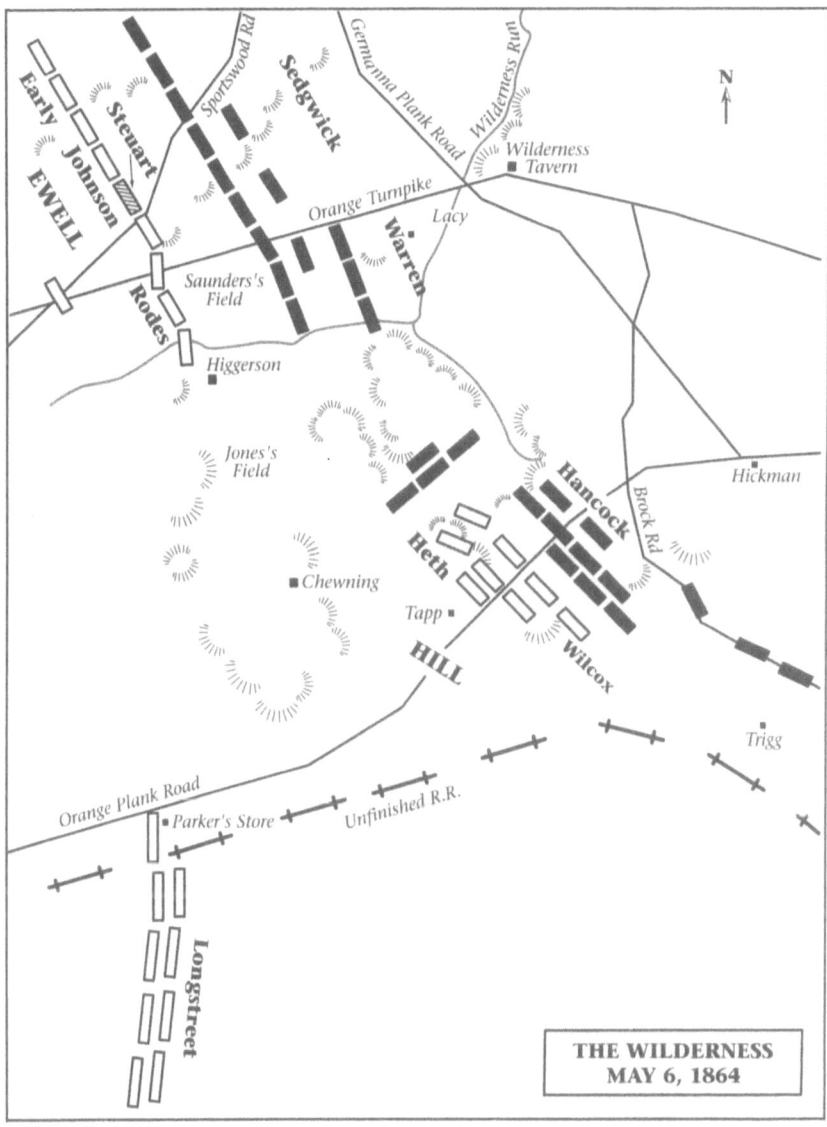

The approximate positions of the Union and Confederate lines in the Wilderness on May 6, 1864, and also showing the location of Steuart's Brigade on the Orange Turnpike.

powder taking each half for a shovel, either with or without an improvised handle. A bayonet served to loosen the dirt, and the shovels followed after. Our men were good wood-cutters and were not slow to fell trees as the basis for the works. The practice they were now getting was to serve them for many weary weeks to come, and it was surprising to see how hastily they threw up trenches in a night and even in a few hours. On this occasion they soon had a good line works and felt satisfied that they could not be driven out. We lost many men in this battle, Adjt. James particularly, losing his right arm early in the engagement.

We had all discussed Grant in camp, and it was well known that he had taken command to hold on and fight until we were worn out. He could lose men and replace them, we could not. Every man lost by us made the line all the weaker, and it was a question of time and endurance which should give up. Our men though were in excellent spirits. If Grant's game was to fight and entrench so would they, and the men as well as the officers caught the spirit of the campaign. Our whole army was extremely weak, and so discouraging was the outlook before the campaign opened knowing the great disparity in numbers, in arms, in food and all that enters into a complete army that General Lee called upon the whole army to observe a whole day of fasting of humiliation and prayer.[11]

We remained on this line but a few days, but in the mean time a heavy battle had been fought by other parts of our army, although Ewell's Corps had made no connection with the line of the other corps.[12] The battles although furious were not decisive. The enemy had merely been kept in check, the fighting quality of Grant's men had been tested and his tactics pretty well learned by both Generals and men.[13] After unsuccessful attempts to break our lines Grant would "sidle" as our men called it,—move by his flank— in the direction of Richmond finding himself at every new turn confronted by the same dirty, hungry, half-clothed but determined men.[14] The fatigue of being in line of battle constantly was severe, and sorely tested the endurance of our men. Especially the sharp shooters composed of picked men, constantly on the alert. They were enterprising and untiring, and did wonderfully good work—and it seemed to be such work as to bring out the best qualities of our men.

> [The Wilderness also made things quite difficult for assistant surgeons like TFW. Getting to the wounded in the thick tangle of undergrowth, often under fire from both sides was no easy task. This was made even more difficult by the fires caused by artillery during the night of the 5th. Many of the wounded, unable to move, burned to death, and the only way to identify to which side they belonged was to turn the body over and check the remains of the uniform closest to the earth. Hospital gangrene was also a serious problem for surgeons after the Battle of the Wilderness, caused by closed-in camps and field hospitals, extreme fatigue, depression, exposure, improper and insufficient food. The distance which wounded had to be transported to the nearest hospitals also contributed to increased cases of gangrene. General

Grant's unrelenting pressure on the Confederate army gave the men no time to recover from the mental and physical exertions of battle and severe cases of battle fatigue resulted giving the field surgeons new problems to deal with. (Cunningham, Doctors in Gray, 115–17, 239)]

Constant firing had set fire to the undergrowth, and the smoke added greatly to the hardships of fighting and marching and loss of sleep and insufficient food. Both armies had a race for Brock Road, Spotsylvania. The marching was very rapid. The Cavalry under Stuart got into position just in time, and bringing up Pott's (N.C. Battery, formerly Latham's), they shot spherical case with very short fuses, the shell exploding at only a few feet from the mouth of the guns. Captain Potts was killed, and several men, and the command fell upon Captain (Dr.) H.G. Flanner. This saved our position, and the infantry came up in good time and formed a line of battle.[15] So close were the two armies that the ground could not be selected, but the men on both sides proceeded to entrench their lines of battle. This was the 8th of May, I think. Sharpshooting continued all the time, but no actual engagement until the 10th.[16]

SPOTSYLVANIA

After the severe march to reach Spottsylvania [Spotsylvania] poor (Lt. Cicero) Craig[e] was greatly overcome by fatigue and I found him overcome by the road side lying down and in an apparently forlorn condition. I advised him to get to the rear and let me treat him, but he doggedly refused, but went to the front as soon as he rested a little. On the 10th of May our Brigade had a fearful fight on the Spottsylvania [Spotsylvania] line, in which Craig[e] was wounded in the fleshy part near the knee. So low was he in health that he was within a few days hopelessly ill and died.[17] Poor fellow. He had often begged me to kill him if he came under my care wounded, and now that he was wounded he fell into the hands of the Corps Surgeon and I merely saw him. Of course I laughed at his whim of desiring to be put to death with drugs for a small wound. He died near the line of battle in a field hospital. We lost several good officers in this battle as well as men. Our Division (Genl. Ed Johnson) filled the "bloody angle" as it is now called, but the "horse shoe", as the men called it then. Our line of breast-works were built just at the line of battle on account of the nearness of the enemy to us, but on this occasion in order to get position for our artillery, the engineer Genl. Martin (Ramrod) Smith included a slight eminence with an angle of works projecting out from our main line. This angle was large enough to hold our Division, about 3,000 men, may be more. It was my duty to get out to the hospital in the rear at night to assist the Surgeon, and return at day-break to the line of battle

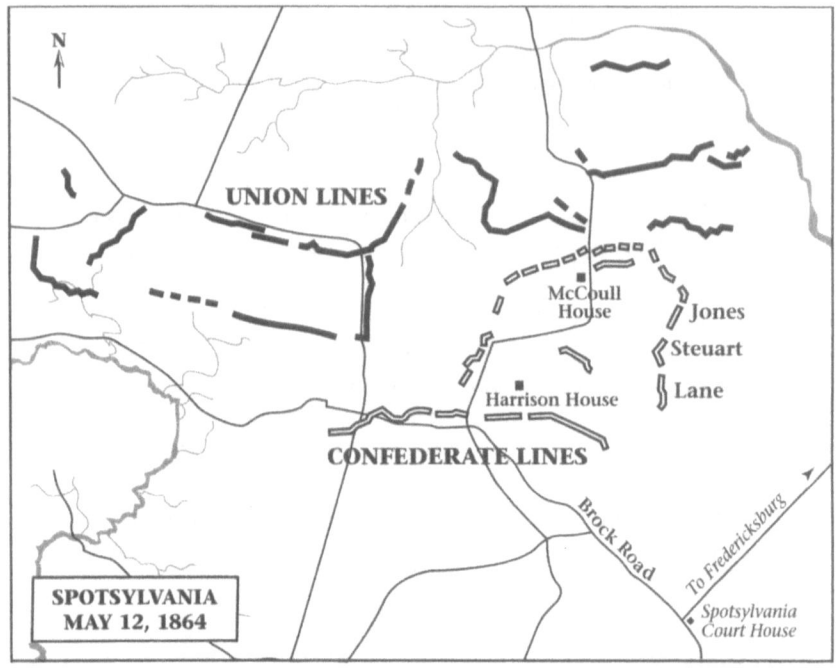

The battlefield at Spotsylvania on May 12, 1864, showing Steuart's position on the right side of the "mule shoe" near where the breakthrough occurred.

again.[18] On the morning of the 12th of May, I was awakened by a tremendous firing and went to the front from the field hospital. When I reached the skirt of woods, which was in good artillery range of our works I saw for the first time a panic among our men. The field was dotted with men coming to the rear, and who were congregating in groups at or near the spot I had reached. Wounded and panic stricken men were coming off the field with fearful descriptions of what had happened. It was so unusual a sight among the men with whom I conversed that I made up my mind that our army was at a great crisis, and that desperate things had to be done.[19]

The weather corresponded with the state of things in our lines. Heavy rains had deluged everything and was still threatening. It was not long before a large group of men had assembled, among them many officers, and the enemy getting our range dropped in a shell or two which created a great panic and scattered most of the men. I learned by this time that our whole Division was captured, including Maj. Genl. Ed Johnson, and Genl. George H. Steuart. At no time did the fortunes of our army seem to be so desperate. General Lee appeared at the point of disaster taking charge of the disorderly crowd of men of many commands, forming them into a line and moving them right to the front. There must have been as many as 1,500 men in this line, and they moved into the charge after they had overcome the first, rather shaky condition, and made a timely and effective onslaught.[20]

The news gradually collected in the excitement and revealed the fact that our Lt. Col. Parsley had been captured, our Maj. Ennett, and nearly all of the 1st and 3rd Regts.[21] Among the wounded were Captain Ned Armstrong, who had his arm shattered, and who by desperate effort escaped to the rear. Poor fellow, his arm was resected and he died of his wound—the first one he had ever received.[22] Capt. John Badger Brown was also wounded and Sergeant Major Bob McRee, son of Dr. James F. McRee, but I believe they were wounded on the 10th of May.[23] Col. H.A. Brown of the 1st Regt. was wounded severely in the chest, and as he fell backward he was caught by Captain Williamson of the 1st. The enemy was advancing and they were both now within his lines. Poor Brown was dismayed at such a desperate wound and a prospect of falling into the enemy's prison, and the tale goes that he said to Captain Williamson: "Williamson, Williamson, ah—ah—ah—read the bu—rial," meaning that he wanted the Burial Service from the Prayer Book. Brown got well, and the enemy's line was driven back, so that he was not taken prisoner.

In all my experience previous to this I had never passed such a day as the 12th. Our army was nearly cut in two, and a whole division captured, and here I was without a regiment, and nothing but a lot of wounded men depressed and gloomy to care for. What was left of our commands, the 1st and 3rd, were ordered to report to Ramseur's N.C. Brigade. For the first time in the history of our regiments we were attached to a N.C. Brigade, and although we were not much now as an organization, and the fragments of the regiment went by the name of the "1st and 3rd," we were better satisfied with the new alliance. General Ramseur had been promoted to be a Maj. Genl. and Col. W.R. Cox was promoted to succeed him as a Brigadier.[24] To add to my gloom I was sent by the Surgeon of the Brigade, G.W. Briggs, to go with a train of wounded men to Hamilton's Station. The journey was an all night one, and the whip-poor-wills were singing their doleful songs in the desolate woods as I trudged all alone on horseback. Late in the evening, it must have been the 19th of May the sound of another heavy engagement was distinctly heard.[25] This time the enemy was repulsed and started off on another sideling movement until they brought up in the neighborhood of Hanover Junction. At Hanover Junction we entrenched as usual, and it was there that I for the first time had occasion to speak to General Lee. He was on horseback and in search of his Chief of Staff Col. W.H. Taylor. All was confusion to me and I could give no information. There was no engagement at Hanover, and as usual we "sidled"—moved by the flank again towards Richmond.

Our Brigade had a sharp engagement at Bethesda Church, in which General Doles was killed. Genl. Doles had once commanded our regiment, that is we were brigaded with him. This was a flank movement in which we sought to attack the enemy's rear. This was our first engagement in Ramseur's, now Cox's Brigade.[26]

At Cold Harbor, near the scene of the first battle in 1862, there was another engagement but we were not needed. The enemy made a blind and reckless attack on our works, which was repulsed with fearful slaughter. The victory was so easy that our men were greatly encouraged. The hardships of daily fighting were somewhat reduced, but the supply of food was so irregular, and the opportunities for cooking so short, and cooking utensils so scarce, that what we had was merely to appease hunger. But we were then veterans of the hardiest type.[27]

The Rev. Mr. Patterson, our Chaplain was with us and fared badly. He required more food than most of us, and fasting was a great hardship. As we got near Richmond he was tempted to beg a bunch of young onions. There was no cooked food and no early promise, so the half starved Chaplain ate with avidity raw onions with salt, to take off the sharp edge of his appetite. Unfortunately the dollar's worth of onions, which were hardly sufficient for him were rejected by an insulted stomach and the poor man had to wait for his camp biscuit and thin slices of fat meat.

We remained in comparative idleness until the 13th June 1864. The blow Grant had received at Cold Harbor dispirited his troops as much as it had encouraged ours. But living in trenches, sleeping on our arms almost literally, was a dreary monotonous business. Our old adversaries Pope, Hooker, and others when they got a good beating, cleared out for a while, giving our army a chance to go into regular camp, and enjoy leisure, and clean clothes and some better food. Not so with Grant. After he was repulsed he lingered around and hugged close to our lines, threatening to go at it again at most any day. Great was our surprise then when we were withdrawn from the trenches, and found that we were part of a new army corps composed of Rodes', Ramseur's and Peagram's Divisions, under General Jubal A. Early.

[General Grant had finally realized that it would be a far more difficult task to defeat Lee's army than he had previously thought. He resorted to tactical offensives and diversionary tactics for the next few weeks after Cold Harbor. Lee learned on June 6 that a force led by General David Hunter had occupied the Shenandoah Valley town of Staunton, the western terminus of the Virginia Central Railroad. Sheridan's forces had also been sent west to join Hunter. To deal with Hunter, Lee sent two of Breckinridge's brigades to the Valley. Lee soon realized that Grant's purpose was to destroy the Shenandoah Valley as a producing center for the Confederate Army and also to break Lee's communications with the Valley by taking out the Virginia Central. Lee had to move to protect the Valley and at the same time prepare himself

for Grant's next move which was to isolate Richmond from the South by capturing Petersburg. (Dowdey, Lee's Last Campaign, 301–17)]

Rodes Division Hospital
Old Battle Field of Cold Harbor
June 10th 1864

Dear Lydia,

I received your letter of the 5th, mailed the 7th in Wilmington, with a great deal of pleasure. It had a comfortable ring of home about it that almost made me feel that I was very near about the *"frog pond."* The thoughts of home for the past week or so have not been few. I am writing you now upon the farm where McLellan [McClellan], the little Yankee Napoleon, had his headquarters when the Battle of Cold Harbor was fought, and in the rear of the field the Yankees camped. The House is now occupied by Gen. Lee as Hd. Qu.[28]

Our hospital camp is in an apple orchard. Let me give you a description of a Hospital Camp, taking our old Brigade as a model. Each Brigade has a hospital wagon and each Div. one for transporting stoves, cooking utensils, tents, etc. Each tent is marked the same as that of the Brigade, and laid out in regular order. One large tent fly is located centrally as a tent for operations. This constitutes a Hospital Camp. The wounded are placed in these tents, and are operated on in such order that suit the case of the patient. When we have no wounded, we of course have shelter for ourselves. But as long as it doesn't rain, I like to sleep out of doors.[29]

There have been some changes lately in our lines. The Yankees seem to be determined to make a desperate effort in the neighborhood, as they take it to be the key to Richmond. Such an attempt would be exactly what we want. We are map[p]ed very strongly at this point, which affords us time to rest and recruit. Men are constantly coming in from the camps of instruction and hospitals swelling our ranks no little. As for my regt. through next week we number but about 30 for duty. Col. Thruston has resumed command and has in addition to his own, the 1st N.C. which number about 40—making a command of 70 men.[30] I have no regular duties to perform now, being sometimes on the field, sometimes in Hospital. During the last week or so we have had two men very badly wounded in our small company. I have never seen more frightful lacerations than these men had.

No one can now complain of Confederate rations. We get a

plenty of everything. Bacon of all sorts, coffee, sugar, molasses, vegetables, and alternately wheat and meal, and sometimes a ration of baker's bread. So you see we are doing very well. In fact, there has been no time since the war began that the men have been better fed than now. There is no one that can grumble about the fare; if grumbling would do any good we might say something about this continual fight. For several days there has been but little fighting. One day the flag of truce was out for the purpose of burying the dead. It was said to be a strange sight (it occured in front of Hoke's Division) when the signal gun announced the commencement of the truce. Previously nothing but sharpshooters had been showing themselves, as everyone who exposed himself was shot at by a hundred muskets. But as soon as the signal was given, three solid lines of blue-dressed Yankees rose as if by magic, and *four* lines of well-dressed Confederates (it was once the fact that the Yankees were better dressed than our men, but it is no longer so). The two contending parties were soon mixing up with each other as though they had not been a few minutes before engaged in deadly strife. The number of Yankees slain were great— I have forgotten the figures.[31]

The enemy is now busily engaged in digging parallels or zigzags, in order to dig us out, as the fire fighting only weakens them to no purpose. The insane idea of accomplishing anything this way would occur to anyone but Grant. In his stubborness consists his greatness. The prospect that this is the last campaign of the war makes our men bear their excessive fatigues with a great deal of fortitude. Our Corps (now Early's) is at present resting, and in reserve. Petersburg is no longer in danger—that is, imminent danger.

Tom Lewis[32] is most certainly a prisoner. I heard yesterday that (Big) Tom Wright was killed in the late Battle of Cold Harbor. Dr. Cromwell has just returned from the Hospital, and reports that my friend Capt. Armstrong was dying when he left, and that Craig[e] was removed to a private house and was getting along well; although he has been desperately sick, he was in fair way to recovery.[33] Dr. C., my Surgeon, is to be assigned to Hospital duty, and I will be in charge, as I am most always.[34]

[The letter ends here, without a signature, indicating that the balance of the letter was probably lost.]

ELEVEN

Early's March on Washington City

On June 12, 1864, the Army of the Potomac began to move out of their lines at Cold Harbor, Virginia, and turn south for the James River and Petersburg. The assault on the Confederate lines at Cold Harbor had been devastating for General Grant, and it would be a mistake he would remember for the rest of his life. In the Wilderness campaign, the Union had lost fifty-four thousand men, and the names the Wilderness, Spotsylvania and Cold Harbor would be etched in blood on the minds of most Americans, North and South. However, "Butcher" Grant, as he was now called, was more determined than ever to press forward towards a victory over Robert E. Lee and his steadily weakening Army of Northern Virginia. Lee's losses in the Wilderness Campaign, though less than Grant's, had far more serious consequences due to dwindling resources in manpower and supplies.

Although a number of army units made stirring declarations of optimism, serious problems faced the Army of Northern Virginia in early 1864. Desertions were increasing at an alarming rate, and many of those were going over to the enemy. One of the primary reasons for the increasing desertions was that of reduced rations. Because of critical difficulties in obtaining provisions for the army, the normal daily rations in early 1864 amounted to three-quarters of a pound of meat—usually salt pork or bacon—and a quarter pound of salt. Even with this

Thomas Fanning Wood, M.D., c. 1864. Probably taken in Richmond just prior to Early's Washington Campaign. Thomas Fanning Wood Collection, Wilmington, N.C.

reduced ration, soldiers often received quarter rations or less. The combat effectiveness of Lee's army was in serious decline and getting worse every day.[1]

General Lee needed a bold plan to ease the Federal pressure on his army, and he had already sent General Jubal "Old Jube" Early and his Second Corps, with approximately eight thousand men, to Lynchburg to help Major General John C. Breckinridge ward off a push by Union General David Hunter, and it would be a bold stroke to send them on northward to threaten Maryland and Washington. A threat to the nation's capital might just cause Grant and Meade to pull back from their determined pursuit of Lee's army and the threat to Richmond. If General Early's small corps could somehow embarrass the Lincoln government by casting doubts about the ability of the North to break the obvious stalemate and bring a final conclusion to this war, there might just be some hope for the survival of the Confederacy. The first mission, to stop Hunter and his push to control the Shenandoah Valley, was absolutely necessary. The second mission, a strike at the Federal capital, was a definite gamble but worth the risk.[2]

TFW and the remnants of the 1st and 3rd North Carolina Infantry Regiments, numbering approximately seventy men, were to play a part in this adventure as members of Brigadier General William R. Cox's brigade and Major General Dodson Ramseur's division. This was a time for glory and pride for Old Jube's Confederates, but it would also prove to be a time of tragedy and sadness. It would be the last grand strategic campaign for the Army of Northern Virginia.

Even though few medical reports exist that cover this campaign, it is certain that the field surgeon had a rough time of it. The blockade of Wilmington was continuously tightening which created critical shortages of medicines and supplies to the front. The lack of proper instruments and drugs necessitated that doctors improvise in the treatment of wounded and sick. Dr. Wood often resorted to the use of natural herbs and plants to help ease pain and suffering. The shortage of quinine caused more concern than that of any other single medicine. Fatigue, poor nutrition, and exposure were still encouraging the spread of diseases like malaria, small pox, and typhoid fever and in the latter stages of the campaign, General Sheridan's systematic destruction of the Shenandoah Valley caused severe shortages of critical fruits and vegetables further weakening the stamina of the Confederate soldier. Dysentery and diarrhea remained in the lead over bullets as a contributor to the mounting casualty lists. Thousands of men in Early's army were without shoes, causing increased straggling and more work for the surgeons. This campaign stretched the army surgeon's ability to the limits and only

General Jubal Anderson Early, who led Lee's Second Corps against Federal General Hunter in the Shenandoah and moved on to threaten Washington in July of 1864. Massachusetts Commandery Military Order of the Loyal Legion and the U.S. Army Military History Institute.

those with imagination and initiative were the least bit effective in easing suffering and keeping the men in fighting condition.

———•———

We left the Richmond area on the 13th June, and started on a march toward Louisa C.H.[3] None of the subordinate commanders knew what it meant, and where we were going, but we were quite confident that General Lee, whose good judgement we trusted implicitly, would not weaken his army without being well assured that he had the advantage over his opponent. The fresh air, the green foliage and pure water of the country was greatly enjoyed after an imprisonment in the trenches since May. On the second day out we passed the battle field of the great cavalry battle between Stuart and the Union cavalry. It was known as the Battle of Catlett's Station, I believe.[4] There were signs of a terrible musketry engagement which defeated Grant's design of uniting his cavalry with (Federal) Genl. Hunter's army then approaching Lynchburg.[5] Of course we knew nothing of this at the time. We reached Charlottesville on the 16th of June. The hospitality of the citizens was unbounded. We halted only a short time in the streets, and our men were surprised with food and tobacco and were shown many kind attentions which were heartily appreciated.

There was intense excitement there, and it was here that we learned that General Hunter was at Lynchburg, threatening the University,[6] and our presence was hailed as their liberators. We took the train at a station beyond Charlottesville to Lynchburg. Our horses being driven over by the turnpike. Our haste was desperate, and we arrived just in the nick of time, for in desperation the local militia [was] composed of the old men and lads, and hospital clerks, nurses and convalescents. On our arrival on 17th June in Lynchburg we went at once into line of battle on the edge of town. Our Brigade was in line at a graveyard, expecting early in the morning to make an attack. In our reduced condition, the 1st and 3rd Regts. were consolidated and I was the only medical officer. Just before day a gunshot sounded near me, and I thought this was to be the opening of the battle, but it turned out to be that a cowardly fellow who shot his finger nearly off, in order to escape the fight. I examined his hand and found it powder-burnt and Col. Thruston directed him to be marched next day under guard. It was very early in the morning when we discovered that the army of Hunter had disappeared, and our army was started out in hot pursuit, on the morning of 18th June.[7]

The morning of June 18th 1864 was hot and dusty when we started in pursuit of Hunter, on the road towards Liberty. In the whole Brigade there was but one horse. This the General rode, then it was ridden "ride and tie" by the commanders of the regiments. The men seemed to enjoy very much the prospect of the doctor's walking, and all along I could hear undertone remarks about it, "Doctor's on foot today boys," and so on. The gait we struck on this march was very rapid, and the dust was almost suffocating, but on I trudged doing as well as any of them. As noon approached the heat became intense and the veterans kept dropping out of ranks over heated and exhausted. I stopped and administered to every one of them, writing permits as required by the regulations, that they would not be arrested as stragglers. This all took time, as each permit had to be written, and water and medicines had to be procured for each, and then trot on to catch up with the line. In the course of the day about 30 men were overcome, and were cared for by me, and when we reached Liberty we had made 27 miles. I think the men were satisfied that I could do a day's hard marching as well as they, and after that I had no more wry faces when I was called upon to pronounce upon the ability of a man for a day's march. It was a part of the duty of medical officers to examine the men and decide what their ability for duty was. The men did not know that I was used to marching, and were surprised that I should be able to keep up. Fortunately our horses came up that night and the next day I was able to enjoy a ride, for my ham-strings were very sore, and I doubt if I could have done as well the next day. But I had already established a reputation for marching.

Hunter's army had destroyed property very wantonly in their hasty retreat, and it seemed to us old soldiers as a most cowardly fight.[8] On the 19th we set out again for Salem, still in pursuit. The Peaks of Otter were in full view from Liberty, and the whole country was beautiful and fertile. But abundant harvests had been destroyed by Hunter, and the pillage of private property was shameful.[9] From Salem we went westward and so continued until the 21st, when we had the mortification of seeing the enemy escaping through Hanging Rock Gap to the Kanawha Valley. I say we saw it, it was only General Ransom's Cavalry that saw the enemy and had a little collision, but captured only a few cassions and wagons.

We rested one day at Salem, and recovered all the men who had been disabled by the heat, and on the 23rd started on the march towards Lexington, and on the same day I got permission to visit or rather go by the natural Bridge. I had so often seen the Natural Bridge in picture books that it was not quite so much of a wonder. It is the shape of an irregular arch, spanning a stream which is at the bottom of a deep cut. I went below the bridge to the stream and collected all the traditions of the locality. One that George Washington threw a stone over the bridge whereupon everybody in the party tried, and fell short more than one half the distance. The stream is walled in by precipitous walls rising almost perpendicularly above it, with slightly jutted edges. The story was that George Washington had climbed this ledge to the top. None of us tried this experiment, but we learned that Henry MacRae, brother of Mr. Don MacRae climbed to a very dangerous point, and finding that he could not get to the top had to be rescued by a rope let down from above. I collected some coarse ferns and lichens from the rocks, and sent them home. This was the beginning of my collection of plants, which I continued afterwards. When I got several specimens I sent them by letter to the Rev. Dr. M.A. Curtis, at Hillsborough for identification, as I knew nothing about systemic botany, and I had no book with me. Dr. C. was very kind and prompt in his replies, and encouraged me to continue.[10]

When we left Salem on our march toward Lexington, our baggage was reduced to just what we could carry on the backs of our horses. This consisted of a fly tent (captured from the enemy) which was in two parts with button holes on one edge and buttons on the other. When we got into camp we cut two forked branches (Y) and a ridge pole. Over this were buttoned the flies, which were stretched and kept in place by pegs and a small trench "scratched" rather than dug, for we had no tools, to lead the water off, in case of rain. Two of us could crawl in, but it was a tight squeeze. The protection was all we needed in good weather. The order of our march was, reveille at 3:45a.m. and the whole column was in motion by 4. We marched until 12 o'clock then went into bivouac for rest and cooking food, and in the cool of the afternoon made a few more miles, and then went into camp for the night. With this order of march we continued for 30 days, during which time we made an average of 20 and a half miles a day, including about three days of rest or partial rest.

We had only one wagon for cooking utensils, one for medicine stores, and one for Brigade Headquarters, and two ambulances, so we were not much encumbered with "implements". In this light marching trim, on the most beautiful roads in the country, we made good time. The road beds were of stone, and they were repaired by breaking lime stone rocks. These were pulverized by the passage of wagons and horses over them, and in dry weather the dust was very bad. We had no rain during all this march for nearly a month, and the dust settled on hair and beard, making us all look like venerable gray heads. Opportunities for bathing of the most superficial sort were very limited and very few of the officers had any other clothing than that we had on. A pair of socks had to be taken off, and washed while the owner went barefooted until they were dried, and they were put on wet or dry according to the time we got to do the laundering. Such a thing was luxury with most men, and many of them went a month without washing. Our meals were cooked at noon rest, which consisted of biscuit made of flour and which tallow[11] was substituted for lard. It was easy enough for a hungry man to get down a warm biscuit, but when they were cold they were not very inviting. The beef had to be boiled and stored away in our haversacks, when it got cold it was far from inviting. In order to make it more palatable the bread was cut up into small bits with the beef, and stewed together in a pan. The addition of an onion would have been a great luxury, but none

Jubal Early's route through the Shenandoah Valley in 1864, leading to the brief engagement before Washington and the retreat back across the Shenandoah River.

were to be had. Our mess had a bag of rye which was parched and a drink was made which we imagined to imitate coffee, but this was because genuine coffee had been so long a stranger to us that we could not even imagine. Sugar was a very rare luxury, and the rye tea drunk hot without sugar, helped lubricate the way for tallow biscuits. But our health was excellent, and the army of veterans was in fine spirits.[12]

On the 25th June we reached Lexington. This town was the seat of the Virginia Military Institute from which many excellent men graduated who were conspicuous in our army. It was also the seat of the Washington University. General T.J. Jackson (Stonewall) had been a professor at the Military Institute and after his death his remains were interred in the cemetary in that town. It was arranged that the Corps should pay respect to the memory of Jackson, by filing past the grave with reversed arms, officers uncovered. Unfortunately, I did not spy the grave until I was nearly out of the enclosure but the whole division to a man were mourners at the grave. Stonewall Jackson was as truly admired and venerated as any man could be by soldiers, and many a vain regret at his death escaped from the lips of the men.

The enemy had destroyed the Virginia Military Institute, General Letcher's house, and a large flour mill. At the Washington College they overturned a statue of Washington, and all of the pillaging and destruction was of a most wanton sort.¹³ The ladies were profuse in their gifts to the soldiers and doubtless inspired confidence in many a tired soldier.

From Lexington we went to Staunton and from Staunton we went to Winchester but saw no enemy. The weather was very hot and the roads were dusty almost to stifling. The good people along the route gave to us of their scanty stores, and added greatly to our former monotonous diet of dried beef and tallow biscuit. One of the men said to General Early that the tallow stuck to the roof of his mouth, so that he expected to have to build a fire on the top of his head to melt it out. This was but a specimen of the course which was abundant among our soldiers, and this is a refined specimen.

We saw no enemy when we got to Bolivar a little village near Bolivar Heights on the Potomac near Harper's Ferry.¹⁴ Some of the Union officers had prepared a Fourth of July dinner, and were enjoying it with some of the ladies of the neighborhood—for in this section there were some people who sympathized with the Federals. It was great fun for our sharpshooters who swooped down upon the gay party, taking some prisoners, and capturing the good things prepared for the feast. Ice-cream, Lemonade, Cake, etc.—such things as many had not tasted for years. This skirmish led to a skirmish in the town of Harpers Ferry. General Max Weber was in command there, and having "bottled him up", General Early crossed the river and marched on to Washington City.¹⁵ We crossed the river at Shepardstown, the same ford which we crossed on our way to Gettysburg.¹⁶ We stayed a day near the battle field of Sharpsburg. There were hardly any signs that a battle had been fought there, although the old Dunker Church was still standing, and the old soldiers could point out where our line was, for it was a very memorable battle in which 21 out of 24 of the "line of file closers"—including all but three officers in the regt. were killed or wounded.

The following are some letters written by me under the signature "U.U.D." They appeared in the *Wilmington Journal* and were read very largely. The description is far from elegant, but the letters will show how much feeling there was on both sides. For the time, they were considered temperate letters.

[The following "letters" are actual newspaper clippings attached to the pages in volume three of TFW's memoirs. Of note is the optimistic tone in these articles, at least at the beginning of the campaign, intended to boost morale at home and cover the rapid deterioration of the Army of Northern Virginia. An explanation of the unusual signature that TFW chose to use to close each letter has not been discovered but could have represented "double-U D" or "WD" for Wood, probably to protect the letter writer from identification. At that time the Confederate Army was critically outnumbered by the enemy on all fronts and the government had issued a warning for soldiers not to discuss sensitive military matters in letters home. The use of initials or pseudonyms was not uncommon during this

period, and names like "Truth," "Ivy Green," "Dodger," and even "Tar Bucket" served as final signatures on many letters to Southern newspapers.]

LEESBURG VA., JULY 14TH 1864
[Publication date in the journal: July 28, 1864]
OUR VISIT TO THE YANKEE CAPITAL WITH INCIDENTS BY THE WAYSIDE

That North Carolina was represented in the late invasion of the enemy's country you already know, but we have to speak more particularly of the representation from Wilmington, whose welfare you have envinced a desire to see promoted, and whose interest we believe is your interest.

The bloody Battle of the Wilderness had decimated our ranks but little, and we had hoped that the fates were turning in our favor, and that the end of the campaign would soon be at hand with but few of our comrades rendered hors du combat.[17] The service that our Regiment did on the 5th and 10th days of May particularly, have passed into history to their credit as well as that of the good old Cape Fear.[18] We want to pass by the history of this part of the campaign, for the capture of 225 of our Regiment on the 12th carries with it many sad recollections—the desperate struggle when the order "Let's fight it out", was given by one, now the victim of retaliation, the overwhelming force of the enemy, and the consequent capture, all the work of a moment, adds new glories and new sorrows to our bloody annals.

We left Richmond on the 13th June, having been idle for several days near the trenches and started towards Louisa C.H., our destination of course unknown to us, but speculations were abundant. In our little squad composed of the 1st and 3rd Regiments, the vacancies were painful. We had never commenced a campaign before with so few. The larger portion lingering in Yankee prisons, two of them under the ceaseless boom of the guns of Charleston; two of them, Capt. E.H.A. and Sergt. Maj. R.F. McR., sleeping the last sleep of death.[19] We exchanged gladly the free air of the country for the foul air of the trenches, and in spite of the casualties to our Regiments, we left Richmond with lighter hearts since the battle of the 12th.

We passed on the second day of our march the battle field upon which our cavalry had fought against a raiding party, sent out from the right wing of the Yankee army to destroy the Virginia Central R.R. and make a junction with Hunter's Cavalry at Charlottesville. They were whipped badly after a severe fight and driven back to their base. We had abundant evidence of the severity of this fight, which drew from the infantry praise, not reluctantly bestowed.[20]

Leaving Louisa C.H. we took the direct road for Charlottesville, and arrived there on the morning of the 16th, a day long to be remembered by us as a bright spot in our soldier life. The morning's march had been a very hot one—we were dashing off at the rate of 25 miles a day—the day we arrived at Charlottesville.

We rested ten minutes in the street to receive the most lavish testimonials of the appreciation of our service to their country by these good people. Refreshments were distributed, tobacco given away at the rate of two or three boxes to a small regiment, and a variety of articles of especial value to soldiers were distributed profusely; kind words, approving smiles, and God speed were given to lighten the burden and heat of the day, and make us feel that although soldiers were no rarity in their town, yet they had not forgotten that though rough and dirty, we were their defenders and fellow citizens. In behalf of the 1st and 3rd North Carolina, we return thanks for the pleasure the good people of Charlottesville caused us and only hope that we have been able in this campaign to render them some material return for their benefactions. We had the pleasure of visiting the University, that noble work which does honor to Jefferson, who conceived, and the state of Virginia which executed the plan of the best school of the country. The halls of the University were vacated, but everything is kept in good repair. Several of the professors still live in the College, and are doing duty in the hospital. We rejoiced to feel that such a noble institution had been saved from the fiendish hands of the vandals.[21]

Our command took the train for Lynchburg on the 17th, and arriving the same evening formed a line of battle near the town. The day was too far spent to attack the enemy, and the next day before light we were making preparations for battle; but the keen Hunter took the precaution to evacuate his position and was in full retreat before we discovered through the smoke of the morning that he had left. And now commenced a chase that caused us the most rapid marching of the war. The first day from Lynchburg, Gordon in front, Rhodes next, and so on, we halted near Liberty, 27 miles from our starting point only to get a little fight out of their rear [Hunter's army] in which General Robert Ransom only was engaged.

From our bivouc near Liberty we could see plainly the Peaks of Otter, the height of the Blue Ridge in Virginia. The mountain scenery of this part of the ridge is by far the most picturesque of the state. The whole country along the line of our march after leaving Liberty, is extremely fertile and groans under the burden of the largest crops ever made in the country. But the despoiling hand of the vandal had cursed the country with desolation. The track of Hunter's retreat was the scene of shameful pillaging and this under his sanction—a Major General in the Union army. The tale of the heedless depredations should not fall heedless on the ears of the country, the attestations of the whole corps of men confirms it. Cattle, chickens, hogs, sheep, and every other thing upon which they could vent their malace were killed and when not eaten left to rot upon the ground. Carriages were destroyed, wagons burned, women insulted, and acts of vandalism (Yankeeism should be the term) which we blush to record. A more hellish set of fiends were never before turned loose in the loveliest valley of Virginia.[22]

Day after day we continued the march in hot pursuit, each evening bringing with it a new hope, that the next day, we would be able to overtake the enemy and administer to him a punishment adequate to his crime. On the evening of the 21st, after a hard day's march, we were mortified to see the demoralized and scattered remnant of Hunter's force clambering up over the mountain going through Hanging Rock Gap in the Allegheny. General Ransom's cavalry succeeded here in taking several wagons and pieces of artillery, burning many pieces and capturing a few prisoners. We made a day's rest at Salem, and on the 23rd we took up the line of march toward Lexington.

Of course no one will imagine that General Lee sent General Early out on a sight seeing expedition, when our "Rebel Capital is beseiged"; but no one will doubt particularly any member of the "TELEGRAPH CORPS" that we did see sights. On the 23rd Breckinridge and Gordon marched by the Natural Bridge, and Rhodes and Ramseur within three miles of it. Permission was given by the General for all mounted officers to visit the great work of nature. No one needs a description of the Natural Bridge; but however grand one has imagined the scenery, he will find the reality to exceed it. It was well worth the weary pilgrimage of ten days march to see the greatest natural wonder in the state. We saw the imaginary eagle in the summit of the archway; the imaginary English Coat of Arms; all formed by lichen which clings to the rocks. We had pointed out to us the letters G. Washington carved in the stone, which were once quite plain, but time has nearly effaced the last vestige of them. A townsman of ours is said to have been critically suspended in attempting to put his name on the ledge above that of the great Washington.

We reached Lexington on the 25th day of June at noon. Every preparation had been made for us to pay a tribute of respect to the grave of our lamented hero—Stonewall Jackson—by his old corps. The whole corps filed by the grave at double ranks, arms reversed and officers dismounted. Everyone uncovered his head at the grave, while sadness was depicted upon the countenances of all, the bands playing some sweet solemn dirges. The grave was profusely ornamented with sweet flowers, while a large national flag, a present from England, floated mournfully over it. The scene was simple but impressive, and caused all fresh regrets that the greatest genius of the war was resting in the grave before his country's liberty was achieved. May God give us more of the genius of Stonewall Jackson.

The ladies of Lexington not only cheered us by their presence on the sidewalk and at the windows, but by distributing to the poor thirsty soldiers something to eat and drink. In the very town of Lexington, the blackened ruins of Governor Letcher's home stood a memorial of the fiendish enemy, and then too, just above the Governor's house, the Lexington Military Institute[23] lay in ruins. A large flour mill on the canal, was also a victim of the torch of the enemy, "because forsooth", it fed the rebels—not the army, but

Confederate citizens. Our army crossed the James at Lexington, fully determined that they would make the enemy suffer retaliation when it should be our fortune to invade. Upon the pedistal of a monument in Lexington the following was inscribed in lead pencil: "We swear we will destroy one College and one Gubernatorial Mansion in the enemy's country, in retaliation for the outrages perpetrated in Lexington." 1st Md. Cavalry.

Nothing of interest transpired in our long march from Lexington to Staunton, and from Staunton to Winchester, except that we were cheered by the unequaled hospitality of the good people of the valley, and luxurated in the good things which we know but few of our people at home can enjoy. We have never seen before such continuous hot weather; and superadded to the excessive heat was the dust. For thirty days we have been upon the tramp from Virginia to Maryland and back and only once have we had a shower. The fatigues in consequence of this protracted drought were very unusual, and yet this corps accomplished in eighteen successive days an average of twenty-three miles a day. And even to the time we formed line of battle under the walls of the Yankee Capital, including our stoppages from every cause, and comprising a space of time of nearly one month, we averaged twenty one and a half miles a day.

On the 4th of July we astonished Max Weber[24] by attacking him in his impregnable fastness upon Arlington and Maryland Heights, around Harper's Ferry from the Virginia side. Here we accomplished an important purpose, although we did not succeed in capturing the place. However no one will ever imagine that we could have captured such a place, after seeing the position—Jackson taught the Yankees that Maryland Heights was the key to Harper's Ferry,[25] and since its first capture they had made the position quite formidable. To accomplish the ultimate design of our campaign it was not necessary that we capture this place, but draw upon Washington for troops, and thereby keep all the Yankees out of our way, by strengthening Harper's Ferry in our rear, and weakening Washington City in our front.

No regular line of battle was engaged in the attack, but our sharpshooters drove the enemy from Bolivar, and part of the town of Harper's Ferry, capturing thereby quite a quantity of commissary stores, even a plenty of luxuries. How strange to see "Confeds" with cigars, sugar, coffee, lemons, whiskey and every thing which the most fastidious soldier could desire. But while we record the deed of daring, which adds page after page of glory to our country's history, we must relate with a degree of shame, which I can't conceal the outrageous conduct of some of our men. We did not blame our sharpshooters for partaking of the 4th of July dinner which the Yankee officers had prepared in Bolivar in honor of their national jubilee, for we know the weakness that Confederates have for a nice dinner when ornamented and illuminated with good wines and fruits, but some stragglers even under the fire of the enemy's guns, plundered private property to a shameful extent. There was legitimate plunder enough in town for all, but stragglers are fastidious brutes, and they could not satiate their greed until they had destroyed a large quantity of illegitimate plunder. You may rest assured that the General took prompt measures to prevent a repetition of the outrage, and that not our army, but our stragglers are charged with this violation of the rules of war.

We crossed the Potomac at Shepardstown on the 5th day of July, leaving Max Weber to shell the empty woods from his secure eminence unable to communicate with Washington City. To say that the whole of the Yankee nation was surprised to see an army entering their territory, which they supposed was fully employed by Grant, would but feebly express the indignation depicted upon the faces of the citizens of Yankee-land as our column marched into their country.

We passed by the ever memorable and sanguinary battlefield of Sharpsburg. We saw the old church riddled with rifle shots, the memorable Antietam Creek, and all of those spots which brought back to those of us who were in the first Maryland campaign, the unwelcome recollections of a hard fought battle, which did more to cripple us than any blow the enemy ever dealt us. We saw the fence of which Lt. C. [Craige] said that the rails of it were kept constantly in the air by the artillery of each side. The opening upon the mountain occupied by McClellan's Signal Corps and more memorable to the 3rd Regiment than any other spot on that field, the place where it fought,—not only fought but maintained its position in the most sanguinary battle of the war against fearful odds, when other regiments had fled from the same field, inflicting upon the enemy a severe castigation, and making a very decided influence upon the issue of the day's battle. It was there our gallant Colonel [William Lord deRosset] was disabled for the war, and the lamented Williams, Meares, Cowan, Quince, Rhodes, McNair, Speight and a host of other gallant men fell, some of whom had never before been under fire.

From Sharpsburg we moved upon Fredrick City by the way of Crampton's Gap, passing through Merry Valley, one of the most lovely spots in Maryland. Every spot of ground throughout the whole valley was under cultivation, groaning with the burden of abundant crops, enjoying undisturbed repose; no work of vandalism to be seen. It was the battle of this Gap, that Col. Lamar of Cobb's Legion fell. At the village of Burketsville [Burkittsville] rests not only the remains of Col. Lamar but a number of our gallant braves.[26]

Our division was rear guard of the corps in Maryland, and the brigades and detachments of brigades, were sent in different directions to watch the various gaps which open into this fertile little valley. On the 9th of July we formed a line of battle near Frederick City at Monocacy Junction. A battle ensued there between our forces and the 6th Army Corps (U.S.) under General Wallace. At sundown Wallace was in full retreat, and we captors of about a hundred prisoners, the enemy leaving about two hundred wounded and a large number of dead upon the field. Our loss was three hundred in our entire corps. Ramseur and Gordon only being partially engaged.[27]

We saw for the first time in this campaign the real sentiment of the people of Maryland. The sad truth is they are sorely oppressed, and with the system of espionage employed by the United States to keep them in subjection we have but little to hope, except by successful occupation of the state. They are with us. We believe today the real original elements of the state are with us, and that their heart's desire is to unite their destiny with ours. Their kindness to us and their prayers for our success, tell us what they feel. Remember, you who stand afar off and call Maryland a Yankee State, that you do her injustice. An anthem would have been sung in every church in Maryland had we been successful in capturing the Yankee Capitol. Had you seen the kind attention of the lovely Maryland ladies, their well wishes and hopes that we would relieve their state from thraldrom, you would have been impressed as this corps was, with the greatest respect and warmest sympathy for this poor, noble state. But alas, she is lost to us and lost to herself. Without we can rescue her by an army, she is destined to be a mere dependency of the United States.[28]

Recruits come in from all parts of the state; whole cavalry brigades were mounted, and the oppressors of the good people of the state—we mean the Lincolnites—were punished, by being forced to donate their horses and provisions for the good of our service. On the 12th day of July we were in line of battle under the forts of Washington City, some distance nearer the Yankee Capitol than Grant had been to ours since his so-called seige of Richmond. The suburban Washingtonians (Secessionists) were quite confident that we would meet but little resistance in the attack; but not one of the most sanguine of us thought we could take this walled city. It was not the design to make an attempt on Washington, to decimate our ranks by an attack upon a place which a handful of men could hold against great odds, and with a shattered army have the Potamac at our backs. The sequel will show why we threatened Washington.

What a record to show the world. Our own capital "beseiged"! "The backbone of the rebellion crushed," and a corps to spare to go into the enemy's country to knock at the gates of his own Capital. Where was Mr. Lincoln, all this time, the men would ask? Some would reply that "he was brushing up his scotch cap for another Hegira." But somebody was at home for at our first approach Mr. Lincoln's Butler (perhaps the Beast)[29] commenced issuing "lampposts", cans of preserves (perhaps grapes)[30] to us, in honor of our arrival. We formed line of battle on the N.W. side of the city and advanced sharpshooters. The enemy opened his heavy guns from the forts, causing but few casualties to us. In fact we have never seen artillery used with such poor effect. With their position the enemy had no excuse for not inflicting severe injury upon us. We employed them busily all the 12th and 13th with our sharpshooters.

The troops we first engaged were evidently citizens, as they were not in uniform; but the soldiers came in afterwards, re-inforcements from Wallace and elsewhere.

While we were engaging the attention of the enemy, at Washington, Col. Bradley Johnston [Johnson], commanding Imboden's Brigade was paying his attentions to Baltimore. He cut the bridges over Powder Mill and Bush Creeks, and destroyed some railroads between Baltimore and Philadelphia, and between Baltimore and Washington. By order of Gen. Johnston [Johnson], Governor Bradford's house[31] was burned in retaliation for the burning of Governor Letcher's house in Lexington and that too, within three or four miles of Baltimore. He also captured about three hundred mules which a dealer was carrying into Washington for the army. So you can readily imagine that General Early's visit to the Yankee country produced no little terror.

To sum up the whole campaign, Early whipped two armies out of the way, one at Lynchburg and one at Fredrick City, passed on to their capitol, made important captures of cattle, horses and mules; subsisted our army upon the enemy eight days, levied upon Fredrick $200,000 in green-backs; and after drawing army re-inforcements from the front of General Lee and harrassed the denizens of Yankee Sodom, recrossed the Potomac leisurely with about four hundred prisoners, with a loss to ourselves of less than 300 men.

Beyond a doubt this has been the most important invasion into the enemy's country, the most advantageous to us, and the most disastrous to the North. Numerically we are stronger than when we entered; many having rallied to the Southern cross. This invasion proves General Early's capacity for commanding an army, and gives him rank among our best corps commanders. If the old gentleman did march us very hard, and if we did say very emphatic things about him when the hot sun was overcoming us, we ask the old gentleman's pardon, for he is the only man who has ever given us a peep at the dome of the Yankee Capitol.

We don't wish to make the last paragraph tell of the disorderly acts of our army, but we must certainly have men in our army whom it would seem are apt scholars of the Yankee depredators. We mention these acts to let the world know that the sacking of houses near our line of battle, the burning of Montgomery Blair's house, were unauthorized acts of exasperated villains, and for which the government is not responsible. Prompt means have been taken, to detect the depredators. We will leave the people of Maryland to say how far we respect their property and rights.

Too much praise cannot be awarded our brave men for their unflinching endurance in this campaign. In spite of the fatigue, our corps is in better condition than when it left Richmond. We shall long remember Early's antiscorbutic campaign, (as it has been facetiously called) all over Virginia and a part of Maryland.

We are now resting in the loveliest part of Virginia, surrounded by kind friends, who are continually exerting themselves for our comfort. God bless these lovely women of the valley.

U.U.D.

[TFW's journal continues. He takes us back to Frederick, Maryland, in July 1864.]

Although the paper clippings here given cover some of the narrative, there is much that was left out.

We marched directly upon Frederick City from Sharpesburg, and there encountered a small force under General Lew Wallace, near Monocacy bridge. Our brigade was not engaged.[32]

I took an unauthorized opportunity to visit Frederick to see what I could get in the way of wearing apparel and eatables and drinkables, and much more from curiosity. I found that there were strict orders for officers not to visit the town. General Early levied a contribution of $200,000 and when the authorities protested and wanted to reduce it, Genl. Early said if they refused he would let his men loose in the town to purchase with Confederate money. This would have been worse than the levy demanded, and the prospect in the latter case was that the U.S. Congress would refund the money to Frederick. The money was paid, and our men were encamped out of town within supporting distance of the part of the army fighting at Monocacy.[33] I saw no officers in the town, and I suppose I escaped arrest because I had on an Asst. Surgeon's uniform, and I was supposed to be on the lookout for the sick. There were some Southern sympathizers, and we made the acquaintance of a lady who knew some of our friends who were at the Catholic Convent School, which was a favorite school with some of our Southern families. In company with these ladies we visited the Convent, and found that the Sisters, as well as the pupils were Southern in their sympathies. There was a Miss Rush there, a sister of Mrs. W.E. Spring and Mrs. Capt. Parker. There was also a Miss Marmion a sister of Dr. George Marmion, who married my cousin Lizzie Wood. The girls came into the reception room to see us. And each one gave us a pocket handkerchief or pin-cushion. We were well fed, and a good lunch was put up for our journey. One of the Sisters was an aunt of Dr. Marmion and afterwards came to Wilmington to the Convent there. The Sisters had been on the house top watching the Battle of Monocacy and were delighted with our victory. When we returned to camp we found the regiment encamped near the field of battle and many of the dead were lying on the ground around us.[34]

Having removed Genl. Wallace from our front we marched directly towards Washington, the weather was very hot and the road exceedingly dusty. We were now well within the enemy's country, far away from a base and our movements had to be rapid. The people all along our march were excited and believed that we were in greater force than we were, and every means was used to spread the report. It became evident to the men that now we were really marching on towards Washington City, and it caused a thrill of excitement. Only a month ago we were about to be penned up in the trenches around Richmond, now we had driven all of the available army from the Federal side from our front, and if we could strike before Genl. Grant could reinforce Washington, we could raise such an alarm as would raise the seige of Petersburg.

The day's march previous to arriving around Washington was prepared with great care. Preparations were made so that no stragglers should be left on the road side. I was detailed to assist a South Carolina Surgeon whose name I forget—to look after the sick and those overcome by the heat. Being cut off from my regiment I had nothing to eat, and in the cool of the day there was not much need of our services. We came to a neat looking farm house, having the name of "Dr. Taylor" neatly cast in iron over the gate. The (S.C.) doctor and I went into the enclosure and took seats under the trees of the avenue leading to the house, waiting for the troops to pass us.

The gentleman of the establishment came out and invited us to his house, and introduced himself as Dr. Taylor. He was a Southern sympathizer and was very cordial in his invitation. He asked us to breakfast for which he apologized, as he had been feeding our men all day. The ladies after breakfast sang and played war songs. Everything was in disorder in the household, and they were evidently under the apprehension that if we failed they would be made to suffer for their disloyalty. The generous host though, did all he could and gave us letters to friends in Washington. So certain did he seem to be that we would take the city without difficulty. He told us of an amusing thing that happened. He went down to the spring to have some conversation with some of our cavalrymen. One of them took quite a fancy to the Doctor's coat, and in an army parlance asked him to "come out of it." The Doctor declined politely whereupon the cavalryman said he would have it, suited his actions to his words, tried to take it by force. The other men stood off and saw "fair play" and the Doctor succeeded in giving him a good drubbing and saved his coat. This outrageous conduct on the part of the cavalry did not dampen his ardor, for he continued to feed our men as long as he had anything to eat.

The work of the S.C. Surgeon and mine was not what we had expected, having had occasion a very few times to administer to exhausted men. There may have been more than we thought, and attention was given to them by the medical officers immediately attached to the commands. We saw the last of the army pass before us before we rejoined our regiments, and when we did they were in line before the City of Washington. We marched on the Rockville Pike passing through the village of Rockville.[35] As we approached the town they commenced shelling from immense guns. They were evidently served by unskillful gunners, as the shells fell into and beyond our wagon trains. I did not get on our line but was told by our sharpshooters that they could see men on the works in their linen dusters and silk hats, evidently citizens who had come to the rescue.[36]

I took up my headquarters at Silver Springs, which was a handsome estate. The houses of Montgomery Blair and a Mr. Roach were near our line.[37] We had a number of seriously wounded men here, but few in the 1st and 3rd N.C. As the fighting progressed it was evident that Washington had been re-inforced by old soldiers.[38] After a day of desultory fighting General Early withdrew from W. marching all night. There was no pursuit and we made our way leisurely. The object of the engagement was to draw away troops from Genl. Lee's front at Petersburg and release our prisoners in Maryland by means of our cavalry, and by the additional assistance of a small fleet (or one vessel it may have been), to attack the prison fort by sea. Our cavalry severed all communications with the North with Washington by rail and created great consternation and alarm. So wide spread were the movements of our army that it was believed by the people of Maryland that Early and A.P. Hill were both with us. We got safely out of Maryland crossing near Leesburg in Virginia and went into camp.[39]

Our men committed depredations in Maryland to some extent, burning the house of Montgomery Blair and plundering the houses of Mr. Roach and Mr. Blair near the lines. It was not sanctioned by General Early. Among the captures was a lot of blank bills, of a defunct bank of Michigan or Wisconsin. Before it was discovered, it was circulated in the army, and the men bought from the farmers, offering their choice between our Confederate money and their stolen notes, and all chose the latter, in such bad repute was our money at the time.

At this period of our campaign we were reduced to the very smallest amount of baggage. During the dry weather we slept out of doors without a tent, and when we started out in the morning at 3:45am we made our toilet by pulling on our boots and mounting, delaying the washing of hands and faces and brushing our teeth, if we did them at all, at the first spring or brook the opportunity offered us. The Valley of Virginia had been badly stripped and plundered, so that provisions were hard to be obtained, and the citizens had to resort to hiding their provisions between the ceiling to keep any food for themselves. To show to what extremeties they were reduced, I recollect to have seen a lot of bees flying in and out of an attic window, and we learned that the farmer had been obliged to carry his bee hives to the attic for security. You will find in the printed letters a sketch of some of our campaigning, but when disasters came I had no heart to write to the papers, and I did not wish to depress the people at home.

THE WILMINGTON JOURNAL
[Publication date in the Journal: August 18, 1864]
THE CONTINUANCE OF GENERAL EARLY'S ANTISCORBUTIC CAMPAIGN

Bivouac near Bunker Hill, Va.
August 4th, 1864

When you last heard from us, we were in the camp between Berryville and Charlestown, with a promise that we should there enjoy the rest and comforts which the hospitable neighborhood offered so abundantly. But our stay was destined to be short.[40]

General Breckinridge's Corps was in position to watch the Charlestown Pike, while Rodes, Ramseur and Gordon of Early's Corps guarded Rocks, Snicker's and Ashby's Gaps. Our cavalry in the meantime was partly on out post duty, and rested in camp to recruit, after their excessive labor in the campaign in the enemy's country.

We purposely omitted to tell you of an exciting mishap which occured on the East side of the Blue Ridge, near Snicker's Gap. Early in the day we had intimation that a force of Yankees, indefinitely stated as to numbers, was hovering about our wagon train. Our train was between two divisions of infantry, but unprotected on the flanks, and marching in single line.

About noon a heavy cloud of dust was raised upon the right of the road, which proved to be a body of cavalry, 200 or 300 strong, a party of Averill's command. We were on the slopes of the hill when the alarm was given of the approach of the enemy. Our column was halted, and having gained the summit of the hill, the action was much more distinct to us than those nearer the clouds of dust being almost impenetrable.

It seemed that this cavalry had been in ambush near the road and as soon as our wagon train came in full view, they put two rifle pieces into position, which soon commenced shelling vigorously, while a squadron of horsemen charged our unprotected train, carrying off about thirty wagons before our infantry came up. Col. Cook (now Gen.) came up with his brigade of Georgians, and pursued the enemy, killing or wounding five or six, and capturing three. All wagons except six, which belonged to General Ransom's Cavalry (MaCausland's Brigade), and which the infantry troops declared to be only loads of calico, were recaptured, together with the mules; the enemy's artillery, and a quantity of small arms were also taken.[41] It is rather doubtful if this boldness of the Yankees did us any harm. We lost only one poor fellow, a wagoneer from Grime[s]'s Brigade, in the skirmish. It was asserted that a Q.M. [Quartermaster] killed a Yankee Sergeant with his own hands, but we heard a "*shooter*" claimed the same thing; and in corroboration of the latter statement General Cook said he (the

Yankee) was killed by one of his men, who threw himself between him and the Yankee when he was attacked unarmed. The scene was quite an exciting one for a few minutes, and had its good effect. It taught a single but important lesson to those who should have known better. An accident of this sort frequently occuring, would put in serious jeopardy our entire transportation, which we assure you is now quite small.

That "*audacious Rebel Chieftain*"—Mosby—passed by our column while we were going through Snicker's Gap. He is Captain General of that section of the country, and is constantly on the alert to inflict some blow upon the Yankees. His name is a terror to every wagon driver and quarter master in this department. He so fully impressed the Maryland people that his little squad was A.P. Hill's advance guard, and that the Second Army Corps was at the mouth of the Monocacy supporting our left flank, that it was actually believed not only by the Washingtonians but by some of our officers. Such a man is worth having.

But to return to our narrative. Our camp was arroused at three o'clock Monday, the 18th of July, by the occasional discharge of artillery, and we were soon enroute for the scene of the conflict. The enemy crossed the Shenandoah at Snicker's Ferry[42] and below, in a considerable force, occupying with his artillery the heights on both sides of the river. We could get no position for artillery, which gave to him the advantage of employing his batteries entirely upon our infantry column. General Rodes engaged the enemy about four o'clock and the tale is soon told. The Yankees were driven pell mell into the river, with a heavy loss in killed and wounded; but few prisoners fell into our hands. Genl. Cox and Grimes lost more heavily than any other Brigade.

We have to lament the death of Col. Owen[s],[43] who fell leading Grimes' Brigade. His remains were disposed in the yard in the venerable old Stone Church near Berryville. Col. Stallings,[44] the gallant commander of the 2nd N.C. Regiment, and Col. Wood,[45] of the 14th N.C. also fell in this battle. These officers were young men of bright promise; veterans of the hardest type, schooled under Anderson and Ramseur by the severest discipline, and with the generous impulse and brilliant daring of true patriots, their memories will ever remain fresh in the hearts of the men of this Brigade. The remains of Col. Wood were buried with appropriate ceremonies at the residence of a patriotic gentleman in Clarke County—Col. Ware's. Col. Stallings' remains were deposited at the churchyard at Berryville, the ceremony at both occasions was performed by Rev. George Patterson, Chaplain of the 3rd N.C. Regiment.

The loss in the 1st and 3rd N.C. was small. Luke Cornegay, Co. D, 3rd N.C. was killed and Private Ennis, Co. K, wounded dangerously; Private Rogers, Co. B, wounded dangerously; Private Edge, Co. C, seriously; Private Biggs, Co. G, wounded in the hand; these men were all of the 3rd N.C. Regiment. We are thankful that our gallant Colonel [Thruston] escaped again the dangers of this battle.[46]

The enemy now made a demonstration towards Front Royal, and we took up line of march through Berryville towards Strasburg, via White Post and Newtown. But arriving at Newtown, on the 21st, after 18 miles march, we found the town in considerable excitement about a battle which had been fought by Major General Ramseur, and of which the most exaggerated disasters were rife. We were ordered up to Ramseur's support, but after marching to Kearnstown we found that he was able not only to hold his position but the enemy was afraid of him.

Without assuming to be a critic on military affairs, we will state the army gossip relative to Genl. Ramseur's favor, and your readers can form their own judgement. Genl. Ramseur was rear guard for our army, and receiving information from the cavalry that a small force was in line in his rear, he advanced upon them. The Genl. failed to discover the presence of the enemy until close upon them, when he rapidly deployed his Brigade but found the enemy's line overlapped his, about the strength of a Brigade. The enemy opened vigorously upon them before they could form, and driving the Brigade on the right, the one next to it the next, and so on, until all, General R.D. Johnson's Brigade inclusive, were forced to retire, leaving four pieces of artillery on the field, but saving the caissons and limbers.

General Johnson had fought the Yankees with such success in his front, that but for his (the enemy's) success on our left, he would have been defeated. The line was soon reformed, however, and the enemy was too discreet to follow up his partial success. We lost a hundred and fifty prisoners and four pieces of artillery, and a few wounded. Among the wounded was Genl. Gaston Lewis, of North Carolina. The disaster, though slight, was the only one which marred the brilliancy of the campaign.[47]

On the 21st we encamped near Strasburg, about the scene of General Jackson's victory over Shields in his brilliant Valley Campaign in 1862.

Early on the morning of the 24th, the bugle sounded forward, and our army was in motion towards Winchester. About 2 o'clock we encountered Cook [Crook] in line of battle, between Kearnstown and Winchester. Coming down upon both flanks at once, Breckinridge on the right and Early on the left, the enemy scarcely made a stand, and was soon flying towards his base on the Potomac. We captured upwards of 200 prisoners, killed and wounded a considerable number, while fifty would cover our entire loss. General Mulligan, of Western notoriety, was mortally wounded and died. He was a brave officer, and undoubtedly a severe loss to the enemy. Since his death he is found only to have a Colonel's commission. Had he lived, however, he would have passed himself off for a Major General, and no doubt, exchanged as much.

Having again cleared the way of Yankees, we were soon on the way again to the Potomac. The tract of the enemy's retreat was strewn with wagons.

When you know that upward of a hundred wagons were destroyed, including caisson, forges and limbers, you can imagine that Cooke's [Crook's] retreat, although over a splendid road, was made in confusion.[48]

After a cavalry skirmish of a few hours, we took possession of Martinsburg, that odious nest of Unionists, and destroyed the railroads and bridges for several miles; pushed on in two or three days to the Potomac, crossed a ford at Williamsport, made important captures of cattle and commissary stores, and returned to rest in camp at Bunker's Hill, a victorious and competent army.

It may not appear to your readers, what this army is accomplishing here, but if they could see the immense amount of wheat, flour and cattle which are collected daily, they would properly appreciate our work. The energy, caution and daring of Genl. Early, entitles him to the distinguished place among the Lieutenant Generals of our army. We can assure that his slanderers are not in the army, but confined to a few out of the army, who are always ready to find fault.

Deserters from the Ohio regiments are coming in small squads daily. Although we are not willing to confide in the statement of any sort of Yankees, they assure us that the spirit of discontent is increasing in their army daily, and that the "new Levy" of troops are guarded carefully to prevent desertion.

We have been placed in a position lately to hear a free expression of Yankee sentiment. The people of the South must not value too much this evidence of discontent among the Yankees. A large party in the North hate the Lincoln dynasty, but they hate us worse, and will hold out to the last hour against us. Repeated disaster can only break down their stubborn determination and establish our supremacy.

Holden now knows where his friends of the army are. An election was held at Martinsburg last Thursday, resulting in upwards of 1,800 votes for Vance, against 136 for Holden. Five men out of ten from the 2nd N.C. Regt., who voted for Holden, deserted the night after the election. Send up your papers to us soon, that we may know the result of the election of the whole State.[49]

U.U.D.

ARMY CORRESPONDENCE FOR THE JOURNAL
[Publication date in the Journal: September 1, 1864]
OUR FOURTH TRANS-POTOMAC CAMPAIGN

Star Fort, Winchester, Va.
Aug. 11th, 1864

The latitude which the Shenandoah Valley affords to armies for maneuvering is so extensive, that an active campaign sometimes degenerates into a game of hide and seek, as in the case of the present one. We were quietly enjoying the passtime of tearing up the Baltimore and Ohio R.R. during the 26th, 27th and 28th days of July, at Martinsburg. After resting leisurely for several days, we moved on towards Falling Water, and encamped in woods between the last named place and the Potomac, and felt around with our cavalry on the other side of the river for the purpose of stirring up the lion in his den.

But on the 5th day of August we commenced in real earnest another invasion of the enemy's country which was our fourth. Genl. Breckinridge and other forces crossed at Shepardstown, and Rodes crossed at Williamsport, the former proceeding towards Sharpsburg, the latter towards Boonesborough.

The enemy had completely "drawn in his horns", so that no vestige of his army could be found by our indefatigable Mosby, and the general impression was that he was making his way towards Petersburg to re-inforce Grant. This being the disposition of the enemy, their whole country would be left open to us to penetrate to its very heart.

We crossed the Potomac at the small town of Williamsport, a depot of the Chesapeake and Ohio Canal of about 3,000 inhabitants. The river was at its very lowest, and the fording easy and pleasant. We pursued the Boonesborough road, a short distance, passing en route St. James College, encamping near the latter institution. Many availed themselves of visiting their Alma Mater. Some of the faculty with most of the students, left upon hearing of our approach. The Rev. Dr. Kerfoot, President of the College, remained the unsuspecting victim of retaliation and did the honors of his house to quite a table full of Rebels of all ranks.

It became the duty of one of these officers (of high rank) to issue the order for the Reverend Doctor's arrest, while partaking of the hospitality of his board.

The Rev. Dr. Boyd of Winchester, was arrested several months ago and held as hostage for a Yankee who afterwards died, and the worthy man is still a prisoner. Genl. Early has quite a keen perception of the quality and quantity of retaliation it takes to overcome the stubborn Yankees, and arrested the Rev. Dr. Kerfoot as a hostage for Dr. Boyd, giving him twenty days to make arrangements.

On the 6th day of August our Brigade was returned to Williamsport to garrison the town. It was our fortune to be in camp upon the Conogeague Creek, about two miles from where it enters into the Potomac, at which place we enjoyed the country hospitality of Maryland and obtained an insight into the politics of the Yankee nation.

There seems to be a determination upon the part of some of the people of Maryland to throw off the restraints which have been placed upon the ballot box. They have but to will it, and they have the power. We heard from a number of Democrats here that they had not been allowed to vote since they cast their vote for Breckinridge. As soon as it is ascertained that the citizen, whoever he may be, intends to vote an anti-administration ticket, a soldier informs him that he cannot vote. Now we hope they will vote regardless of the wishes and desires of the Yankees. The truth is, every town in the North had its company of provost guards whose high prerogative it was to elect the proper persons to vote; but now, all of these companies have been called in to attend to more urgent business about Richmond. So it would seem some prospect still remains for the people to exercise their rights. The Democrats, however, seemed not to have concentrated upon any man, but seemed determined to support some "anti-war" nominee. The people of the border have learned to treat both Yankees and Confederates with so much simplicity that it is extremely hard to tell one's real sentiments from his conversation. They are certainly in an uncomfortable position. One said a few days ago, "the Yankees come and take my horses and the Rebels come and take my wheat, and I do not know who is my friend." It was suggested to the gentleman that he had better espouse the cause of one or the other even if he had no feeling in the matter.

The 7th day of Aug. found nearly all of our army encamped in and about the beautiful little valley, which is watered by this same creek, the Conogeague. It is sometimes called by the name of this stream. Everything is seen by us when we invade under the most disadvantageous circumstances. Every industrial pursuit is checked, except where here and there a commissary has a flour mill in operation. All horses not taken by us or the enemy, (for the Yankees steal from the Marylanders) are carried to the neighboring mountain to be secreted and the same of cattle.

One would be a little surprised to see the alacrity with which the "anti-war" Democrats take our money, and even these which once regarded it as trash are more inclined to give it a more respectable consideration and put it aside for future reference.

The burning of Chambersburg caused a great deal of consternation among the people of the Cumberland Valley. While some denounced it with a great deal of violence, others said that it was but what they could expect. Nothing is needed to stop the house burning by the Yankees except an unflinching determination to retaliate—house for house, and town for town, and no one is more conscious of the fact than Genl. Early.[50] Even now from the mountains can be seen the smoking track of the enemy advancing up the Valley, finishing his develish work of destruction.

On the 8th our entire army re-crossed the Potomac at Williamsport, having accomplished nothing more than to procure some subsistence, making a reconnaissance in force, to ascertain who and what the enemy was, and making a feint towards the Yankee Capitol.

Another object also was accomplished. General McCausland and General Bradley Johnson were making an extensive raid in the Cumberland Valley. They had just burned Chambersburg, had made a feint towards Cumberland City and were being followed up briskly by a superior force. They made their way out again, having had but one collision, and were in bivouac on the South branch of the Potomac near Moorefield.

It is so easy to do injustice to cavalry knowing so little of their service, that we will endeavor to state the plain case, in the affair near Moorefield, without comments. It seems that McCausland and Johnson were in bivouac, with the usual picket in their front. On the morning of the 7th the enemy made a sudden descent upon their camp, without any intimation of his approach, and without encountering any pickets, and scattered the whole command. It was a complete and unfortunate surprise, Genl. Johnson making his escape upon a bare back horse. One member of the command says the enemy flanked their pickets, and came in between their line and the camp. The Col. whom we understand commanded the picket, was wounded and captured. The entire loss was 300 men, four pieces of artillery, 35 killed and wounded, while the statement about the capture of horses is so conflicting the truth cannot be arrived at. It is true however, "that we watch our horses right close when they are turned out to graze."[51]

We hailed the result of the election in our state, as the proudest triumph in the annals of her history. Let her slanderers hang their heads, for she has shown the world, what her sons knew before, that she is a staunch upholder of the Confederate cause. We rejoice to announce that the 1st, 3rd and 4th N.C. Regiments did not cast a vote for Holden.

The vanguard of the enemy attacked our vanguard on the evening of the 11th. Sheridan was the attacking party. General Gordon soon repulsed the attack, driving the enemy back in confusion. The 6th, 8th, 19th U.S. "Corps de Armee", have been reorganized and retain the name of the 6th under General Wright. The Second Corps (Hancock) . . . are also in the Valley.[52]

U.U.D.

FROM OUR ARMY CORRESPONDENT
[Publication date in the Journal: September 8, 1864]
FURTHER OPERATIONS IN THE LOWER VALLEY—
THE BATTLES OF THE SHARPSHOOTERS

In Bivouac near Charleston, Va.
August 23rd, 1864

We are now nearly upon the sight of the spot upon which that archfanatic, John Brown, expiated his crime upon the gallows, watching the enemy in his strong position upon Maryland Heights. The whole slope of the hill is white with tents, while the Yankee flag floats defiantly from the works on its summit; it is safe there under the protection of hundred pounder guns which cannot be charged.

After making a retrogade movement up the Valley to Strasburg on the 14th, entrenching there in that narrow pass formed by the Massonutton on the East and Little North Mountain on the West, inviting the advance of our reinforced enemy, we sailed out on the 17th and came up with him at Milltown Mills, a short distance from Winchester. The enemy took a strong position on that line of hills on the west side of Winchester, and was attacked just before sunset by Warton's (Breckinridge's) and Ramseur's Divisions. The fight was quite a spirited one, but of short duration, resulting in the capture of 300 prisoners, and killing about thirteen; our loss was eight killed. The enemy retreated all night, going into camp around Charleston.

The track of the enemy from Charleston to Winchester was a scene of renewed outrages. The few standing barns and granaries were burned, as well as the stacks of wheat standing in the fields. The same destruction marking his track from Front Royal to Berryville. At Milltown a fine flour mill was destroyed. These are but the indications of the desperations of the barbarous foe, who failing to hold this country by honorable warfare is determined to drive us from it by destroying all of the subsistence here.

But the blow only falls heavily upon these down-trodden people of the valley; they bear up under it with a heroism and fortitude worthy of emulation.

We left our camp at Bunker Hill at sunrise of the morning of the 21st. Rodes, Gordon, Ramseur, and Breckinridge taking the Charleston Turnpike, and our other corps taking the Winchester and Charleston grade. About ten o'clock we encountered the enemy near Charleston close to his encampment. When our sharpshooters came upon them, their wagons and ambulances were in part apparently unaware of our proximity. Brisk skirmishing ensued during the entire day between our sharpshooters, supported here and there by a regular line of battle, and a regular line of the enemy. The engagement was severe during the whole day and is the heaviest which this division has seen during the Valley Campaign, except perhaps, at Washington.

The enemy retreated from his entrenchments during the night carrying from the field all of his wounded which would number about 200. The number of dead we have not heard estimated, but graves are numerous. Our loss in wounded was about 90; and of killed few—perhaps 20. The enemy skirmished the next day through Charleston with his cavalry and afterwards an orderly and creditable retreat under cover of the heavy guns on the heights.

This battle was fought almost entirely by the sharpshooters corps, supported in several places by Col. Kenen's 43rd N.C., Col. Peeble's 44th Georgia, and Col. Clarke's 30th N.C. in our front. This corps has done more extra service during the campaign than any other portion of the army, and their cool bravery and efficiency has been the admiration of the several brigades from which they are detailed for this important duty.

We saw the New York Herald of the 18th yesterday, which announced in a mysterious manner that Genl. Sheridan's army was about to drive the Rebels out of the Valley, and in a few days Lynchburg would fall into their hands. We have no map at hand but would ask if there is a Lynchburg in Maryland.

We know that the news will be stale, but we would call attention to the interest that Wilmington is attracting, as the only port which the U.S. squadron has to blockade, and a proposed plan for closing the port permanently, which is contained in the N.Y. Herald of the 18th.

The people of Charleston witnessed the first execution of Abolitionists, and since that time they have been called upon to witness much bloodshed in their very streets, in a war, the natural sequence of John Brown's raid. A more devoted and earnest people never enlisted in any cause than these. They have sent scores of good soldiers to our armies; they have fed our hungry; nursed our sick and wounded, and have set an example of unflinching determination in our cause, that their neighbors in Martinsburg might follow with credit.

In sight of us stands the ruins of Col. Andrew Hunter's house which was burned by order of Genl. Hunter, his relative, and the order written by the notorious Porte Crayon (Strother) his nephew, (Hunter's A.G.), in retaliation for the burning of houses in Maryland.[53]

Many citizens were arrested and carried off when the enemy evacuated the town, upon some flimsy pretense. The Yankees hope that by incarceration they will subdue the lofty spirit of the leading men of the border, and thereby hasten our return to the Union. This is their theory, but the practical influence of such treatment does not sustain it. A lady remarked while our skirmishers were fighting through the town: "The Yankees tell us they hate us and we are proud of it!"

The morning of the 24th was one of some excitement in camp. We are in bivouac on the crest of a crescent shaped hill and in front of us about two miles is our line of skirmishers, in a parallel to this, on the right and left of the Harper's Ferry Road. Between those two lines is a corn field, paid for by the yankees, and in which our men have been gathering corn for a day or so. But this morning about noon, an attack was made upon our sharpshooters in front, with a simultaneous dash of the cavalry down upon our right flank into this field upon our men. They were rather keen for the enemy having observed them as they filed out of a point of woods on the hill beyond, and got a considerable start in the chase. The pursuit was a hot one, the excited Yankees commanding: "Halt, Halt Surrender, You d—— rascals." But our men have too great a horror of Yankee prisons and continued their flight, sticking tenaciously to their loads of corn, while the Yankees beat the air lustily with their sabers, and fired their carbines wildly; but this only stimulated the exertions of our men. At this opportune moment Col. Nelson's artillery opened from our line with his superb Napoleons, and scattered the bold cavaleer all over the field, from which they afterwards retreated to their line.

This corps has never before fought such a demoralized army as the one which now confronts us. They have not in one instance, during the campaign, ventured to give us general battle, and it has required little more than a division of our army to achieve the victories of each battle. Devastation to the country and destruction to transportation and implements of war have marked the retreating enemy from Lynchburg to Salem, and from Strasburg to Charlestown. The HUNDRED DAY MEN (Recruits obligated for only one hundred days of service) have deserted after every battle, thrown away their arms and sought refuge in the friendly hills of West Virginia, and they now stand an army of dastards, crouching under the heights waiting for another opportunity to apply the torch to our homes and granaries as soon as we retire.

But we do not make vain boasts when we say we are able to hold this territory, as long as we are not needed else where. We are essentially "an army of occupation and masters of the Shenandoah Valley."

Mosby's late attack upon the Yankee trains in the Page Valley shows that he is not yet intimidated. Although the Yankees deny in their newspapers that he captured their major P.M. with a load of green backs, yet our Rebel guerilla is the veritable owner of the pile. Mosby is our "left bower".[54]

U.U.D.

FROM OUR ARMY CORRESPONDENT
[Publication date in the Journal: September 15, 1864]
A RECONNAISSANCE IN FORCE—A RAID CHECKED—
OUR CAVALRY—ANOTHER RUNNING FIGHT

Bunker Hill, Va.
August 31st, 1864

When we last wrote we had two divisions of infantry watching the enemy upon the heights, from which lofty eminence he was busy shelling our lines, while our sharpshooters kept up a continual firing from their strong barricade, without doing more than to keep themselves and the enemy on the alert. We saw very few wounded, and but one dead man.

The next day, the 25th, our army changed its position, moving out from Sharpstown, via Leetown, and encountered the enemy between the latter place and Shepardstown. Wharton's Division of Breckinridge's Corps was in front, and upon arriving near the enemy, deployed sharpshooters. The enemy came dashing down upon this feeble line with his cavalry column and succeeded in breaking it, and causing some confusion in the line of battle. Artillery fire rapidly succeeded the charge, and the enemy went dashing on towards our column of infantry. But rapidly recovering their temporary confusion, a bold front was given, and he retired without getting in very dangerous proximity to our line. The spirit with which the dash was made, and the prompt cooperation of the enemy's artillery, did a considerable amount of damage to us before it was fully realized what the character of the force really was.

A vigerous pursuit now commenced. But any one who had witnessed the pursuit of cavalry by infantry, know how extremely futile such cases are. On, on, our heavy columns pressed, at quick time, our advance firing an occasional shot at the enemy's retreating column, until about sundown. We had succeeded in cutting off a small body and had walled them in by three heavy columns of infantry. Night now came on and closed the scene; the nimble horsemen slipped through our fingers under cover of night, and forded the Potomac at Shepardstown. In a fit of exasperation we fired a few rounds of artillery ammunition into the woods on the opposite shore, with the hope of killing anything that might be there; tired and chagrined we gave up the chase, and were glad to partake of a refreshing sleep and promised the enemy to make it up the next time we encountered his infantry.

Our loss was more important and heavier than that of the enemy, while the whole affair could not be dignified with the name of a fight. We lost a Colonel from Wharton's Division and one from Gordon's, killed, and two other wounded.

There is no doubt, though, that an important raid was checked in the encounter. From what we could learn, The Yankee cavalry, estimated about 10,000 (it was no doubt less), expected to slip out between our left flank and the mountain, and go right up the Valley, with the prospect of destroying all of our stores, and making their escape into the Kanawha Valley. The acute military perception of Genl. Early is equalled to all such maneuvers of the enemy, and nothing but hard fighting will accomplish what they expect to gain by trickery.

The uncertain reports of an unreliable cavalry as to the force in our front, while we were in line at Bunker Hill, caused Genl. Rodes with his division, to make a reconnaissance in force toward Martinsburg on the 31st. The distance between the two places is ten miles and no general skirmishing took place until we mounted the hills which skirt Martinsburg. We here encountered Averill's [Averell's] cavalry, and after an exciting running fight, drove them beyond town. The force there was asertained to be entirely cavalry, about 30,000 strong. The good ladies of the town met with us with good cheer and kindly salutation. Both men and beast enjoyed the stay of nearly a day in town, and left in glee.

The only capture of any importance was that of Lt. Col. J. Barleycorn, a deserter from our army since the Battle of Mannassas. He was in full Yankee uniform, dressed in the height of fashion, having the odor Bouquet d'Orleans, about him. So furious were our men upon seeing him, that they rushed en mass, and cut him to death, in spite of an attempt by our Generals to show him respect due a prisoner of his rank. Had he lived, a court marshal would have decided his fate, the poor fellow's life was terminated ignominiously. Seeing they could not refrain the fury of the men, the officers cordially joined in the work of death.

Movements of the enemy upon our right flank, necessitated a counter movement by us on the 2nd, and Early's Corps fell back to the point where the Jordan Spring's Road intersects the Valley Turnpike. Rode's was the rear division.

About 11 o'clock there was a heavy cloud of dust in the rear of our column and soon came our cavalry dashing furiously to our rear, hatless and covered with dust, evidently "what they called demoralized." It seems that they had been left to bring up the rear, they were pressed, and fired in retreat until they had reached our former picket post between Larksville [possibly Darksville] and Bunker Hill, and finding no infantry post there to support them, the retreat became a route, and they ran away leaving their wagons and cattle to the enemy. Battle's brigade came up to their assistance, but after all the damage was done.

Skirmishing ensued on our line during the entire day of the 3rd, and the cavalry on this occasion made a very creditable fight, retrieving the disgrace of the day before; while upon the wing composed of R.H. Anderson's troops. an engagement occured between the contending forces near Berryville in which engagement we lost six men and carried the enemy's works.[55]

The cavalry arm of the Army of the Valley District is sadly inefficient, and often prevents the infantry from achieving successes. When our cavalry returned from Maryland there was no better armed and equipped body of troops in our services; but they had been unrestricted, untramelled by discipline, glutted with successes and plunder, allowed the freest license in the enemy's country and then lapsed into indolence and carelessness, which caused their defeat at Moorefield, and subsequent inefficiency. Well armed, mounted and disciplined in the campaign of this valley, cavalry would be very valuable; but as it is, a heavy tax upon the patience of the infantry whom they caused trouble by false alarms, and the country which they feed upon. Now that our whole campaign has degenerated into cavalry hunting we need good cavalry to do it, for we assure you we are tired of performing the duties of both arms of the service.

The infantry of Sheridan's army has entrenched itself near Berryville and will probably remain there until charged out or mustered out of the service; their prudential principles keep them close behind their works being already forced to acknowledge this to be the "Valley of Humiliation" to them.

On the evening of the 6th, we had another chase after cavalry, which for exciting interest to all concerned was the most important which has occured in the Valley. Our cavalry commenced the engagement upon a line at right angles to the Valley Turnpike, about 5 miles from Winchester. They behaved well, but were forced to recoil before the superior strength of the enemy. But just at the right time Rodes' Division was sent in to support, and a few volleys changed the tide of battle and now a chase commenced. The enemy's cavalry was well trained, and kept up an orderly running fight, with the "hungry Rebels" yelling like hounds in the chase, close upon their heels. A furious rain storm now came on, pelting our men right in the face, but on they pressed, seemingly invigorated by the fury of the storm. Our artillery was far in the rear, being distanced by our fleet foot cavalry, but the enemy used his batteries, with no other effect however, than to keep the vultures well to the rear.

But with all the running and yelling and firing, we lacked the fleetness of horses. The darkness of night enveloped pursuer and pursued now, and the bugle called us off the chase. And then it seemed that the very flood gates of heaven were opened. The storm raged with increased violence; disappointed and fatigued, our wet column retraced their steps for a camp ground, yelling as terrifically as though they were celebrating some jubilee. But the Rebel yell means many things. It is heard in the chase; it is heard when the fatigue has been excessive; it is the greeting of a General, and the index of an unbroken spirit of our noble army.

The result of the encounter was but the capture of perhaps one hundred prisoners, and death to a small number of the enemy. Our loss would not exceed ten or fifteen and but one man killed.

The Yankees are endeavoring to crowd their cavalry past our right, in order to make a raid in our rear between Winchester and Woodstock. But the ways are not left open—not even the back door. If the infantry of Sheridan's army still continues to make the cavalry do all the fighting, and our cavalry makes us do all on our side, Gov. Vance will have to send us up "Isenberg Pontoons"[56] for barefooted men are becoming numerous.

The storm is still raging here, and in a few days we will all be stuck in the mud.

U.U.D.

Up to the 19th of September 1864 we had been masters of the Valley.[57] Our victories constantly drew troops from Grant's front at Petersburg and it became necessary that we should be beaten. The Northern army was reinforced, until their cavalry numbered as many troops as the whole of our army. It was evident therefore that our army must be maneuvered with superior skill or be beaten. At the date mentioned, our small army was divided, one half being at Bunker Hill, the other at Stevenson's Station near Winchester. I belong to Rodes' Division (Ramseur's old, now Cox's Brigade) and we were ordered to march towards Winchester, and as we neared the town we heard the roaring of cannon and sharp musketry; Genl. Rodes pushed on. I was riding at his side talking very pleasantly and took the good opportunity to tell him that his order "that the position of the Asst. Surgeon in the time of battle should be with the line of file closers" could not be carried out. That few Surgeons had the coolness to dress a wound under fire, and that it was rarer still to find a wounded man who could get away who would stop to have his wound dressed. His only reply was, "you have heard my order" and changed the subject. In a few minutes our whole division was faced to the front, General Rodes with them and a terrific fight took place. In a very few minutes he was killed, falling almost in the arms of Col. Thruston of our Regiment. He was wet with his blood. It was a desperate fight, with General Ramseur holding the line until he was nearly exhausted, and when our Division came up we drove the enemy quite briskly but they were too strong for us and our cavalry gave way on our left flank. Soon the enemy poured in, and it was a scamper to avoid being captured. I had on a "Yankee" blouse, my coat being so badly worn, I found it convenient because it had so many pockets, I could stuff away sponges and bandages, etc. But I remember that General Sheridan had issued an order that any "Rebel"—that is Confederate Soldier—who was found with their uniform (Union) on, would be shot on the spot—at any rate that was our news and I felt uncomfortable and made good my escape. The army was driven back so rapidly that the retreat was turned into a stampede. Such confusion I never saw, and why Sheridan did not capture the whole army I cannot see. I was told by Col. Thruston that Col. Nelson with his battalion of artillery brought up the rear, without the support of any organized body of troops, only such men as on their individual impulse stood by him. In this Col. Nelson lost only one gun which was so disabled he could not bring it off.[58]

Our Brigade had often supported his battalion and there was a good feeling—a feeling of mutual admiration but this day he was deserted. I recollect afterwards when we were entrenched at Fisher's Hill after this battle, that our men cheered Col. Nelson as he passed by but he did not like the compliment, and retorted, "but boys you deserted me at Winchester"—it was a stinging rebuke.[59] No one can form any idea of a stampede of an army. Wagons four abreast driven at the greatest speed mule flesh is capable of, by crazy drivers, cursing, whipping, spurring, lashing furiously with their reins, driving pell mell rushing into each other. Now and then one overturns his wagon, he stops for nothing, cuts his saddle mules out of the team and rushes wildly off without hardly looking behind; and leaving the rest to take care of themselves. Interspersed in the hubbub are infantry soldiers, bare headed cavalrymen, droves of cattle, limber chests, camp followers, all pushing to the rear with all the speed they could muster. Excited officers turning every now and then, and although showing in their actions more panic than the fleeing men—ordering to "halt", "rally', and after stopping long enough to hear an-

General Robert Emmett Rodes, led the division to which the 3rd North Carolina belonged until he was mortally wounded at Winchester on September 19, 1864. Massachusetts Commandery Military Order of the Loyal Legion and the U.S. Army Military History Institute.

other shell explode, racing to the rear like they were possessed. If it is dangerous to march to the front under fire, it is more dangerous to retreat, especially when a retreat becomes a panic. I was on foot, my horse having been taken to the rear for safety, and after getting out of immediate danger of capture, I trudged along at a slow pace. An excited cavalry Major ordered me to halt and made a little rallying speech to me and those about me, but I saw the same fellow after that galloping to the rear with great speed. We were not pursued very closely, and it was ascertained that we had not lost as heavily as was supposed at first, and the morale of our army seemed to be restored.[60]

We retreated towards New Market, an old town in the Valley, inhabited largely by German Lutherans and their descendants. Dr. Casper C. Henkel, formerly Senior Surgeon of Steuart's Brigade lived there, and I made a pleasant visit to his house, sometime previously. We took up our line at Rood's [Rude's] Hill overlooking the beautiful farm of Mr. Meam [Meem].[61] It was a farm apparently a mile square, quite level, remarkable for the mountain country. He had hay enough and to spare for our army and wheat in abundance. We entrenched on the edge of this hill and spent a day or so in quietness. The cavalry finally engaged us to occupy our attention, when it was discovered that their infantry was coming in on both sides of the mountain to cut off our retreat. We could see the flash of their bayonets away off in the mountain pass. General Early formed his army into two hollow squares with the artillery in the center. One division would fight until the other located artillery in the rear, and then retreat and we came off the field in this way. A correspondent of the New York Herald described it as equal to a holiday drill, so cool and precise was every movement.[62] We reached the point where the Kiezel Town Road enters the Valley Turnpike just in time to retreat by this road. This we did without much loss. But the retreat by the Kiezel Town Road was exceedingly rough, made more so by the comparison with the beautiful smooth road of the turnpike we had left. We retreated until we had reached the neighborhood of Waynesville and Port Republic, the scene of Stonewall Jackson's Campaign of 1862. Here we were joined by R.H. Anderson's Division and after resting awhile we proceeded down the Valley again towards Winchester.

ARMY CORRESPONDENCE OF THE JOURNAL
[Date of Publishing: October 27, 1864]
BATTLE OF WINCHESTER NO. 3; BATTLE OF STRASBURG;
RETREAT FROM NEW MARKET

Bivouac near Port Republic
September 26th, 1864

The past week has been of eventful interest in the history of this campaign in the Valley, and the news would have been forwarded to your columns but for the late order issued by the A & I G,[63] requiring a month to transpire between the occurance of an event and the account thereof.

On the 17th Generals Rodes' and Gordon's divisions left camp at two o'clock, P.M., and proceeded towards Martinsburg upon another reconnaissance—Rodes' division was left near Bunker Hill, guarding the roads which lead from Harper's Ferry while General Gordon made a raid upon Martinsburg to secure cattle and forage reported there in large quantities. The entire affair was a failure, for there were no stores there, and except driving a few cavalry out of the town there was no engagement. We will close the curtain upon the scenes of dissipation which came to our ears; no soldiers can indulge their appetites to such an extent, and be effecient, and it is now time that officers high in authority should notice its demoralizing tendency.

On Sunday, the 18th, General Gordon returned, and joining Rodes at Bunker Hill, went into camp about six miles from Winchester. The same evening General Ramseur had an engagement with the enemy's cavalry on the Berryville Road, repulsing them.

On the morning of the 19th the firing was resumed about sunrise at Winchester and General Rodes' division was put in motion towards the latter place. Arriving there we found the rest of the army partially engaged, and the line of battle was hurriedly formed and advanced, Gen. Rodes leading in person. The account which states that "Rodes was in camp and being surprised was killed rallying his men" is without foundation. At the time of General Rodes' death his division was advancing in an orderly and effective charge.

Some account of our line must first be given, that you may obtain an idea of the battle. The left was composed of General Lomax's division of cavalry, made up of Imboden's, Johnson's and Vaughn's brigades. This line crossed the Martinsburg Turnpike, the extreme left resting upon Apple Pie Ridge. There was an interval between the right of the cavalry and the left of the infantry column, and then came Rodes' division, then Ramseur's division and Fitz Hugh Lee's division on the extreme right, the whole line forming an arc of a circle, covering the Berryville and Martinsburg Road, with the fortified heights (Apple Pie Ridge) in the rear.

When Rodes came upon the field Ramseur moved to the right, Gordon formed on the left of Rodes, and in this line the battle opened. With the usual dash of our troops the line went forward with a rush and drove the enemy pell-mell before them. Here it was that our noble Major General fell, pierced through the brain with a minnie ball.[64] Everything was now going well. We captured two hundred prisoners and about *nine* stands of colors, when a portion of the line advancing farther than the rest came under an enfilade fire upon both flanks, and was forced to retire to the common line. The repulse was quite a decisive one to the enemy, and the opposition in our front afterwards was but feeble. In fact, we learn from a reliable source, that the enemy's wagon train was ordered to the rear, under strong guard, preparatory to a retreat.

Averill's [Averell's] cavalry had been skirmishing for some time with Lomax's cavalry, and about two o'clock the fire gradually advanced and increased in rapidity until the smoke of muskets was in full view from the centre of the line, and giving way. And now a commotion commenced in the rear, but not a moment too soon, for Lomax's division came streaming out and in perfect rout. The whole field was alive with flying cavalrymen, wounded men and ambulances.

Just at this time Breckinridge's division rushed at double quick time from the centre, and formed on the left, with the hope of checking the tide of battle; but all efforts to check our retreating horsemen availed nothing; all entreaties and threats were used, but the disgraceful panic only increased. Seeing this successful onslaught on our left, columns of infantry came up to support the cavalry, and although we were partially successful in checking the retreat, our whole column was again driven back. The fight was one of desperation; the enemy was flushed with success, and struck boldly at the vital part and the day was lost.

The retreat of the whole army now commenced, and it was one of disorder. Our army is not used to retreating, and the fight in retreating was but feeble and disorganized. Fortunately, the sun went down upon our misfortune and saved us from further loss.

We have not one single word of commendation for our infantry, but for Fitz Hugh Lee's cavalry and the artillery. It may be said, however, in extenuation of the discreditable action of our army, that our cavalry had allowed the enemy to come in their rear before any confusion was caused, and even amist all the disorder which the breaking of such an important part of a line as the flank had caused, our infantry was cool, and formed an orderly line, but failed to arrest the panic. No considerable bodies of the Army of Northern Virginia have ever before been thrown into confusion. It is a remarkable fact that our army has never known *defeat*, and this can be ascribed to no other cause than the personal bravery of officers and men. But no one can say that our men are less brave now than ever, for individual acts of bravery were shown during the battle of the 19th inst. not less brilliant than any in the war. But the number of men panic stricken was sufficient to keep our lines in a constant state of disorder, vacillating from point to point, in spite of the efforts of our gallant Generals to keep them steady.

The Moorefield surprise had not yet been overcome by two of the brigades composing Lomax's division, and to their care was entrusted what is usually considered important—the flank.

After all, though, the broad shoulders of the commanding General will have to bear the blame, and the historian many years hence will no doubt form quite a different opinion from any entertained now of the affair. We can say they saved the balance of the army from a severe loss; the former our wagon train, the latter our combined infantry. Had all done their duty as unflinchingly as the artillery troops, our colors would not now be drooped in dishonor. Four pieces of artillery only were lost, and one of these was brought off the field, though unserviceable. In killed and wounded our loss is quite vague; many supposed lost have since come in. Gen. Fitz Hugh Lee was wounded, though not seriously. Our gallant Colonel, S.D. Thruston, was painfully, though not seriously wounded, quite early in the engagement. He was fortunate enough to escape capture. Capt. J. P. Cobb, senior officer of the 21 N.C. Troops, had his leg fractured so badly as to necessitate amputation; he was captured. Col. R. Bennett and Major Lambeth of the 14th N.C. are both prisoners—the latter wounded. Gen. Godwin of Hoke's old brigade, and formerly Colonel of the celebrated conscript regiment—the 57th—was killed.[65]

We retreated to our old position at Strasburg, arriving there on the morning of the 20th. The array of battle in this position was little changed from that at Winchester, Lomax's division on the left flank.

Properly supported, this position is one of great strength. This is the narrowest point in the Valley. The Massenutten rises up between the Blue Ridge and the Little North Mountains, dividing the Page Valley on the East from the Valley proper. in this narrow pass is Fisher's Hill, a commanding position, the right of it forming a natural defense, entirely unapproachable. Three main roads traverse the Valley in nearly parallel lines. The Turnpike, Middle and Back Roads; the latter is close under the North Mountain, and was generally conceived to be the accessible way to our left flank.

On Wednesday, the 21st, the enemy made a vigorous attempt to dislodge Peagram's sharpshooters from their position, charging them three times with their line of battle, but without success. Skirmishing was kept up upon different portions of the line during the entire day.

The next day about noon, heavy columns of the enemy's infantry filed through the woods upon Middle Road, and massed upon our right and left centre, preparatory to the onslaught.

All anxiety and apprehension was felt during the day, for fear the enemy would mass upon the left flank, and sweep our weak cavalry from their position. The enemy showed no disposition to strike us in front, but kept patiently maneuvering his lines. Late in the day a small party of the enemy's cavalry came rushing down from the mountains in a charge, in the rear of the left flank of our cavalry, and simultaneously an attack was made in front of the left. A few shots were exchanged, but our miserable cavalry broke and fled, leaving their artillery. Gen. Ramseur (commanding Rodes' old division) withdrew Cox's brigade from the centre, and moved it hastily to recover the disaster to the left, in an attempt to drive the enemy back. But the disaster was irretrievable; the enemy poured in upon the flanks and rear, and a confused effort to restore the line only resulted in further disaster.

But the demoralization of the preceding day manifested itself, and another confused retreat again commenced, and on this occasion our artillery, not so easily whipped, continued firing, until a large number of pieces fell into the hands of the enemy (from 12 to 14 pieces). A few of our troops acted well, but for the army its action was not at all creditable. The real cause of our disaster at Fisher's Hill was quite obvious. The troops present were insufficient to hold the line, and confidence was nowhere felt by the troops in their ability to hold the position. The morale of the command was very poor, and everything in prime condition for the enemy to gain just such a victory as a little ingenuity could devise. The enemy did but little fighting, and accomplished all by strategy.

Our army took up position in front of Mt. Jackson on the morning of the 23rd, and after a brisk day's skirmish we retired to Rose Hill, a commanding position between New Market and Mt. Jackson. This new position, although good, was easily flanked, and as was expected, it was perceived that the enemy was pushing our cavalry on the left, and we commenced to retire.

The maneuver by which means we retired in the face of the enemy, in open day, was well conducted and tested the courage of our troops more than a line-of-battle engagement. The retreating army formed three sides of a square artillery, ambulances and ordinance wagons in the centre. The enemy opened on us with his artillery from his position near New Market, and an artillery duel was kept up during the day, with an intermission when a change of position became necessary. The action of our artillery was credible; both officers and men showed skill and courage, and kept the enemy at bay. The casualties of the day were very small, and it was with a degree of satisfaction that we reflected upon our successful retirement. Lieut. M. Charles, Co. C, 1st N.C. was painfully wounded in the face.

On Sunday, the 27th, we went into bivouac near Port Republic, on the East side of the South branch of the Shenandoah, and at the mouth of Brown's Gap. This vicinity is one of exceeding interest. It was here that our lamented Jackson fought the battles of Cross Keys and Port Republic and commenced his successful career.[66]

South River flows between the Blue Ridge on the East and a small range of hills on the West, and drives many mills of various kinds. In this small range of hills is one of the great natural curiosities in Virginia—*Weir's Cave*.[67]

We commenced another cavalry chase on the 27th and drove the enemy from his position about Cave Hill, capturing some prisoners. Mr. Mohler, the gentleman who owns the cave, states that on the opening of our attack, that nearly all of the cavalry officers were in the cave—but we couldn't catch them in so plain a trap.

Porte Crayon in his "Virginia Illustrated" has described graphically Weir's Cave, and established his reputation as an artist.[68]

We visited the house of the owner of the cave to procure a guide to point out the objects of interest but the old gentleman told us the Yankees had destroyed his candles, and committed so many depredations he couldn't leave home. But we were not to be so easily foiled, and our small party, Lieut. B———e and Adjutant T.C.J. and your correspondent, without a guide started on our expedition.[69]

Arriving at the mouth of the cave we found several gentlemen just leaving, who had been piloted by an enterprising bare-footed "rebel", and he gladly undertook to be our guide. Our candles were so short that we only saw a few main points: *"Fat Man's Misery"*, *"Niagara Falls"*, *"Job's Turkey"*, *"Jacob's Ladder"*, etc. The scenery of this cave is said to be more chaste than that of Mammouth Cave, but far smaller. A large number of the army visited it, one party carrying the Brass Band of the 4th N.C. The music heard in an adjoining chamber was soft and melodious sounding and reverberating through these numerous subterranean halls like a grand organ in a Cathedral. No one will attempt a description of this beautiful natural wonder after Porte Crayon, as he exhausted the subject. Weir's Cave though now has a historic interest, having been visited by the armies of Jackson and Early as well as by Vandals.

The future has some bright rays of hope for us.

U.U.D.

We again found ourselves encamped about the 15th of Oct. on Fisher's Hill near Strausburg. The enemy thought we had retreated out of the Valley, and was about withdrawing some of his troops. Genl. Early had a council of war and an attack was determined upon. At night on the 18th of October we were put in line of march and the strictest silence was enjoined. Cups and canteens were thrown away and we commenced a march through the defiles of the mountain. It was so dark by the denseness of the foliage that we had to take the road in faith. It was nothing but bridle path, and at times it was so steep I had to dismount and lead my horse. Thus we trudged away all night, every now and then the Adj. Theo. C. James giving orders in a whisper to keep the strictest silence. It was a frosty night and while we were in motion we were comfortable. At daybreak we debauched upon the plain a few hundred yards from Cedar Creek. Thus we halted and waited until a few hundred cavalry filed past us. It was now cold and I tried to keep warm by walking up and down the length of our line. My fine black overcoat got me again into trouble. Col. Forsythe, of Ala.[70] whom I knew very well, halted me. He demanded who I was, but I thought it was a joke. But he showed me he was in earnest when I opened my overcoat and showed him my uniform and face. He said a spy was supposed to be in our lines, and I filled the description. We had some pleasant chat. It was about daybreak, 19 October. The sharp crack of rifles sounded in the direction the cavalry had gone and we were rushed forward and across Cedar Creek upon the left flank of the enemy. It was very exciting. Our cavalry had surprised their outposts, and we were nearly upon their flank when some wild shots were fired. Our Corps got safely over and our line drove the enemy pell mell. Maj. H.W. Miller, our Commissary Officer went over with us, although his duty was in the rear. We were riding along together when I stopped to dress the wounds of Sergt. Major Taylor who had been shot accidently. While in the midst of it, a large troop of the enemy's cavalry rode up behind us, and we were soon between two fires. While our line was busily engaged we heard firing on our left, and in a very short time we had driven the enemy's lines off the field and captured all of their artillery. It was a brilliant victory. The conception I have since heard was Genl. J.B. Gordon's. Simultaneous with our attack, another Corps attacked in the center, and all the cavalry on their right, the combination having been carried out with great promptness and precision.

The excitement of this attack was great even to old soldiers. Up to this point nothing had failed. The enemy had abandoned his artillery to the amount of about sixteen pieces (I write from memory) and left the field strewn with wagons, loaded with commissary and sutlers' stores, and the usual camp plunder, much of which had been carried off from houses in and around Middletown. Many of our men were very needy, lacking shoes and other needful things, and there were many plunderers in the camps of the enemy. I have seen quite as many other battlefields, but where every man was needed to prolong the line in our front, and prepare for the reaction which we might certainly look for. Our final line was made beyond the little village of Middletown, and we set down to wait and see what the enemy would do about it.[71]

I was sitting on my horse on the turnpike late that afternoon, the sun was about an hour, talking with some medical friends. A woman had harnessed a straggling horse to a wagon, and had been out on the battlefield bringing in plunder, some of which was furniture taken from her house. We were standing by looking on, for our work with the wounded was over, when one or two shells went crashing over our heads, and one struck her horse, breaking his front legs.

The tide of battle grew stronger and nearer, until the whole of our line had as much as it could do to keep position. Signs of panic were early evident, and I rode back to the hospital and gave the warning. The field in the rear of the line was an open one, offering very little shelter for a retreating line. When I reached the field hospital which was South of Cedar Creek, I could see our lines melting away, until the whole field was dotted with men, only here and there an organized line was stemming the tide. Major Ennett had just returned from his long imprisonment after his capture on the 10th May at Spottsylvania [Spotsylvania]. He was in poor health and I advised him not to take command in the confusion but to await developments. He had brought me from home a new pair of cavalry boots and two bottles of gin and some other small articles. I lightened my baggage by discarding my old boots and pulling on the new ones, and divided my gin with a friend, and hastened the preparation of striking hospital tents and sending the wounded to the rear. We had not completed the preparations when the shells were whistling over our heads, the enemy having advanced two or three miles from where they first began the afternoon attack. All was over with us and we hurried the wounded to the rear as fast as possible. Poor Sgt. Major Edwards who had been wounded early in the morning was trying to make his way to the rear, hobbling between two men. He dreaded being captured so I dismounted and put him on my horse. By this time we had to step up lively as the enemy's cavalry was pushing on like a torrent. Edwards was a happy man, but poor me. (I met Sgt. Major Edwards in May 1888, in Wilson. He was a man of about 40, stout, wealthy and prosperous.) I discovered too late that my new boots had not been rid of the tacks, and they were sharp and long. As I walked along briskly, I was gigged at every step, until I could hear the "goosh, goosh" of the blood in my boots. I tried the gin to help me along for I could not bear being taken prisoner, and it was only late at night that Ennett and I had some one else make a fire in the woods and went into camp. The night was cold and frosty and poor Ennett was attacked with rheumatism—the acute sort which attacks the joints—and when the remnant of the army was mustered the next day he could not take com-

General Stephen Dodson Ramseur took over Rode's division after General Rodes's death and was wounded and captured at the Battle of Cedar Creek on October 19, 1864. He subsequently died of his wounds the following day. U.S. Military Institute.

mand. Fortunately he had a most excellent officer in Captain William H. Thompson, of Sampson Co. and of the 1st Regt. He was exceptional for cool courage and devotion to duty and for the confidence he inspired among his men.

I have not been able to give from memory the numerous movements of our army in all of this active campaign by Genl. Early. I will relate a battle which occured on the 20th September.

We were strongly entrenched on Fisher's Hill. Here the Valley of Virginia narrows into a point about four miles wide, with the Massonutton Mt. on one side and the Little North Mt. on the West side. Our line was short but excellently located as far as the infantry was concerned, but on our extreme left under the Little North Mountain was posted our cavalry under Genl. Lomax. The enemy swept by them turning their flank, and then there began a stampede. The cavalry came in wild disorder through Little North Mountain, some on horses, some on limber chests, creating the wildest panic.[72] Our infantry though were sullen and determined. The Rev. Mr. Power of S.C., a brave and Godly man, seeing the conflict that was about to ensue, besought the men to rally but without effect.[73] Finally he with the assistance of others belonging to the hospital staff threw up a barrier of fence rails to keep them from running to the rear, and it was amusing to see these frightened fellows coming down this road full speed and finding it blocked, course around and then stop. Finally after a good many were trapped this way, they pulled down Mr. Power's barrier and retreated with the renewed stimulus of the firing from the front. The First and Third regiments now, not larger than a big company behaved very handsomely on this field under Capt. Thompson (now of Taylor's Bridge in Sampson Co., living July 31st 1888). As the enemy doubled up our flank, confusion and route ensued. Ramseur's Brigade now under General Cox, (now Judge Cox and member of Congress from the Raleigh District). . . .

> [Here the journal ends abruptly, half way through the third book, with no explanation. Evidently TFW just stopped writing temporarily after deciding that he was well enough to leave the sick bed and resume his practice of medicine after the long year of convalescence. He stopped writing in July of 1888 and never continued his memoir. Thomas Fanning Wood died four years later on August 22, 1892.
>
> The regiment returned to Petersburg and went into winter quarters at Swift Creek, about three miles north of the city. Here the regiment remained until the middle of March when it was ordered into the trenches in front of Petersburg. At this point, Major General Bryan Grimes commanded the division, General Cox commanded the brigade and Lieutenant-Colonel Parsley the regiment. They took part in an attack on the enemy lines on March 24, as part of Gordon's corps, opposite Hare's Hill. The division surprised and captured the enemy's pickets and entered the main lines. They occupied the enemy's works for some distance on either side of Hare's Hill and held them for about five hours, finally being driven back with heavy loss. After heavy fighting during the next few days, the army began a withdrawal from the lines around Petersburg on April 3rd and began a march towards Amelia Courthouse. The division was assigned as the rear guard and carried on a running fight with Federal cavalry the whole way. On the afternoon of the 6th, at Sailor's Creek, near Farmville, Virginia, a general engagement took place and the Confederates, overwhelmed by superior numbers, retreated across the bridge at Farmville. It was here that Lieutenant-Colonel William Parsley was killed by a minnie ball in the head. Major William T. Ennett assumed command of the 1st and 3rd North Carolina Regiments. The division continued towards Lynchburg on a parallel road to that of the enemy. They reached Appomattox Court House on Saturday evening, April 8, and bivouacked until the middle of the night when they were ordered to the front to open the road to Lynchburg, presently being occupied by the enemy in large force. At sunrise on Sunday morning, April 9, Grimes's division engaged a large body of Federal cavalry, supported by infantry, and drove them more than a mile, capturing a battery and a number of prisoners. While engaged in this pursuit they were ordered back to the valley to form a line of defense. As they were retiring, the enemy cavalry attacked, and General Cox calmly or-

dered his men to turn about to face the enemy. The last volley fired by the Army of Northern Virginia in the Civil War was fired by these North Carolina troops, the 3rd Regiment among that number. On leaving this valley they learned the Army of Northern Virginia had surrendered.[74]

The fragment of the 1st and 3rd Regiments was bivouacked with Cox's brigade, Grimes's division, Gordon's corps, and prepared the muster rolls for the final surrender. On the morning of April 12th they, along with Lieutenant Thomas Fanning Wood, M.D., stacked their arms, dispersed on foot, many ragged and without shoes, and made their way back to their homes throughout North Carolina. Dr. Wood traveled home to Wilmington accompanied by General William Cox and Captain James Metts.

The Honor Roll for the 3rd North Carolina is quite distinctive and tragic. Colonel Gaston Meares, killed in the Battle of Malvern Hill; Captain Thomas E. Armstrong, killed in the Battle of Chancellorsville; Captain John Van Bokkelen, wounded at Chancellorsville and died of intestinal fever shortly after; Lieutenants Tobias Garrison, Henry A. Potter, and Thomas Kelly, killed in the Battle of Gettysburg; Captain Edward H. Armstrong, Lieutenant Cicero H. Craige, and Sergeant-Major Robert C. McRee, killed in the Battle of Spotsylvania; Lieutenant Colonel William M. Parsley, killed in the Battle of Sailor's Creek, and a host of valiant non-commissioned officers and privates who gave their lives under the banner of the Confederacy.

Of the nine friends who had shared a mess with Dr. Wood from February of 1863, when he had joined the 3rd North Carolina, only James Metts was with him at the final surrender at Appomattox Court House. Metts had been wounded and captured at Gettysburg, July 2, 1863, exchanged on September 21, 1864, and finally paroled at Appomattox on April 9, 1865. John Van Bokkelen, Ned Armstrong, and Cicero Craige were dead. Dr. Joshua Walker had been transferred to hospital duty on March 30, 1863. William Barr was wounded at Chancellorsville on May 3, 1863, and his resignation was accepted on February 10, 1864. James Clarke was wounded at Payne's Farm on November 27, 1863, and resigned on March 17, 1864, with chronic rheumatism. George Patterson finished the war as a senior chaplain at Chimborazo Hospital in Richmond and after Appomattox moved to Wilmington for several years as minister of the Protestant Episcopal Church. He then moved to Memphis and began a career in the Calvary Episcopal Church. He also served for a time as chaplain of St. Mary's Episcopal School for Girls. He remained a close friend to TFW and officiated at both of his weddings and the funerals of his first wife and two boys. John Cowan was captured at Spotsylvania, May 10, 1864, and released at Fort Delaware on May 26, 1865.[75] Stephen Decatur Thruston was wounded four times, the last time was September 9, 1864 at Winchester, when he was shot through both hips, completely disabling him and ending his military career. He moved to Dallas in 1872 where he practiced medicine until his death.][76]

Notes

Abbreviations

BCF	Battle Cry of Freedom
BW	The Battle of the Wilderness, May 5–6, 1864
C1863	Chancellorsville 1863, The Souls of The Brave
CBA	Chancellorsville: The Battle and Its Aftermath
CCFR	Chronicles of the Cape Fear River
DG	Doctors in Gray
GG	Generals in Gray
HRBNC	Histories of the Several Regiments and Battalions from North Carolina in the Great War, 1861–1865
JERW	Jubal Early's Raid on Washington, 1864
LCFHSB	Lower Cape Fear Historical Society Bulletin
LL	Lee's Lieutenants
LLC Lee's	Last Campaign
MBW	Monocacy—The Battle that Saved Washington
MHCG	Medical Histories of Confederate Generals
MSHCW	Medical and Surgical History of the Civil War
NCMJ	North Carolina Medical Journal
NCT	North Carolina Troops, 1861–1865, A Roster
SRML	Some Recollections of My Life
TFW	Thomas Fanning Wood
TGR	To the Gates of Richmond
WC	The Wilmington Campaign
WFS	"The Woods–Father and Son"

Preface

1. TFW, *North Carolina Medical Journal* 52 no. 4 (Apr. 1991): 167–73.
2. He had established his office in the basement of his home at the corner of Second and Chestnut Streets in Wilmington, North Carolina, so it was natural for patients and associates to visit him there.
3. The first one hundred twenty pages of this journal which TFW called "Some recollections of my life written for my children during my confinement with aneurism beginning 25th April, 1886," involved his early childhood in Wilmington and his determination to become a physician.
4. Janet K. Seapker, "Wood Works, The Architectural Creations and Personal Histories of John Coffin and of Robert Barclay Wood," *Lower Cape Fear Historical Society Bulletin* 39, no. 1.
5. *Wilmington Herald*, Sept. 22, 1855.
6. In June of 1853, R. B. Wood established a partnership with his son-in-law N. B. Vincent to run the Carolina Hotel. The partnership lasted only one year, and in June 1854, Vincent and B. B. Brown took over the management of the hotel. The Wood brothers owned the hotel until 1857 when they sold it to John McRae. LCFHSB 39, no. 1.

7. This was a serious matter and was probably kept within the family. There is no mention in the community records of Richard's escape or the family's involvement. This is a personal recollection by TFW from Some Recollections of My Life, Thomas Fanning Wood Collection, William Madison Randall Library, Univ. of North Carolina at Wilmington.
8. *LCFHSB* 9, no 1.
9. Wood, SRML, vol. 1: 93–95.
10. James Sprunt, *Chronicles of the Cape Fear River* (Raleigh: Edwards & Broughton, 1916), 255.
11. TFW read his Bible. In the New Testament, Thomas, one of the disciples of Jesus, is also known as Didymus, which means "the twin." "Thomas" means "twin" in Aramaic and Didymus means "twin" in Greek. The New Testament Thomas is generally known as Doubting Thomas since he refused to believe the resurrection unless he verified it himself. Bible, King James Version. *The Messenger* was published by a Mrs. Bumpass, widow of a Methodist minister. TFW began writing for the newspaper because he became interested in the Reformation after reading D'Aubigne's *History of the Reformation*. TFW, SRML, vol. 1: 70.
12. Dr. James Fergus McRee, Jr. was also a prominent physician in North Carolina and was chairman of the committee which established the North Carolina Medical Society in 1849. *Medicine in North Carolina* 2: 354–55.
13. MSHCW, v–viii.
14. MSHCW claims that 700,000 men died from wounds and sickness. The National Library of Medicine—*Medicine of the Civil War* in their exhibit booklet of 1973—claims total deaths of 617,528.
15. MSHCW, iii–iv. H. H. Cunningham, *Doctors in Gray* (Cloucester: Peter Smith, 1970), 184–210.
16. Robert E. Denney, *Civil War Medicine: Care and Comfort of the Wounded* (New York: Sterling Publishing, 1995), 10.
17. Family records; New Hanover County census, 1870; St. James Church Historical Records.
18. Jane Zimmerman, "The Formative Years of the North Carolina Board of Health, 1877–1893," *The North Carolina Historical Review* 21, no. 1 (Jan. 1944): 3–6.
19. Autobiographical sketch of Thomas Fanning Wood, Manuscript Collection, William Madison Randall Library, Univ. of North Carolina at Wilmington.
20. Diane Cobb Cashman, *The Lonely Road* (Wilmington: Medical Society of New Hanover, Brunswick and Pender Counties, 1976), 38.
21. George Cooper, M.D., "The Woods—Father and Son," *Southern Medicine and Surgery* 90, no. 12 (Dec. 1928): 789.
22. WFS, Memoriam, 13–16.
23. WFS, 4–9.
24. Zimmerman, "The Formative Years of the North Carolina Board of Health," 3–5.
25. Edward Warren, M.D., *A Doctor's Experiences in Three Continents* (Cushings & Bailey Publishers, 1885), 309.
26. *Wilmington Star News* article taped to the inside of TFW's personal copy of the book. No date on the article.
27. *NCMJ*, vol. 52, no. 4: 171–72.
28. WFS, 8.

Chapter 1. Mr. Erambert's Drugstore

1. *LCFHSB*, vol. 9, no. 1: 5.
2. TFW, The Population Analyzed, Thomas Fanning Wood Collection, William Madison Randall Library, Univ. of North Carolina at Wilmington, 12–15.
3. *LCFHSB*, vol. 9, no. 1: 7.
4. *SRML*, 55–61.
5. *SRML*, 101–7.
6. Louis B. Erambert was the son of A. J. and Martha Erambert. He was 24 years old when TFW worked for him in the drug store. Erambert would die on September 27, 1862, of yellow fever. *Wilmington Weekly Journal*, Oct. 2, 1862.
7. Dried rhizome and roots of a yellow-flowered European gentian, G. lutea, sometimes used as a tonic. *American Heritage Dictionary*, Third Edition, 757.
8. *NCMJ* was first published in 1858 by Dr. Warren and was interrupted in 1861 by the outbreak of the war. TFW resumed publication in 1878. Dr. Warren later served as a professor at the Medical College of Virginia and during the war was appointed as medical inspector of the hospitals of northern Virginia. He served as a special representative of North Carolina's Governor, Zebulon Vance, in the surrender of Raleigh to General Sherman in the final days of the war. Years later he was awarded France's Order of the Legion of Honor and, in 1882, was appointed the commander of the Osmanieh by the Khedive of Egypt. Warren, 309, 335, 534, 537.
9. *Paroira's Materia Medica and Therapeutics*, 1851.
10. In addition to this published piece, he conducted a number of other experiments while at Erambert's, most as a result of reading articles in *The American Journal of Pharmacopoeia*. Though inexperienced, he conducted experiments for the preparation of propylamin and gelsemina (a chemical made from the powdered roots of yellow jasmine), as well as studies of bi-nitro-sulphide of iron. He also began to classify different medicinal herbs and plants, especially those in the Cape Fear region. This interest in botany would continue throughout the war and would become an important benefit in his professional life. Thomas Fanning Wood Medical Notes, 1861. North Carolina State Archives. PC1346.4.
11. The anterior wire splint was a suspensory apparatus invented by Dr. Nathan Ryno Smith, chair of surgery, Univ. of Maryland. It was used extensively by both Confederate and Union surgeons during the war for the treatment of fractures of the lower extremities. *DG*, 235.
12. On Saturday night, March 9, 1861, at 10:00 P.M., A. J. Costin was shot by Pinckney Shelly, just outside the drug store on Market Street. When Lewis Erambert tried to break up the growing fight, he was seriously wounded by Shelly, fracturing his thighbone. Shelly surrendered to authorities the next day. *The Daily Journal*, Mar. 11, 1861. There seemed to be confused and conflicting testimony, but the case was bound over for trial, and a bond was set at five hundred dollars for each shooting. *The Daily Journal*, Mar. 18, 1861.
13. South Carolina signed the Ordinance of Secession on December 20, 1860. Fort Sumter was fired upon by batteries at Fort Johnson on April 12, 1861. TFW, Wilmington in the Great Struggle from 1861 to 1865, Thomas Fanning Wood Collection, William Madison Randall Library, Univ. of North Carolina at Wilmington, 14–21.

14. In August of 1862, the town of Wilmington was vulnerable to yellow fever and other contagious diseases. The military occupation, the laxity of municipal control, the constant movement of troops and the non-enforcement of quarantine regulations opened the city to infection from blockade runners arriving daily from Nassau. From a biographical sketch of Dr. James H. Dickson by TFW, *NCMJ* (1874).
15. The older citizens of Wilmington were more devoted to the Union and reluctant to break the bonds, but after the total failure of the Peace Conference in Washington City in February of 1861, Representative George Davis gave his judgement that "the Union could only be preserved with dishonor to the South." CCFR, 271.
16. As the population divided and the Union sentiment established an unpopular stronghold with the forming of Cape Fear Minute Men, an organization called The Committee of Safety was formed to protect private property and ultimately to escort Union sympathizers out of town. TFW, The Committee of Safety—1861, Thomas Fanning Wood Collection, William Madison Randall Library, Univ. of North Carolina at Wilmington, 3–8.
17. Mary Ann Wilbur (1815–1888) and Agnes Fanning Wood (1837–1867). Agnes was married to Nathaniel B. Vincent, a partner with R. B. and J. C. Wood in the Carolina Hotel.

CHAPTER 2. JOINING THE RIFLE GUARDS

1. CCFR, 277.
2. Chris E. Fonvielle, *The Wilmington Campaign* (Campbell: Savas Publishing Co., 1997), 33.
3. Radcliffe was connected with the engineering department of the Cape Fear defenses when he was elected colonel of the 8th Regiment of Volunteers on July 18, 1861. He had been principal of a military school in Wilmington previous to the war and was an excellent drillmaster and disciplinarian. On the reorganization of the 8th into the 18th State Troops on April 24, 1862, he was not re-elected but became colonel of the 61st North Carolina Regiment. CCFR, 307.
4. Col. Oliver Pendleton Meares was made captain of the Wilmington Rifle Guards in 1861, and when the 8th Regiment was reorganized after twelve months, Meares assumed the rank of a lieutenant colonel. In August 1862 he became commissary of the 61st Regiment. After the war he became a judge. CCFR, 343.
5. George Tait was elected major of the 8th Regiment in July 1861, resigned his commission, and joined Company K of the 40th Regiment, stationed at a battery near Federal Point Lighthouse. In 1863 when the 40th was organized as the Third Artillery, he was appointed lieutenant colonel. In 1865, he resigned his commission to take over as colonel of the 69th North Carolina Regiment. CCFR, 307.
6. It was rumored that a U.S. revenue cutter, either the *Forward* or the *Harriet Lane*, was rushing troops to garrison Fort Caswell, much as Maj. Robert Anderson had done at Fort Sumter on December 26, 1860. WC, 33.
7. Volunteers led by John J. Hedrick forced the surrender of Ft. Johnson at Smithville from Ord. Sgt. James Reilly. Hedrick and a crowd of volunteers and citizens from Smithville rowed across the harbor and took possession of Fort Caswell from its caretaker, Sgt. Frederick Dardingkiller. WC, 33.
8. Craig's Wharf was located almost a mile north of the fort on the Cape Fear River side of the peninsula. WC, 35.
9. In the middle of September 1861, Companies F and I of the 18h Regiment were sent to Fort Fisher at the mouth of the Cape Fear River, and Company K was sent across

New Inlet channel to a battery on Zeke's Island. A few weeks later the other seven companies joined F and I and began to build the foundation for Fort Fisher. This fort was to be one of the last strongholds of the Confederacy. Walter Clark, *Histories of the Several Regiments and Battalions from North Carolina in the Great War, 1861–1865* (E. M. Uzzell, 1901), vol. 2: 17-19.
10. In 1861, Fort Fisher was a lonely and isolated place surrounded by huge sand bastions and plagued with mosquitoes, deer flies and sand gnats. It was five miles northeast of Smithville across the harbor and more than nineteen miles south of Wilmington. It was quite difficult to drill in the soft sand and the general conditions led to looser discipline from the officers. *WC*, 73-74.
11. It is quite probable that these young men were not yet accustomed to the strict discipline of the military life and tended to create juvenile criticisms of anyone in authority. This was a dangerous and foolish prank, but these sort of attitudes would disappear quickly as the young soldiers faced their first battles.
12. Both brothers, Robert Barclay and John Coffin Wood, had agreed to work for Major W. H. Whiting and help build Fort Fisher on Federal Point. *LCFHSB*, vol. 39, no. 1: 6.
13. Company K was sent back across the New Inlet channel to a battery on Zeke's Island where they remained until they rejoined the regiment on the way to Kinston, North Carolina, in March 1862. *HRBNC*, vol. 2: 17-19.
14. The Agostini family were some of the first truck farmers in the Wilmington area, and their farms were located on the Little Bridge Road near San Souci Plantation. *CCFR*, 169.
15. Dr. Moses John deRosset was assistant surgeon at Bellevue Hospital in New York and resigned his commission to come South and was commissioned assistant surgeon in the Confederate Army serving with Jackson in the Valley Campaign. Later, he served as one of the surgeons in charge of the hospital at Baptist College, Richmond. *CCFR*, 294.
16. Early in the war, many new soldiers had similar concerns as TFW about faith, church and morality. War inevitably dented the faith of many Civil War participants, especially in the early years. Religious unrest was spreading throughout the country. The major religious denominations were the first large organized groups in American society to face the issue of slavery. With secession, these churches became the first casualties of the war. Although several denominations, like the Episcopal Church, managed to hold together through much of the slavery crisis, secession tore most of churches apart. Fear, distrust, and confusion began to associate itself with the church on both sides of the conflict. New soldiers, leaving the restraints of home and loved ones, were vulnerable. Cast as soldiers in a novel environment, an environment that alternated between apathy and loneliness on one hand and excitement and danger on the other, these new soldiers found it easy to wander from the moral path. Once most of these men experienced the terror of battle, their need for home-learned Christian principles returned, and ardent crusades for Christ among soldiers on both sides occurred frequently during the latter part of the war. James I. Robertson, Jr., *Soldiers Blue and Gray* (Columbia: Univ. of South Carolina Press, 1988), 171-74.

CHAPTER 3. THE REGIMENT MOVES TO SOUTH CAROLINA

1. *HRBNC*, vol. 2: 18.
2. The American Hotel occupied a series of connected buildings at King Street and George Street.

3. The regiment was ordered to move to Pocataligo, midway between Charleston and Savannah to guard the lagoons on the coast below the Coosaw River. *HRBNC*, vol. 2: 18.
4. Coosawhatchie was a crossroads town on the Charleston & Savannah Railroad beside the Coosawhatchie River. It was approximately five miles west of Beaufort and five miles south of Pocataligo. *Civil War Atlas*, p. 91, plate 4.
5. Port Royal is located between the Broad River, which flows into Port Royal Sound, and the Coosaw River, which flows into St. Helena Sound.
6. The 18th was joined at Camp Stephens on the Huguenin Farm by Trenholm's battery and Colonel John C. Calhoun's regiment of cavalry, sometimes under the command of Brigadier General Robert E. Lee whose headquarters was two or three miles away. *HRBNC*, vol. 2: 18.
7. John Barry, born in New Hanover County, enlisted as a private in Company I, 8th Regiment, and on reorganization was elected captain of the company. He was wounded at Frayser's Farm, Virginia, in 1862 and was promoted to Major. After the fall of Col. Purdie in June 1863, he became colonel of the regiment. *CCFR*, 303.
8. William A. Wooster, private, Company I, 18th Regiment, was killed in the Seven Days Battles around Richmond. He was one of the brightest young men of Cape Fear and was commissioned lieutenant before he was killed. *CCFR*, 367.
9. Dr. James A. Miller was the surgeon of the 18th Regiment and went on to become surgeon of the brigade and then the division. He finally became district surgeon of the district of the Cape Fear. *CCFR*, 346.
10. Captain Robert Williams was the commander of the Rifle Guards but later resigned and was appointed purser of the blockade runner *Index*. He died of yellow fever while serving on the blockade runner. *CCFR*, 366.
11. Matthew Laspeyre was born in New Hanover County, North Carolina, and was by occupation a machinist prior to enlisting at the age of twenty-one. He was elected first lieutenant on July 20, 1861. He was defeated for reelection when the regiment was reorganized on April 24, 1862, possibly due to his command attitude described by TFW. Louis Manarin, *North Carolina Troops, 1861–1865, A Roster* (Raleigh: North Carolina Division of Archives & History, 1989), vol. 6: 401.
12. Dr. William James Harriss Bellamy was born in Wilmington and enlisted as a private in Company I, 18th Regiment on August 20, 1861. He was wounded at Gaines Mill, Virginia, on June 27, 1862 and discharged in 1863. He raised a company of volunteers from Brunswick County. He continued his study of medicine and eventually received his medical degree from the University of New York in 1869. Diane Cobb Cashman, *The History of the Bellamy Mansion* (research report, Jan. 1990), 78.
13. As a child TFW's family visited a cousin, Thomas Coffin, at his plantation near Beaufort, South Carolina, while Robert Barclay Wood helped build the first lighthouse on Hunting Island. Mr. Fripp's plantation on Morgan Island was just west of Coffin's, across the Morgan River from St. Helenaville and just to the east of Coosaw Island. SRML, 83–105.

CHAPTER 4. VIRGINIA AND THE SEVEN DAYS BATTLES

1. Brigadier Gen. Robert Ransom's brigade was part of Maj. Gen. Benjamin Huger's division in Maj. General John B. Magruder's command and consisted of the 24th North Carolina, the 25th North Carolina, the 26th North Carolina, the 31st North Carolina, and the 48th North Carolina. The 49th North Carolina, Branch's bri-

Notes to pages 24–26   197

gade, was part of Maj. Gen. A. P. Hill's Light Division in Maj. Gen. Thomas J. Jackson's corps. Stephen Sears, *To The Gates of Richmond* (New York: Ticknor & Fields, 1992), 385-91.
2. *TGR*, 5–11.
3. General Ambrose E. Burnside and a force of eight thousand Federals landed at Slocum's Creek to begin their attempt to capture the town of New Bern, North Carolina. The Confederate defenders under Maj. Gen. L. O'B. Branch, unable to hold the town, fell back to Kinston, North Carolina. *NCT*, vol. 6: 295.
4. The exact strength of Branch's command at this time is unclear, but the brigade was one of the largest in the army. One of the regiments, as of May 27, numbered 890 muskets. O.R., ser. 1, vol. 11, pt. I, p. 743.
5. William J. Hardee's published manual, *Rifle and Infantry Tactics*, was so highly thought of that both Union and Confederate forces used it during the war. Both sides also relied heavily on Winfield Scott's three-volume *Infantry Tactics*. Robertson, 48.
6. In the Spring of 1861, both Northerners and Southerners believed that one or two battles fought somewhere in the border states of Virginia or Kentucky would settle the whole issue. For that reason the enlistment periods were set for three months in the North and one year in the South. At this point in the war, a good many soldiers worried that peace would come before they got their first taste of battle. Robertson, 4.
7. Though brief, this was an exciting opportunity for TFW. He had the opportunity to learn more about medical practice, continue his experiments from Erambert's and study natural remedies in the landscape. TFW Notes. North Carolina. State Archives. PC1346.4
8. Robert H. Cowan, a native of Wilmington, was first chosen lieutenant colonel of the 3rd Regiment but was elected colonel of the 18th in the spring of 1882. He was greatly respected by all of the men in the regiment and was successful in bringing the unit up to top efficiency. He was wounded severely in the Seven Days Battles around Richmond and was disabled from service. He resigned in November 1862. *CCFR*, 299–300.
9. Thomas James Purdie was born in Bladen County where he resided as a farmer prior to enlisting at the age of thirty. He was elected first lieutenant on April 26, 1861, and was elected captain on July 26, 1861. On March 24, 1862, he was elected lieutenant colonel of the 18th North Carolina and later served as colonel of the regiment. *NCT*, vol. 6: 412.
10. Forney George had been serving as captain of Company C and was promoted to major on March 6, 1862, and transferred to the Field and Staff. He was wounded at Cedar Mountain, Virginia, on August 9, 1862. He returned to duty and was promoted to lieutenant colonel. He was wounded again at Chancellorsville, Virginia, on May 3, 1863, and resigned from the army. *NCT*, vol. 6: 306.
11. General McClellan was moving his Third and Fourth Corps upstream along the southern bank of the Chickahominy River in an effort to uncover more crossing sites and build more bridges so that he could shift most of his army across the river and move his siege guns along the rail road to the very gates of Richmond. He received word that the Confederates were advancing a force of seventeen thousand men towards Hanover Court House. He believed this report even though his cavalry reduced that number to six thousand and sent General Fitz John Porter with his troops toward Hanover Court House. *TGR*, 113–14.
12. Captain Willie J. Sikes was born in Bladen County and was by occupation a farmer

prior to enlisting at the age of 33. He was elected second lieutenant on May 3, 1861, and to captain on April 24, 1862. He was killed at Hanover Court House on April 24, 1862. *NCT*, vol. 6: 322.

13. General Branch had his six North Carolina regiments—approximately four thousand men—four miles southwest of Hanover Court House, at Peake's Crossing. He was charged with guarding the Virginia Central Railroad, Richmond's main link with the Shenandoah Valley. General Branch's background was congressional politics rather than the military, and his only previous command was the failed defense of New Bern. McClellan grew apprehensive and assigned his favorite general, Fitz John Porter to clear his flank of possible threat by the Confederates. Porter expected to find the main Confederate force at Hanover Court House and marched past Branch's troops at Peake's Crossing. General Branch misjudged the Union numbers and gave battle when the wiser course would have been to retreat. He threw all five regiments against the Yankee rear guard with the Eighteenth in the lead. The fight became a fierce fire fight between the two forces, and soon Porter's main force arrived and drove the Confederates back in defeat. The count of Confederate dead and wounded is incomplete, but the numbers probably totaled nearly three hundred. Branch lost 731 men captured. *TGR*, 114–17.

14. Brigadier General James Ewell Brown (Jeb) Stuart with twelve hundred cavalry troops conducted a secret reconnaissance mission that would take him on a complete circuit of McClellan's army. It was a journey that would become one of the lasting legends of the Confederacy. *TGR*, 168–73.

15. The 28th North Carolina was ordered to hold the crossing at Taliaferro's Mill on the road to Mechanicsville. General Porter moved on this crossing and the 18th and 37th North Carolina Regiments were sent to reinforce the 28th. The 18th made a direct attack on Porter's front line and drove it back until repeated Federal volleys took their toll. The 18th lost heavily in this action with some companies losing as much as fifty per cent in killed and wounded. This engagement earned the regiment the title "The Bloody 18th." *HRBNC*, vol. 2: 20.

16. Wood contracted a severe case of Chickahominy fever which was probably a strain of malaria, typhoid, or typhus. Numerous fevers cut through the green troops on both sides during their stay in the swamps and bogs along the Chickahominy River in 1862. Ten Union generals, including General McClellan himself, became seriously ill of disease during this campaign. In the Confederate Army, at least six generals were incapacitated by illness. *TGR*, 163–64.

17. Lt. Joseph P. Bridger was born in Hertford County and was by occupation a bookkeeper prior to enlisting at the age of twenty-one. He was mustered in as a private and was appointed second lieutenant on April 24, 1862. He was promoted to first lieutenant on June 30, 1862, and was wounded at Frayser's Farm, Virginia, on the same day. He was convalescent through August 1863 and was then promoted to assistant quartermaster (captain) and assigned to post duty. *NCT*, vol. 6: 400.

18. Early in the war, the time required for soldiers to recover from illness or injury was not as tightly monitored as it was later when shortages of trained men began to effect the tactical strength of the army. By 1863, TFW would not be allowed to accompany Lt. Bridger to the Richmond hospital but would have been sent back to his regiment after a reasonable period of convalescence. *DG*, 92–98.

Chapter 5. Richmond

1. *DG*, 37–39.
2. Dr. Samuel Preston Moore was an efficient and energetic Surgeon General and made an outstanding contribution to the improvement of medicine in the Confederate army. He insisted that medical examining boards use the highest standards in interviewing prospective surgeons and organized a network of field, divisional and general hospitals as well as pharmaceutical laboratories. Dr. Otis Manson, surgeon-in-charge of Hospital No. 24, had named the hospital after Dr. Moore, but the Surgeon General would have preferred a larger hospital to bear his name—probably Winder Hospital. Below Moore Hospital was Rocketts, a busy wartime landing, loading troops and supplies for locations on the lower James River. Prisoner-of-war vessels put in here. *Medical and Surgical History of the Civil War* (Wilmington: Broadfoot Publishing, 1990), vol. 1: vii.
3. Dr. Otis Frederick Manson was born in Richmond, Virginia, in 1822 and graduated in medicine from Hampden-Sydney College in Richmond. He moved to North Carolina to practice and became involved in research to perfect the treatment of malarial diseases. He was one of the early members of the fledgling North Carolina Medical Society and presented a number of noted papers on malarial pneumonia and remittent fever. In 1859 Dr. Manson was chosen by the North Carolina Medical Society as a member of the first Board of Medical Examiners. Governor Zebulon B. Vance selected him to head up the new Moore Hospital in Richmond in July 1862. Dr. Manson had a great influence on TFW and was the catalyst for Wood's life-long interest in viral diseases. *NCMJ*, 21, no. 3, 150–62.
4. Dr. William George Thomas was a distinguished surgeon from Tarboro and Wilmington and was charter member of the North Carolina Medical Society, 1849, as well as its first secretary. He was a general practitioner and obstetrician pioneering in surgery of vesico-vaginal fistula, using wire sutures and duck-bill speculum. *Medicine in North Carolina*, 672.
5. Manson obviously recognized Wood's talent and passion for the study of medicine, and there was an acute shortage of trained physicians at that time. A distinct relationship had been developed between the Confederate Medical Department and the Medical College of Virginia. By order of the surgeon general, a certain number of carefully chosen young gentlemen were annually appointed hospital stewards with the privilege of attending the lectures at the Richmond Medical College. On graduation, letters of invitation were issued for examination for appointment as assistant surgeons. *DG*, 36.
6. Hospital stewards were authorized by Congress in May 1861 and held the rank of sergeant. Appointees were to be skilled in pharmacy and to possess such qualities as honesty, reliability, intelligence and temperance. The steward was responsible for the cleanliness of the wards and kitchens, patients, and all articles in use. *DG*, 75–76.
7. TFW's full case book has not been found, but recently a small notebook was found, in the North Carolina State Archives, containing descriptions of six cases that he handled at Moore Hospital after he was commissioned assistant surgeon, with dates and treatments. TFW Medical Notes. North Carolina State Archives. PC1346.4.
8. Dr. Edward Warren was Surgeon General of the State of North Carolina. *DG*, 250.
9. *Traité d'anatomie pathologique*, Lebert's French work on pathology, *NCMJ*, 21, no. 3, 159.
10. Dr. Manson's views of the therapeutics of quinine were soon known in Richmond

and were met with much opposition. He claimed that quinine could be a significant factor in the cure or recovery of pneumonia. In 1882 he published a small volume entitled "A *Treatise on the Physiological and Therapeutic Action of the Sulphate of Quinine.*" This work and subsequent experiments received broad support throughout the medical community. *NCMJ,* 21, no. 3, 160–61.
11. Dr. Manson's work in the treatment of smallpox had a significant influence on TFW and was a motivating factor in his development of the first smallpox hospital for free blacks in Wilmington after the war.
12. No information seems to be available as to her reason for leaving the city but it could, as TFW notes, have something to do with her brother, General John Gibbon, being commander, Fourth Brigade, First Division, Third U.S. Army Corps.
13. Captain Eugene Grissom was commander of Company D, 30th North Carolina Regiment and received a brevet promotion (increase in rank without an increase in pay) to major by Governor Vance after the Seven Days Battles. *NCT,* vol. 10: 495.
14. Professor Alexander Dimitry offered friendship and support to TFW during his time at Moore Hospital. Hugo's *Les Misérables* was quite popular throughout the South, and the Southern people identified with the plight of the common man in the French Revolution. During the early years of the Civil War, most Southerners referred to the Army of Northern Virginia as "Lee's Miserables." There were several translations done in Richmond during those years. *Richmond Historical Society.*
15. In 1862, because of the increasing intensity of the war and the desperate need for surgeons in the field, the Medical College of Virginia shortened its sessions and graduated two classes in one year rather than one. *DG,* 36.
16. Esculapius is the Greek god of medicine.
17. Dr. James Brown McCaw was an able and efficient medical man. He was commandant and medical head of Chimborazo Hospital while on the faculty of the Medical College of Virginia. He later served as the editor of the *Confederate States Medical and Surgical Journal* in 1864 and 1865. He headed up a number of medical committees and boards during and after the war and was committed to the treatment and prevention of contagious diseases throughout his entire career. *DG,* 29–63.
18. TFW's sister Agnes Fanning Wood, twenty-six years old. She was married to Nathaniel B. Vincent in 1852.
19. TFW's sister Mary Frances Wood, twenty. In 1866, Mary Frances married Robert Houston, a second lieutenant in Company D of the Third North Carolina Regiment.
20. Edward J. Moore, sergeant, previously served in Company I of the 18th North Carolina and was transferred to Company H with the rank of private. He was promoted to corporal on October 1, 1862. Wounded at Fredericksburg on December 13, 1862, he was promoted to sergeant on January 1, 1863. He was reported absent wounded on light duty through February 1865. *NCT,* vol. 6: 386.
21. Richmond E. Lloyd was born in Bladen County and was a student prior to enlisting in the 18th North Carolina at age nineteen. He mustered in as a private and was promoted to corporal in October 1862. He was wounded at Fredericksburg on December 13, 1862. He was promoted to sergeant in August 1863 while absent wounded and discharged on February 1, 1864, because of disability. *NCT,* vol. 6: 385.
22. Captain Robert McRae, previously served as captain of Company C of the 7th North Carolina and appointed major on January 6, 1863, and transferred to Field & Staff.

He resigned on February 24, 1863, because of gunshot wound of the neck received at Ox Hill, Virginia, on September 1, 1862. He died on December 28, 1864. *NCT*, vol. 4: 405.
23. Hugh Walker Gardner was appointed surgeon on July 11, 1862, and served on the staff of the 18th North Carolina Regiment. He was reportedly transferred to the 33rd North Carolina Regiment in the summer of 1862. *NCT*, vol. 6: 307.
24. The worst of the diseases in the army at that time was known as the Chickahominy fever, later to be called the James River fever, and involved malaria, typhoid, or typhus or other of the numerous fevers associated with the swampy battlefields of the Virginia peninsula. *TGR*, 163.
25. Dr. M. John deRossett was from Wilmington and had been an assistant surgeon at Bellevue Hospital in New York. He resigned his commission and came south and served with Stonewall Jackson in the Valley Campaign. He was transferred to Richmond and later served as one of the surgeons in charge of the hospital at Baptist College, Richmond. *CCFR*, 294.
26. TFW, Medical Notes, 1861. North Carolina State Archives. PC1346.4.
27. The Confederate Army medical examining boards were authorized by the Surgeon General and the Secretary of War. These boards were thorough, complete and eminently practical considering the medical knowledge and standards of the day. Each applicant was required to answer a number of written questions within a specific time frame and under the supervision of the secretary of the board. This being done, he was submitted to an oral examination to the satisfaction of the assembled board. It was an extremely challenging review and a good number of practicing physicians failed to pass the examination. Deering J. Roberts, M.D., *Confederate Medical Department*, URL: www.civilwarhome.com/confederatemedical.htm.
28. The American Hotel was located at the corner of Eleventh and Main Streets.

CHAPTER 6. THE NEW ASSISTANT SURGEON

1. *MSHCW*, vol. 1: iv.
2. The epidemic was officially declared over in December of 1862. During that time fifteen hundred citizens of Wilmington caught the fever and 654 died. There was confusion in the cemetery death records and not all Negro deaths were recorded, making it probable that the death toll was higher. TFW's old employer, Lewis Erambert died in this epidemic. Cobb, *The Lonely Road*, 31.
3. The states of Maryland, Kentucky, and Missouri contained large and resolute secessionist minorities. A slight twist in events, and passions might have enabled this faction to prevail, adding 45 percent to the white population and military manpower and 80 percent to the manufacturing capacity of the Confederacy. Control of Maryland was crucial, for the state enclosed Washington on three sides and its allegiance could determine the capitol's fate in the early days of the war. James M. McPherson, *Battle Cry of Freedom* (New York: Macmillan, 1994), 284–90.
4. The worst epidemic of small pox hit the Army of Northern Virginia following the Antietam Campaign, and the infection's source has never been fully determined. Although it had been more than sixty years since the English physician Edward Jenner demonstrated that small pox could be prevented by vaccination, most individuals in America, especially in the army, had not been vaccinated. The use of vaccine crusts or scabs, especially those taken from the arms of children, was the most popular treatment

in the army accompanied by at least a fifteen day quarantine in special receiving hospitals. Some attempt was made by Confederate surgeon Hunter Holmes McGuire to obtain bovine virus for vaccination, but most physicians were suspicious of this method. They believed the cowpox virus "may develop in the persons to whom it is immediately applied, a form of the disease in itself infectious." *DG*, 195–99.

5. Howard's Grove hospital in Richmond was originally designated to handle wounded soldiers from Georgia, South Carolina, Florida, and Alabama, but in 1862 the small pox epidemic necessitated the assignment of quarantined patients to specific hospitals. Howard's Grove was designated a small pox hospital. *DG*, 53–85.

6. The formation of the characteristic scab or crust at the site of the vaccination, commonly called "eruption." Russell L. Cecil, A *Textbook of Medicine* (London: W. B. Saunders Co., 1942), 45–62.

7. Rocketts, located at the eastern end of the city below Chimborazo Hospital, was a busy wartime landing, loading troops and supplies for locations on the lower James River. The area was mostly low income, occupied by dock workers, general laborers and transients. The incidents of disease and illness in this area were high. *MSHCW*, vol. 1: vii.

8. This was Early's campaign on Washington, June 12–18, 1864.

9. Brigadier General William R. Cox, Rodes's division, formally General Stephen D. Ramseur's brigade.

10. Richmond, at the time, was crowded with soldiers on leave, convalescents, traveling merchants, seamen, and questionable characters of all sorts. Rowdiness, drunkenness, and crime were widespread. Anticipating the need for drastic action, the Confederate Congress passed a bill in secret session authorizing martial law in Richmond. It included suspension of the writ of habeas corpus. Passports were required for persons entering or leaving the city. Virginius Dabney, *Richmond: The Story of a City* (Charlottesville: Univ. Press of Virginia, 1990), 170–71.

11. James A. Seddon was secretary of war for the Confederacy from November 21, 1862, until February 4, 1865. *TGR*, 200.

12. The Spottswood Hotel was located at the corner of Main and Eighth Streets. It was the social and political center of Confederate Richmond. Jefferson Davis, his cabinet members, and their families stayed there after their arrival in 1861 until permanent homes could be found. Richard M. Lee, *General Lee's City* (McLean: EPM Publications, 1987), 148.

13. These were really two separate hotels. Both were located at Franklin and Fourteenth Streets. The Ballard House on the northeast corner and the Exchange Hotel on the southeast corner were both owned by John B. Ballard. An upstairs passage over Franklin Street connected the two hotels. Lee, 140.

14. This soldier's home was established for North Carolina soldiers under authorization of Governor Vance. The need was so great that Dr. Manson and Dr. Murphy eventually opened it to soldiers from other states. Dr. Murphy had served under Dr Manson as ward master at Moore Hospital, graduating from the Medical College, and was appointed in early 1863 to supervise the North Carolina Soldier's Home. The home won admiration for both Dr. Manson and Dr. Murphy for their "economy of management, the satisfactory way in which food was prepared for hungry travellers going to and from the battlefields." Dr. Murphy later became the founder of the Rugby Academy in Wilmington, Delaware. *NCMJ* 21, no.3, 160.

15. Both General Lee and President Davis occasionally attended Broad Street Methodist Church which was located at Broad and Tenth Street. Lee, 77.
16. The Association of Army and Navy Surgeons of the Confederate States was created by Surgeon General Moore in the summer of 1863 to stimulate needed discussion and publication on medical subjects. Most of the medical societies and professional journals had been shut down because of the war. Dr. Moore was the association's first president. *DG*, 29.
17. Suppuration is the formation or discharge of pus.
18. Dr. Lafayette Guild was an industrious and dedicated physician. He did not hesitate to challenge authority if it meant better conditions and comfort for sick and wounded soldiers. He criticized the army's policy for granting furloughs and discharges since a large number of soldiers became permanently disabled for field service due to the neglect of their wounds after being sent home too soon. He pushed for a change in regulations that would allow two assistant surgeons for each regiment rather than only one. He worked diligently to reorganize the ambulance system in the army. He worked with Northern surgeons, after the Battle of Malvern Hill, to help concentrate their efforts where surgical aid could be more efficient. He was an untiring inspiration to Confederate surgeons on the field and in hospitals. After the war Dr. Guild fought yellow fever as quarantine inspector for the port of Mobile until his premature death in 1870. *DG*, 93–272.
19. Hamilton's Crossing is about four miles south of Fredericksburg near the crossing over the Massaponax River. The time that TFW was reporting to army headquarters was shortly after the Battle of Fredericksburg.
20. Dr. Hunter Holmes McGuire was medical director of Stonewall Jackson's command. Both the 3rd North Carolina and the 18th North Carolina were Wilmington regiments and part of Jackson's command. The 3rd belonged to D. H. Hill's division and the 18th was in A. P. Hill's division. *TGR*, 386–87.
21. The Marye home is located on the heights immediately west of Fredericksburg and north of Hazel Run, known as "Marye's Heights." The heights played a major part in the Confederate defensive operation during the Battle of Fredericksburg.
22. The Alsop house was located about three and one quarter miles northwest of the Marye home. This is quite a walk in the snow, and it is quite possible that he got a ride on an army wagon. *Civil War Atlas*, plate 41.
23. Either Henry C. Wood or James H. Wood, both captains in Company D, 37th Virginia Regiment and promoted to major. Neither was a relation of TFW. Janet B. Hewett, *Roster of Confederate Soldiers, 1861–1865* (Wilmington: Broadfoot Publishing Co., 1997), vol. 16: 454–55.
24. Guiney's Station is approximately twelve miles south of Fredericksburg on the Richmond, Fredericksburg, and Potomac Railroad. It is assumed that TFW traveled to Guiney's Station by rail. *Civil War Atlas*, plate 45.
25. The home of Richard Corbin was a spacious house near Moss Neck, between Fredericksburg and Port Royal. Jackson had originally intended to remain overnight but the family encouraged him to stay and he did, for three months. The Corbin family entertained Generals Lee, Stuart, Jackson and members of their staffs at Christmas. Ernest B. Furguson, *Chancellorsville 1863, The Souls of The Brave* (New York: Knopf, 1992), 83.
26. Joshua C. Walker was from New Hanover County in North Carolina and had been

appointed second assistant surgeon on May 16, 1861. The rank of second assistant surgeon was dropped on August 20, 1861, and he was appointed assistant surgeon as of September 2, 1861. *NCT*, vol. 3: 488.
27. At this time he was commander of the district of Cape Fear.
28. Located on the west bank of the Rappahannock, seven miles north of Port Royal.
29. Captain Edward H. Rhodes was from Onslow County and was the commander of Company G, 3rd North Carolina Regiment. He was thirty years old when he was killed. He was shot through the knee and heart at Sharpsburg and died on September 17, 1862. *NCT*, vol. 3: 554.
30. New assistant surgeons were not well thought of by most men in the army. They were perceived to be under-trained and inexperienced, which was mostly the case. TFW's new uniform with his two rows of gold braid on the coat sleeves and bright stars on the collar of his tunic probably added to the awkward appearance of this new physician on his horse with no tail. *Confederate Medical Department*, 3.
31. Prior to this, the 3rd North Carolina Regiment was part of Major D. H. Hill's division but was now changed to Jackson's old division, commanded by Major General Isaac Ridgeway Trimble. Trimble was recovering from a painful wound received at Groveton, and it was questionable whether he would be fit enough to command a division. Brig. Gen. W. B. Taliaferro, as senior brigadier in Jackson's old division, felt that he should have received a divisional command. When he did not get it, he decided to seek a transfer. To succeed Taliaferro, Jackson appointed Brigadier General Raleigh E. Colston. The 1st and 3rd North Carolina, along with the 10th, 23rd, and 27th Virginia Regiments, formed this new brigade. Douglas Southall Freeman, *Lee's Lieutenants, A Study in Command* (New York: Charles Scribner's Sons, 1944), vol. 3: 414–505.
32. A letter appeared in the *Wilmington Daily Journal* on April 24, 1863, signed by a member of the 3rd North Carolina Regiment calling himself ZETA. "Since I last wrote you there has been a few appointments, ... Dr. Wood has been assigned to this regiment, to fill the vacancy occasioned by the transfer of Dr. Walker. We all regretted very much to lose Dr. Walker, but in as much as he did leave, we are proud that one so able and kind as Dr. Wood takes his place."
33. Dr. James Fergus McRee was a physician from New Hanover County with whom TFW studied as a young student in Wilmington. He was appointed an army surgeon on May 16, 1861. He was reassigned to a surgical position in Salisbury, North Carolina in May 1863. He later served as surgeon to the 28th North Carolina Regiment. *NCT*, vol. 3: 488.
34. TFW's sisters, Agnes Fanning Wood, twenty-six years old, and Mary Frances Wood, twenty.
35. Joseph L. Jacobs was born in New Hanover County and enlisted as a private in the 18th North Carolina at the age of nineteen. He was appointed second lieutenant on December 11, 1862. He was wounded at Chancellorsville on May 3, 1863. He was reported absent wounded until he was dropped from the rolls of the company on April 26, 1864. *NCT*, 6, 401.
36. George Williams enlisted in New Hanover County on January 15, 1862, and was appointed hospital steward and assigned to the 3rd North Carolina Regiment. He died at a hospital in Charlottesville, Virginia, on September 23, 1864 of "diarrhoea acute." *NCT*, vol. 3: 489.
37. Medical officers in the field held surgeon's call or sick call, early every morning,

usually 15 minutes or so after reveille. The ailing of each company were marched to the hospital by a noncommissioned officer, probably the hospital steward, and the assistant surgeon examined each man. Diagnosis was rapidly arrived at, usually by intuition, and treatment was made with drugs that happened to be in the knapsack or with natural remedies. *DG*, 111.
38. Stephen D. Thruston was transferred from Company B of the 3rd North Carolina to major on July 1, 1862. He was promoted to lieutenant colonel on March 26, 1863, and took command of the 3rd North Carolina Regiment. He was wounded at Chancellorsville and promoted to colonel on October 3, 1863. *NCT*, vol. 3: 487.
39. *Ile*, or, rather, oil.
40. A vesicle is a fluid-filled blister formed in or beneath the skin.
41. An acute viral infection characterized by inflammation of the sensory ganglia of certain spinal or cranial nerves and the eruption of vesicles along the affected nerve path. *American Heritage Dictionary*, 1665.
42. Edward George Earle Lytton (Bulwer-Lytton) was an English novelist and dramatist during the mid-1800s. He served as a member of Parliament and was colonial secretary from 1858 to 1859. Among his most popular books were *The Last Days of Pompeii* (1843), *Eugene Aram* (1832), and *The Last of the Barons* (1843). He wrote *A Strange Story* in 1862. *Benét's Reader's Encyclopedia*, 139.
43. A card game similar to bridge, played with a full deck by two teams of two players. The last card dealt indicated trump, tricks of four cards are played, and a point is scored for every trick over six won by each team.
44. Dolman, a woman's garment having cape-like arm pieces, popular in the 1880s. *American Heritage Dictionary*, 549.
45. George Patterson resided in Washington County as a minister of the Protestant Episcopal Church. Previous to being appointed chaplain to the 3rd North Carolina, he served as chaplain to the 11th North Carolina Regiment. He joined the 3rd North Carolina on February 11, 1863. *NCT*, vol. 3: 489.
46. Smithville is across the Cape Fear River from Fort Fisher.
47. Steven Decatur Thruston was born in Virginia on November 28, 1833, and was only ten when his father died. He attended the University of Virginia and studied medicine at the University of Pennsylvania. He settled in Wilmington to practice medicine and married there. He was married twice and had two children from his first marriage, both of whom died before him. He was a member of the Wilmington Light Infantry, who were the first to respond to the Governor's call for troops. He was appointed major to rank from July 1, 1862, and was wounded in the chest at Sharpsburg on September 17, 1862, but remained on duty. He was promoted to lieutenant colonel on March 26, 1863, three months after the Battle of Fredericksburg. *The Confederate Veteran*, 14 (1907): 40. TFW spells his name "Thurston" in his memoirs, but both *NCT* and *HRBNC* spell the name "Thruston." To prevent confusion, I have corrected the spelling in this book.
48. J. Pembroke Jones, a prominent officer in the United States Navy, resigned his commission and joined the Confederate Navy. He was first lieutenant commanding the iron-clad sloop-of-war *Raleigh*, which attacked and broke the Cape Fear blockade. He served with distinction in several departments of the Confederate Navy and after the war was employed by the Argentine Republic developing military defenses. *CCFR*, 326–27.
49. Gaston Meares, when quite a young man, moved to the west from Wilmington and

engaged in the Mexican War attaining the rank of colonel. Upon the secession of North Carolina, he reported to the governor for duty and was immediately commissioned a colonel and given the 3rd North Carolina. Col. Meares was an inspired leader, respected by his superior officers, beloved by his subordinates, and admired by his men. At Malvern Hill, July 1, 1863, while on foot in front of the line, he was instantly killed by shrapnel from an artillery shell. His brother-in-law, Major William L. deRosset, succeeded him. CCFR, 296.

50. William Lord deRosset was a member of one of the oldest and most prominent families of Wilmington. He was the eldest of six sons of Dr. Armand J. deRosset and in 1861 was appointed captain of the Wilmington Light Infantry. He led the light infantry in the occupation of Fort Caswell on the Cape Fear River. When the Constitutional Convention authorized the formation of ten regiments from North Carolina, he was commissioned major of the 3rd Regiment. Succeeding Col. Meares as commander of the 3rd, he led the regiment into the Battle of Sharpsburg in September 1862, where he was seriously wounded in the thigh and hip. Finding himself permanently disabled, he resigned and was enrolled in another branch of the service. CCFR, 296–97.

51. William H. Quince was from New Hanover County and was appointed as second lieutenant at the age of twenty-four on May 16, 1861. He was promoted to first lieutenant on February 21, 1862. He was killed at Sharpsburg on September 17, 1862. NCT, vol. 3: 555.

52. William Murdock Parsley was appointed as major to rank from December 10, 1862. He was promoted to lieutenant colonel to rank from October 3, 1863. NCT, vol. 3: 487–88.

53. John Badger Brown enlisted in New Hanover County on May 23, 1861. He was appointed first lieutenant to rank from May 16, 1861. He was wounded at Malvern Hill, Virginia, on July 1, 1862 and promoted to captain to rank from the same date. NCT, vol. 3: 501.

54. Henry W. Horne resided in Cumberland County where he enlisted at age twenty-five on May 23, 1861. He was appointed second lieutenant to rank from May 16, 1861, and to first lieutenant on November 22, 1861. He was promoted to captain to rank from May 23, 1862, and was wounded in the thigh during the Battle of Sharpsburg on September 17, 1862. NCT, vol. 3: 511.

55. Charles Peter Mallett resided in Cumberland County where he enlisted at age sixteen on June 4, 1861. He was appointed third lieutenant to rank from May 16, 1861 and promoted to second lieutenant on November 22, 1861. He was promoted to first lieutenant on May 23, 1862, right after the Battle of Front Royal and was wounded at Malvern Hill on July 1, 1862. NCT, vol. 3: 511.

56. Thomas E. Armstrong was promoted to captain on September 17, 1862. He was killed at Chancellorsville, May 3, 1863, rather than Sharpsburg as TFW indicates. NCT, vol. 3: 583.

57. Edward Hall Armstrong was one of TFW's closest friends. He was born in New Hanover County where he resided as a farmer. He enlisted at age twenty-one on February 1, 1862, while he was in his third year at the University of North Carolina. He was appointed second lieutenant on July 1, 1862, and promoted to captain on September 17, 1862, succeeding captain Edward H. Rhodes as company commander of Company G after Rhodes was killed at Sharpsburg. He was one of only three officers in his regiment to emerge unscathed from Sharpsburg. NCT, vol. 3: 554.

58. William Thomas Ennett was transferred from Company E of the 3rd North Carolina upon his appointment as major to rank from October 3, 1863, after the resignation of Col. deRosset. He was wounded in the thigh at Sharpsburg on September 17, 1862. *NCT*, vol. 3: 511.
59. Cicero Craige was another close friend to TFW. He was from New Hanover County and had enlisted as a private on July 3, 1861, at the age of twenty-three in Company D, 1st Regiment Georgia Infantry (Ramsey's). He rose through the ranks and was appointed second lieutenant in the 3rd North Carolina Regiment on July 1, 1862, and promoted first lieutenant on October 9, 1863. *NCT*, vol. 3: 578.
60. Theodore M. Sikes resided in Bladen County where he enlisted at age twenty-three on July 15, 1862. He was sent to the hospital July 14 through October 31, 1862 and the muster roll on May 15, 1863 reported, "died in hospital Richmond, date not known." *NCT*, vol. 3: 564.
61. Edward J. Garrison resided in New Hanover County where he enlisted at age twenty-one on June 6, 1861. He was mustered in as a sergeant and promoted to first sergeant in January 1862. He was appointed second lieutenant to rank from August 8, 1862, and promoted to first lieutenant on December 10, 1862. *NCT*, vol. 3: 544.
62. James Henry Albritton resided in Greene County and was appointed second lieutenant at age twenty-one to rank from May 16, 1861, and to first lieutenant from January 16, 1862. He was wounded at Malvern Hill on July 1, 1862. He was promoted to captain to rank from September 7, 1862, while on sick furlough at home. He returned to his company by January–February 1863. *NCT*, vol. 3: 490.
63. Theodore James transferred from Company C, 59th North Carolina Regiment upon appointment as adjutant with the rank of first lieutenant on March 14, 1863, to rank from January 26, 1863. *NCT*, vol. 1: 488.
64. "First" is 1st North Carolina Regiment.
65. He was appointed captain on January 29, 1863, and transferred to Field & Staff, Third North Carolina. In September 1864 he was assigned to command the ordnance train for Rodes's division and remained in that job until March 10, 1865. He was paroled at Salisbury, North Carolina on May 1, 1865. *NCT*, vol. 1: 488.
66. Very seldom were these numbers accurate. A serious shortage of ambulances and steady deterioration of the few railroads needed to transport ill soldiers increased with each passing month of the struggle. The steady advance of the Union armies beginning in late 1862 forced the Confederates to shift hospitals from one site to another, always with diminishing returns. The South was faced with caring for more than three million cases of disease and wounds in an invaded and blockaded country. Surgeon Lafayette Guild complained in July 1862, "that one of the most serious problems confronting the army as a whole was that of transportation." *MSHCW*, vol. 1: vii.
67. The assistant surgeon was in charge of the regiment's Infirmary Corps who accompanied the ambulances and acted as orderlies. A member of the Infirmary Corps assisted each surgeon in the field by carrying a canteen of water, a tin cup, and a knapsack containing lint, bandages, sponges, tourniquets, four splints, chloroform, morphine and a pint bottle of alcoholic stimulants. *DG*, 14.
68. George Hume "Maryland" Steuart was born in Baltimore, Maryland in 1828 and graduated from West Point when he was nineteen years old. After routine cavalry service on the frontier, he resigned his commission and was appointed captain of cavalry in the Confederate Army. After First Manassas he was appointed colonel of the First

Maryland Infantry. Promoted to brigadier general on March 6, 1862, he commanded a brigade of four Virginia regiments and his old Maryland regiment in Ewell's division during the Valley Campaign. He was seriously wounded at Cross Keys, struck in the neck and back by grapeshot or a canister breaking his collar bone, and disabled for some time. After Chancellorsville he assumed command of Colston's brigade and at Gettysburg he led the brigade (including the 3rd North Carolina) in Edward Johnson's division of the Second Corps and continued until he and most of his command were captured in the "Mule Shoe" at Spotsylvania. Ezra J. Warner, *Generals in Gray* (Baton Rouge: Louisiana State Univ. Press, 1987), 290. See also note 52, Chapter Seven.

69. Morton's Ford is about thirty-three miles west of Fredericksburg on the Rapidan River.
70. John Cowan was transferred from Company I, with TFW, to the 3rd North Carolina and was appointed second lieutenant On September 17, 1863, he was promoted to first lieutenant and then to captain on June 22, 1863. He was captured at the Wilderness on May 10, 1864, and confined to Ft. Delaware. He was released at Ft. Delaware after taking the Oath of Allegiance on May 26, 1865. NCT, vol. 1: 522.
71. TFW's sister Mary Frances Wood.
72. TFW's sister and her husband, Nathaniel B. Vincent.
73. The Richmond bread riot occurred on April 2, 1863, as a result of the widespread hunger in Richmond and throughout the South. A mob demanded bread from the Richmond authorities, and the disturbance quickly turned into more general looting and disorder. Although President Davis and the militia eventually dispersed the crowd without bloodshed, the news of the event was circulated throughout the country. It was not a critical disturbance, but it was representative of economic difficulties facing the South. *American Heritage CD-ROM series*, Disk 1 (Byron Preiss Multimedia Co. and American Heritage, 1995).
74. The Enrollment Act of 1863 (Mar. 3, 1863) was designed by the Democrats mainly as a device to stimulate volunteering by the threat of draft. It did have some success but with such inefficiency, corruption, and perceived injustice that it became one of the most divisive issues of the war. Congress authorized a Provost Marshal's Bureau in the War Department to enforce conscription. Their task was to enroll every male citizen and immigrant who had filed for citizenship aged twenty to twenty-five. Of the men chosen in the drafts, more than one-fifth (161,000 of 776,000) failed to report—fleeing instead to the West, Canada, or to the woods. Of those who did report, one-eighth were sent home because of already filled quotas and 522,000 were exempted for physical or mental disabilities. Of the 207,000 men who were drafted, 87,000 paid a commutation fee (three hundred dollars) and 74,000 furnished substitutes. There were numerous opportunities for fraud, error, and injustice by corrupt and incompetent officials. BCF, 600–602.
75. Tim refers to his younger brother Alfred Wood, and Herbert is the son of Nat and Agnes Vincent.
76. "Poor Craig" is Cicero Craige, First Lieutenant.
77. His brother, Robert Barclay Wood, Jr., was appointed deputy clerk and master in equity, April 9, 1863. *The Wilmington Daily Journal*, Apr. 9, 1863.
78. "R." is TFW's brother Robert.
79. The Waverley novels were a series of thirty-two novels and tales by Sir Walter Scott. The first novel, *Waverley*, gave the series its name. *Reader's Encyclopedia*, 1050.
80. "That boy" is Herbert Vincent, son of N. B. & Agnes Wood Vincent.

Chapter 7. The Battle of Chancellorsville

1. Dietary deficiency including the lack of sufficient vegetable rations caused widespread cases of scurvy in the army, appearing as early as January 1862. With the commencement of spring, General Lee ordered a daily detail from each regiment "to gather sassafras buds, wild onions, garlic, lamb's quarter, water cress and poke sprouts" to supplement the ration, but the supply obtained was not sufficient to overcome the deficiency. *DG*, 206–7.
2. Gen. Raleigh Edward Colston was a Frenchman by birth and the adopted son of a Virginia physician; he graduated from VMI in 1846. He remained at the institute as a professor of French until 1861 when he was appointed colonel of the Sixteenth Virginia Infantry. He commanded a brigade in the Peninsular Campaign and in April 1863 was assigned a brigade in Stonewall Jackson's corps. *GG*, 58–59.
3. Colston was in command of the division. Col. E. T. H. Warren was in command of the brigade. Lt. Col. S. D. Thruston commanded the Third North Carolina Regiment. *C1863*, 362.
4. The march to Fredericksburg began April 29, 1863.
5. Lee and Jackson met Hooker's flanking force near the Chancellor House on May 1, 1863. With the battle stalled, Lee decided to send Jackson around Hooker's right flank by the way of back roads—Furnace and Brock's Roads, to attack Howard's corps on the Orange Plank Road—May 2, 1863. TFW seems to blend the two movements together but on May 1, Jackson's corps moved to Chancellorsville. On May 2, the corps began its movement around Hooker's flank. *C1863*, 151–55.
6. "The Major" is Major William T. Ennett.
7. As the troops settled into route step, the columns lengthened despite urging to close up. This was a long, winding route with little to ease the line of march. Jackson's twenty-six thousand men moved down this narrow lane, four abreast—three divisions, fifteen brigades, seventy regiments which covered six miles of road even without the inevitable stretch-out between troops and units. Added to this column were sixteen batteries of artillery, plus ammunition wagons and ambulances. *C1863*, 145.
8. Colston's division was in the second line of the attack with Warren's brigade on the right, straddling the Orange Turnpike, and Jones on the left. The 3rd North Carolina was part of Warren's brigade, moving forward on the right side of the Turnpike. *C1863*, 167–69.
9. The Eleventh Corps was mostly made up of Germans and had been recently commanded by General Franz Sigel who was also German-born. He was a career soldier who had fought in Germany's revolution before being exiled. His men were proud of their heritage and had a boastful toast, "I fights mit Sigel." General Hooker decided to use the Eleventh Corps, now under the command of Gen. Oliver Otis Howard, to anchor the extreme right wing of his line. The sudden and unexpected attack by Jackson's force slammed into Howard's Eleventh Corps sending them scrambling to the rear. Howard was taken totally by surprise and was unable to stop his fleeing soldiers. *C1863*, 91, 172–82.
10. It was the assistant surgeon's duty to be as close to the front lines as possible to apply bandages and plaster, administer stimulants (usually whisky) and load the badly wounded in the ambulances for transportation to the field hospital. No elaborate surgical procedure was undertaken unless there was an urgent need for it. Jackson's sudden attack caused Hooker's right wing to retreat so rapidly that they overran

their own field hospitals leaving many Union wounded mixed with Confederate wounded for the surgeons to care for. The attack moved so quickly that most of the medical services were left far behind caring for wounded of both armies. Gary W. Gallagher, *Chancellorsville: The Battle and Its Aftermath* (Chapel Hill: Univ. of North Carolina Press, 1996), 182–94.

11. Dr. Lucius C. Coke was transferred from Company G of the 1st North Carolina Regiment upon appointment as assistant surgeon to rank from June 12, 1862. TFW and Dr. Coke were able to work the front lines together because the 1st and 3rd North Carolina were usually bivouacked and formed up for battle together. NCT, vol. 2: 142.

12. During the attack, the first and second lines merged in the confusion of the thick undergrowth and the forward momentum. By the time the attack was halted, the first and third regiments were on the front lines. Evidently TFW and Dr. Coke had moved out in front of their lines and were near the Van Wert house, which is why they found no regimental wounded, only Union wounded. At about this time General Colston was attempting to reorganize his division, and the 1st and 3rd were pulled back to the second line. The doctors were very near the spot where A. P. Hill's staff was fired upon. CBA, 111–21. Battlefield study and conversations with park officials also indicate that this was likely.

13. This change in command took place prior to the opening of the Battle of Chancellorsville. Warren was severely wounded leading the initial attack on the night of May 2nd and Col. Titus V. Williams had taken command of the brigade. Williams was hit on the next day and Lt. Col. Hamilton A. Brown assumed command. C1863, 226–29.

14. TFW is referring to Thomas Jefferson Capps the ambulance driver for the 3rd North Carolina and probably Richard Ward, a private in Company A, who also served as an ambulance driver when needed. NCT, vol. 3: 499–500, 673.

15. Family oral history has described TFW's position as very near the place where Jackson was wounded. TFW is said to have been attending Union wounded when a Confederate officer approached and asked for assistance for a downed officer. TFW declined, being in the middle of attending to wounded and not knowing it was Jackson who was down.

16. Thomas Jefferson Capps was designated an ambulance driver for the 3rd North Carolina Regiment assigned to Company E. According to a letter that he wrote on November 21, 1883, which was published in the *Wilmington Daily Review* of December 1, 1883, he confirms driving the ambulance in which Stonewall Jackson was carried to the field hospital on May 2, 1863. It is unclear whether this was the ambulance that carried the General from just behind the Confederate lines to the first stopping point at Dowdell's Tavern or the three-and-a-half miles to the corps hospital near Wilderness Tavern, or both. It has been believed by some historians that one ambulance belonged to Marcellus Moorman's horse artillery. NCT, vol. 3: 673.

17. The general was carried through the lines by litter, over extremely difficult terrain and was dropped twice, further damaging his left arm and causing great pain. He was helped into Capps's ambulance, which drove him to the rear, probably down a branch of the Hazel Grove Road to Dowdall's Tavern, the Orange Turnpike home of Baptist cleric Melzi Chancellor just east of the Wilderness Church. At Dowdall's Tavern, Dr. Hunter McGuire joined them and stopped the flow of blood from Jackson's wound. They con-

tinued the brutal three and a half mile trip to the field hospital at Wilderness Tavern where Jackson's left arm was removed. Eight days later, on May 10, 1863, General Stonewall Jackson died of pneumonia at Fairfield, Virginia. *C1863*, 211–16.
18. James Ewell Brown Stuart was the bold cavalier but had never had to manage a mass of infantry struggling through a wilderness of thorns and thick brush. This was against every principal of the fast-moving cavalry. On the night of the 2nd, Stewart Stuart had not heard of Jackson's intention to thrust north and cut Hooker off from the Rappahannock fords; his only instruction had been to "do what he thought best." He decided to carefully probe the enemy position and wait reassurance from Lee or detailed reports before committing himself. The opportunity was lost and the Union still had a way out. The battle on the 3rd was brutal and bloody, but the Union forces were pushed back off Chancellor Hill and into defensive lines behind Orange Plank Road. *C1863*, 220–44.
19. The Lacy House called "Elwood" was a 1799 farmhouse that still exists and is owned by the National Park Service. The house was used as HQ for Gen. Warren and Gen. Burnside during the Battle of the Wilderness. Stonewall Jackson's arm is buried in the cemetery there. TFW was probably working at Wilderness Tavern hospital less than one half mile away; it was the division and corps hospital following the attack on the 2nd. The hospital was approximately three and a half miles behind the lines. National Park Service.
20. Probably either Vaucleuse Mine or Greenwood Mine which were the sources of ore for Catherine's Furnace. National Park Service.
21. The Federals retreated over U.S. Ford.
22. On Sunday the 3rd, the regiment was formed on the right of the Plank Road, and advancing , captured the first line of the enemy's works. The portion of these works that crossed a ravine and swamp, a favorable position for the enemy, was assaulted three times by the Confederates before it finally held. During one of these assaults Col. Thruston was wounded, and the command shifted to Lt. Col. Parsley, who was also wounded but remained in command throughout the Pennsylvania Campaign. The 3rd North Carolina participated in the last two of these charges. It was then that Gen. J. E. B. Stuart, who was now in command of Jackson's corps, ordered the whole line forward. The enemy's earthworks were carried by storm and many pieces of artillery were captured. The Chancellor House was now in full view and the captured guns were turned on the enemy. Soon the Chancellor House was in flames and Hooker's army was withdrawing. *HRBNC*, vol. 1: 192–93.
23. "This day" being 1887 and represents Confederate Memorial Day.
24. Out of 802 men, Warren's brigade suffered 128 killed, 594 wounded and 80 missing. *C1863*, 362.
25. "Caledonia Forge" is Catherine's Furnace. National Park Service.
26. An "old saw-pit" where they recovered Union medical supplies was Kalmbach's sawmill.
27. Dr. Edward R. Squibb established the Drug Manufacturer's Laboratory at Brooklyn, New York, Navy Yard in 1852. He perfected a large-scale production method for manufacturing ether and chloroform, and his firm turned out enormous quantities of painkillers for the war. In 1858 he was severely injured in an ether explosion and fire at the Laboratory. He started his own drug company in 1859. Joseph J. Fucini, *Entrepreneurs: Men and Women Behind Famous Brand Names and How They Made It* (G. K. Hall), 242.

28. U.S. Ford was used. National Park Service.
29. Dr. Asch came over on May 10 with orders from Dr. Jonathan Letterman, Medical Director, Army of the Potomac, to take charge of the Union hospitals and wounded. Dr. George Suckley, Medical Director of the Eleventh Corps (Gen. Howard), however, had already been put in charge of the hospitals by the Confederate authorities. He had been captured on May 3. Frank Whitehouse, "A Michigan Surgeon at Chancellorsville," *University of Michigan Medical Bulletin* 29 (1963). Under the truce, twenty-six Union surgeons, along with five wagons laden with blankets, beef, and medical supplies, headed over the river to Chancellorsville. More than two thousand rations crossed at United States Ford while six hundred more rations headed to Banks Ford. Twenty-six Federal surgeons who had been taken prisoner or had chosen to stay behind, worked closely with their Confederate counterparts to treat the wounded on both sides. The 1st and 3rd North Carolina Regiments were designated to remain behind to coordinate this operation. On the morning of May 15, the last wounded Federals—1,160 in number—crossed the Rappahannock into Union lines. CBA, 191.
30. "Greenbacks" were new one dollar paper bill issued by the United States Government.
31. "The old Branch Brigade" is 18th North Carolina Regiment.
32. Gen. Stuart ordered a dawn attack on May 8 against the Union line, spearheaded by Hill's division, now commanded by Gen. Henry Heth. Col. Thomas James Purdie, staff officer with the 18th North Carolina was killed in this attack, trying to rally the troops. Twelve regimental officers were killed or wounded in this engagement. HRBNC, vol. 3: 37.
33. Gutta-percha is a special gum from the island of Borneo, that proved to be a suitable insulation for underwater telegraph cables. Its discoverer, Dr. John Craven, demonstrated its use in 1857 by transmitting telegraph messages beneath various streams and rivers. *First Search web site* (www.ref.oclc.org).
34. The regiment lost 39 killed, 175 wounded and 17 missing at Chancellorsville. NCT, vol. 3: 483.
35. Dr. Walker Washington served as surgeon to the 3rd North Carolina from June 30, to September 30, 1863, when he was "transferred to post duty." NCT, vol. 3: 488.
36. TFW's hospital steward referred to here is probably George Williams.
37. TFW's "double" cousin, Daniel Haines. He was the grandson of Daniel and Hettie Wells (Fanning) Wood.
38. This statement shows his immaturity as it is in marked contrast with the descriptions of the events in his recollections some twenty-one years later.
39. The "Oath" is the oath of allegiance to the U.S.
40. The newspaper here is the *Wilmington Journal*.
41. It is interesting that TFW makes such disparaging remarks about Jackson. It is rare that we see negative comments about the general from soldiers in the field, especially just after his death. Jackson's death devastated Gen. Lee but these comments become more feasible if you consider the feelings of the men at the time. Under Lee's leadership, they had once again defeated a vastly superior enemy force and sent them scurrying off the field for safety. The feeling of invincibility was spreading throughout the Army of Northern Virginia and as horrible as this battle had been, most of the men believed that with General Lee at the helm they could not be defeated. TFW might have been trying to convince his parents and himself that even though Jackson was gone, the army was still strong and ready to meet the enemy on any battlefield.

42. James Foreman Clarke was a lieutenant with Company G, transferred from Field & Staff upon his appointment as second lieutenant on September 17, 1862. He would be wounded at Payne's Farm, Virginia on November 21, 1863, and would resign in 1864 due to "chronic rheumatism." *NCT*, vol. 3: 554.
43. It is assumed that this refers to his hopes to go before the Army Board of Examiners to be appointed surgeon to replace Dr. McRee. After this letter Dr. Washington assumed the duties as regimental surgeon.
44. Charles R. Banks, first lieutenant. Enlisted in Cumberland County at age twenty-six on September 2, 1863. Appointed first lieutenant to rank from date of enlistment. *NCT*, vol. 3: 354.
45. "Dan H." is Daniel Haines, TFW's cousin. See also note 39 above.
46. David Thally, Private. Resided in Duplin County and enlisted in Brunswick County at age twenty-one, April 16, 1862. Later captured at Fort Fisher on January 15, 1865, and confined at Elmira, New York until paroled for exchange on February 20, 1865. *NCT*, vol. 1: 288.
47. Nancy Swain (Wilber) McLaurin, sister of TFW's mother, born August 12, 1823, at Nantucket, Mass. Married Joe McLaurin at Wilmington where she died March 1, 1900. Family Bible.
48. Dr. Dabney Herndon served as surgeon to the 3rd North Carolina while on duty with the 1st North Carolina Regiment. *NCT*, vol. 3: 488.
49. Dr. Otis Manson and his assistant, Dr. S. W. Murphy, attempted throughout the war to get TFW assigned to Moore Hospital or another hospital in Richmond.
50. It had been decided that General Raleigh Edward Colston was not fit to command a brigade, and he was transferred. He then served under General Beauregard in the defense of Petersburg and subsequently at Lynchburg. George Hume "Maryland" Steuart was given command of his brigade. It was thought that Steuart could be utilized as an old regular army man to take the Virginia–North Carolina brigade of Colston. Experience had indicated that where an officer well-schooled in the "old army" took a brigade that had regiments from one or more states, rivalries usually ended. *LL*, vol. 2: 702. George Hume "Maryland" Steuart graduated from West Point in 1848, thirty-seventh in a class of thirty-eight. He became lieutenant colonel of the 1st Maryland Infantry and after First Manassas succeeded Arnold Elzey as colonel. Promoted to brigadier general, he commanded a brigade of four Virginia regiments and his old Maryland regiment during the Valley Campaign with Stonewall Jackson. He was seriously wounded at Cross Keys and was disabled for some time prior to assuming command of Colston's brigade after Chancellorsville. *GG*, 290–91. Jack D. Welsh, M.D., *Medical Histories of Confederate Generals* (Kent, Ohio: Kent State Univ. Press, 1995), 204. See also note 69, chap. 6.
51. It is assumed that TFW is talking about General J. E. B. Stuart who took temporary command of Jackson's corps when the general was wounded.
52. The smallpox and yellow fever epidemics of 1862 had taken their toll on Wilmington, and the blockade had finally begun to put a strangle hold on the city's economy.
53. Alfred V. Wood, TFW's younger brother.
54. Lumberton, North Carolina, where the writer's family was refugeed from Wilmington because of the yellow fever epidemic.
55. Lydia Summerhays Wood, the writer's sister who married N. B. Vincent.
56. TFW's uncle, John Coffin Wood (1809–1873) of Wilmington.

Chapter 8. The Gettysburg Campaign

1. *HRBNC*, vol. 1: 193.
2. Van Bokkelen was commander of Company D, 3rd North Carolina Regiment, and he was stricken with typhoid fever.
3. The march began on June 5, 1863.
4. The division left Hamilton's Crossing on June 5 and moved with the corps towards Winchester, crossing the Blue Ridge at Chester Gap. Leaving camp at Cedarville on the morning of June 13, they moved down the Front Royal and Winchester Turnpike. General Ewell sent Major General Jubal Early's division down the valley turnpike to gain the heights west of Winchester—June 13. Johnson's division proceeded to within four miles of Winchester, where it encountered the Federal forces of General Robert H. Milroy. Johnson's mission was to engage the enemy's attention on the right while Early moved in on the left to deliver the main attack. That evening, Johnson received orders to move further to the right and get behind the town and cut off the Federal line of retreat. After a brief but intense engagement at Jordon Springs, involving Steuart's brigade and another, more than twenty-five hundred enemy troops threw down their arms and surrendered. *HRBNC*, vol. 1: 194.
5. The regiment lost four killed and ten wounded—including Lieutenant Cicero Craige wounded. *HRBNC*, vol. 1: 194.
6. Dehydration was a serious problem on long marches during the summer months, and it could thin the ranks quickly if not dealt with. Most regiments had their assistant surgeons and medical staffs, armed with canteens of water, follow the march to give the men some relief and keep them on their feet.
7. Opium was used for its narcotic and analgesic effects. Camphor was obtained from the wood of Cinnamomum camphora, an evergreen tree. It was applied topically to the skin as an antipruritic and anti-infective. It was prepared as camphor-water, spirit of camphor, and as a liniment. Taken orally, it supposedly had a useful effect in treating cholera, diarrhea, vomiting, stomach pains, typhoid and eruptive fevers. It was also used to relieve pain when needed for conditions such as myalgia, toothache or gangrene. *MHCG*, 264, 275.
8. The preceding paragraph is from a manuscript written by TFW for a civic speech, just prior to beginning his Recollections in 1886. TFW, An Assistant Surgeon's Recollections of the Gettysburg Campaign (manuscript written on or about 1886), Thomas Fanning Wood Collection, William Madison Randall Library, Univ. of North Carolina at Wilmington.
9. Kitchen Powers, was born in New Hanover County and resided as a farmer in Onslow County prior to enlisting on June 1, 1861, at the age of thirty-four. He was mustered as a sergeant and was appointed second lieutenant on August 1, 1862, in the 3rd North Carolina. He was promoted to first lieutenant in October of 1862, and to captain in May 1863, on the last day of the Battle of Chancellorsville. *NCT*, vol. 3: 589.
10. George Rouse was a private in Company D, 3rd North Carolina. He was from New Hanover where he enlisted on May 27, 1861, at the age of thirty-two. He was captured at South Mountain, Maryland, just prior to the Battle of Sharpsburg and was paroled and exchanged on November 10, 1862. He was killed at Winchester on June 15, 1863. *NCT*, vol. 3: 531.
11. Johnson's division captured between twenty-three hundred and twenty-six hundred prisoners. *NCT*, vol. 3: 484.

12. Hamilton A. Brown transferred from Company B of the 1st North Carolina upon his appointment as lieutenant colonel on July 8, 1862. He wasn't promoted to colonel until December 14, 1863. NCT, vol. 2: 141.
13. The regiment crossed the Potomac on June 18, 1863, and went into camp near Dunkard Church on the old battlefield at Sharpsburg. NCT, vol. 3: 484.
14. They lost a total of 330 dead or wounded out of 520, and only 3 officers out of 27 were left standing. HRBNC, vol. 1: 189.
15. On June 19, 1863, as a tribute to the officers and men of the 3rd North Carolina who were lost at Sharpsburg, the 1st and 3rd North Carolina Regiments assembled, with arms reversed, and marched to the old battlefield where Rev. George Patterson read burial services. A detail of men under the command of Lieutenant James I. Metts fired a military salute over the spot where their bodies were buried. HRBNC, vol. 2: 194.
16. This was after the defeat of Milroy's force at Winchester in June. Many of the Union surgeons had remained behind with the wounded and had been taken prisoner.
17. Many of the serious hospital infections—gangrene, tetanus, erysipelas, and pyaemia—had their beginnings on the battlefield, reinforced by dedicated field surgeons with inadequate supplies and limited knowledge. Dirty bandages, used scalpels, and improper dressings in the field were compounded by lengthy exposure, damp and cold conditions, and usually long and painful ambulance rides to the division hospital. By the time most wounded men made it to the hospital, various infections had already taken hold. DG, 236–42.
18. Sponges were not only used over and over to clean wounds but often became scarce. Linen and cotton rags were used instead, sometimes boiled and washed out but mostly just rinsed. To create more absorbent material, old linen was scraped with a knife to make lint or raw cotton was baked in an oven until it was charred. Most of these were necessary expedients and not the most effective treatment. DG, 221–35. Silk gauze and dressings were made in the Palestinian city of Gaza, where the name *gauze* is derived, as early as the 1700s. The cotton gin was introduced to Europe and the Middle East around 1840, and absorbent cotton gauze began to be manufactured in the early 1850s. The medical profession, on both sides, was too diverted by the war to focus on improvements from overseas. The American pharmaceutical company, Johnson & Johnson, began importing and selling absorbent cotton gauze in the 1870s. To be absorbent enough for surgical needs, the fiber count of the gauze had to be twenty to forty-four threads per inch with a weight of 17.2 to 44.5 grams per yard. Fielding H. Garrison, *Garrison's History of Medicine*, 4th ed. (Philadelphia: W. B. Saunders, 1967).
19. The preceding three paragraphs are from An Assistant Surgeon's Recollections of the Gettysburg Campaign. See also note 8, this chapter.
20. Throughout TFW's narrative is the approval of Lee's order that caused many Confederates to feel morally superior to the degenerate Yankees who had burned and looted the South. The purpose of Lee's order was not altogether to protect the property of Pennsylvanians but was also intended to preserve the morale and discipline of his army in enemy territory. Unfortunately, many Confederates did not live up to their moral responsibilities in this campaign. They acted just like the Yankees. The Gettysburg Campaign saw its share of looting, intimidation and needless destruction.
21. Battle of Chancellorsville, May 2, 1883.
22. The 6th Alabama was part of Gen. Robert E. Rodes brigade, D. H. Hill's division, during the Seven Days Battles before Richmond. The colonel of the 6th

Alabama at the Battle of Seven Pines was John Bell Gordon. The 6th was criticized unfairly for its performance at Seven Pines if that is the battle that TFW is referring to. During the Confederate assault, the 6th was on the right and became exposed to heavy Union fire. Rodes ordered them to pull back, and in doing so, the 12th Alabama and the heavy artillery battalion also retired in some confusion. Col. Gordon listed every one of his field officers killed in this assault. The 6th took 632 men into the battle and only 259 survived unhurt, a casualty rate of fifty-nine percent. Col. Rodes was wounded in this action, and Col. Gordon assumed command of the brigade. O.R. ser. 1, vol. 11, pt. 1: pp. 971–80.

23. Dr. Robert B. Drane was rector of St. James Episcopal Church in Wilmington and sacrificed his life in the yellow fever epidemic of 1862 by remaining with his flock in town and serving the sick and needy instead of refuging. CCFR, 608–9.

24. Lee's army was spread out, and he was without the reconnaissance support of Jeb Stuart. General Henry Heth was in command of a division in A. P. Hill's corps, and on June 30 he decided to send four regiments under James Johnston Pettigrew to the little town of Gettysburg in search of shoes and other supplies. They spotted a Federal cavalry and withdrew before being spotted. When the incident was reported to Gen. Hill, he doubted that it was much more than a small detachment when in reality they had run across part of Gen. John Buford's two full brigades of cavalry. Lee's latest reports placed the Federal army at Middleburg, still in camp. Heth returned to Gettysburg with his division on the morning of July 1 and collided with Buford's cavalry and the contest soon developed into a major engagement. Heth was joined by Hill and later by Lee. Gen. Lee, finally realizing that he had engaged an advance element of Meade's army, began to recall his army. Gary W. Gallagher, *The First Day at Gettysburg: Essays on Confederate and Union Leadership* (Kent, Ohio: Kent State Univ. Press, 1992), 30–47.

25. General Benjamin Butler was commander of the occupation troops in New Orleans after its fall to the Federals in 1862. Butler's cruel and unjust treatment of civilians brought out strong protests directed at any Federal soldier. His order of May 15 that any woman who persisted in the practice of insulting Northern soldiers "shall be regarded and held liable to be treated as a woman of the town plying her avocation" brought out the wrath of the entire South. Southerners and Europeans chose to interpret the law as a barbarous license for Northern soldiers to treat refined ladies as prostitutes. BCF, 550–53.

26. Having witnessed the destruction of an invading army, most Southern soldiers had achieved an attitude of moral superiority over their enemy, as so often is the case in war. The Union's burning and looting of the Southern countryside gave the Confederates more reason to hate the Yankees. General Lee's order prohibiting misconduct concerning civilian property was primarily intended to maintain discipline and prevent widespread retaliation. The psychological strain of now being the invader and the moral outrage over the enemy's destruction to their homeland caused many Confederate soldiers to disobey their commander's order and seek retribution. TFW repeatedly refers to the horror of senseless enemy destruction but is rather astonished when the destruction is by Confederate hands.

27. Edward "Old Allegheny" Johnson was born at Salisbury, Virginia, and moved to Kentucky as a child. A graduate of West Point in the class of 1838, he saw service in the Seminole War and in Mexico where he was brevetted captain and major for

gallant service in the field. He entered into Confederate service as colonel of the 12th Georgia Infantry. He was promoted brigadier general on December 13, 1861 and major general on February 28, 1863. Johnson participated in the Valley Campaign where he was severely wounded, and he was given Stonewall Jackson's old division at Gettysburg. GG, 158–59.

28. After a tough fight, the Federals were pushed back through the town and as darkness approached, Meade took up a defensive position on Cemetery Ridge. As Confederate units arrived at Gettysburg, they were moved through and around the town to take up positions facing Cemetery Hill. Johnson's division was assigned the left flank of the army facing Culp's Hill. Both Ewell and Early have received criticism for not following through with an attack on Cemetery Hill on the night of July 1. Both men felt that, considering the growing darkness, the strong enemy position, fragmented positions of their own troops and the fact that many of their key units were still on the road to Gettysburg, a further pursuit would be unwise. Bruce Catton, *Gettysburg: The Final Fury* (New York: Doubleday, 1974),10–20.

29. This field dressing station was probably located at the Christian Benner farm, a 208-acre family farm which occupied land just northeast of Culp's Hill, south of the Hanover Road and about one thousand feet east of Rock Creek. Gettysburg National Battlefield Park. Christian Benner's second son celebrated his nineteenth birthday in July of 1863 and witnessed the 2nd of July on Culp's Hill. He watched as the Confederate troops drove the Federal forces from their works and heard the piercing Rebel yell. He watched as the wounded began to be brought back and laid them on the floor of their kitchen, and up in the barn, and out in the yard. He watched in horror as doctors amputated limbs in great numbers and discarded the severed parts out in the yard. On July 4, he found two dead Rebels lying in back of the barn, and they were not buried until the next day. Gregory A. Coco, *A Vast Sea of Misery: A History and Guide to the Union and Confederate Field Hospitals at Gettysburg, July 1–November 20, 1863* (Gettysburg: Thomas Publications, 1988), 115–16.

30. Late in the afternoon, at the sound of Longstreet's artillery, Ewell ordered Gen. Johnson's batteries to open on Cemetery Hill. Johnson's artillery was Snowden Andrews's Maryland battalion to which the Rockbridge artillery was added. Andrews was still recovering from his wounds, and Maj. Joseph W. Latimer directed his guns. The Union batteries answered immediately, sighting on Benner's Hill and taking heavy casualties. *LL*, vol. 3: 129.

31. Persuaded by his military commanders that Ewell's corps lacked the strength to capture the high ground on the enemy's right, Lee decided that Longstreet's corps would spearhead the attack on the second, hitting the Union left. Ewell's primary mission would be to pin down the Federal forces on Culp's Hill and Cemetery Hill, on the Union right, preventing them from going to the aid of Federal units being attacked by Longstreet. Waiting for orders to engage, Ewell's corps remained inactive most of the 2nd when they could have possibly made a significant difference on the Union right, which was critically under strength as Meade buttressed his line on Cemetery Hill. Late in the afternoon as Ewell began his artillery bombardment of Cemetery Hill, he decided to turn the demonstration into an assault. He sent word to Early to follow Johnson in an attack on Culp's Hill. Gary W. Gallagher, *The Second Day at Gettysburg: Essays on Confederate and Union Leadership* (Kent, Ohio: Kent State Univ. Press, 1993), 1–32. About six o'clock on the afternoon of the 2nd, after the heavy

artillery bombardment, the division was ordered forward over Rock Creek to assault the Federal positions on the hill. The brigade (Steuart's) was on the extreme left of the advancing line, and the 3rd North Carolina was placed on the right of the brigade. As the brigade advanced, the three regiments on the left gained and occupied the first line of enemy entrenchments, after those Union troops had been shifted to help cover Little Round Top, but the 3rd North Carolina was unprotected and exposed to heavy fire. At this time the 1st North Carolina was sent up to support the 3rd and a general assault was launched on the second line of works. This assault failed but the Confederates held the line. During the night, the 1st North Carolina was withdrawn, and members of the 3rd alternated positions with troops behind the breastworks. *NCT*, vol. 3: 484.
32. Christian Benner's farm. The boy was probably Christian Benner's nineteen year old son.
33. TFW is probably referring to John C. McIlhenny who was a first lieutenant in Company E, Light Artillery, 10th Regiment, North Carolina Troops who was from Wilmington but had relatives in Gettysburg. *CCFR*, 340.
34. TFW is now speaking about the third day, July 3. Gen. Ewell, who was ordered to attack the enemy's right as a support for the main thrust on the Union center, began his artillery assault shortly after dawn. He followed with an all out attack on the Federal line still holding Culp's Hill. Unfortunately, this was far too soon for the forces on Seminary Ridge to take advantage of its diversion. Steuart's brigade was formed at right angles to the line of works to attack a Federal force on the Confederate left. Again, the 3rd North Carolina was placed on the right of the brigade. During the advance, the left of the brigade failed to maintain its position and the right, being in advance, suffered concentrated fire, and finally fell back. The whole line retired and rallied behind a stone wall which ran parallel to the breastworks. Here they remained about an hour until they were withdrawn to Rock Creek where they stayed the rest of the day. *NCT*, vol. 3: 484.
35. The last charge of the third day was brutal for the 3rd North Carolina. They were caught on the right with no protection of breastworks as did the other regiments. By the time they moved to the join the balance of the brigade to participate in the assault, their ranks were already severely thinned. The regiment suffered more in killed and wounded than in any of the many battles in which it was engaged. *HRBNC*, vol. 1: 197. Entering the battle with 548 guns, it was reduced by 218 men in killed and wounded. Reports listed 48 killed, 140 wounded and 30 missing, making it one of the 20 regiments with the greatest losses. John W. Busey and David G. Martin, *Regimental Strengths and Losses at Gettysburg* (Hightstown: Longstreet House, 1994), 285. Col. Parsley, Capt. E. H. Armstrong, and Lieut. Lyon were the only line officers not killed or wounded. *HRBNC*, vol. 1: 197. Lt. Edward J. Garrison and Lt. Henry W. Potter were killed during the assault on Culp's Hill on July 2, 1863. Lt. Thomas J. Kelly was wounded on July 2 and died in the hospital on July 9, 1863. Captain James Isaac Metts was wounded on July 2 and was captured on July 4 when the hospital was occupied by Federal troops. *NCT*, vol. 3: 501–70.
36. The division hospital was located at the Daniel Lady Farm, a little over one-half mile east of Rock Creek on the north side of the Hanover Road. There is evidence that this site was also a bivouac and headquarters for Generals Richard Ewell (Second Corps) and John B. Gordon. Coco, 116.
37. Lieutenant Colonel James R. Herbert was commanding officer of the 2nd Mary-

land Infantry when he was wounded on Culp's Hill and taken prisoner when the hospital was occupied by Federal forces. Major William W. Goldsborough was assistant in command of the 2nd Maryland Infantry and was wounded on Culp's Hill on July 2 and also taken prisoner. *Confederate Military History: Extended Edition* (Wilmington: Broadfoot Publishing, 1987), vol. 2: 296–97. General J. M. Jones received a flesh wound in the thigh on the second day, during the assault on the first line of the Federal entrenchment. Because of excessive bleeding, he had to be carried off the field giving up his command. MHCG, 122.

38. The failure to break the Federal center by the Pickett-Pettigrew charge during the afternoon of July 3, necessitated withdrawal. Johnson's division was withdrawn across Rock Creek and retired through the town to a position north and west of Gettysburg during the night of July 3. On July 5, the division started the march back to Virginia by way of Waynesboro to Hagerstown. Here a line of battle was established but no engagement occurred. On the night of July 13, the division re-crossed the Potomac and marched to a point near Martinsburg. NCT, vol. 3: 484.

39. The Confederate wounded left behind in field hospitals fared far better than those who were carried with the army in ambulance trains. The retreat from Gettysburg proved to be a harrowing experience for all concerned but especially for the wounded and attending physicians. The jolting trip over rough roads was bad enough but the wagons were continuously attacked by enemy raiding parties, who destroyed many of the wagons leaving the wounded to suffer without transportation. Most of the wagons and ambulances moved on July 4 through Cashtown Pass and Greenwood to Williamsport, Maryland, on the Potomac. Brigadier General John Imboden provided escort for this entourage with twenty-one hundred cavalry. Gary W. Gallagher, *The Third Day at Gettysburg & Beyond* (Chapel Hill: Univ. of North Carolina Press, 1994), 161–65.

40. Darkness, confusion and indecision on the afternoon of the 3rd prevented Gen. Meade from following up Lee's withdrawal with a counterattack. That night Gen. Lee made plans for a withdrawal from Gettysburg, and after remaining in position most of the day on the 4th, unchallenged by the Union army, he sent his infantry toward the mountains with Hill in the lead followed by Longstreet and Ewell. They moved in heavy rain towards Hagerstown, Maryland, and then south to Williamsport to cross the Potomac. Finally on the 6th, Meade ordered his Chief of Staff, Maj. Gen. Daniel Butterfield, to prepare for pursuit. Lee's rearguard arrived at Hagerstown on the 7th and constructed a defensive perimeter around the town. After several days of indecision, Meade finally decided to launch a reconnaissance in force on July 14, but Lee had already decided to abandon his lines and cross the Potomac to safety. The Potomac had dropped enough to allow Ewell's infantry to wade across at Williamsport. Two divisions of the Third Corps were preparing to escape when their rearguard were attacked by Union cavalry. Brigadier General J. Johnston Pettigrew was killed and as many as one thousand other Confederates became casualties. Gallagher, *The Third Day at Gettysburg and Beyond*, 161–75.

41. When the Confederate wounded arrived in Williamsport, they were finally moved across the swollen Potomac on rafts and ferry boats. An ambulance line was then organized by the Richmond Ambulance Committee which moved the wounded to trains connecting to Richmond and some were transported to hospitals in the valley. DG, 119–22.

42. Orange Court House is approximately twenty miles southwest of Culpepper Court House on the Rapidan River.
43. An excellent overview of the Gettysburg Campaign is provided in the three books by Gary W. Gallagher: *The First Day at Gettysburg: Essays on Confederate and Union Leadership*, *The Second Day at Gettysburg: Essays on Confederate and Union Leadership*, and *The Third Day at Gettysburg & Beyond*.
44. Dr. William F. Stewart was assigned to the regiment from June 30 to September 30, 1863, and transferred to Charlotte Court House, Virginia, by order of the surgeon general in November of 1863. *NCT*, vol. 3: 488.
45. Lumberton, North Carolina, where Robert B. Wood purchased property and where the family remained for the better part of six years.
46. "W." is Wilmington.
47. "Mr. P" is Rev. George Patterson.
48. TFW was delayed in Richmond.
49. General Lee's medical director was Dr. Hunter Maguire.
50. A friend of Rev. Patterson was Samuel B. Mordecai, son of Jacob and Judith (Myers) Mordecai, born c. 1790. 1850 Census of Richmond.
51. Both Murphy and Sherrod were close associates of TFW's mentor Dr. Otis Manson. Murphy was the director of the North Carolina Soldier's Home in Richmond.
52. Captain Richard Langdon was assistant quartermaster of the 3rd North Carolina Regiment. *NCT*, vol. 3: 488.
53. Tim was TFW's youngest brother, Alfred V. Wood (1853–1927). The Dickens vogue at this time probably accounted for the nickname. Aggie was TFW's sister, Agnes Fanning Wood (1837–1867).
54. Instead of Hill, General Longstreet, after strong lobbying on his part, was sent to Tennessee to reinforce General Braxton Bragg, stalled in front of Chattanooga, facing Union Generals W. S. Rosecrans and A. E. Burnside.
55. TFW was approximately twenty-three miles west of Fredericksburg on the Rapidan River.
56. "Bertie" is Herbert Vincent (1861–1866), son of N. B. and Agnes (Aggie) Wood Vincent.

Chapter 9. The Winter of 1863 and the Turning Tide

1. *LL*, vol. 3: 238–47.
2. A. P. Hill suffered 1,360 losses. Cooke's brigade lost 700 men killed, wounded or captured and Kirkland lost 602, of whom nearly half surrendered. Both Cooke and Kirkland were badly wounded. With Meade strongly entrenched and the Confederate supply lines overextended, General Lee withdrew on October 18. *LL*, 245–46.
3. TFW is referring to Brigadier General Alfred Iverson, Jr. He was colonel of the 20th North Carolina Infantry and was promoted to brigadier in November 1862. He commanded a brigade in Rodes's division, Second Corps at both Chancellorsville and Gettysburg. *MHCG*, 110.
4. Mitchell's Ford is just west of Fredericksburg on the Rapidan River.
5. "W." is Warrenton.
6. Bristoe Station is on the Orange & Alexandria Railroad.
7. This was General Warren's attack from the railroad cut.
8. During the assault, General Heth reported a large number of Federal troops on his

right and was certain that if he moved forward, they would take him in the flank. Hill ordered Heth forward, thinking that Anderson was coming up to protect Heth's flank. No blame for this disaster was placed on Harry Heth by Confederate authorities. He had acted according to direct orders from Hill and had taken sufficient steps to ensure that the danger to the flank of the attacking column was known to the corps commander. *LL*, 244–46.

9. The fruits of their adventure had been to drive the Yankees away from Richmond.
10. "Q.M. Dept. C.S." stands for Quartermaster's Department.
11. "A. N. Va." Stands for Army of Northern Virginia.
12. John Minor Botts was a U.S. congressman from Virginia and avowed neutral. He was arrested, along with thirty others, in March 1862, for treason against the Confederacy. *BCF*, 434.
13. Henry Flanner enlisted at Camp Wyatt at the age of twenty-three on October 26, 1861. He was appointed second lieutenant to rank from May 1, 1862, and transferred to Company H, 40th North Carolina Regiment (3rd Regiment North Carolina Artillery) *NCT*, vol. 6: 405.
14. Five miles northeast of Culpepper Court House on the Orange & Alexandria Railroad. Perry Kirkley Davis, *Military Atlas of the Civil War* (Fairfax Press, 1983), plate 23, no. 4.
15. "O &A" is the Orange & Alexandria RR.
16. TFW's mother was to go to Wilmington from Lumberton.
17. "A.Q.M." is Assistant Quartermaster.
18. Col. John Decatur Barry, commander of the 18th North Carolina Regiment.
19. Dr. Stewart was transferred to Charlotte Court House, Virginia, November 1863. *NCT*, vol. 3: 488.
20. Benjamin M. Cromwell, M.D. was assigned to the 3rd North Carolina and reported on April 6, 1864. He was captured at Winchester, Virginia, on September 19, 1864 and was confined at Old Capitol Prison, Washington, D.C. He was transferred to Fort Delaware on December 7, 1864, and then to Fort Monroe on December 9. He was exchanged on January 6, 1865, and furloughed, returning to the regiment. He was paroled with the regiment at Appomattox Court House on April 9, 1865. *NCT*, vol. 3: 488.
21. On November 26 the Federal army crossed the lower Rapidan and turned west to meet Lee's army. Lee thought the enemy was heading south and moved to strike their flank. On November 27 the two armies met at Payne's Farm. The 3rd North Carolina was formed up and moved forward in the thick undergrowth. They struck the enemy where their line crossed the road. The action was quite sharp for a short time but the Confederates charged, driving three lines of the enemy before them. The pursuit followed for about eight hundred yards, and it was discovered that the enemy was turning the 3rd's left. Col. Thruston adjusted the front, but three companies on the right failed to hear the command and did not follow, subsequently forming on the 1st North Carolina. The remaining companies were outnumbered, and they retired to the field beyond the road, where a temporary work had been thrown up. The 3rd remained in that position until the Federals retired. The losses of the regiment were reported as 99 men killed, wounded and captured. Report by Colonel Stephen D. Thruston, Commander 3rd N.C. Regiment. *NCT*, vol. 3: 484–85.

22. A creek that flows into the Rapidan River near Mitchell's Ford. *Military Atlas of the Civil War*, plate 23, no. 4.
23. "W. Qrs." is winter quarters.
24. The soldiers in the ranks often made the surgeons the butt of their jokes, but just as often they picked on the adjutants, supply officers and all others who were not in the ranks. The medical corps was no place for cowards however; the surgeon was a true non-combatant and was forbidden to engage in any action which was not strictly in the line of duty. He carried no weapon of war and his attention during battle was usually focused on the wounded and not on protecting himself. During an engagement, the assistant surgeon was on the front lines or immediately behind so as to treat the newly wounded and evacuate them to the field hospital as soon as possible. During the march the assistant surgeon usually took his place at the rear of the unit to care for dropouts and return them to the line of march expediently. The ambulance train was always an easy target for enemy raiders on the march, and to protect the wounded, the ambulance train was often placed in the center of the line of march. Any attack on the train would split the forces and cause confusion. *DG*, 111–22.
25. The regiment reported ninety-nine men killed, wounded, and captured. *NCT*, vol. 3: 485.
26. The new and more strict conscription measures passed by the Confederate Congress failed to produce many new capable soldiers. Many were too fresh from a protected lifestyle to adjust to the severity of war and the professionalism at that stage in the conflict. Others when retreating with veterans were seized with panic and ran, never to be heard from again. All too many never really made an effort to adjust and simply waited for a chance to slip away. It was far more difficult to assimilate these raw recruits into this battle-tested, veteran army than it had been earlier in the war. A much more effective conscription plan was the extension of the draft age to create a reserve force in each state. All men aged seventeen and those between forty-six and fifty were drafted into state reserve forces which could be mobilized if needed in a local emergency. In 1864 the Confederacy raised fifty thousand reserves for the army. Hattaway Herman and Archer Jones, *How the North Won: A Military History of the Civil War* (Champaign: Univ. of Illinois Press, 1983), 531–33. Early in the war, North Carolina Governor, Zebulon Vance, had opposed conscription but at this late date he fully supported the new conscription measures and once again provided significant numbers of men for service in the Confederate army. *BCF*, 691–98.
27. Private Jesse Hinshaw was born in Yadkin County where he made a living as a farmer. He enlisted at the age of thirty on October 27, 1863. He was discharged from the army on March 14, 1864, because of a disability labeled "a state of mental imbecility bordering on idiocy, and a caracature of spine." *NCT*, vol. 3: 571.
28. Food, clothing and shelter were essential elements of survival that allowed a fighting soldier the opportunity to prepare physically and mentally for the terror of the battlefield. At this stage in the war there existed a severe shortage of these essential elements in the Army of Northern Virginia which made it even tougher on the new conscript. Foraging for even the most meager meal, building a lean-to from pine poles and tree branches, and traveling the hard, rocky roads of Virginia in bare feet became a serious deterrent for this new conscript to remain in the army. The Confederate supply system was notoriously inefficient, and soldiers in the field often went without. Impressment for military use was supported by the military, and the

Confederate soldier stretched this approval as far as possible to survive. The Confederate soldier did not intend to go hungry if food was available, and new conscripts had to learn quickly to survive.
29. Many cases of sickness and disease were reported among these new conscripts, just as new recruits fell to disease earlier in the war. Medical standards were relaxed for these conscripts due to the need to replenish the thinned ranks. Closely associated with weak conscription requirements was the background of these new men. Most of them were farm boys who had never been subjected to communicable diseases of childhood—chicken pox, measles, mumps, diphtheria, and scarlet fever. Such diseases quickly took hold and once again threatened epidemics in the camps. These farm boys were far more susceptible to these diseases than men from urban areas. MSHCW, iv.
30. Orange Court House is about seven miles northeast of Gordonsville near the Rapidan River. *Military Atlas of the Civil War*, plate 23, no. 4.
31. Whist is a card game ancestral to bridge, played with a full deck by two teams of two players, in which the last card dealt indicates trump. Tricks of four cards are played and a point is scored for each trick over six won by each team. There is no bidding and no dummy. Albert H. Morehead, *Hoyle's Rules of Games* (New York: Penguin, 1983), 33.
32. Irving C. Stone was born in New York and resided as a teacher in Beaufort County, North Carolina before he enlisted at the age of twenty-four. He was mustered in as a sergeant and was promoted to first sergeant within eight months. He was appointed to second lieutenant on August 1, 1862. He was wounded at Chancellorsville on May 3, 1863, and promoted to first lieutenant the next month. He was promoted to captain to rank from October 9, 1863, and was captured at Spotsylvania Court House on May 12, 1864, with most of the 3rd North Carolina NCT, vol. 3: 578.
33. Captain Edward Hall Armstrong, commander of Company G.
34. "Chapel Hill pranks" refers to student pranks typical at the University of North Carolina at Chapel Hill.
35. Lt. Col. William M. Parsley, Commanding Officer of the 3rd North Carolina—Captain John L. Cantwell—Maj. William T. Ennett.
36. Col. John L. Cantwell served as a produce broker for Adams Express Company before the war and was also secretary of the Wilmington Produce Exchange. He served for many years as secretary of the Chamber of Commerce where he maintained a careful and sometimes exaggerated regard for official detail. During the war he fought in most of the major battles as part of the 3rd North Carolina and was captured in the "Bloody Angle" at Spotsylvania Courthouse with most of his regiment. As a prisoner, he was purposely exposed, with six hundred other Confederate officers, to almost certain death in a violent cross-fire on Morris Island. He never forgot this experience and kept a detailed record of it including a list of the fifty-nine other officers in a small notebook which he carried in his pocket and closely guarded for the rest of his life. CCFR, 300–301.
37. Franking means to put an official mark—in this case his name—on a letter so it can be sent for free. During the Civil War, soldiers on both sides had the privilege of franking but the postage had to be paid by the addressee.
38. Rations issued by the Confederate Commissary Departments, if they ever got to the troops, ranged from poor quality to downright unsafe, especially in the latter years of the war. Deteriorating railroads and supply wagon trains continuously hassled by

enemy scouts, kept the supply of rations always late getting to troops on the march. Most of the men were ultimately resigned to foraging for themselves whenever they grew hungry. Considering the combination of irregular and unbalanced diet, the ignorance of proper cooking methods and the preference of the troops for frying everything in heavy grease, it is understandable that so much illness existed with the army in the field. Rations or the lack of rations were one of the worst problems encountered by surgeons in the effort to keep the army healthy and effective. Robertson, 64–66.
39. "Orange C.H." is Orange Court House.
40. "Tim" is Alfred V. Wood, TFW's younger brother.
41. "W." is Wilmington.
42. Robert Barclay Wood, Jr., TFW's brother.
43. Captain Richard F. Langdon, Regimental Quartermaster.
44. Moore Hospital, TFW's old training ground in Richmond.
45. "His" pants are Ennett's pants in this sentence.
46. The "long roll beat" are drums, calling the troops to parade.
47. The *Spectator* and *Tatler* were popular 18th Century English periodicals with essays covering politics, literature, and social gossip. The *Guardian* was a Manchester weekly established by Charles Prestwich Scott in 1821 and supported the Liberal party, lobbying for social reforms. By 1855 it had become a daily and one of the world's most respected newspapers. *Encyclopedia Americana*, vol. 24: 427, 442; vol. 25: 464–65.

CHAPTER 10. THE WILDERNESS CAMPAIGN

1. An excellent monograph on the Battle of the Wilderness is Gordon C. Rhea's *The Battle of the Wilderness, May 5–6, 1864* (Baton Rouge: Louisiana State Univ. Press, 1994). This note references page 21.
2. Thomas J. Armstrong private papers, Univ. of North Carolina at Wilmington. Dated Mar. 30, 1864.
3. Armstrong private papers, Apr. 8, 1864.
4. BW, 46–60.
5. BW, 67–86.
6. "Our old field of battle" is Chancellorsville.
7. Brigadier General John Marshall Jones had received a flesh wound in the thigh at Gettysburg in the attack on Culp's Hill and returned to the army in September, 1863. He received a serious wound to the head in November at the Battle of Payne's Farm but reported back in a few days to resume command. His brigade would open the fight in the Wilderness on May 5, 1864. MHCG, 122.
8. Around 6:00 A.M. on May 5, Ewell's advance force, Johnson's division, spotted federal columns crossing the Turnpike just ahead of them. Halting his columns, Johnson ordered Jones's advance brigade to deploy on either side of the turnpike and began to form his other brigades for battle. Aware of Ewell's approach, Meade turned to meet him at the intersection of the Brock Road and the Orange Turnpike. The Federal Fifth Corps struck first in the center but were repulsed by Ewell's corps at Saunders Field on the Orange Turnpike. When first contact had been made with the enemy, and as Ewell began to redeploy his troops, the enemy launched an attack in the thick tangle of the forest which routed Jones's brigade and seriously threatened the destruction of the support brigade under the command of General Cullen Andrews

Battle. General Jones was killed while trying to rally his broken regiments. Battle's brigade, though confused, held fast. General Steuart's brigade moved in on the left of the threatened brigade—with the 3rd North Carolina on the right—and General Robert Rodes sent two brigades to reinforce Battle's right. The whole line moved forward to repulse the Federal attack and in the move, Steuart's brigade captured the 146th New York infantry regiment and two guns. *BW*, 115–71.
9. Winslow's Battery D, First New York Artillery.
10. Lee's prediction of the effect that the Wilderness would have on the heavily burdened, strung-out enemy column was quite accurate, and Grant had done exactly as he expected, but Lee's outnumbered forces could not hold the initiative for long. Ewell's corps suffered greatly in this series of attacks, but due to superb leadership and remarkable determination, the line held. In the afternoon after repeated attacks from both sides, the fight shifted from Ewell's front to the right, and A. P. Hill became heavily engaged. Ewell reformed his troops, protected his flanks and threw up strong fortifications before nightfall. The Union advance on the Orange Plank Road, by General Hancock's corps, eventually ground to a halt under heavy pressure from Hill's Confederates. The fighting on the fifth ended in a stalemate and both sides fortified their positions for the night. The day which had begun with a promise of victory for Grant's army had ended in bitterness and defeat. *BW*, 187–250.
11. To take advantage of the weakened right side of the Confederate line, Grant ordered a massive attack by Hancock's corps, augmented by Burnside's Ninth Corps, for dawn on May 6. Federal troops broke the center of Lee's outnumbered lines along the Orange Plank Road, but General Longstreet arrived with his corps just in time, and attacked with John Gregg's Texas brigade in the lead, driving General Hancock's Federal troops on the Federal left, back to the Brock Road. On the Confederate left, both sides had spent the morning of May 6 attacking and counter-attacking until exhaustion and confusion had created a stalemate. Steuart's brigade solidly held the center of Ewell's line just north of the Orange Turnpike. General Gordon had discovered that the Federal right was uncovered and by late afternoon had received permission to attack the Federal flank. Once again, the dense forest of the Wilderness created confusion and breakdowns in communication, and the Rebel assault soon faltered. The Federals held on until nightfall and the Battle of the Wilderness was basically over. *BW*, 283–425.
12. Ewell's corps was entrenched on either side of the Orange Turnpike and Hill's corps covered the Orange Plank Road. With the exception of the brief time that Ramseur's brigade tried to fill the gap between the two forces, a distance of approximately two miles separated the two wings of Lee's army. Grant tried to take advantage of this hole in the Confederate line on May 6 but was never able to accomplish it.
13. *BW*.
14. Having reached an impasse between the two opposing forces, and deciding that Lee could not be beaten in this environment, Grant decided to move his army out of the Wilderness. He, however, did not withdraw but instead moved to the left ("sidled") towards Spotsylvania on May 7, to try and get around Lee's right flank and position himself between the Confederates and Richmond. Lee began to move his army quickly towards Spotsylvania by parallel roads to cover his flank. Fitzhugh Lee's delaying tactics at the Alsop farm on May 8 enabled General Richard H. Anderson's corps to reach Laurel Hill, west of Spotsylvania Court House, just minutes ahead of the Federal army

and make a stand. Gordon C. Rhea, *The Battles for Spotsylvania Court House and The Road to Yellow Tavern* (Baton Rouge: Louisiana State Univ. Press, 1997), 21–47.

15. Captain John R. Potts's battery was part of Major John C. Haskell's artillery battalion who arrived at the Spindle Farm on the Brock Road with Stuart and Anderson's forces and arranged his batteries in echelon, each supporting the others. At one time during the ensuing battle, on May 8, with the U.S. Fifth Corps, Potts's North Carolina guns were firing in three different directions. Potts was killed along with half of his men, but officers and orderlies continued to service the guns with Captain Flanner in command. Rhea, *The Battles for Spotsylvania Court House*, 55–56, 360.

16. TFW is referring to his regiment. The 3rd North Carolina saw little or no action until the 10th. As his army arrived on the battlefield, Lee placed them in line on Laurel Hill to meet the probable Federal assault. Lee shifted Heth's and Mahone's divisions to the left to attack Hancock's line along the Po River, leaving Early with just one division to hold Spotsylvania Courthouse. Early had taken command of Hill's Corp because General Hill was too ill to take the field. Ewell's corps was placed in the middle with Johnson's division to hold that portion of the line resembling an inverted V which became known as the "Muleshoe" Salient. Steuart's brigade was on the right or northeast side of the Muleshoe with Colonel William Witcher's brigade on the left and on the right was Brigadier General James H. Lane's brigade of Hill's corps. *NCT*, vol. 3: 485.

17. Lt. Cicero H. Craige died on July 9, 1864, of the wound received on May 10, 1864. *NCT*, vol. 3: 578.

18. Little is known about the location of the Confederate field hospitals at Spotsylvania especially the forward hospitals, but it is conceivable that brigade hospital was in the Trigg House about a mile to the rear of Steuart's line. Spotsylvania National Battlefield Park.

19. Late on the afternoon of the 10th, Colonel Emory Upton's Union brigade broke through the line at Dole's brigade on the left side of the Muleshoe. Several regiments from Steuart's brigade, including the 3rd North Carolina, were moved over to reinforce the breach. After a sharp fight the Union was repulsed. Col. Thruston was seriously wounded and Lt. Col. Parsley took command of the regiment. It was here that Cicero Craige was wounded. At dawn on the 12th, a massive attack by Hancock's Second Corps was made on Johnson's division, occupying the east side of the Muleshoe. The Federals broke through at the point of the apex held by Col. William Witcher's (formerly J. M. Jones) brigade, striking the 1st and then the 3rd North Carolina and finally capturing the entire division. The prisoners taken by the Federals numbered three thousand including Major General Edward Johnson and Brigadier General George Steuart. Rhea, *The Battles for Spotsylvania Court House*, 161–237.

20. Lee struck back with a series of brutal counterattacks that resulted in a massive struggle for the "Bloody Angle." The desperate hand-to-hand combat continued for twenty-two hours, but the Confederate line held. During this series of counterattacks, General Lee rode ahead to hurry Nat Harris's Mississippians forward to Rode's assistance. In his urgency to hurry the men he moved to the head of the column with General Harris, and they suddenly came under heavy artillery fire. Just as in the Wilderness, the men began to yell "Go back, General Lee, go back." Calmly he announced, "If you will promise to drive those people from our works, I will go back." Clifford Dowdey, *Lee's*

Last Campaign (New York: Bonanza Books, 1993), 209–11. Early on the 13th Lee ordered the survivors of this ordeal to pull back out of the Muleshoe and establish a new line. The Federals had taken a strategic position away from the Confederates but were unable to turn the victory to their advantage. In two weeks, the Union had lost eighteen thousand men and the Confederate casualties were almost twelve thousand men. Ewell's Second Corps had lost approximately fifty-five hundred men. Rhea, *The Battles for Spotsylvania Court House*, 243–311.

21. All but about thirty men in the 3rd North Carolina regiment were killed or captured, including most of its officers. *NCT*, vol. 3: 485.
22. Captain Edward Armstrong was slightly wounded during the attack on May 10 and again severely on the 12th when the entire division was overwhelmed. Captain Armstrong's body servant, Mose, in a letter to his mother on May 21 says: "Master Edward's co. was all taken but four & himself makes five. Master Ned was slightly wounded on the 10th in the rite breast. The ball did not enter but bruised smartly and on the 12th he was severely wounded in his upper left arm and was resected and since he wished that he would of had it taken off and the doctor thinks now too that it would have been best to had it taken off but they are agoing to try to save it now. Night before last it commenced to bleeding and they begin to think that his arm would have to be taken off. Now at this time he seems to be in good spiret but he is helpless. He can't walk nor can't read. We had him to toat two miles & 1/2 on a litter." Ned Armstrong died June 7, 1864. Letter from Mose—May 21, 1864, Thomas J. Armstrong private papers, Univ. of North Carolina at Wilmington.
23. Captain John Badger Brown was wounded on May 10, 1864, and didn't return to the regiment until November of 1864. *NCT*, vol. 3: 501. Sergeant Major Robert C. McRee was wounded on the 10th and died of complications from that wound on June 6, 1864. *NCT*, vol. 3: 571. Ned Armstrong mentions in his last letter to his father that Sgt. R. C. McRee is there in the hospital with him and the surgeon did not think he would live. Thomas J. Armstrong private papers, Univ. of North Carolina at Wilmington—May 28, 1864.
24. As TFW mentions, the division was now headed by Major General Stephen Dodson Ramseur. On the 12th a ball had passed through his right arm below the elbow and although painfully wounded he refused to leave the field. On the 14th he had some difficulty and could not keep up with the troops but by the 19th he was able to lead the attack against the Federal right flank. He assumed command of Jubal Early's division in late May. The 3rd North Carolina was brigaded with the 1st, 2nd, 4th and 14th North Carolina Regiments in Ramseur's old brigade, now commanded by Brigadier General William R. Cox from Scotland Neck, North Carolina. Cox was given the temporary rank of brigadier general in May and was assigned to command the brigade on June 4, 1864. *NCT*, vol. 3: 485.
25. On May 18, General Grant decided to take one more shot at Lee's lines, thinking that the Confederate shift to the right might have weakened the left, held by Ewell's corps. He tried a repeat of Hancock's pre-dawn attack at the salient but it failed and proved costly for the Union. On the 19th General Lee ordered Ewell's Second Corps to probe the Federal left. General Ewell was not fit to command this operation and managed to get entangled with a sizeable body of enemy troops. Rodes and Gordon struck a Union force at the Harris Farm, just north of the Ni River, and finding a fresh division of heavy artillery, the push came to a halt. *LLC*, 224–25.

26. On May 21, General Grant once more began extending his army to the left towards the Chickahominy, seriously stretching Lee's resources. Grant was moving in a semi-circular route that would bring him closer to Richmond and force Lee to pull back to remain between Grant and the Confederate capitol. The one possible hope of preventing this extension of Grant's left was to strike a blow hard enough to halt the move. There was a brief engagement at Jerico Mills on the North Anna River but neither side benefited. On May 30th at Bethesda Church near Cold Harbor, Jubal Early, now commanding the Second Corps after Ewell's reassignment to Richmond, moved to attack the Federal left. Unfortunately he went in head on, without proper reconnaissance and coordination with the First Corps, and it resulted in a bloody repulse and cost many valuable Confederate lives. *LL*, vol. 3: 502. Brigadier General George Pierce Doles, brigade commander in Rode's division, was killed near Bethesda Church, on June 2, 1864, while supervising the entrenchment of his line. A sharpshooter's bullet passed through his left chest. *MHCG*, 55.
27. During the Battle of Cold Harbor, June 3, 1864, Early's corps (formerly Ewell's) came under attack by General A. E. Burnside's Ninth Corps and part of Major General Gouverneur K. Warren's Fifth Corps. The three-day battle for advantage and position culminated in a general assault that lasted less than an hour. Warren's corps struck the line held by Rode's division and was repulsed. Repeated Federal attacks on the strongly entrenched Confederate line were turned back with heavy casualties. These advances were beaten back so efficiently that many Confederate troops never saw action. Cold Harbor represented a dramatic change in world warfare. This was modern war. No longer would masses of trained soldiers charge across open fields to close with waiting lines of heavily entrenched enemy troops. The accuracy of modern firepower and advantage strong defensive positions had effectively tipped the scales against the brute power of superior numbers. The old massed assaults of Napoleonic Wars, so popular with Civil War leaders on both sides, came to an end at Cold Harbor. Grant's losses numbered almost fifteen thousand in killed and wounded to the Confederate's seventeen hundred. *LLC*, 291–300.
28. He is referring to the first Battle of Cold Harbor, June 27, 1862, during the Seven Days Battles. According to the National Park Service, Lee's headquarters at that time were probably located in or near the William Gaines farm to the right of Cold Harbor Road, just west of the crossing of Powhite Creek at Gaines Mill. The home was called "Powhite."
29. Because Richmond was so near the front at Cold Harbor—approximately ten miles—most of the wounded from the battle of June 3rd had already been transported to hospitals in city by the 10th. Most of the brigade and division hospitals had settled into a normal routine dealing with fatigue, improper diet and camp diseases.
30. Col. Thruston was wounded on May 10 at Spotsylvania but returned in early June to assume command of the remnants of both North Carolina regiments. *NCT*, vol. 3: 487.
31. Seven thousand Union troops were lost in eight minutes, the greatest slaughter in the shortest time in the entire war.
32. Captain Thomas Case Lewis served as company commander of Company I, 18th North Carolina Regiment. He had been wounded at Chancellorsville on May 2, 1863, and returned to duty on September 1, 1863. He was captured at Spotsylvania Court House on May 12, 1864, and confined at Fort Delaware until transferred to Hilton Head, South Carolina, on August 20, 1864. He remained a prisoner until

June 16, 1865, when he was released after taking the Oath of Allegiance. *NCT*, vol. 6: 400.
33. Edward Hall Armstrong died on June 7, 1864, and Cicero H. Craige died on July 9, 1864.
34. Dr. Benjamin M. Cromwell had been assigned to the regiment on April 6, 1864, just prior to the Battle of the Wilderness. He replaced Dr. Dabney Herndon who served as temporary surgeon for the 3rd North Carolina while on duty with the 1st North Carolina. *NCT*, vol. 3: 488.

CHAPTER 11. EARLY'S MARCH ON WASHINGTON CITY

1. J. Tracy Power, *Lee's Miserables* (Chapel Hill: Univ. of North Carolina Press, 1998), 6–7.
2. B. Franklin Cooling, *Monocacy—The Battle that Saved Washington* (Shippensburg: White Mane Publishing Co., 1997), 2–11.
3. Louisa Court House is on the Virginia Central Railroad, twenty-six miles east of Charlottesville, Virginia.
4. It is assumed TFW is talking about General Stuart's raid on Union General Pope's headquarters at Catlett Station in August of 1862, just prior to Second Manassas. *LL*, 68–70.
5. TFW is referring here to the recent engagement in May, 1864. The Shenandoah Valley was troubling to General Grant. The Confederates had used the Valley repeatedly as an invasion route into Maryland and Pennsylvania. He had sent General Franz Sigel with eighty-nine hundred troops up the Valley until General Breckinridge challenged the advance on May 15, 1864. Grant replaced Sigel with Major General David Hunter who continued the push up the Valley with twelve thousand soldiers. The Confederates attempted to halt the drive with a small force of fifty-six hundred men under Major General William "Grumble" Jones. Hunter attacked the town of Piedmont on June 5 and the Confederate defense crumbled. General Jones was killed and the Confederates lost sixteen hundred men. Hunter pressed on to Lexington where he burned the Virginia Military Institute before pressing on towards Lynchburg. Breckinridge hurriedly set up a defense line around Lynchburg and awaited Early's arrival. Benjamin Franklin Cooling, *Jubal Early's Raid on Washington, 1864* (Baltimore: Nautical & Aviation Publishing, 1989), 10–25.
6. There was no university in Lynchburg. TFW was probably referring to the University of Virginia in Charlottesville.
7. Finding himself outnumbered by Early's and Breckinridge's fourteen thousand combined troops, Hunter decided to retreat, claiming a shortage of ammunition. Fearing that Early's pursuit would block off the Valley route, he fell back through the Kanawha Valley into the West Virginia mountains, leaving the Shenandoah Valley clear for Early's advance northward. *JERW*, 12–14.
8. General Grant ordered Hunter to "scorch the earth." Grant believed that if he could deny the Confederates the use of the Valley, which they termed the "Breadbasket of the South," it would create significant hardships for the Rebel army and hasten its destruction. Hunter was instructed to "make all the Valley south of the B&O a desert." Grant clearly indicated that his order did not include destroying homes and personal property of civilians, but Hunter chose to ignore this directive and destroyed many private homes throughout the Valley. Charles C. Osborne, *Jubal: The*

Life and Times of General Jubal A. Early, CSA (Baton Rouge: Louisiana State Univ. Press), 299–300.

9. General Early's cavalry under Gen. Ransom caught up with Hunter's retreating column at Salem, Virginia, and, after destroying several batteries of artillery in a sharp fight, they broke off pursuit as Hunter took to the mountains. *JERW*, 12–13.
10. The Rev. Moses Ashley Curtis, D.D., was one of the foremost botanists in the country in the mid-1800s. He specialized in the vegetation of the Southern Allegheny Mountains and during the war was instrumental in cataloguing edible fungi which helped provide nourishment for the troops in the field. He served as a mentor for TFW who later became one of North Carolina's leading botanists. TFW published a book in 1886 titled *Wilmington Flora* which he dedicated to Moses Curtis. Thomas Fanning Wood, A Sketch of the Botanical Work of the Rev. Moses Ashley Curtis, D.D., *Journal of the Elisha Mitchell Scientific Society* 2 (May 22, 1885): 9–31.
11. Tallow is hard fat obtained from cattle, sheep or horses and was used in foodstuffs or to make candles, leather dressing, soap and lubricants.
12. The Union blockade of Confederate seaports, especially Wilmington, was making it more difficult to get supplies into the South and thus to the troops in the field. Early was also moving rapidly into enemy territory leaving his base of supply, such as it was, behind in Virginia.
13. Hunter's troops not only burned the college buildings of VMI and the home of John Letcher, who had been Virginia's Governor at the time of secession, but he allowed his men to remove books from the library and generally steal from the people in the town. *LLC*, 311. The Union troops had also desecrated Stonewall Jackson's grave by damaging the site and removing the head and foot boards. *JERW*, 16.
14. As Early's army approached the Potomac at Harpers Ferry, their mission was clear: capture the Federal reserve division which guarded the railroad and supply dumps, then destroy the Baltimore and Ohio Railroad, the means by which Hunter might return and threaten Early's rear. General Franz Sigel commanded some 5,000 to 6,000 troops protecting Martinsburg and the B&O Railroad. Brigadier General Max Weber had another 580 cavalry and infantry protecting Harpers Ferry. *JERW*, 24–25.
15. Early had carefully planned the operation against Martinsburg and Harpers Ferry to capture both Sigel's and Weber's forces but experienced stiffer resistance than expected and suffered from poorly coordinated leadership. Sigel was able to withdraw his men from Harpers Ferry and consolidate his force with Weber's men on Maryland Heights across the Potomac from Harpers Ferry. Gordon's and Ramseur's regiments began to take advantage of the spoils of war and were consumed with plundering and pillaging the Federal commissary stores and remains of the Fourth of July celebration. Early's senior officers nearly lost control of the situation and it took some time to regain order. *JERW*, 25–27.
16. Early desperately wanted to repeat Stonewall Jackson's feat of capturing the entire garrison at Harpers Ferry just two years before but could not. The Federal resistance from Maryland Heights prevented Early from accomplishing this, and he realized it was time to move on. They crossed the Potomac on July 5 and 6 and they moved through Sharpsburg to Hagerstown, Boonsboro, and Frederick. On the afternoon of the 6th Early received a message from General Lee extending his mission. An estimated fifteen thousand to twenty thousand Confederate prisoners were being held at Point Lookout, south of Baltimore. These men were sorely needed to help rein-

force Lee's thinly stretched lines at Petersburg, and he asked that General Early attempt a joint rescue attempt with the Confederate Navy. Maryland Brigadier General Bradley T. Johnson and his cavalry would provide the land contingent. July 12 was the designated day of liberation so Early must move quickly to Frederick City where Johnson would split from the army and move toward Baltimore while the rest of Early's troops would proceed to Washington City. *MBW*, 30, 54–56.

17. "hors de combat"—disabled or out of action.
18. May 5 being the initial engagement between Ewell's corps and Warren's Fifth Corps during the Battle of the Wilderness and May 10 being the initial attack on the Muleshoe at Spotsylvania by Col. Emory Upton's Union brigade.
19. Captain Edward H. Armstrong and Sergeant-Major Robert C. McRee were killed at Spotsylvania.
20. TFW is talking about the cavalry engagement on June 5, 1864, between General William E. "Grumble" Jones's cavalry and Federal General Hunter's forces at Piedmont, Virginia. General Jones was killed in this engagement.
21. TFW is talking about the University of Virginia in Charlottesville.
22. In addition to his cousin's home, Hunter burned the home of Edmund J. Lee, a distant cousin of Robert E. Lee, a home where Hunter's own niece, Helen, had spent a short time. Osbourne, *Jubal: The Life and Times*, 300.
23. TFW is talking about the Virginia Military Institute.
24. Brigadier General Max Weber's contingent of 580 Union infantry and cavalry protecting Harpers Ferry.
25. Stonewall Jackson had taken Harpers Ferry on September 15, 1862, by shelling the town from Loudoun Heights.
26. Col. John H. Lamar, popular commander of the 61st Georgia was killed during the Battle of Monocacy on July 9, 1864. *MBW*, 148.
27. This is not quite an accurate picture of this engagement and will be discussed later in this chapter. While true that Ramseur did not commit his entire corps to cover the Georgetown Pike bridge, Gordon was fully engaged on the right of the line and forced the retreat by General Wallace's forces.
28. Most historical accounts contradict TFW as to Maryland's sentiments by 1864. There were many Southern sympathizers in the state, certainly, and even Maryland units fighting for the Confederate army but the state was definitely Union and the area around Frederick was the strong Union part of Maryland. These scruffy rebels entering their state did not inspire confidence and purchases with Confederate script did not win popularity. Jubal Early's ransoming of Frederick as a vendetta to make the North pay for the destruction of the Virginia countryside did not win many Marylanders over to the South. It is obvious that TFW and his comrades saw what they wanted to see and the local townspeople cheering for the rebel army did not represent the sentiments of the population of that part of Maryland.
29. TFW is sarcastically referring to General Ben Butler whom the citizens of New Orleans called "the Beast."
30. He is talking about grape shot rounds from cannons.
31. Maryland Governor Augustus Bradford. General Early later suggested that he condoned the burning of the Bradford residence as well as the mansion of Montgomery Blair outside Washington but claimed he had not ordered either act. *JERW*, 220.
32. On July 7 and 8, Major General Lewis "Lew" Wallace and Brigadier General Erastus B.

Tyler attempted to block Early's progress by throwing up a defense line west of Frederick, Maryland. Seriously outnumbered and waiting for reinforcements, Wallace abandoned the Frederick line and pulled back across the Monocacy and set up a stronger defense line on the eastern bank blocking the major road to Washington. On the 9th there was a stubborn fight led by Rodes and Ramseur at the key crossings of the Monocacy River. General Cox's brigade with the 3rd North Carolina Regiment was held in reserve. After a brutal day's fight, Brigadier General John McCausland's cavalry led a push across the Monocacy to strike the left of the Federal line. This bold strike was followed by an attack on the Federal left by Major General John B. Gordon's division which pushed the Union line back across the Washington Pike. Gordon's attack overwhelmed Wallace's smaller force and Wallace was compelled to retreat towards Baltimore. Early's march toward Washington continued on the 10th, and General Bradley T. Johnson headed for Baltimore. What makes this battle so important is that Wallace succeeded in delaying Early for several days giving Washington just enough time to prepare for the Confederate invasion and for desperately needed reinforcements to arrive from the Petersburg front. MBW, 76–85, 111–55.

33. Early wanted this border state community to feel "his wrath" in retaliation for similar acts by Federal forces in Virginia. He imposed a financial levy of two hundred thousand dollars or his men would burn down the city. The specific demand was for two hundred thousand dollars "in current money for the use of the army," or fifty thousand dollars in material goods at current prices for each of their respective departments. The officers also demanded twenty thousand pounds of bacon, six thousand pounds of sugar, three thousand pounds each of coffee and salt and five hundred pounds of flour. This assessment for a town of only eight thousand residents was a bit steep and other assessments in Maryland (Hagerstown and Middletown) had been far less, but they agreed to pay. The full payment came with a "gentleman's agreement" that all property in the city, including that belonging to the Federal Government would be spared. Early's officers attempted to honor this agreement but rebel scavengers liberated a good bit of private and government property before the army left Frederick. MBW, 97–99.

34. After the Federal army had retreated, Early's men were in no shape to continue the march and encamped on the battlefield for the night. TFW and his fellow surgeons had their hands full that night. The Federals, in their hasty retreat, were forced to leave their wounded behind to be cared for by the Confederates. Every house and barn in the area became a temporary field hospital, and the dead of both sides were interred on the battlefield. (After the war the bodies were moved to Antietam National Cemetery and Mount Olivet Cemetery in Frederick.) JERW, 78–79.

35. Rockville is eleven miles north west of Washington on the Metropolitan Railroad. O. R. Atlas, plate 27.

36. Early's corps approached Washington from the north west along the Rockville Pike and established a line on July 11 from Fort Reno on the right, on the Old Georgetown Pike, to Fort Lincoln on the left, near the Anacosta River. Rodes's division, along with Ramseur's and Gordon's faced Fort Stevens on Seventh Street or Georgia Ave. President Lincoln observed the siege from Fort Stevens and nearly lost his life there. JERW, 110–13.

37. Silver Spring was the elegant estate of Francis Preston Blair, famous newspaper editor and former member of President Jackson's "Kitchen Cabinet." General Early

established his headquarters here. This home was spared due to intercession of General John Breckinridge who had enjoyed the family's hospitality on numerous occasions. Montgomery Blair was the U.S. Postmaster General and his country estate, called Falkland, was very near his father's home. Falkland was burned but Early denied ordering its destruction. Margaret Leech, *Reveille in Washington* (New York: Harper & Brothers, 1941), 39.

38. Wallace's engagement at Monocacy had delayed Early long enough to give General Grant time to send three brigades from the Sixth Corps and a brigade from the Nineteenth Corps by transport from City Point to Washington. By noon on the 11th they had begun to land at the Washington wharves. *MBW*, 190–91.
39. By July 12 the brigades from the Sixth and Nineteenth Corps had arrived at the front. In an effort to protect the President who insisted on observing from Fort Stevens, General Wright and General McCook launched an offensive aimed at pushing back the Rebel sharpshooters. On the evening of the 12th, Early decided that the Washington defenses were too formidable and withdrew his troops from their lines and began a force-march for the upper Potomac crossings. General Bradley Johnson's mission to threaten Baltimore and free the prisoners at Point Lookout was not successful. They destroyed bridges, track and telegraph lines along the Northern Central Railroad and the Philadelphia & Wilmington Railroad and severed all communications between Washington and the North, but on the 12th Johnson received a message from Early that the Point Lookout operation was cancelled and to rejoin the main army at Washington. *MBW*, 190–99.
40. Early retreated back across the Potomac near Poolesville on the morning of July 14 with approximately twelve thousand men, in excess of one thousand captured horses plus two thousand other livestock and over two hundred thousand dollars in cash. *MBW*, 199.
41. This was probably Federal Colonel William Tibbit's attack near Purcellville which resulted in the capture of over one hundred horses, some eighty wagons and ambulances and over fifty prisoners. If infantry support had been available, Tibbit might have accomplished even more. *JERW*, 194–95.
42. TFW was obviously referring to the enemy moving through Snicker's Gap and crossing the Shenandoah at Castleman's Ferry.
43. Colonel William Allison Owens, 52nd North Carolina Regiment.
44. Colonel Walter Scott Stallings led the 2nd North Carolina Regiment.
45. Colonel James Hall Wood, 14th North Carolina.
46. This engagement was an attempt to prevent Federal Colonel Joseph Thoburn's division of Hunter's army from crossing the Shenandoah River at Castleman's Ferry. Rodes attacked the Federal position and without support Thoburn had to withdraw back across the River. Both sides suffered heavily in this two hour engagement at Cool Spring Farm with the Federals losing approximately four hundred men and the Confederates almost that many. *JERW*, 200–201.
47. This engagement was at Stephenson's Depot or Rutherford's Farm near Winchester on July 21. Ramseur, receiving reports that he faced a small reconnaissance force, rushed headlong into premature combat with General Averell's entire division. William Averell's Federal forces smashed into Ramseur's left, turning the flank and the Confederates fled in confusion. Ramseur lost four guns and some 450 men killed, wounded or captured. Osborne, *Jubal: The Life and Times*, 301.

48. The Yankee losses in this engagement were 1,185 with nearly 500 captured. Seventy-two wagons and twelve caissons were destroyed. *JERW*, 209–11.
49. In the 1862 race for Governor, William Woods Holden supported Zebulon Vance as a candidate. Vance was elected and he and Holden became friends and allies. By 1863, however, Holden was promoting the peace campaign which was opposed by Vance and the armed forces. Holden and Vance split on the issue and ran against each other. Vance was re-elected in 1864. From the army, Vance received 13,209 votes to Holden's 1,824; and in the civilian vote Vance received 44,856 to Holden's 12,647. Holden was appointed Governor in 1865 and was elected in 1868. Vance was re-elected in 1877. Glenn Tucker, *Zeb Vance: Champion of Personal Freedom* (Indianapolis: Bobbs-Merrill, 1965), chaps. 11 and 23. William C. Harris, *William Woods Holden: Firebrand of North Carolina Politics* (Baton Rouge: Louisiana State Univ. Press, 1987), chaps. 6 and 7.
50. Early was determined to ransom several Northern towns to reimburse Virginia families who had lost their homes to Hunter's men. On July 30, General John McCausland with about 2,800 men was sent to Chambersburg to demand a ransom of $500,000 in greenbacks or $100,000 in gold. The Chambersburg leaders could not raise that much money, and McCausland insisted that he had to carry out his orders. The Rebels spread kerosene and set fire to many buildings in the town. McCausland's men looted stores, robbed citizens and broke into private homes. More than 400 buildings and 274 private homes were destroyed with property damage exceeding $1,600.00. One third of the 6,000 inhabitants were rendered homeless. *JERW*, 216–18.
51. After the burning of Chambersburg, Averell pursued the Confederates across the Potomac and surprised them in their encampment. At the time McCausland was at a friend's house in Moorefield. The actual loss for McCausland and Johnson was over 500 men and 678 horses. It was a disaster that almost destroyed the effectiveness of Early's mounted arm for future service. *JERW*, 220.
52. After the second Battle of Kernstown, which cleared the northern end of the Valley of Federal resistance, General Grant finally became concerned. With Confederate control of the Valley, Lee's army had a continued resource for food and a clear pathway to again carry the war to the doorstep of the Union Capitol. On August 2, 1864, Grant appointed General Philip H. Sheridan commander of the combined forces of the Middle Department and the Departments of Washington, D.C., Susquehanna, and West Virginia. General Hunter resigned. This new fighting force ultimately became known as the Army of the Shenandoah. Sheridan's orders from Grant were to "follow the enemy to the death." Jeffry D. Wert, *From Winchester to Cedar Creek* (Mechanicsburg: Stackpole Books, 1997), 8–19.
53. "Porte Crayon" was the pen name for David Hunter Strother, one of the best known graphic artists in the country in the mid 1800s. He was a regular contributor to *Harper's Monthly*, both as an illustrator and writer. In the Civil War, he served as a topographer and staff officer to several Union Generals and was General Hunter's Adjutant General during Early's campaign. *Strother Family Genealogy*, Internet.
54. TFW seems to be symbolically comparing Mosby to Early by using the term "left bower" from the popular army card game of euchre. The left bower is the knave or jack of the other suit of the same color as the trump, being next to the right bower in value.
55. To help Early gain an advantage in the Valley, Lee sent Maj. Gen. Richard H. Anderson, in temporary charge of Longstreet's First Corps, with the thirty-five hundred-

man division of Maj. Gen. Joseph B. Kershaw and a battalion of artillery under Col. Wilfred E. Cutshaw. Osborne, 313–25.
56. I have been unable to discover the meaning of "Isenberg Pontoons," but it is obviously a derogatory statement referring to Gov. Vance and the fact that so many soldiers were without shoes. There was no shoe manufacturer named Isenberg, at the time, nor anyone of that name connected with the Governor.
57. After a month of skirmishing up and down the Valley, Early was convinced that he could continue to out maneuver Sheridan and ultimately gain the upper hand. On September 14 Lee asked that Anderson's and Kershaw's troops, his vital reinforcements, be returned to the Army of Northern Virginia. Even after losing these vital reinforcements, Early remained confident—too confident—that he could master Sheridan. Osborne, 328–32.
58. Early had split his army, with Ramseur on the Berryville Pike to Winchester and the rest of the corps at Stephenson's Depot on the Valley Pike. Sheridan's plan was to cross the Opequon at dawn on the 19th and attack Ramseur, cutting him off from the rest of Early's force. On the morning of September 19, General Early had heard that the Federals had forced a crossing of the Opequon Creek, and he immediately ordered Rodes up to support Ramseur. Ramseur, heavily outnumbered, was able to hold on until Rodes arrived and took the position on the left of the line. Gordon soon arrived and filled in on Rodes's left. The Confederate line held and a gap opened up in the Federal advance. Gordon and Rodes had just conferred about possible counterattack when an artillery shell burst over General Rodes head and he was struck by a fragment and was thrown from his horse. He died a few hours later. After a brief and vigorous assault, the Federals began to fall back until Evan's brigade (the left flank of Gordon's division), meeting a heavy fire, was checked and driven back. The artillery made a bold stand and was soon supported by Rodes's brigade and the Federals were driven back. Suddenly the Federal cavalry attacked Early's left and McCausland's brigade began to retire in disorder. Early tried to send Breckinridge to the left to stop the Federal advance, but unfortunately the withdrawal of the cavalry had unnerved the men up and down the line, and they began to make for the rear. Once again the artillery attempted to hold the line, but it was too late. The retreat became a near panic through Winchester with a brief rally just south of town and a more orderly retreat some twenty miles to Fisher's Hill. Osborne, 333–40.
59. General Early tried to rally his retreating army south of Strasburg at Fisher's Hill. He was hotly pursued by Sheridan. The Federal army made a token assault on Early's entrenched line and Sheridan sent Crook's corps around the Confederate left, along the face of Little North Mountain. Early was surprised on September 22 as the Federal troops descended on his left flank sending the Confederate cavalry once again fleeing their defenses. *The Atlas of the Civil War*, 188–89.
60. Despite the brutal defeats that Early had suffered in September, his record showed significant success as well as disaster. The campaign begun at Lynchburg in June had achieved a great deal. Early had succeeded in pulling the entire Sixth Corps from the Army of the Potomac which was an infantry force larger than his own total strength. He had occupied General Sheridan and one division of cavalry from the James River and had forced Grant to send the troops of Crook and Averell against him who could have been effectively used against Confederate supply lines. This was a notable achievement considering Early at no time during the campaign had

more than 13,200 infantry and about 3,700 cavalry against General Sheridan's army of over 40,000 troops.
61. Rude's Hill is approximately six miles northeast of New Market. The farm was called Meem's Bottoms and was located on a peninsula of land between the North Fork of the Shenandoah River and Smith's Creek. *Civil War Atlas.*
62. This action took place on Saturday, September 24, and it was indeed an orderly retreat. As Sheridan sent brigades around the flanks of the Confederates on Rude's Hill, Early began a parade-ground smooth retreat. Odd-numbered brigades in each division went first, moving down the Turnpike and then re-deploying. Then even-numbered brigades retired from Rude's Hill, moving back through the newly formed lines to form their own two miles further south. Wert, 133–34.
63. This stands for Adjutant & Inspector General who at that time was General Samuel Cooper. The National Park Service.
64. General Rodes was struck behind the ear by a shell fragment rather than a minnié ball, and he died within a few hours. *MHCG*, 188.
65. Brigadier General Archibald Campbell Godwin recruited the 57th North Carolina Infantry, which he led at the Battle of Fredericksburg in December 1862. He was captured with most of his command at the Rappahannock Bridge in November 1863. He was exchanged and promoted to Brigadier General and served with Ramseur's division in the Valley Campaign. He was killed by a shell fragment at Winchester on September 19, 1864. *GG*, 108.
66. The Battles of Cross Keys, June 8, 1862, and Port Republic, June 9, 1863, were part of Jackson's famous Valley Campaign against Federal Generals Frémont and Shields which gave him control of the Valley.
67. TFW is talking about Weyer's Cave, now called the Grand Caverns, between Staunton and Harrisonburg, Virginia.
68. "Porte Crayon" or David Strother published an illustrated travelogue in 1854 entitled *Virginia Illustrated* in which he described Weyer's Cave and the surrounding countryside in some detail, both in words and illustrations. *The Strother Family Genealogy.*
69. The editor was unable to identify Lieut. B——e in either the 1st, 3rd or 14th North Carolina Infantry. He could have been from another brigade. Adjutant T.C.J. refers to Adjutant Theodore C. James with the 3rd North Carolina Regiment.
70. Colonel Charles M. Forsythe was commander of the 3rd Alabama Infantry. *Confederate Military History* 8: 59.
71. After the defeat at Fisher's Hill, Lee had returned Kershaw's thirty-one hundred men to Early, and on October 5, Thomas Rosser arrived with his brigade to reinforce Fitz Lee's cavalry. Even after a succession of setbacks, Early was still confident that he could accomplish a final triumphant victory over the Federal army. On October 13 he found Sheridan's army camped along Cedar Creek and he prepared for an offensive. Early crossed Cedar Creek at dawn on October 19 and launched a surprise attack on Sheridan's camp with the forces of Rosser, Gordon, and Kershaw. Sheridan was absent from the army at the time having been called to Washington for a conference. The attack was initially successful. By 8 o'clock Early's men had captured all of the Union artillery, almost two thousand prisoners, and the Federals were in full retreat. The Federal Sixth Corps held firm and eventually stopped the retreat. General Gordon held the left flank and, finding it dangerously vulnerable, had to extend

his line so that a gap opened between two of his brigades. About 3'oclock Sheridan returned after a wild ride through the countryside and rallying his troops, launched a devastating attack into the gap in Gordon's line that ended up in a Confederate route. While attempting to slow the attack, General Ramseur was mortally wounded and captured. Brigadier General Bryan Grimes was temporarily assigned to command the division. Thus when the Second Corps regrouped at New Market after this defeat at Cedar Creek, the 3rd North Carolina Regiment was in Cox's brigade, Grimes's division. At the Battle of Cedar Creek, the Federal losses totaled 5,995 in killed and wounded and the Confederates over 4,000. *NCT*, vol. 3: 486. General Ramseur received a minor wound and the fire was so intense that he had two horses killed under him. As he was mounting his third horse, he was hit in the chest with a ball. He was taken prisoner south of Strasburg and taken to Belle Grove, Phillip Sheridan's headquarters. He died the following day. *MHCG*, 180.

72. TFW is referring again to the fight at Winchester on September 19, 1864, where the Confederate left under General McCausland came under a heavy attack and the entire line began to retire.
73. The Reverend William C. Power was a member of the staff of the 14th North Carolina Infantry Regiment, Cox's brigade, the same brigade as the 1st and 3rd North Carolina. *NCT*, vol. 5: 395.
74. *NCT*, vol. 3: 486–87.
75. *HRBNC*, vol. 1: 212–14.
76. *The Confederate Veteran* 14 (1907): 40.

BIBLIOGRAPHY

ARTICLES, MANUSCRIPTS, AND PRIVATE PAPERS

Apperson Diary. An account by a Seventh Virginia hospital steward at Chancellorsville. Virginia Historical Society.

Armstrong, Thomas J. Civil War Papers of Captain Edward Armstrong. Manuscript Collection, William Madison Randall Library, Univ. of North Carolina at Wilmington.

Cashman, Diane Cobb. "The History of the Bellamy Mansion." Unpublished research report. Jan. 1990. Property of the Bellamy Mansion, Wilmington, N.C.

Cooper, George, M.D. "The Woods–Father and Son." *Southern Medicine and Surgery* 90, no. 12 (Dec. 1928).

deRosset, William Lord. Civil War papers and Letters. Manuscript Dept., Univ. of North Carolina at Chapel Hill.

McLendon, William W. "Edenborough Medical College." *Medicine in North Carolina*. Raleigh: North Carolina Medical Society, 1972.

Medicine of the Civil War. Exhibit booklet. National Library of Medicine, 1973.

Metts, James. Civil War papers and letters. Manuscript Dept., Univ. of North Carolina at Chapel Hill.

Norton, J. W. Roy. "History of Public Health in North Carolina." *Medicine in North Carolina*, 581–622, Raleigh: North Carolina Medical Society, 1972.

Parsley, William Murdock. Civil War papers. Manuscript Dept., Univ. of North Carolina at Chapel Hill.

Seapker, Janet K. "Wood Works." *Lower Cape Fear Historical Society Bulletin* 39 (1994), no. 1.

Shingleton, E. Daniel. "Article on Thomas Fanning Wood." *North Carolina Medical Journal* 52, no. 4 (Apr. 1991).

Thruston, Col. S. D. "Report of the Conduct of General George H. Steuart's Brigade from the 5th to the 12th of May, 1864." *Southern Historical Society Papers* 14.

Washburn, B. E. *A History of the North Carolina State Board of Health*. Raleigh: North Carolina State Board of Health, 1966.

Whitehouse, Frank. "A Michigan Surgeon at Chancellorsville." *University of Michigan Medical Bulletin* 29 (1963).

Whitehead, M., M.D. *Report of the Secretary of the North Carolina Board of Health*. Wilmington, N.C., Sept. 4, 1884.

Wood, Thomas Fanning. An Assistant Surgeon's Recollections of the Gettysburg Campaign (manuscript written on or about 1886). Thomas Fanning Wood Collection, William Madison Randall Library, Univ. of North Carolina at Wilmington.

―――. Autobiographical sketch of Thomas Fanning Wood. Manuscript Collection, William Madison Randall Library, Univ. of North Carolina at Wilmington.

―――. The Committee of Safety–1861. Thomas Fanning Wood Collection, William Madison Randall Library, Univ. of North Carolina at Wilmington.

―――. Letters from Thomas Fanning Wood as correspondent (under the initials U.U.D.). *The Wilmington Journal* (1865).

―――. The letters of Thomas Fanning Wood to his parents & siblings from the front—1863–1864. Family collection of Alfred V. Wood.

―――. "Otis Frederick Manson, M.D." *North Carolina Medical Journal* 21 (1888).

———. The Population Analyzed. Thomas Fanning Wood Collection, William Madison Randall Library, Univ. of North Carolina at Wilmington.
———. "A Sketch of the Botanical Work of the Rev. Moses Ashley Curtis, D.D." *Journal of the Elisha Mitchell Scientific Society* 2 (May 22, 1885):9–31.
———. Some Recollections of My Life Written for My Children, 1886. Thomas Fanning Wood Collection, William Madison Randall Library, Univ. of North Carolina at Wilmington.
———. Wilmington in the Great Struggle from 1861 to 1865. Thomas Fanning Wood Collection, William Madison Randall Library, Univ. of North Carolina at Wilmington.
Zimmerman, Jane. "The Formative Years of the North Carolina Board of Health, 1877–1893." *The North Carolina Historical Review* 21, no. 1 (Jan. 1944).

Books and Magazines

Busey, John W. and David G. Martin. *Regimental Strengths and Losses at Gettysburg*. Hightstown: Longstreet House, 1994.
Cashman, Diane Cobb. *The Lonely Road*. Wilmington: Medical Society of New Hanover, Brunswick and Pender Counties, 1976.
Catton, Bruce. *Gettysburg: The Final Fury*. New York: Doubleday, 1974.
Clark, Walter. *Histories of the Several Regiments and Battalions from North Carolina in the Great War, 1861–1865*. E. M. Uzzell, 1901.
Coco, Gregory A. *A Vast Sea of Misery: A History and Guide to the Union and Confederate Field Hospitals at Gettysburg, July 1– November 20, 1863*. Gettysburg: Thomas Publications, 1988.
The Confederate Veteran. 14 (1907): 40.
Cooling, Benjamin Franklin. *Jubal Early's Raid on Washington, 1864*. Baltimore: Nautical & Aviation Publishing, 1989.
———. *Monocacy: The Battle that Saved Washington*. Shippensburg: White Mane Publishing Co., 1997.
Cunningham, H. H. *Doctors in Gray*. Gloucester: Peter Smith, 1970.
Dabney, Virginius. *Richmond: The Story of a City*. Charlottesville: Univ. Press of Virginia, 1990.
Dammann, Gordon, M.D. *Pictorial Encyclopedia of Civil War Medical Instruments and Equipment*. Missoula: Pictorial Histories Publishing Co., 1996.
Denney, Robert E. *Civil War Medicine: Care and Comfort of the Wounded*. New York: Sterling Publishing, 1995.
Dowdey, Clifford. *Lee's Last Campaign*. New York: Bonanza Books, 1993.
Evans, Clement A. *Confederate Military History*. Wilmington: Broadfoot Publishing, 1987.
Fonvielle, Chris E., Jr., *The Wilmington Campaign: Last Rays of Departing Hope*. Campbell: Savas Publishing Co., 1997.
Freeman, Douglas Southall. *Lee's Lieutenants, A Study in Command*. New York: Charles Scribner's Sons, 1944. Vol. 3.
Fucini, Joseph J. *Entrepreneurs: Men and Women Behind Famous Brand Names and How They Made It*. G. K. Hall.
Furgurson, Ernest B. *Ashes of Glory: Richmond at War*. New York: Vintage Books, 1997.
———. *Chancellorsville 1863, The Souls of the Brave*. New York: Knopf, 1992.
Gallagher, Gary W. *Chancellorsville, The Battle and Its Aftermath*. Chapel Hill: Univ. of North Carolina Press, 1996.

———. *The First Day at Gettysburg: Essays on Confederate and Union Leadership.* Kent, Ohio: Kent State Univ. Press, 1992.
———. *The Second Day at Gettysburg: Essays on Confederate and Union leadership.* Kent, Ohio: Kent State Univ. Press, 1993.
———. *The Third Day at Gettysburg & Beyond.* Chapel Hill: Univ. of North Carolina Press, 1994.
———. *The Wilderness Campaign.* Chapel Hill: Univ. of North Carolina Press, 1997.
Garrison, Fielding H. *Garrison's History of Medicine.* 4th ed. Philadelphia: W. B. Saunders, 1967.
Goodman, Louis, M.D. *The Pharmacological Basis of Therapeutics.* New York: Macmillan, 1941.
Gunn, J. C., M.D. *Domestic Medicine.* Louisville: Allston Mygatt, 1840.
Harris, William C. *William Woods Holden: Firebrand of North Carolina Politics.* Baton Rouge: Louisiana State Univ. Press, 1987.
Herman, Hattaway, and Archer Jones. *How the North Won: A Military History of the Civil War.* Champaign: Univ. of Illinois Press, 1983.
Holt, Daniel. *A Surgeon's Civil War.* Kent: Kent State Univ. Press, 1994.
Jackson, Mary Anna. *Life and Letters of General Thomas J. Jackson.* New York: Harper & Brothers, 1892.
Jones, Archer. *Civil War Command and Strategy.* Indianapolis: Free Press, 1992.
Lee, Richard M. *General Lee's City.* McLean: EPM Publications, 1987.
Leech, Margaret. *Reveille in Washington.* New York: Harper & Brothers, 1941.
Manarin, Louis. *North Carolina Troops, 1861–1865, A Roster.* Raleigh: North Carolina Division of Archives & History, 1989.
McCaw, James B., M.D. *Confederate States Medical and Surgical Journal.* San Francisco: Norman Publishing, 1992.
McPherson, James M. *The Atlas of the Civil War.* New York: Macmillan, 1994.
———. *Battle Cry of Freedom.* New York: Ballantine, 1988.
———. *Drawn With The Sword.* New York: Oxford Univ. Press, 1996.
———. *For Cause & Comrades.* New York: Oxford Univ. Press, 1997.
Mitchell, Reid. *Civil War Soldiers.* New York: Penguin, 1988.
Osborne, Charles C. *Jubal: The Life and Times of General Jubal A. Early, CSA.* Baton Rouge: Louisiana State Univ. Press, 1992.
Pierce, R. V., M.D. *Common Sense Medical Adviser.* Buffalo: World's Dispensary Printing Office and Bindery, 1895.
Power, J. Tracy. *Lee's Miserables.* Chapel Hill: Univ. of North Carolina Press, 1998.
Rhea, Gordon C. *The Battle of the Wilderness, May 5–6, 1864.* Baton Rouge: Louisiana State Univ. Press, 1994.
———. *The Battles for Spotsylvania Court House and The Road to Yellow Tavern.* Baton Rouge: Louisiana State Univ. Press, 1997.
Robertson, James I., Jr. *Soldiers Blue and Gray.* Columbia: Univ. of South Carolina Press, 1988.
Ryan, David D. *A Yankee Spy in Richmond.* Mechanicsburg: Stackpole Books, 1996.
Sears, Stephen. *To The Gates of Richmond.* New York: Ticknor & Fields, 1992.
Sprunt, James. *Chronicles of the Cape Fear River.* Raleigh: Edwards & Broughton, 1916.
Straubing, Harold Elk. *In Hospital and Camp.* Harrisburg: Stackpole Books, 1993.
Thruston, Stephen D. "Report by Colonel Stephen D. Thruston, Commander 3rd N.C. Regiment." ed. Louis Manarin. *North Carolina Troops, 1861–1865, A Roster.* Raleigh: North Carolina Division of Archives & History, 1989.

Tucker, Glenn. *Zeb Vance: Champion of Personal Freedom*. Indianapolis: Bobbs-Merrill, 1965.
Warner, Ezra J. *Generals in Gray*. Baton Rouge: Louisiana State Univ. Press, 1987.
Warren, Edward M.D. *A Doctor's Experiences in Three Continents*. Cushings & Bailey Publishers, 1885.
Welsh, Jack D., M.D. *Medical Histories of Confederate Generals*. Kent, Ohio: Kent State Univ. Press, 1995.
Wert, Jeffry D. *From Winchester to Cedar Creek*. Mechanicsburg: Stackpole Books, 1997.
Wheeler, Richard. *Lee's Terrible Swift Sword*. New York: Harper Collins, 1992.
Wilbur, C. Keith, M.D. *Civil War Medicine, 1861–1865*. Old Saybrook: Globe Pequot Press, 1998.
Wood, Thomas Fanning, ed. *North Carolina Medical Journal*. Wilmington: Jackson & Bell, Publishers, 1886–1892.
Woodworth, Steven E. *Jefferson Davis and His Generals*. Lawrence: Univ. Press of Kansas, 1990.

OTHER SOURCES

American Heritage Civil War CD-ROM Series, Disc 1. Byron Preiss Multimedia Co. and American Heritage, 1995.
American Heritage Dictionary. Third Edition. New York: Houghton Mifflin Co., 1992.
Archives. Calvary Episcopal Church, Memphis, Tenn.
Archives. Richmond National Battlefield Park, Robert E. L. Krick, Historian.
Benét's Reader's Encyclopedia. New York: Harper & Row, 1965.
Cecil, Russell L. *A Textbook of Medicine*. London: W. B. Saunders Co., 1942.
Confederate Military History: Extended Edition. Wilmington, N.C.: Broadfoot Publishing, 1987. Vol. 2.
Davis, Perry Kirkley. *The Official Military Atlas of the Civil War*. New York: Fairfax Press, 1983.
1850 Census, New Hanover County, N.C.
1870 Census, New Hanover County, N.C.
Encyclopedia Americana. Grolier, 1993.
First Search web site. URL: www.ref.oclc.org
Hewett, Janet B. *Roster of Confederate Soldiers*. Wilmington: Broadfoot Publishing Co., 1997. Vol. 16
Medical and Surgical History of the Civil War. Vols. 1, 10. Wilmington: Broadfoot Publishing, 1990.
Morehead, Albert H. *Hoyle's Rules of Games*. New York: Penguin, 1983.
New Hanover County Deeds.
Roberts, Deering J. *Confederate Medical Department*. URL: www.civilwarhome.com/confederatemedical.htm.
St. James Church Historical Records. Vol. 2. Wilmington, N.C.: St. James Church.
Strother Family Genealogy. URL: jefferson.village.virginia.edu/vshadow2/porte.crayon/porte.html.
The War of the Rebellion: A Compilation of the Official Records of the Union and Confederate Armies. Washington: Government Printing Office, 1884.
The Wilmington Daily Journal. July 14, 1864; Aug. 18, 1864; Sept. 1, 1864; Sept. 8, 1864; Sept. 15, 1864; Oct. 27, 1864; Feb. 23, 1866; Feb. 20, 1867; July 12, 1870.

INDEX

Abattis, Chancellorsville, 78
Absorbent cotton, 98
Agostini, Pierre, 15
Albritton, Capt. James Henry, TFW bio., 64
Ambulance Corps, 66, 67
American Hotel, Charleston, S.C., 18
American Hotel, Richmond, 48
American Public Health Association, xx
Amputations, on the battlefield, xvi
Anderson, Gen. Richard H., engagement near Berryville, 176
Aneurysm of the aorta, Dr. Wood's illness, xi, xxi
Apostolic Succession, 86
Apothecary, Moore Hospital, 33
Appomattox, Va., xvi
Armstrong, Capt. Edward, Chancellorsville, 79; letters to his father, 136; reported as dying, 146; shooting through hand, 108; Spotsylvania, 143; visit to Tom Armstrong's grave, 83
Armstrong, Capt. Edward Hall, 122, 128; smoke out, 128
Armstrong, Edward H., photo, 62
Armstrong, Edward, TFW's first mess, 52
Armstrong, Capt. Thomas, grave at Chancellorsville, 83; killed at Chancellorsville, 78
Armstrong, Capt. Thomas E., TFW bio., 61, 62
Army and Navy Surgeons Medical Association, 50
Army and Navy Surgeons Medical Journal, 50
Army of the Potomac, grand review near Port Royal, 71; Hooker's command, 73
Army Rubeola, TFW's treatment notes, 41
Asche, Dr. Morris J., Union medical officer in command at Chancellorsville, 81

Averell, Gen. William, Battle of Winchester, 181; engagement at Martinsburg, 175; operations in the Valley, 165

Ballard's Exchange, hotel in Richmond, 48
Barleycorn, Lt.Col. J., capture near Martinsburg, 175, 176
Barr, Lt. William H., TFW's first mess, 52
Barry, Col. John D., 20, 24, 25, 111
Barry, Col. John Decatur Barry, 121
Battle of Bristoe Station, 117, 118
Battle of Castleman's Ferry, 166
Battle of Catlett's Station, 150
Battle of Cedar Creek, 185–88
Battle of Chancellorsville, xvi, 73–90
Battle of Cold Harbor, xvi, 144
Battle of Coosaw River, 20
Battle of Fisher's Hill, 178, 179, 183
Battle of Gettysburg, xvi
Battle of Hanover Courthouse, xv, 26, 27
Battle of Lynchburg, 150, 151
Battle of Mechanicsville, 28, 29
Battle of Monocacy, 159, 160
Battle of Payne's Farm, 122, 124; regimental losses, 122, 123
Battle of Spotsylvania, 141–43
Battle of the Wilderness, 138–41
Battle of Winchester, 177–79; against Gen. Milroy's forces, 92–96
Bellamy, Dr. William James Harriss, 18th N.C. Regiment, 22, 196n
Bethesda Church, Battle of, 143, 144
Blair, Montgomery, burning of his home, 161
Bloody Angle, 141
Botts, J. Minor, plantation, 119
Bowden, John N., TFW's first tent mates, 13
Boyd's Landing, Coosaw River, 21
Branch, Gen. Lawrence O'Bryan, command of North Carolina brigade in New Bern, 23

243

Index

Brandy Station, Cavalry fight, 118; defensive line after Gettysburg, 116
Breckinridge, Gen. John C., Battle of Winchester, 181; defend the valley, 144; Lynchburg, 148; retreat from Washington, 165
Brigade Hospital, near Cold Harbor, 145, 146
Briggs, Surg. G. W., Spotsylvania, 143
Brown, Capt. John Badger, raised a company in Duplin County, 58; regimental staff mess, 68; TFW bio., 60, 61; wounded, 1
Brown, John, site of the gallows, 171
Brown, Col. Hamilton A., pursuit at Winchester, 96; wounded, 143
Brown, Maj. Hamilton A., command of brigade after Chancellorsville, 81
Brown, Sgt. Maj. T. W., 19
Butler, Gen. Benjamin F., conduct in New Orleans, 103

Caledonia Forge, Union lines at Chancellorsville, 81
Caledonia Mine, Chancellorsville field hospital, 79
Caledonia Pass, Thad Stevens' Coal Mines, 103
Camp Stephens, Coosawhatchie, S.C., 22
Campbell, Dr. H. F., TFW's oral exam, 42
Camphor, making powders on pummel of saddle, 94
Cantwell, Capt. John L., Officer of the Day, 129; wrestling, 128
Cantwell, Col. John L., 13th Regiment North Carolina Militia, 11; record of his imprisonment, 223n
Cape Fear Minute Men, 7
Cape Fear River, Fort Fisher, xii, xiv
Capps, Thomas Jefferson, Ambulance Corps, 67; Jackson's ambulance driver, 78
Carolina Hotel, xii, xiv, 8; location of Erambert's Drug Store, xv
Carpenter, Phil, TFW's first tent mates, 13
Chambersburg, Pa., burning of the town, 170; occupied during Gettysburg Campaign, 99
Chancellor House, buried knapsacks, 81
Charleston, S.C., temporary assignment, 18
Chickahominy fever, Dr. Hugh Walker Gardner, 40; TFW's ailment, xv, 29
Chiselden's Anatomy, xiv
Chloroform, surgeon's supplies, 97
Christian Benner Farm, field dressing station, photo, 106, 217n
Citadel College, Col. James D. Radcliff, 15
Clark, Dr. James, TFW's first mess, 52
Coffin, Thomas A., Coffin Point Plantation, xiv
Coke, Dr. Lucas, busy with the wounded, 107; established field dressing station at Culp's Hill, 104, 105; share surgeon's case during Gettysburg Campaign, 97
Coke, Dr. Lucius C., assisted TFW at Chancellorsville, 76
Colston, Gen. Raleigh Edward, assumed command of Trimble's division, 77; Chancellorsville, 74; transferred, 87
Colston, Gen., relieved of command, 93
Committee of Safety, xv, 11
Confederate Army Board of Medical Examiners, examination for asst. surgeon, xvi, 41, 42; invitation to appear for examination, 40
Confederate Medical Department, shortages during Gettysburg Campaign, 97
Confederate Memorial Day, 80
Conscripts, 124–26
Cooke, Gen. John, Bristoe Station, 116, 118
Cooper, Dr. George M., xviii
Coosaw River, 19
Coosawhatchie, S.C., deployment in 1861, 15, 19
Costin, Jack, shot by "Pink" Shelly, 6
Cowan, Capt. John, 69, 102
Cowan, Col. R. H., Gordonsville, Va., 27; Kinston, 24

Cowan, John, TFW's first mess, 52
Cox, Col. William R., promoted to Brig. Gen., 143; Valley Campaign, 148
Cox, Gen. William R., Battle of Cedar Creek, 188; release at Appomattox, 189
Craig's Wharf, 194n
Craige, Capt. Thomas, 127
Craige, Cicero, wounded at Spotsylvania, 146
Craige, Lt. Cicero, 127, 128; Christmas celebration, 132; letters of protest, 134; new clothing, 127; Spotsylvania, 141; wounded at Winchester, 95
Craige, Lt. Cicero H., TFW bio., 63, 64; under arrest, 71
Cromwell, Dr. Benjamin M., assigned to hospital duty after Spotsylvania, 146; replaced Dr. Stewart, 122
Cronly & Morris, Richmond auctioneers, 48
Crook, Gen. George, defeat near Winchester, 167, 168
Culp's Hill, xvi, establishing the line, 104
Curtis, Dr. M. A., plant specimens, 152

Dardingkiller, Sgt. Frederick, surrender of Fort Caswell, 11
Darwin's Zoonomia, xiv
Davis, Hon. George, visit to Moore Hospital, 44
DeRosset, Dr. Moses John, 16; assistant at Moore's Hospital, 40; his commission, 195n
DeRosset, Lt. Armond L., TFW bio., 64
DeRosset, Maj. William Lord, election of officers, 59; Sharpsburg, 159
DeRossett, Col. William, breaking up gambling, 126
Dickson, Dr. James H., 6
Didymus, Thomas, TFW's pen name, xv
Dimitry, Professor Alexander, translation of *Les Miserables*, 36, 37, 200n
Doles, Gen. George, killed, 143
Dover's Powder, xiv, 95
Drane, Dr. Robert B., died of yellow fever in Wilmington, 101

Draper's Physiology, xiv
Dunglison's Medical Dictionary, xiv
Dysentery, xiv, 149; in camp after Chancellorsville, 85

Early, Gen. Jubal A., 87; attack on Winchester, 93; Chancellorsville, 73; Valley Campaign, xvi, xxi, 148–88, 154, 157
Early, Gen. Jubal, Battle of Cedar Creek, 187; ransom of Frederick, Md., 162
18th North Carolina Regiment, xv, 12; organization, 17
8th North Carolina Volunteers, xv
8th Volunteers, regimental numbering change, 17
Ellis, Gov. John W., 11, 12
Elwood, Stonewall's arm buried there, 211n
Ennett, Capt. William Thomas, captured, 143; returned from imprisonment, 186; TFW bio, 63
Ennett, Maj. William Thomas, 133; in command of the 3rd N.C., 188; rheumatism, 186; switching uniforms, 133; wrestling, 128
Enrollment Act of 1863, inefficiency and corruption, 208n
Erambert, Louis B., xv, 4–9
Erambert, Louis E., his confinement, 17; purchase of drugs, 25
Ewell, Gen. Richard E., Battle of Bristoe Station, 117; gathering R.R. iron, 120
Ewell, Gen. Richard S., Bristoe Station, 116; command of Second Corps,, 93; defense of Richmond, 113; offensive into enemy territory, 92; photo, 93; Wilderness Campaign, 137, 174

Federal Point, xiv, 17
Flanner, Capt. H. G. in command of Pott's battery, 141
Flemming, Warner L., steward of Moore Hospital, 46
Forsythe, Col. Charles M., confusion over the overcoat, 185
Fort Caswell, xiv, 12; Cape Fear River, 11

246 Index

Fort Fisher, xiv, xv, 15; first encampment, 13
Fort Johnson, Cape Fear River, 11
Fort Sumter, xv, 6
Franking, 129
Fripp, John, Morgan Island, 22
Front Street Methodist Church, Wilmington, N.C., 3, 4
Fuller, Adelia Powell, TFW's first wife, xvii

Gardner, Dr. Hugh Walker, abcess of the liver, 40
Garrison, Lt. Edward J. "Tobe," killed at Gettysburg, 107; TFW bio., 64
General Hospital No. 24, Moore Hospital, 32
Gentian, extract of, 5
George, Maj. Forney, Kinston, 24
German Volunteers, 12
Gettysburg Campaign, 91–114
Gibbon, Dr. Robert, brother of Union General Gibbon, 36
Gibson, Dr. Charles Bell, professor, Medical College of Virginia, 1862, 37, 38
Goldsborough, Maj. William W., wounded at Gettysburg, 107
Gordon, Gen. John B., Battle of Cedar Creek, 185; Battle of Monocacy, 160; Battle of Winchester, 181; raid on Martinsburg, 180; Valley Campaign 1864, 156
Gordonsville, Va., 25; encampment, 27
Grant, Gen. Ulysses S. Grant, in command of all Union armies, 135; Cold Harbor, 144, 147; Lee's strategy, 116; promotion to Lt. Gen., 115; siege of Washington City, 160; Wilderness, 137, 138, 140;
Granville's lotion, treatment for TFW's eyes, 8
Greenbacks, in abundance at Chancellorsville, 83
Grimes, Gen. Bryan, command of the division, 188
Grissom, Capt. Eugene, North Carolina surgeon, 36
Guardian, reading material, 134

Guild, Dr. Lafayette, criticized army policy, 203n; medical director, Army of Northern Virginia, 51
Gutta-Percha Telegraph, at Chancellorsville, 83

Haines, Henry S., superintendent of the Charleston Savannah Railroad, 18
Hall, Eli W., xiv
Halleck, Henry W., reassigned as Chief of Staff, 115
Hallett, Sgt. B. A., 25, 26
Hamilton's Crossing, camp after Chancellorsville, 84; reporting to the field, 51
Hancock, Gen., Wilderness, 137
Hanging Rock Gap, Valley Campaign, 151
Hanover Courthouse, 23
Hanover Junction, Wilderness Campaign, 143
Hardee, Gen. William J., *Rifle and Infantry Tactics*, 197n
Harper's Ferry, Valley Campaign 1864, 154, 158
Harriet Lane, reinforcement of Fort Caswell, 12
Hedrick, John J., command of the Wilmington Rifle Guards, 11; surrender of Fort Johnson, 194n
Henkel, Dr. Casper C., senior surgeon in Steuart's Brigade, 179
Herbert, Col. James R., wounded at Gettysburg, 107
Herndon, Dr. Dabney, appointed temporary surgeon to 3rd N.C., 87; stayed behind with wounded at Gettysburg, 108
Heth, Gen. Henry, Battle of Bristoe Station, 119
Hill, Gen. Ambrose Powell, 85, 87, 113; Bristoe Station, 116, 117; enemy movements prior to Chancellorsville, 71; first day at Gettysburg, 102, 104; offensive into enemy territory, 92; wounded at Chancellorsville, 78
Hill, General Daniel Harvey, Battle of Bristoe Station, 118, 119

Hinshaw, Jesse, 124, 125
Holden, Gov. William Woods, his dispute with Gov. Vance, 234n
Holden, William Woods, 1865 governor's election, 168, 171
Hooker, Gen. Joseph, Chancellorsville, 73, 75, 91; Jackson's flanking movement, 75, 81
Horne, Capt, H. W., TFW bio, 61
Hospital Gangrene, Battle of the Wilderness, 140
Howard, Gen. Oliver Otis, Jackson's flanking movement, 76
Howard's Grove, 25
Howard's Grove Hospital, smallpox hospital in Richmond, 45
Hunter, Gen. David, burning of Col. Andrew Hunter's home, 173; Lynchburg, 148, 150, 151; Shenandoah Valley, 144; Valley Campaign 1864, 156
Hunting Island, xiv

Ipecac, xiv
Ivenson, Gen. Alfred, Battle of Bristoe Station, 117

Jackson, Gen. Thomas J., cemetery at Lexington, 153, 157; death, 80, 81, 83, 85; location of Corps prior to Chancellorsville, 52; map showing where he was wounded, 77; move to reinforce, 25; move to stop Hooker at Chancellorsville, 73, 74, 75; night reconnaissance at Chancellorsville, 76, 77; wounded, 78
Jacobs, John L., TFW's first tent mates, 13
James Island, bivouac, 18
James, Adj. Theodore C., Cedar Creek, 184; lost his arm, 140; regimental staff mess, 68; TFW bio, 64–66; visit to Tom Armstrong's grave, 83
Johnson, Col. Bradley, burning of Gov. Bradford's home, 161; intended attack on Lookout Point Prison, 161
Johnson, Gen. Bradley, burning of Chambersburg, 170

Johnson, Gen. Edward "Alleghany," 87, 122, 137; assigned to command Stonewall division, 92, 93; captured, 142; Gettysburg, 104; marking of ambulances at Gettysburg, 102; Spotsylvania, 141
Johnson, Gen. Robert D., engagement at Kernstown., 167
Jones, Gen. John Marshall, attack on Winchester, 93; command of Second Brigade, Second Corps, 92; Wilderness Campaign, 137, 138
Joynes, Dr. L. J., professor, Medical College of Virginia, 1862, 37, 38

Kanawha Valley Campaign, 151
Kelly, Lt. Tom, died of wounds at Gettysburg, 108
Kinston, N.C., Gen. Branch's command, 23–25
Kirkland, Gen. William, Bristoe Station, 116, 118

La Fiever Typhoide, 35
Langdon, Capt. Richard F., 112, 121, 132; photo, 66
Laspeyre, Lt. Matthew, 21, 22
Lee, Gen. Fitz Hugh, confusion at Winchester, 182; on the right at Winchester, 181; wounded at Winchester, 182
Lee, Gen. Robert E., 89; Battle of Bristoe Station, 117, 119, 128; Chancellorsville, 73, 82; church, 137, 138; command of department at Coosawhatchie, 22; day of fasting, 140; decides on offensive move into enemy territory, 92; formed a line at Hagerstown, 108; Gettysburg, 102; Grant's new objective, 116; HQ near Cold Harbor, 145; loss of Jackson, 85; orders granting furloughs, 110; recommendation from officers of 3rd N.C., 87; shortages, 135; Spotsylvania, 142, 143; strict orders on the march, 99; suspends executions, 114; Valley Campaign, 150, 157

Les Miserables, translation of, 37
Letcher, Gov., ruins of house, 157, 161
Lewis, Tom, TFW's friend captured at Spotsylvania, 146
Locust Grove, Wilderness Campaign, 138
Lomax, Gen. Lunsford, Battle of Winchester, 181
Longstreet, Gen. James, offensive into enemy territory, 92
Louisa Courthouse, Valley Campaign, 150
Lumberton, N.C., Wood's temporary home, xvii, 89

Maguire, Dr. Hunter, application for TFW's transfer, 111, 112
Malaria, 149
Mallard, Jack, TFW's first tent mates, 13
Mallett, Lt. Charles Peter, 61
Manson, Dr. Otis, 39, 44, 50; advisor to N.C. *Medical Journal*, xix; application for TFW's transfer, 111; director of Moore Hospital, xv, xvi, 32, 33; his son Willie, 37; medical library, 34; recommendation to Medical College, 37; soldier's home in Richmond, 49
Marmion, Dr. George, sister in Frederick convent, 162
Marye House, reporting to the regiment, 51
Masonboro Sound, family refuge in Wilmington, N.C., 44
McCarthy, Gerald, book on plants growing in Wilmington area, xx
McCausland, Gen. John, burning of Chambersburg, 170
McCaw, Dr. James Brown, Chimborazo Hospital, 200n; professor, Medical College of Virginia, 1862, 37, 38
McDowell, Rep. Thomas, visit to Moore Hospital, 44
McGuire, Dr. Hunter, advisor to *N.C. Medical Journal*, xix;
McGuire, Dr. Hunter Holmes, assignment to the 3rd North Carolina Regiment, 51, 52; reported movement of the Corps, 53; reporting for duty, 52

McIlhenny, T. C., farm at Gettysburg, 106
McRee, Dr. James F., Jr., xv, 4, 6; Ambulance Corps, 67; orders to assist at Chancellorsville, 78; retired from the regiment, 83, 84; surgeon of 3rd N.C. Regiment, 52, 54, 55
McRee, Sgt. Maj. Robert, death at Payne's Farm, 123; wounded, 143
Meade, Gen. George Gordon, remain in charge of the Army of the Potomac, 116; sent XI & XII Corps to reinforce Rosecrans, 116; Wilderness, 136
Meares, Capt. O. P., Wilmington Rifle Guards, 12
Meares, Col. Gaston, 59; First Colonel of 3rd N.C. Regiment, 56
Meares, Col. Oliver Pendleton, 18th N.C. Regiment, 21; Kinston, 24; Wilmington Rifle Guards, 194n
Medical College of Virginia, 34; attending lectures, 47; studies begin, 37
Medical Society of Army & Navy Surgeons Meeting, 112
Meginney, Levin, Odd Fellows School, xiii
Messenger, The, xv
Metts, James I., release at Appomattox, 189; baptized in Potomac River, 104; TFW's first mess, 52; wounded at Gettysburg, 107, 108
Miller, Dr. James A., 21; 18th N.C. Regiment, 196n; requested TFW's help, 27
Miller, Maj. Harry, Battle of Cedar Creek, 185
Miller, Maj. Harry, supplying food, 108
Milroy, Gen. Robert H., Second Battle of Winchester, 93, 94, 95
Mitchell's Ford, encampment, 117
Moore Hospital, xv, xvi, 31, 46, 133; political visitors, 44; TFW's attempt for assignment, 50; training in the treatment of small pox, xviii
Moore, Surgeon General Samuel Preston, 32, 39, 44, 50; order for distribution of supplies, 36

Moorefield, Confederate defeat, 171
Mordecai, Mr. Samuel B., 112
Morgan Island, S.C., 22
Morphine, 95
Mosby, Col. John Singleton, Early's Valley Campaign, 166
Moss Neck, picket station for 3rd N.C., April 1863, 70
Mulligan, Col. James, death in the valley, 167
Murphy, Dr. S. W., soldier's home in Richmond, 49, 112; stay in Richmond, 112
Myers, Adj. Charles D., Battle of Coosaw River, 20

Natural Bridge, Valley Campaign, 151, 157
Nelson, Col. William, artillery support at Battle of Winchester, 178
New Bern, N.C., orders to deploy, 23
North Carolina Board of Medical Examiners, Dr. Wood elected to, xviii; Manson's membership, 32; TFW's medical license, xviii
North Carolina Medical Journal, xix; first published, 193n; TFW's first article, 5
North Carolina Medical Society, Dr. Wood's membership, xviii
North Carolina State Board of Health, xviii

Opium, 95; making powders on pummel of saddle, 94
Orange Court House, camp after Gettysburg, 109; winter quarters, 126, 130
Orange Courthouse, encampment, 135
Orange Plank Road, Jackson's flanking movement, 75
Owens, Col. William Allison, death at Castleman's Ferry, 166
Oxide of silver, 4

Paroira's Therapeutics, 5
Parsley, William M., baptised, 85; captured, 143; Christmas celebration, 131; command of 3rd N.C. Regiment, 92; killed at Sailor's Creek, 188; photo, 60; switching uniforms, 133; TFW bio, 59, 60; wrestling, 128, 129
Patterson, Rev. George, 68, 107, 111; Apostolic Succession, 61; attends dying Union soldier, 81, 82; baptism, 85, 104, 136; calls upon Episcopal minister in Shepardstown, 97; correspondence with Wilmington newspaper, 85; fasting services, 110; Gettysburg mess, 103; ill at Cold Harbor, 144; living on fresh vegetables and fruit, 88; nightly prayers, 127; photo, 57; sermon, 69; service for Col. Stallings, 166; sharing quarters at Chancellorsville, 82; sharing quarters in ambulance, 84; TFW bio, 56, 57; TFW's first mess, 52
Paxton, Gen. Elisha Franklin "Bull," command of Stonewall Brigade, 92
Peachy, Dr. St. George, TFW's oral exam, 42
Peaks of Otter, Valley Campaign,151
Pellagra, Edward Jenner Wood, xx
Pender, Gen. W. Dorsey, removed from command, 87
Peticolas, Dr., Confederate Army Board of Medical Examiners, 40; professor, Medical College of Virginia, 1862, 37, 38; TFW's oral exam, 42
Port Royal, S.C., 22; fall to Union forces, 17
Porter, Gen. Fitz John, Battle of Hanover Courthouse, 27
Pott's Battery, action at the Spindle Farm, 226n
Powers, Lt. Kitchen, wounded at Winchester, 95
Provost Martial, passes for traveling in Richmond, 47
Purdie, Col. Thomas James, killed, 83
Purdie, Lt. Col.. Thomas James, Kinston, 24

Quinine, 95; shortage, 149; treatment of malarial fever, 34

250 Index

Radcliff, James D., 19; assembly of troops at Ft. Fisher, 14; Battle of Coosaw River, 20
Radcliffe, James S., organization of the 18th North Carolina Regiment, 12
Ramseur, Gen. Steven Dodson, Battle of Fisher's Hill, 183; Battle of Monocacy, 160; Battle of Winchester, 181; engagement at Kernstown, 167; engagement on Berryville Road, 176; holding the line at Winchester, 178; promoted to Maj. Gen., 143; Valley Campaign, 148
Ransom, Gen. Robert, ambush in the Valley, 165; command of North Carolina brigade in New Bern, 23; Valley Campaign, 151, 156
Rations, Cold Harbor, 145, 146
Regiments: 1st N.C., Spotsylvania, 143, 144; 1st N.C., Valley Campaign, 148, 150; Union, 146th N.Y., 138; 10th Virginia, Colston's Brigade, 75; 18th N.C., wounding of Gen. Jackson, 83; 1st N.C. Regiment, Battle of Bristoe Station, 117; 1st N.C. Regiment, Chancellorsville, 76; 1st N.C., Colston's Brigade, 75; 1st NC, 1865 Governor's Election, 171; 23rd Virginia, Colston's Brigade, 75; 2nd N.C. Regiment, Battle of Bristoe Station, 117; 37th Virginia, Colston's Brigade, 75; 3rd N.C. Regiment, Battle of Bristoe Station, 117; 3rd N.C., Chancellorsville, 73–90; 3rd N.C., losses at Gettysburg, 107; 3rd N.C., losses at Sharpsburg, 106; 4th N.C., 1865 governor's election, 171; 64th N.C. Regiment, 129; 6th Alabama, behavior at Seven Days Battle, 100; 7th N.C. Regiment, Battle of Hanover Courthouse, 27; 7th N.C. Regiment, Seven Days Battle before Richmond, 28; 7th N.C., 24
Reilly, Ord. Sgt. James, surrender of Fort Caswell, 12
Religious revivals, the Wilderness, 136

Reynolds, Gen. John F., killed at Gettysburg, 104
Richmond, 31–42
Rocketts, cases of smallpox, 45; James River landing, 202n; Richmond river front, 32; TFW's temporary practice, 46
Rodes, Gen. Robert E., Battle of Winchester, 179; death during the Battle of Winchester, 178, 180, 181; occupied barracks at Carlisle, 102; reconnaissance near Martinsburg, 175; Valley Campaign 1864, 156
Royal College of Physicians and Surgeons of London, xx
Rude's Hill, Early's retreat, 179

Saint James Episcopal Church, 3
Scotch Boys, 13
Sedgwick, Gen. John, Hooker's plan for Chancellorsville, 73
Siege of Washington City, 160–61
Seven Days Battle before Richmond, 28, 36, 40; wounded in Richmond, 31
Seven Days Battles in front of Richmond, xv
Sharpsburg, Va., passing through during Gettysburg Campaign, 97; Valley Campaign 1864, 154
Shelly, "Pink," wounded Louis Erambert, 6
Sheridan, Gen. Phil, assigned to take command of Union cavalry, 116; captured uniform order, 178
Sherman, Gen. William Tecumseh, assigned to command of western armies, 115
Shingles, 55
Sigel, Gen. Franz, Jackson's attack at Chancellorsville, 76
Skinker's Neck, 55; location of regiment when TFW reported for duty, 52
Skinner, Capt. Sam W., brother-in-law of Louis Erambert, 29
Small Pox, 149; breakout in Moore Hospital, 44, 45; hospital in Wilmington, N.C., xviii; TFW's

Index   251

symptoms, 45; vaccination, 201n; Wilmington epidemic, xviii, 35
Smith, Gen. Martin "Ramrod," Spotsylvania, 141
Smith, Jeff, TFW's first tent mates, 13
Smith's Anterior Splint, 5
Spectator, reading material, 134
Spotsylvania Courthouse, 142
Spottswood Hotel, Richmond, 48
Sprue, Edward Jenner Wood, xx
Sprunt, Mary Kennedy, TFW's second wife, xx
Squibb, Dr. Edward R., captured medical supplies, 81
St. James College, arrest of college president, 169
St. James Episcopal Church, xii
Stallings, Lt. Col. Walter Scott, death at Castleman's Ferry, 166
Steamer Kate, brought Yellow Fever to Wilmington, 7
Steuart, Gen. George H., 112; assumes command, 87; captured, 142; charging up Culp's Hill, 106; Christmas celebration, 131; command of Colston's brigade, 92; dealing with law breakers, 125; farmers complaining about stolen horses, 100; fasting services in his quarters, 110; Louisiana brigade, 67; marking of ambulances at Gettysburg, 102; photo, 94; spelling of his name, xxii; stopped the furloughs of officers, 114; Wilderness Campaign, 137
Stewart, Dr. William F., 121, 122
Stone, Lt. Irving C., 127
Strother, David Hunter, Porte Crayon and Weyer's Cave, 173, 184
Stuart, Dr. William F., new regimental surgeon, 109
Stuart, Gen. James Ewell Brown, 88; assumes command of the Second Corps, 78; in church, 138; march around McClelland's army, 27
Surgeon's call, TFW's first, 54,55
Surgeon's pocket case, photo, 98; TFW's secures his first, 98

Swift Run Gap, 25
Sykes, Gen. George, Union Sixth Corps at Bristoe Station, 116

Tait, Capt. George, 18th North Carolina Regiment, 12
Taliaferro, Gen. W. B., TFW's brigade assignment, 52
Tallow, making biscuits, 152
Tatler, reading material, 134
Taylor, Col. W. H., Spotsylvania, 143
Thomas, Dr. William George, 32
Thompson, Capt. William H., replaced Maj. Ennett, 187
Thruston, Col. Stephen Decatur, 127, 129, 134; appointment as commander of 3rd N.C. Regiment, 53; Battle of Payne's Farm, 124; Battle of Winchester, 178; Christmas celebration, 131; Cold Harbor, 145, 150, 151; dealing with conscripts, 125; dealing with gambling, 126; draw-poker, 61; punishment of Craige, 134; regimental staff mess, 68; spelling of his name, xxii; TFW bio., 57–59; wounded at Chancellorsville, 78; wounded at Winchester, 182
Trimble, Gen. Isaac Ridgeway, assignment to his division, 52; disabled at Chancellorsville, 77
Tucker, Dr. David, professor, Medical College of Virginia, 1862, 37, 38
Typhoid Fever, 149; subject of TFW's written exam, 41; TFW's notes concerning confusion with Typhus, 40, 41

University of North Carolina, xiii
University of Virginia, 150
U.S. Ford, Hooker's retreat from Chancellorsville, 79
U.S. Ford, interview Union surgeons after Chancellorsville, 81, 85

Van Bokkelen, Capt. John F. S., photo, 55; TFW bio., 55, 56; TFW's first mess, 52

Index

VanBokkelen, Capt., stricken with typhoid fever, 92, 93
Vance, Gov. Zebulon B., controversy over Capt. Eugene Grissom, 36; 1865 governor's election, 168; establishment of North Carolina Hospital, 31; visit to Moore Hospital, 34
Venus Fly Trap, xx
Vincent, Agnes Fanning Wood, TFW's sister, 8, 39, 70, 90
Vincent, Nathaniel B., married TFW's sister Agnes, 70
Virginia Central Railroad, Valley Campaign 1864, 155
Virginia Medical College, attending lectures, 32
Virginia Military Institute, 74, 153, 157

Walker, Dr. Joshua C., asst. surgeon of 3rd N.C. Regiment, 52; his return to N.C. and Marine Hospital, 52
Wallace, Gen. Lew, Battle of Monocacy, 159, 160, 162; reinforcements for Washington, 161
Walter, Thomas U., dome for U.S. Capitol, xii
Warren, Col. E. T. H., command of Colston's brigade, 77, 78
Warren, Dr. Edward, 69; controversy over Capt. Eugene Grissom, 36; founder of N.C. *Medical Journal*, xix, 5; visit to Moore Hospital, 34
Warren, Gen. Gouverneur, Bristoe Station, 116; Wilderness, 137
Warrenton Springs, encampment, 118
Washington, Dr. Walker, 104; appointed as new regimental surgeon, 84, 87; division hospital at Gettysburg, 107; Gettysburg mess, 103; new regimental surgeon, 88; preparation for Gettysburg Campaign, 92; resigned, 109
Washington, George, natural bridge, 151, 157
Weber, Gen Max, Valley Campaign 1864, 154, 158
Wellford, Dr. B., medical case in Rockets, 46; professor, Medical College of Virginia, 1862, 37, 38

Wellford, Dr. John, advisor to N.C. *Medical Journal*, xix
Weyer's Cave, 184
Whist, 127
Whiting, W. H. C., Dr. Joshua Walker's brother-in-law, 52; Hunting Island light house, xiv
Wilderness Tavern, TFW's first amputation, 79
Williams, Capt. Robert, Company I commander, 21, 22
Williams, George W., hospital steward, 53
Williams, Thomas H., xiv
Wilmington, N.C., blockade, 149; TFW's medical practice, xvii; silk braid for the overcoat, 132
Wilmington Journal, 154–84
Wilmington Light Infantry, 11
Wilmington Rifle Guards, xv, 11
Wilmington Scotch Boys, 12
Winchester, captured greenbacks, 102
Wood, Alfred V., TFW's younger brother, 89
Wood, Col. James Hall, death at Castleman's Ferry, 166
Wood, Dr. Edward Jenner, TFW's son, xx
Wood, John C., xiv, 3, 90; building casements at Fort Fisher, 15
Wood, John C., R. B. & J. C. Wood Builders, xii
Wood, John Fuller, TFW's son, xvii
Wood, Lydia Summerhays, letter from TFW, 90, 110
Wood, Mary Francis, TFW's sister, 39, 70; letter from TFW, 88, 110
Wood, Robert Barclay, xii, xiv, 3, 7, 8
Wood, Robert Barclay, Jr., appointed deputy clerk & master, xiv, 71; letter from TFW, 38, 39; letter from TFW after Chancellorsville, 84, 85; TFW letters, xxi
Wood, Thomas Powell, TFW's son, xvii
Wright, Tom, TFW's friend killed at Cold Harbor, 146

Yellow Fever, Wilmington epidemic in 1862, 7, 44

www.ingramcontent.com/pod-product-compliance
Lightning Source LLC
Chambersburg PA
CBHW030310080526
44584CB00012B/507